Fairport by Fairport

with Nigel Schofield

Δ88

First published in the United Kingdom in 2012 by Rocket 88,
an imprint of Essential Works Limited
29 Clerkenwell Green, London ECIR ODU

This edition first published in 2013

The text for *Fairport by Fairport* was written by Nigel Schofield

All interviews conducted and compiled by Nigel Schofield

Illustrations by Eugen Slavik

ISBN: 978-1-906615-48-2

Printed in Italy by Castelli Bolis Poligrafiche

Printed using cover and paper materials certified
by the Forest Stewardship Council

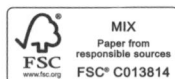

MIX
Paper from
responsible sources
FSC
www.fsc.org
FSC® C013814

fairportconventionbook.com
rocket88books.com

1 3 5 7 9 10 8 6 4 2

Contents

Dedication

This history of Fairport Convention is dedicated to the memory of actor and musician Geoffrey Hughes, 1944-2012

Acknowledgements

Most importantly, I would like to thank members of Fairport past and present for the music that has been a key element in the soundtrack of my life for the past four and a half decades. In addition, thanks for time, patience and a warm welcome each time we sat down over the years to conduct the interviews – which make up the majority of this volume.

Thanks also to the countless friends, fans and family of Fairport who have shared music and memories. Thanks to Russell Beecher for asking me to write this book, to Simon, Peggy, Ric, Chris and Gerry for recommending me for the task, and to my editors Mal Peachey and Dipli Saikia who have shown patience, imagination and diligent attention to detail in turning my lengthy and meandering drafts into a succinct text.

Thanks to Mike and Helen, my most regular Cropredy companions, and also to John, Rosie, Tim, Lucy, Neil and Ken, not forgetting 20,000 others who watch the moon rise over the field each August.

Finally, thank you and 'without whom' to Christine, for love, support, companionship and tirelessly tackling many drafts of this and other volumes without complaining about having read it before!

Nigel Schofield
September 2012

Who's Who

Quotes from members and ex-members of Fairport Convention are identified by a single name throughout the book. They are taken from interviews conducted over 42 years (1970-2012). This list identifies all Fairport members cited in the text; it is *not* a complete list of Fairport members.

ASHLEY	Ashley Hutchings 1967–1969	PEGGY	Dave Pegg 1970–present
SIMON	Simon Nicol 1967–1971; 1976-present	TREVOR	Trevor Lucas 1972–1976
RICHARD	Richard Thompson 1967–1970	JERRY	Jerry Donahue 1972–1976
JUDY	Judy Dyble 1967–1968	BRUCE	Bruce Rowland 1975–1980
SANDY	Sandy Denny 1968–1969; 1974–1976	RIC	Ric Sanders 1985–present
DM	Dave Mattacks 1969–1971; 1972–1976; 1980–1998	MAART	Maartin Allcock 1985–1996
		CHRIS	Chris Leslie 1996–present
SWARB	Dave Swarbrick 1969–1981	GERRY	Gerry Conway 1998–present

Introduction

In 2012, Fairport Convention celebrated the 45th anniversary of their formation.

This book presents the story of Fairport's journey, its highs and lows, ups and downs, tragedies and triumphs, told through interviews conducted over the last 42 years, capturing the recollections of the many musicians who have been part of the Convention.

I first saw Fairport Convention perform in 1969, when the band was less than two years old and had already gone through a number of significant changes in line-up and musical direction. Almost every year since then, I have seen them perform live at an amazing range of locations, from the festival at Cropredy and similar sites to the intimate confines of the recording studio and the domestic front room. I first interviewed the band – or at least Daves Pegg and Swarbrick – in 1970. In the ensuing years, I interviewed almost every long-term member and ex-member of the band. I have drawn on those interviews, and interviews with a host of other friends, fans and folkies from the music scene to tell Fairport's epic story.

When drawing up lists of best / most important / most influential albums in the history of recorded music, respected publications simply cannot agree, but they always include at least one by Fairport Convention: for *Rolling Stone* it is *What We Did on Our Holidays*; *Mojo* and *Melody Maker* opt for *Unhalfbricking*; while listeners of Radio 2 and readers of the NME chose *Liege & Lief*. In 1969, Fairport scored their only hit in the singles chart and also featured in the headlines of both the music and national press for tragic reasons. That year, Fairport recorded a catalogue of songs that would become classics and stand them in good stead for the next four decades: 'Genesis Hall', 'Crazy Man Michael', 'Who Knows Where the Time Goes', 'Matty Groves', and 'Meet on the Ledge'. Sadly, in May of 1969, the band suffered a fatal motor accident that almost ended their career before it had properly started.

Each member of Fairport has his or her own story to tell about their experiences as part of the 'family'. Wherever possible, this story of Fairport Convention is narrated through the words and recollections of those who have been a part of the band. Not all recollections concur: they often 'view the scene from a different angle'. Only when recollections have been at variance with demonstrable facts have I amended what has been said – ensuring that events reported are physically viable (no matter how hard you try you cannot play in Sydney in the afternoon and San Francisco the same night!); and checking that references to record releases and publications are accurate (one long-serving member of the band consistently neglects to include the first album in calculations of releases – "That's 'cos I never had that one, y'see").

The band has faced its demise on several occasions, coped with several untimely losses and commercial crises, and achieved its legendary status with none of the usual trappings of music business success. When listeners to BBC Radio 2 were asked to pick 'the most influential folk album of all time' and 'all-time favourite folk song' in 2007, both their choices came from Fairport's back catalogue.

Fairport is a band haunted by anomaly. Most people, including Radio 2 listeners, will agree they are a folk act, yet very little of their repertoire is traditional. Unlike other long-lasting rock acts, there is no constant presence: even Simon Nicol, who was there on day one and was the band's frontman in the second decade of the 21st century, took time out in the Seventies. Dave Pegg, who joined in 1970 – at the point when most chroniclers reckon the band's zenith had just been achieved – has been a member for the longest (if broken) period.

Some of the individuals most famously associated with the band, notably Sandy Denny and Richard Thompson, were part of Fairport for a very short span of the band's timeline, though as Richard has remarked, once you have been part of "the greatest folk-rock band in the world", you never truly sever ties with it. In this volume, we'll take verbal snapshots of crucial moments in

Fairport's career and explore how these reflect the complex and fascinating lifespan of one of the most influential bands of all time.

RICHARD: Fairport is the Hotel California of rock music: you can check out any time you like, but you can never leave.

SIMON: Richard left Fairport at the start of 1971 and has been playing with us ever since.

ASHLEY: It is strange to think that Fairport was a band started by a bass player and run from his home. A dozen years later it became a band continued by his successor on bass and run from his home. I started the whole thing off and ultimately, in more ways than one, Dave Pegg became my replacement.

SANDY: Fairport will always be more than a band. I was a member of Fairport on two separate occasions, but a band so similar to Fairport backed me on record and on stage so regularly that I feel never to have not been a part of Fairport.

SWARB: *Smiddyburn* (1981), one of my solo albums, reunited the 1970 line-up of Fairport. That wasn't who Fairport were at the time and, in fact, there may not even have been a Fairport at that juncture.

RIC: There have been versions of The Albion Band that have been described as 'more Fairport than Fairport'. People assume I ended up joining the band because I'd been in a version of The Albions with Simon and DM: in fact, it was because my father knew Peggy's dad.

RICHARD: You know with people who've been in Fairport that you're dealing with a safe pair of hands on stage. That's why I've used Fairporters when I've put together bands from British players.

PEGGY: An amazing number of people who've been in Fairport were also members of Jethro Tull – I played in both bands for years; then there's Maart, Gerry, DM, Ric. The Dylan Project was basically Fairport with P J Wright and Steve Gibbons.

JOHN PEEL: By most normal ways of estimating such things, Fairport were never a successful band. But their influence, as a group and as individuals, has been enormous. There are only a couple of degrees of separation between them and most major figures in rock music.

Fairport Convention have created a unique, vibrant, memorable and living catalogue of songs and memories for band members and fans alike. This book tells the story of a journey that Fairport made from the living room of a family house, through the byways and highways of Britain, across the world and back again to a place that they call home, for at least a few days each summer: Cropredy.

CHAPTER ONE

Fortis Green to Home Field

Fortismere Avenue is a leafy suburban road, running north to south from Fortis Green Road to Grand Avenue in the Muswell Hill district of North London. At its northern end, right on the junction, sits Fairport, a large residential house and former doctors' surgery. At different times, it has been the home of Simon Nicol, Ashley Hutchings, and the original Fairport Convention.

SIMON: It's a big house with quite a considerable garden behind it. The downstairs was the home of the medical practice, which had three doctors, one of them my father. There was the surgery itself, a big waiting room, and an office / dispensary unit. There was also a housekeeper's room, and a kitchen. That gives you an indication of the footprint of the house. The Nicol family had the two upper storeys, which were big enough for a family with four kids. The top attic room was big enough to have a full-size ping-pong table that you could cycle around. There were always two bicycles stored in the room.

ASHLEY: I was working for a publishing firm in the centre of London at the time, and I wanted somewhere that made it easy to commute to work. Because I was leader of two or three different bands, I also wanted somewhere that was a good base for rehearsing. Fairport was ideal.

SIMON: My father was the senior partner, but after his death the practice passed into the care of one of the others. The Nicol family moved out and the upper floors were divided into flats. Though we didn't own the building, my mother became responsible for the lease. She decided to rent it out to get some money in, and we moved to our own flat, about 50 yards down the road. My dad, though I love him to bits, was no more financially responsible than I am and he didn't believe in the value of property, which is why we didn't own Fairport. They had moved there in 1947, after he had completed his time in the RAF, and they were offered several opportunities to own the house; on one occasion he could have bought it for £750. After his death, mum had to get a job, and to cover her obligation to service the lease on Fairport she began renting it out as student-type accommodation. One of her tenants was Ashley Hutchings.

WEDNESDAY 6 JULY, 1966
'J B' (PUBLIC BAR)

Ashley Hutchings returns home from a visit to the local pub and, as he is in the habit of doing, brings his diary up to date: 'Called on Si[mon Nicol] and suggested we form a folk-rock group with him and Rich Thompson. We agreed to give it a go.'

Today, thanks partly to the groundbreaking work of Fairport Convention, folk-rock has evolved from the way Tyger, Si and Rich defined it back in 1966. The term was being used then in the music press to describe an American phenomenon – the Byrds' Beatle-esque electrification of Dylan, Seeger and American folk songs; the overdubbed hit versions of Simon and Garfunkel's early songs like 'Sounds of Silence'; and even the all-out rock Dylan was creating with The Hawks (soon to be The Band). Dylan's 1966 world tour had ended in May with three weeks of concerts that stretched the length of the UK (Bristol, Cardiff, Birmingham, Leicester, Sheffield, Manchester [the famous "Judas!" concert], Glasgow, Edinburgh, Newcastle and, on 26 and 27 May, the Royal Albert Hall). The music press was still reporting the fallout from those gigs.

Ashley wasn't proposing a radical new musical start or a major change of direction, even if that is what it became. Rather, he helped create what would be one of a string of bands he organised and managed. Already known as a mover and shaker on the local scene, he could usually come up with a live act that would fit most venue managers' needs. Want a blues band? Budget won't stretch to Mayall or The Yardbirds? Ashley could supply Dr K's Blues Band. Then there was Still Waters, offering, as the name suggests, a more mellow sound. Tim Turner's Narration were a prototype prog rock act. Their name came from the man who provided the voiceover for the *Look at Life* documentary series screened before the main feature at Odeon Cinemas, like the one in Highgate where Simon Nicol was a trainee projectionist. The Ethnic Shuffle Orchestra had a nice line in jug band music inspired by The Lovin' Spoonful and Jim Kweskin's Jug Band. There was also a nameless quartet of Ashley, Simon, Richard and Judy Dyble that sometimes played at folk clubs.

JUDY: It's sometimes assumed I was part of Fairport from the start. But, although I had played in a couple of Ashley's bands, when he put together the very first Fairport, I wasn't asked. I was their first real lead vocalist, though.

Just as he would later with The Albion Band, Ashley turned to his address book to create from the many musicians he knew a line-up for the emerging folk-rock scene. Among them were Simon Nicol, first recruited because he owned a 12-string guitar, and Richard Thompson, already gaining a reputation as a lead guitarist. Ashley sometimes stood in as bass player in Richard's school band, Emil and The Detectives, when their normal bass player, Hugh Cornwell, was unavailable (he later became a founder member of The Stranglers). Others included Geoff Krivit who sometimes played with John Mayall, and the mysterious 'Willy', a kazoo blower who had played bass in Roy Everett's Blueshounds, featuring guitarist Dave Pegg.

None of these bands had a permanent line-up and, as discussion about the folk-rock group developed, it became clear that this could be a proper band with a regular line-up, bringing together the best of the musicians that Ashley played with. Ashley, Simon and Shaun Frater – three members of The Ethnic Shuffle Orchestra – were joined by Richard Thompson, whose lead guitar swiftly became the band's unique selling point. Like all of Ashley's bands, they rehearsed in the large room that he rented in Fairport.

SIMON: It's passed into legend that Ashley painted one room red and this was where Fairport Convention first played together, rehearsing what would become our live set.

Richard Lewis suggested Fairport Convention as a name, emulating the names of bands emerging from the West Coast music scene such as the Grateful Dead, Buffalo Springfield, Jefferson Airplane.

THE FIRST GIG: 27 MAY, 1967
ST MICHAEL'S CHURCH HALL, GOLDERS GREEN

Ten months after the suggestion of forming a folk-rock group was made, Fairport Convention gave their first public performance. The *Melody Maker* gig guide for the previous couple of weeks had carried a listing which read: 'Fairport Convention stays home again, patiently awaiting bookings (TUD 0718)'. It was the phone number for Fairport, the house and the band.

The list for Saturday 27 May, however, just below 'A ball at BLUESVILLE '67', showed an ad inviting readers to 'Be Converted!!! Fairport Convention happen'.

The band that appeared that night was a quartet. Ashley was bass player and clearly the band's leader; Richard and Simon played guitar, though they had a mandolin and fiddle to hand; Shaun Frater played drums. For six shillings admission the audience was treated to, among other songs, Love's '7 and 7 Is', Dylan's 'My Back Pages' (learned from The Byrds' version), and a Chuck Berry number. That night set a pattern for Fairport that would continue throughout their existence. Not only did they play their own versions of other people's songs, but after the gig they also made the acquaintance of someone who would become an important part of the line-up. In a band once noted for its turnover of membership, Shaun holds the record for the shortest tenure after being asked to leave at the end of the first gig. He was replaced by Martin Lamble who had watched the gig, loved the arcane choice of music, and approached them as they were packing up. A try-out secured him his place.

It was the first of a string of similar personnel changes, with new members originating among the Fairport audience. Others include Dave Pegg at Mothers in Birmingham, Maartin Allcock in West

Yorkshire, Gerry Conway at the Royal Festival Hall, Chris Leslie in Banbury, and Ric Sanders at Cropredy.

Second Weekend in August, Home Field, Cropredy

Every year, up to 20,000 fans gather in the small Oxfordshire village of Cropredy to attend the three-day festival curated and headlined by Fairport Convention. The event is a highlight of every Fairport fan's year. Even those unable to attend scrutinise setlists and reviews published in music magazines or online for details of returning ex-members, surprise superstar guests, and back-catalogue rarities dusted down for the occasion.

The Cropredy Festival began in 1976 in a back garden. However, since the early Eighties, it has taken place in a field at Home Farm that provides a natural amphitheatre. More than anything, the festival – an artistic, organisational and, significantly, financial triumph – represents Fairport's ability to 'begin to continue', a phrase first used about them in 1969 when they were, for the first time, on the brink of ceasing to exist. In 1979, faced with a transformed music scene in which they seemed no longer to have a place, they held their farewell gig at Cropredy Festival, but instead of marking an ending, it began a new era for them.

PEGGY: After that farewell concert, someone suggested we try an annual reunion. Cropredy was home turf for us all at the time, so logistics weren't a problem. Christine, my wife at the time, and I agreed to take on the task of organising it. That developed into organising the second reunion and the annual festivals after that, then the occasional gig, the short tours, the longer tours, the album releases, and so on.

So began the annual meeting of what, at times, became a confusing and constantly changing line-up of Fairports. They were so plagued by comings and goings early in their history that one of the band's first serious chroniclers labelled it The Fairport Confusion.

MARK RADCLIFFE: It's amazing that Fairport, a band who – let's face it – were never a huge commercial success, year in year out can pull a crowd of 20,000.

BOB HARRIS: Fairport are one of those few bands where speaking of a family is really valid. Like any family, they don't always get on, but there is a deep and special bond that goes beyond friendship. When they suffer a loss, whether it's a band member or someone from the team or a loyal fan, it hurts and it increases that bond.

6 FEBRUARY, 1969
BRADFORD UNIVERSITY

My association with Fairport began on a freezing northern night with a concert at Bradford University, where I saw them by accident. As a regular listener to John Peel's show on Radio 1 and a reader of both *NME* and *Melody Maker*, their name was familiar to me. But it was the fact that John Peel would be hosting an evening at my local university, playing records and featuring three acts, that drew me down to the campus that chilly February evening.

My first sight of Fairport came during a sound-check, through a door accidentally left open. They were playing 'Nottamun Town' which I recognised from Shirley Collins and Davey Graham's album *Folk Roots New Routes*.

Three hours later they looked little different from the way they had when they set up. They didn't play 'Nottamun Town', but the set included 'Meet on the Ledge', 'Suzanne', 'Book Song' ("there's a cello on the record, so tonight you'll have to imagine that bit"), and 'Percy's Song'.

SIMON: It was one of our first forays into Yorkshire – and this was before the M1 made it a simple journey – at not the best time of year to be travelling the roads of Britain. We'd actually made the journey seven days earlier, due to a mix-up with the booking, but didn't play that time.

What I saw that night was a long way from the showbiz flash of package tours I had been used to, with their short sets and Music Hall values. Nor could I compare it to the earnest and rather studiedly amateur folk club I attended most weeks. Instead, here was a group who made little attempt to project to the audience, performing with an intensity that clearly gave them great satisfaction.

The overall impression was of professionalism and modesty. They were great, but didn't seem to realise it – or if they did, they didn't care. Each seemed to have found his or her own way of hiding on stage: Iain Matthews behind his congas, Martin sitting low behind his drumkit with cymbals tilted to display almost full discs, Richard upstage and almost offstage most of the time, Ashley sepulchral in dark clothes, intensely still and seemingly able to find unlit places to stand even on the brightly lit stage, Simon hidden behind a personal curtain of hair, and Sandy Denny upfront – her eyes closed, the mic in front of her face.

As for the sound they made, it was unique, an intricate and delicate blend.

The notes in my diary for that night identified 'bass, drums, male singer, female singer', etc. The names came later. Next day, suitably impressed, I went along to Valances [Electrical and Music Store] to purchase my first of many Fairport albums. I went along the racks to find LPs by artists beginning with F. I flicked back through them… Marianne Faithful, Percy Faith and His Orchestra, Adam Faith. Then, there they were, two LPs by Fairport Convention, on two different record labels. Both sleeves were dark. One showed the band around a table where the only illumination was a Tiffany lamp, the image wrapped around the sleeve – as if someone had planned to create a gatefold but the budget had been cut.

The other was even odder: the reverse showed the band in a shot which could have been taken the night before; the front was (again) largely black with a chaotic cartoon of the band performing alongside lots of other incidentals – a Transit bouncing along a road, Harvey the roadie who would figure horribly in Fairport's saga in three months' time, sparks, cables, and a section of the National Grid. Naturally my eyes were drawn to a small sign bearing the word Bradford, an odd bit of serendipity. It turned out it was the name of the German Shepherd who featured both front and rear.

While I hadn't caught the names of the various band members in mumbled and often off-mic stage announcements, I had learned the lead singer was called Sandy. The Tiffany lamp album (Fairport's first) didn't have anyone called Sandy on it. That, and the word 'Bradford' on the second sleeve, ensured I went home with a copy of *What We Did on Our Holidays* under my arm.

What We Did on Our Holidays

Island
January 1969

SIDE 1:

- 'Fotheringay'
- 'Mr Lacey'
- 'Book Song'
- 'The Lord Is in This Place'
- 'No Man's Land'
- 'I'll Keep It With Mine'

SIDE 2:

- 'Eastern Rain'
- 'Nottamun Town'
- 'Tale in Hard Time'
- 'She Moves Through the Fair'
- 'Meet on the Ledge'
- 'End of a Holiday'

Holidays was Fairport's second LP, and the first to feature Sandy Denny on lead vocals. At this point she shared vocal duties with Ian Matthews, who had just changed his name from Ian MacDonald; later, he would add a second 'i' to his first name. It had songs by Joni Mitchell and Dylan. I knew the Dylan track was obscure because I owned every Dylan album from his bluesy debut to the recently released *John Wesley Harding* and it wasn't on any of them. I'd hoped for a copy of their sublime version of 'Suzanne', but would have to wait seven years for that. There were two 'traditional' songs, but everything else had been written by the band. 'Meet on the Ledge' felt like a classic song. It had the advantage of familiarity because I had already heard it two or three times on Radio 1. Richard's two other songs seemed removed from run-of-the-mill popular music – even their titles were drawn from another era. A couple of years later, when my sister, a New Seekers fan, turned up with a copy of *New Colours*, I took great delight in being able to tell her where 'No Man's Land' came from. 'Fotheringay' sounded like a folk song.

When I added Fairport's second album to my record collection – soon followed by their first, third, and fourth albums – it was a pretty eclectic shelf of vinyl. There was a complete set of Beatles LPS, most of the Stones albums, Dusty Springfield, Scott Walker, a fair section of rock from Cream to the Small Faces, the classical section embraced Mahler, Mozart and Tchaikovsky, and crackly but playable were some ancient rock 'n' roll albums bought for me years before as requested birthday gifts – Buddy, Don 'n' Phil, Elvis, Chuck. But the biggest section, growing all the time, was my folk collection. Many of the LPS had been bought at the folk club, where visiting performers would usually have their latest release to peddle during the interval: here you'd find Shirley Collins and Davy Graham, TOPIC compilations of 'source singers', Martin Carthy, the Ian Campbell Folk Group (both with Dave Swarbrick), The Young Tradition, Pentangle and its solo members, Ralph McTell, The Incredible String Band, Bert Lloyd, Ewan MacColl and Peggy Seeger, Pete Seeger, Joan Baez, as well as less familiar names such as Jackie and Bridie, Bob and Ron Copper, and Sweeney's Men. Naturally, because I regarded Fairport as a rock band, I was interested to see how they tackled the two traditional songs on the album. I remember being thrilled by the evocative eeriness of both 'Nottamun Town' and 'She Moves Through the Fair': my diary reads, 'grt v(ersions) of trad songs: hope they decide to do more.'

In the two years that the group had then existed, Fairport had built itself a reputation as one of the most promising bands on the scene, described by Pete Frame in the lead article of the first edition of *ZigZag* magazine as being 'like a growing city, phagocytically swallowing the peripheral satellite towns. He added that their new album '[towered] like an aardvark over an ant colony' of all other releases so far that year.

By May 1969, they had recorded three albums and changed from being a covers band to producing their own very high quality material. They had already lost their first drummer and both their lead vocalists – Iain Matthews was in the process of setting up Southern Comfort, Judy Dyble had worked with Giles, Giles and Fripp, the group that became King Crimson, and had recently formed Trader Horne. Judy's replacement Sandy Denny had received accolades as one of the country's finest female singers. Her folk credentials saw Fairport being increasingly accepted by the folk audience. As they moved from support act to headliners in 1969, they often found that the acts booked to support them were established folk artists, which was the start of a trend that continued throughout their career.

What We Did With Sandy Denny

In May 1969, *What We Did on Our Holidays* represented the range of what Fairport could do. It was a tentative first step towards folk-rock. The American singer-songwriters whose music still represented a large element of their live and radio sets were represented by a song apiece from Dylan and Joni Mitchell, whose 'Eastern Rain' was learned from a demo that came via producer (and manager) Joe Boyd. Joni did not go on to release the song herself, and her website directs us to Fairport's version.

JONI MITCHELL: Some versions of my songs were released by other singers before I recorded them, sometimes definitively. Sometimes, every singer-songwriter has to admit "They did it better than I ever will."

The songs on the album that are band originals are intriguing and inventive.

SANDY: The first album with Fairport was partly intended to show the variety of what we could do. There're a lot of different styles from traditional folk to Richard's rockier songs. We wanted to show what we could do musically so we included a track with Richard playing slide guitar that we'd recorded in a church; he played accordion on a couple of songs. I played keyboards – harpsichord as well as piano. Simon played violin, dulcimer, and the autoharp that Judy used to play.

JUDY: When I was asked to leave Fairport, one of the things that really upset me was having to give back the autoharp. An autoharp is a pretty obscure instrument, but this was an electric one. There can't have been many of those in the UK.

ASHLEY: The original autoharp was a rather battered acoustic instrument. We rigged a pick-up using parts cannibalised from a telephone. It was good practice for what we would have to do with Swarb's acoustic fiddle.

The original autoharp was not up to the demands of going on the road and being played by three different band members. ("A case would have helped," offers Simon.) In the end it fell apart, and was replaced by a brand new black electric autoharp, bought for the band by John Peel. Sandy's 'Fotheringay' was a recent rewrite of an earlier song called 'A Boxful of Treasures'. Al Stewart was there at the moment of transformation, which took place backstage at Central Hall, Westminster, on 19 July, 1968. It was two months to the day since Sandy had joined Fairport. In that time, they had played the usual London venues (Sandy's first gig with them being at Middle Earth) and travelled as far afield as York and Whittlesey, where Ashley had had his interest in folk traditions tweaked by a conversation about the local Straw Bear. They'd done a couple of radio sessions. There had been one abortive session for the next album, when they had recorded a version of Eric Anderson's 'Close the Door Lightly'. Sandy had also continued to fulfil solo commitments including a session for the BBC's *My Kind of Folk*. The Central Hall concert was her most prestigious gig with Fairport to date, though.

AL STEWART: It was a charity gig for human rights. The folk community could always be relied upon to donate their services. When I went into the dressing room, Fairport were in a huddle working on 'Fotheringay'. Sandy was finishing the lyrics. I was interested because, like Richard and Sandy, I had Scottish roots, even though I grew up in Dorset. Anyone who knows my music will also know that I am fascinated by history.

SANDY: I've never found it easy to write. Ashley made it clear he expected the members of 'his' band to write songs, though. 'Fotheringay' came out of my interest in Mary Queen of Scots. I was fascinated by what it must have been like to spend all those years as a prisoner, like Rapunzel or The Lady of Shalott.

The Sunday Times had recently serialised excerpts from Antonia Fraser's biography of the Scottish Queen and this may have been a source of inspiration for Sandy.

SANDY: I've always been fascinated by the history of Scotland. I am naturally drawn to tragic heroines. There is something about the sound of the word Fotheringay that is particularly beautiful. It was for the latter reason that we [later] chose it as a name for the band. We realised afterwards that our albums would be filed under F in record racks, right along-side Fairport.

The mock Tudor stateliness of 'Fotheringay' is immediately followed by the 12-bar rock onslaught of 'Mr Lacey'.

ASHLEY: Although he is quite a well-known figure in the alternative art world, to me Bruce Lacey was just a neighbour. He lived round the corner from Fairport – the house, that is. He built little robots which we recorded for the instrumental break on the track.

Bruce Lacey's career included work with The Goons, The Alberts, and The Beatles (a cameo appearance as 'indoor gardener' in *Help!*). A madcap inventor and a true eccentric, he was the originator of what became, in the Nineties, a Fairport catchphrase: "It may be rubbish but at least it's British rubbish." He has been cited as an influence by entertainers including The Bonzo Dog Doo-Dah Band and The Young Ones, and anyone who remembers Michael Bentine's *It's a Square World* will doubtless recall the animated 'flea circuses' which were invented, developed, and created by Bruce Lacey. At the other end of the scale, two of his works are owned by the Tate Gallery and there have been in-depth retrospectives at several British museums associated with modern art.

Aside from featuring on the original track, Professor Lacey has often joined Fairport on stage to perform 'Mr Lacey' at Cropredy. Perhaps surprisingly, it is the only song in Fairport's studio repertoire to be credited entirely to Ashley Hutchings.

ASHLEY: We wanted to include more of our own material on the second album. That was a conscious policy. Aside from Martin, everyone in the band has a composer credit on that LP. 'Mr Lacey' predated Fairport, a jokey collision of a very English character and a classic American music form.

The British blues boom – from which sprang The Yardbirds, The Animals, Cream, Fleetwood Mac, Chicken Shack, Jethro Tull, Free, Led Zeppelin and many other bands – was ripe for parody. The

Liverpool Scene, The Bonzos and The Beatles all had a pop at it, as did Fleetwood Mac's Jeremy Spencer with 'Mean Blues'.

After a brief interlude for chamber music – the cello-accompanied 'Book Song' – comes 'The Lord Is in This Place', a spooky improvisation around a Blind Willie Johnson song, 'Dark Was the Night'. Unlike the rest of the album, it was recorded in St Peter's Westbourne Grove, a former church that had been converted to a venue for recording religious albums. The location suggested the title, which is a paraphrase of the words uttered by Jacob after his vision of the stairway to heaven in Genesis, chapter 28:

> And Jacob awaked out of his sleep, and he said, "Surely the LORD is in this place; and I knew it not."

Rolling Stone contributor Greil Marcus wrote in his obituary of Sandy that the song's eerie mood and departing footsteps came to mind as soon as he heard the news of her death. It has the sound of a couple of buskers, like the ones Fairport had heard late one night in Covent Garden. As the acoustic guitar plays, three pennies are dropped (by Fairport biographer and friend Kingsley Abbott) and (Martin Lamble's) footsteps walk into the distance; echoey atmospherics suggest rain-damped pavements and sodium-lit darkness. John Tams would consciously evoke a similar mood when recording a version of The Beatles' 'Girl' for the BBC many years later.

'Meet on the Ledge' has an iconic status in Fairport's history. Eloquently defined by the band's first biographer Kingsley Abbott as "Fairport's family song", it has been dissected, described and interpreted in many ways – though never by its composer Richard Thompson, who has resolutely drawn a veil over its creation and symbolism. Richard's best introduction to the song was in the midst of an acoustic set of new songs in the early Eighties. Relatively taciturn, letting the music speak for itself, he seemed to pause to consider what to do next and said, simply, "I used to be in a group once."

Since the early Eighties, Fairport have always used 'Meet on the Ledge' to end every performance. *What We Did on Our Holidays* closes with 'End of a Holiday' which, as its title suggests, is a brief coda. An instrumental lasting just over a minute, it is a Simon Nicol composition and as such a rare number.

SIMON: It began life as a tune for some lyrics that Iain had written, but the two elements didn't gel somehow, so it became a little orphan instrumental. Years later, it found a new home as the intro to 'Matty Groves'. There was pressure on bands to write their own material in the Sixties. I probably made it to the album because my compositional output had never been what anyone would call prolific. When you're in a band with Richard and Sandy, you have a pretty impossible standard to match.

There are two further songs written entirely by Richard Thompson ('No Man's Land' and 'Tale in Hard Time'). 'Book Song' was written with Iain Matthews while 'The Lord Is in This Place' is credited to Richard and Ashley. The man who had first got the band noticed with the inventiveness of his guitar work also played the accordion and the dulcimer on the album. While he took lead vocals on some songs live, it was felt that the group's official singers should be the only lead singers on disc.

The album's two remaining tracks provide a hint of things to come. Both were familiar as 'trad arr' songs and had been recorded on several occasions. Despite its American source, 'Nottamun Town' is generally believed to be English. Ashley has described it as "an old magic song using the device of riddles," adding that the language reminds him of Mummers' plays. It has variously been described as symbolic allegory, nonsense rhyme, fragmented ballad, and allusive satire. Most recordings of the song are versions of a recording by the Ritchie Family of Hazard County, Kentucky. For Fairport, it provided a vehicle for a brief foray into that short-lived phenomenon of raga-rock. When they played it live, the song concluded with exchanges between guitar and bongos that were reminiscent of Indian classical music. That extended coda crystallised an approach that was later developed for Fairport's reinvention of big ballads on their next two albums. Remarkably, it is the first Fairport recording of a traditional song to include a violin, in this case played by Simon Nicol.

'She Moves Through the Fair' is based on the melody of a traditional Irish air, its lyric written by the Irish poet Padraic Colum. Fairport were far from the first act to assume this exquisite pastiche is actually from the tradition. It was first published anonymously in 1909, and the poet claimed authorship in a collection of poems called *Wild Earth* in 1921. The song was a particular favourite of the

Irish traditional singer Margaret Barry, who attempted to inclu
whenever she was recorded or appeared on television. The earli
recording of her singing it was made by Ewan MacColl in 1955. On
some versions she accompanies herself on the banjo; others are totally *a capella*. In a *Melody Maker* interview following the second
time Sandy topped their annual poll for Best Female Vocalist, she
named Margaret Barry as one of her "favourite singers and biggest
influences." The song had also been recorded by another singer she
had similarly named the previous year, Anne Briggs. It seemed an
essential part of the repertoire of Celtic traditional singers, having
been recorded by Francis McPeake, Belle Stewart, Dominic Behan
and Paddie Bell. Fairport's version is eerie and spatial: Simon's
guitar echoes as it is slapped near the bridge while Richard's weaves
luminous lead patterns around it; and Martin and Ashley on
cymbal and bass "bubble and swirl like the mist over a night-time
peat marsh," as John Peel described it. We can be certain that Sandy
brought this song to the table. She had already recorded a demo
in 1967 that suggests the way the song might go, before she even
considered joining Fairport. It was one of the few old songs she
chose to revive when she rejoined Fairport in the mid-Eighties.
Richard Thompson, too, has occasionally included it in acoustic
live sets.

All Our Own Artwork

While touring the country, travelling from college to college,
Fairport members tried various ways to pass the time 'creatively'.
Their artistic efforts were not solely confined to music, as the sleeve
for their second album proves.

SIMON: Because we were relatively well brought up, we didn't
rampage and smash things up, as some bands have been
known to do. The sleeve of *What We Did on Our Holidays*
shows we could actually be quite creative, I think.

SANDY: It's very much a group effort, and a reflection of our
sense of humour and sense of boredom while waiting to go
on stage at a gig.

ASHLEY: If you had a long journey to a concert and you had to allow time for setting up, it often meant you had a good while to kill. Lots of things have come out of that time – songs, arrangements, musical collaborations, album titles and, in this case, album sleeves.

SIMON: Our dressing room was normally a classroom and had a large moveable blackboard. There was also a lot of chalk. A big black space, something to draw on it with – it was too tempting!

SANDY: We began with cartoons, drawing ourselves, or each other. Sometimes making the portraits less and less flattering. Then we began to fill out space around it, adding in details and objects and words that meant something to us, or little in-jokes.

ASHLEY: It was a bit of fun, something to amuse ourselves with. We laughed out loud as various things took shape.

SIMON: Everything, including almost, the kitchen sink, went in there. Ivory towers, electricity, our roadie, the van, even his dog Bradford.

SANDY: Someone once described the sleeve as a "cut price monochrome *Sergeant Pepper*": I think we were a bit insulted at the time but it is a pretty accurate description. It wasn't drawn as an album sleeve, it was light relief, a way of avoiding boredom. I had done something similar for the first Strawbs LP, the one that wasn't released – *All Our Own Work*.

SIMON: I think it was the following day that someone realised our creative experiment might just be worth preserving. Somebody was despatched with a camera to wherever it was…

ASHLEY: Bournemouth, I believe. Incredibly, it was still there. No one had wiped the board. And so it became the sleeve of our second album. It might just be the cheapest piece of original art ever to grace a long-playing record.

Everyone expected *What We Did on Our Holidays* to establish Fairport as a major act. The music press and the record industry were convinced that 'Meet on the Ledge', their first single for Island, would be a hit. When he launched the underground music magazine *ZigZag* in April 1969, Pete Frame turned the album into a test case to demonstrate how the music business and music fans got it wrong: 'The ecstatic plaudits I expected to see when their album came out never appeared. Inexplicable.'

But, against the odds, as they would for the rest of their career, Fairport wrested success and viability from unexpected areas. Unlike many bands, they have always been able to make playing live profitable. Occasions when this was not the case, usually connected to ambitious or misinformed overseas sojourns, are, to this day, still spoken of as surprising exceptions or ridiculous errors of judgement.

They played all the major clubs in London and beyond – Middle Earth, UFO, Blaises, the Marquee, etc. They were invited to play most of the first wave of British music festivals including the Sunbury Pop Festival at Kempton Park, the Isle of White Festival, and free festivals in Hyde Park and at Parliament Hill Fields. In September and November 1968, they were chosen as a representative band at the Festival of Contemporary Song, which began with a concert at the Royal Festival Hall and then played large venues around the country; also on the bill were Joni Mitchell, Jackson C Frank (Sandy's former boyfriend) and Al Stewart.

AL STEWART: I knew the Fairports quite well in the early days. Richard, Simon and Martin all played on my second album, though as they used to say back then, their names were altered for contractual reasons.

Al was just one of the musicians who recognised the high calibre of Fairport's musical skills. Although Richard's guitar talents were the most in demand, Fairport members could be heard, as the Sixties drew to a close, on albums by Nick Drake, Marc Ellington, The Young Tradition and The Incredible String Band. Session work would continue to be a source of income for Fairport members throughout their career.

SIMON: When Peggy set up Woodworm Studios at Barford

St Michael, Fairport effectively became the house band. When someone needed backing, various members of the band would be brought in. It harked back to our early days in London, when you could pick up session work at lots of London studios.

Fairport's other regular studio visits were to the recording facilities of BBC Radio.

JOHN WALTERS: Radio 1 originally operated under strict needle-time restrictions. In addition, we had an agreement with the Musicians' Union to include a certain amount of session work. These were long-standing BBC agreements that Radio 1 inherited when it started in 1967. A band like Fairport was ideal for lots of reasons: they were local and not very expensive (sadly, to a producer they were key factors), more importantly they were professional, efficient. They always arrived rehearsed. They were nice people.

JOHN PEEL: I always liked Fairport. They were a nice bunch. They didn't try to prove anything beyond the fact that they were a truly fine band. As someone overseeing sessions, it was good that no matter how often they were booked, they always had new songs to offer. It wasn't simply a matter of plugging the latest LP.

ASHLEY: We tried not to repeat ourselves on those sessions. Radio 1 had a huge audience and influence back then. We realised that radio allowed us a way to showcase what we could do. There were some things we learned for radio sessions and never played again. You can't make a simple assumption that the BBC sessions represent what Fairport was like live back then, any more than you can make that assumption based on our albums. They were different situations.

JOHN PEEL: There were some very odd things: Richard Thompson's version of 'Lady Is a Tramp' that we actually used as a competition, a parody of 'Light My Fire' and a very odd Christmas country song that I think was a band original.

Ashley, the man who once created bands to suit the occasion, retained the bespoke approach for Fairport. A 'big vision' was forming – and it was one that would change his life. For now, those regular BBC sessions were another welcome source of income. Because Ashley was on good terms with the recording engineers, he also managed to secure, quite illegitimately, a good quality copy of each session.

Years later, these would be repackaged into a self-bootleg called *Heyday*. This collection had a life of its own, eventually mutating through vinyl version, CD reissues, expanded CD version, box set, and a 'Best of the box set'. Today, we are used to bonus tracks, archivist box sets, 'At the BBC' compilations, and off-air transcription releases. However, it was Ashley's cassette mail order that started the whole thing off.

SIMON: Though we couldn't say so at the time, they were copies of our BBC sessions. We used to ask for a copy of our recordings as an effective souvenir. It was only a few years later that Ashley had the idea of assembling some of the more significant tracks on cassette. This was then manufactured by Simon Stable who was running a cassette duplication business. He was Judy Dyble's husband and obviously we had kept in touch with Judy. It's another example of how Fairport tend to keep things within the family. It was all very unofficial.

JOHN PEEL: I am assured *Peel Sessions* is now a recognised genre in the world of record collectors… Ashley Hutchings was the man who started it all.

ASHLEY: They were recordings I was proud of. They represent an alternative history of one phase of Fairport's career. It was good to be able to bring them into the canon by playing a *Heyday* set at Cropredy.

Heyday, originally released in 1976, is a bookend to the first phase of Fairport's career.

ASHLEY: We started out, as you'd expect, with smaller clubs and less salubrious venues. Our second gig – where Martin

Lamble made his debut with Fairport – was at Happening 44 in Soho. It was a strip club that also put on rock bands.

Details of Fairport's early days have filtered through into a number of Richard Thompson's songs, from the mock Tudor houses of the band's home turf to the squatters in Genesis Hall. While his songs are not strictly autobiographical – and he is insulted by those who interpret them literally – his life experience does inform his writing. Jack Braceland, the shady character who owned Happening 44, can be detected in the words of 'Cooksferry Queen', for instance. 'Josef Locke' recounts an encounter in the early hours after a gig at Middle Earth, when an Irishman accosted the young musicians, claiming to be the legendary Irish singer fallen on hard times.

RICHARD: It was an incident which made a real impression – one of those late night/early mornings in Covent Garden. There was always a curious mix of people. There was this character who claimed to be Josef Locke. I don't know if he was, or if he believed he was. That's not what was important.

To prove his claim, the strange Irishman sang a song.

RICHARD: As I recall, he wasn't bad. And then he was gone.

UFO

In the late Sixties, cultures collided in the small hours of a London morning.

RICHARD: The Middle Earth club used to be in Covent Garden amid all the workers from Covent Garden market, plus the people going to and from the opera. So you had these three cultures which would all intermingle at the sausage sandwich stall on the corner. People in tails and evening dress, market guys in white coats, and freaks in Afghans all mixing together.

ASHLEY: You'd stagger out of a late-night gig at Middle Earth and encounter this strange mix of people.

Fairport's original plan, as shared with their local paper in July 1967, was to gig no more than three nights a week, which would allow them time to rehearse, work on new material, and have some time off. They informed the paper that they were already earning enough to give up their day jobs. They were very quickly in demand at London's more famous clubs.

JERRY DONAHUE: I first saw Fairport at The Marquee Club in 1967. They made quite an impression. They were very to-gether for such a young band. Little did I think I would join the band a few years later, even if no one I saw that night would still be in the group by the time I was recruited.

On 28 July, 1967, the band played at The UFO Club on London's Tottenham Court Road. On their debut at the prestigious under-ground venue, they were the support for Pink Floyd. The Floyd were effectively the club's resident band, and already had a large star-studded fan following. 'Arnold Layne' had been a hit, 'See Emily Play' was in the charts, and their debut album was to be re-leased in exactly a week's time – the gig was a kind of album launch for them.

GEORGE HARRISON: When we were recording *Sergeant Pepper*, Pink Floyd were in the next studio working on their first LP. We'd pop in to see how things were going and we struck a friendship. As a musician, I was impressed with their ap-proach to playing and Paul was fascinated by the technical things they were doing in the studio. Even as a Beatle, you could go to some of the clubs in London without any hassle. I went along to see Floyd at The UFO when they launched their album. Fairport Convention were playing and I was amazed by how well Richard Thompson played.

Pink Floyd had just returned to their home turf following a tour where, to their horror, they had been treated like a pop band and expected to perform their current hit. Their set that night at The UFO included the first performance of 'Reaction in G', an extended protest against their recent tour. 'Pow R. Toc H.' and 'Astronomy Dominé' were also performed.

RICHARD: The audiences in those London clubs of the late Sixties were pretty open-minded. The same bill might include something very Pop-y, like The Move, a singer-songwriter with an acoustic guitar, a band like Fairport playing West Coast-y stuff, a rock or blues band, or something 'far-out and groovy' like the Floyd with their extended improvisations.

ASHLEY: Fairport was a pretty eclectic band. We could turn our hand to most kinds of music, even in the early days.

SIMON: I'm pleased to say musical flexibility has remained one of Fairport's strong points. One of the great things about Cropredy is the fact that we accompany guests who join us for the set: we've played everything from skiffle to heavy metal. It's very easy to carve up our 45 years into sections and it makes sense to do so in many ways, but it should never be forgotten that the things that made Fairport what it was back in the late Sixties are very much what Fairport is about in the 2010s. There is a consistency about it.

That night at The UFO Club has become part of the Fairport myth – one of those turning points without which popular music would be a different place. Like Sam Phillips overhearing Elvis recording a song for his mum, or Raymond Jones walking into NEMS in Liverpool to try to buy an import German Beatles single, Joe Boyd's discovery of Fairport that night blends real events and convenient legend. An American, Joe Boyd was 25 when he first encountered the band. He had previously been instrumental in tracking down blues musicians long thought deceased and bringing them to New York to play before adoring younger generations; been part of the team that staged the Newport Folk Festival; and in 1965 he had led the stage crew that set up for Dylan's controversial electric debut. Dylan was backed by the Paul Butterfield Blues Band, whom Boyd had signed to Elektra, a folk label that had recruited him as a talent scout with a view to expanding the appeal of its catalogue. Transferring to the label's London office, he formed what was arguably the first supergroup to record tracks for a planned Electric Blues Project compilation LP – the line-up including Eric Clapton, Paul Jones, Steve Winwood, Jack Bruce and Pete York. He signed British folk acts to record for Elektra, including The Incredible

String Band. He formed the Witchseason Management Company to handle the artists he was discovering in England, and produced Pink Floyd's debut single. Boyd also helped establish The UFO Club with John Hopkins.

Despite many accounts which place him at The UFO on the night of Fairport's debut – experiencing some kind of epiphany when Richard began to play a Butterfield Blues Band track – Boyd had in fact known the band for most of their then relatively short existence.

JOE BOYD: I'd been down to Gerrard Street and seen Fairport at Happening 44. At that point, I didn't see much to set them apart from the crowd, beyond Richard's guitar playing. This was shortly after Judy had been invited to join.

Fairport's first lead vocalist, Judy Dyble, was recruited after their debut at St Michael's Church hall had made it clear that, whatever else the band had to offer, it was somewhat lacking in the vocal department. Judy was a librarian at Wood Green Library at the time, a near neighbour of Ashley, and a singer with her own amateur group, The Folkmen. She had been part of a folk group that Ashley occasionally drew together.

JUDY: I'd known Tyger and Simon since I was about 15. Our local music scene was quite small and paths crossed regularly. I sat in on a couple of their jug bands and folk groups. One day, I was at a concert and Ashley asked whether I'd like to join the band he'd formed. This was a professional act, which would mean giving up my job and becoming a full-time musician.

Barely two months later Judy found herself with Fairport, playing support to Pink Floyd at The UFO.

ASHLEY: It would have been a carefully considered set. Bands were not always meticulous about drawing up setlists, and would often decide what they were going to play when they got on stage. I tried to make sure Fairport never fell into that trap. This was a chance to reach a new audience. Because of Pink Floyd's reputation for improvisation, we probably included a couple of things to show off our instrumental skill – or Richard, as he was known.

The set that night included 'Lay Down Your Weary Tune', 'Flower Lady' by Phil Ochs, Jefferson Airplane's 'Plastic Fantastic Lover', and 'East/West', which had been released a year earlier as the title track to the second album by the Paul Butterfield Blues Band. This was no note-for-note copy of the impressive guitar showcase, though: part way through Richard segued seamlessly into an excerpt of the theme to *Children's Favourites*.

JOE BOYD: I winced when they started a version of The Butterfield Blues Band's 'East/West'. These were middle class kids from North London. Then Richard started to play. I could not believe that I was listening to a 17-year-old playing Mike Bloomfield's solo perfectly. At that moment, I said to myself, "This is what I am going to do for the next few years."

The results of that encounter were duly reported in *The Hornsey Journal* on 11 August, 1967. Under the heading 'Pop Group's First Disc Is on the Way', the article explained how 'a Muswell Hill pop group, The Fairport Convention' had been spotted by 'Mr Joe Boyd, a recording manager' when they played at 'The UFO Club, Tottenham Court Road, last Friday'. Of such local reportage are legends and inaccurate timelines made. Remarkably, the article described Fairport's music as 'American West coast songs, folk-rock, blues, and some of their own numbers.'

SIMON: When Fairport started there was no mystique, no barrier between the audience and the bands who populated those early gigs in places like Mothers and Middle Earth. You didn't sneak in through the back door and emerge from the dressing room (always assuming the venue where you were playing had either of those things) with your stage gear on. You'd be in the crowd. You'd get up on stage. When the set was over, you'd join the crowd again or go over to the bar and get a drink. We never made a conscious decision to avoid the whole rock-star mystique thing. It just didn't seem relevant. That's why we always make ourselves available after gigs. That's why we don't hide backstage at Cropredy, and why we encourage others not to do it either.

Fairport's prospects had definitely gone up a notch. Now there was talk of proper headline appearances, a recording contract, and a hit single. However, the evolving band found that Judy's vocal style was too restrained and understated for the direction in which Fairport were heading. The immediate solution was to add a second vocalist. Ashley recruited Iain Matthews. Following a short career in football, Matthews had become the backing vocalist in the UK surf band Pyramid, supplementing his income by working as a roadie, in which capacity – when carting equipment for Denny Laine – he had heard Fairport when they played a large pop concert at the Saville Theatre on 7 October, 1967. Shortly thereafter, he joined the band at Sound Techniques Recording Studio, where they were working on potential tracks for a single.

JUDY: Iain Matthews joined us as we were making the album. I think the first thing he did with us was to record those whispery vocal bits on 'If I Had a Ribbon Bow', which became our first single. I didn't feel threatened by him joining. Mostly he took on the duet parts that had previously been sung by Richard. He was a lot easier to sing with than Richard!

Fairport recorded some demos as potential singles, including 'Both Sides Now'. This, somewhat cryptically given Fairport's version had never been released, was one of the songs Judy chose to sing when she reunited with Fairport at Cropredy in 1981. Judy Collins eventually had a hit with the song in 1968, the B-side of which was her version of 'Who Knows Where the Time Goes'.

24 NOVEMBER, 1967
MAIDA VALE STUDIOS

It was a dark, sleet-filled Friday when the six-piece Fairport recorded their first (of many) BBC radio sessions. Unlike most of the recordings Fairport were to make for BBC Radio 1, this no longer survives. They recorded two songs, both ultimately to be included on their debut album: 'One Sure Thing' and 'Chelsea Morning'.

JUDY: We played everything live. A week later, the session was broadcast. They pronounced my surname wrong and my mum rang the BBC to complain.

The session was for *Top Gear*, the first rock show on Radio 1, which itself had been on air less than two months. The show was soon to become wholly associated with John Peel, but initially the BBC would not trust such a maverick on his own, and so he shared presentation duties with Tommy Vance. It was Vance who, in introducing the session, called them "the English Jefferson Airplane".

ASHLEY: It was obvious and a bit cheap… guitar-based band, folk influences, twin male and female vocals.

RICHARD: There were a couple of events when we appeared alongside Jefferson Airplane – festivals – I doubt anyone would actually have confused us.

Some band members took greater exception to the comparison than others. Judy Dyble in her first interview with *Disc* declared, "Anyone who dares to compare us with the Jefferson Airplane will be pelted with bad herrings." That was probably the most strident the delightful Miss Dyble ever got.

SIMON: To be fair, I did used to sing 'Plastic Fantastic Lover'.

Fairport were never so easily categorisable, and listening to their LPs gives only a partial impression of what they were about. Setlists, arrangements and lead vocals on albums were different from those on radio sessions or on stage.

SIMON: Different members of the band taking lead vocals on a song was a result of playing a series of sets in one night. It was a way of giving the band's 'real singers' a break. I certainly wasn't doing any singing that would have made it as far as the recording studio. Even Richard or Ashley, who were the band's songwriters, handed their songs over to Iain or Judy or Sandy to record.
    In the early days of the first Fairport line-up, one of the regular gigs that we had in London was playing at the Speakeasy in Margaret Street. It was at the time a hip nightclub, popular with the mainstream music business. All sorts of the great and good from the industry would drop in – people from the BBC and showbiz stars. I have a particularly vivid memory of

Cilla Black dancing in front of Fairport as we played. What a frightening sight.

Also spotted in the same audience were Eric Clapton, Jimi Hendrix, Eric Burdon and Georgie Fame.

GEORGIE FAME: I was always impressed by Fairport's musicianship, not just Richard Thompson as a guitarist but the way the whole band worked as a tight unit.

Fairport had come a long way from their debut on 27 May, playing to 20 people in a local church hall, to Cilla dancing at the Speakeasy on 14 December, 1967 – where Jimi Hendrix became entwined with Fairport.

SIMON: Lots of underground bands of our vintage would play there. You'd do a couple of 40-minute sets in the course of an evening. It didn't open till about ten o'clock at night – so I suppose it was literally a nightclub. Jimi Hendrix would often call by, especially after he'd done a gig himself – he was still part of the pop scene then – and he'd stand by the bar drinking vodkas and tonics or smoking interesting cigarettes. It was very obvious that he was a great admirer of Richard Thompson's playing (the feeling was mutual, incidentally); he also loved to get up on stage. He clearly didn't want to play Richard's guitar next to me, so whenever he got up, I handed my guitar to him and they'd play together. He and Richard would find some common ground – some blues, a bit of Chuck Berry, something by Dylan, or a Beatles song. It was mainly about the two of them playing together and it allowed everyone else to take it a bit easier – especially me, of course.

One Fairport-Hendrix collaboration recalled by those lucky enough to have witnessed it was a version of 'Like a Rolling Stone', during which Jimi and Richard traded solos to extend the song – already of a considerable length – to "the best part of half an hour".

ASHLEY: We'd established ourselves as a live act. We'd shown we could handle radio sessions. That left television, which Fairport never really mastered, and records.

CHAPTER TWO

'If I Had a Ribbon Bow'

Advertised with a delightful graphic of a ribbon-bowed girl in profile, who could just as easily have been from the Twenties as from the Sixties, 'If I Had a Ribbon Bow' (Track Records) became Fairport Convention's first-ever release on 23 February, 1968. Not everyone in the band agreed that this jazzy old song really represented what Fairport were about. It had been recorded on 10 August, 1967, so had waited around for a while as the band and Joe Boyd decided which song to release before placing it with a suitable record company.

SIMON: We made our debut on Track, which was The Who's label and had artists like Arthur Brown, John's Children with Marc Bolan, and Jimi Hendrix. Then we moved to Island, run by Chris Blackwell, who had added the London underground to his fascination with Jamaican music. He was busily signing up significant acts on the scene. So Fairport began by being signed to the two most significant indies of their day. When we first started recording, Joe Boyd certainly held all the cards so far as experience went. I don't mean just recording experience, but life experience as well. He seemed to be almost a generation older – though he still looks younger than I do, even now. On top of that, he was American, which was quite a big deal in the mid-Sixties.

'Ribbon Bow' is a beautifully produced single: layered harmonies; clear, ringing acoustic stringed instruments; a jazzy, fluid guitar break from Richard; session player Tristan Fry on vibraphone; and the sexiest sigh ever recorded. Given Fairport's growing reputation, the single was extensively reviewed, one of those debut singles that everyone waited for.

Many of the reviews focused on the Twenties feel of the track. In fact, the tune dated from 1936 and was written as a pastiche folk song (not the last Fairport would commit to tape). The original recording was by Maxine Sullivan, but Fairport almost certainly got it from the American revival singers who seemed curiously drawn to it: they would have had access to it via recordings by Carolyn Hester and Karen Dalton, both of whom were in Richard Lewis' extensive collection. NME damned with faint praise when they called it 'undemanding, quiet, melodic and appealing'. Chris Welch in *Melody Maker* spent half his review telling readers how Martin Lamble had insulted him at the Speakeasy, before concluding Fairport '[were] deserving of great success and they swing along like Benny Goodman (1935 version)'. The single, however, received limited airplay. In the days of the pirate radio station, it was exactly the kind of left-field record that Big L or Radio England might have picked up and turned into a hit. But the pirates had been scuttled after the passing of the Marine Offences Act earlier that year, and if one didn't make the Radio 1 playlist, one's record simply wasn't heard over the British airwaves. Desperate to plug the single, Fairport included both the A- and B-side ('If [Stomp]') in a John Peel session on 3 March, along with 'Time Will Show the Wiser', the opening song on their debut album on Polydor (of which Track Records was a subsidiary), due for release on 1 June.

Bye-Bye, Love

Fairport began casting their net wider. They appeared on French television. They appeared at a television festival in Montreux playing a 40-minute set. On 5 May, they travelled to Rome to play at the International Pop Festival. It was, by agreement, Judy's final gig with the band.

JUDY: The band stayed on – hobnobbing with The Byrds – but

I flew back alone. I didn't return to the stage to take a bow. I didn't say goodbye. I was disappointed, hurt and angry.

SIMON: The shy Miss Dyble! Judy was a reluctant frontperson for a band. She was never overly confident about what she did. She didn't have that stage-cool yearning to be at the front of the stage, chasing the limelight. She certainly had a willowy charm and physical grace. She was an interesting dimension to the band's overall sound. It was ear-catching. She always looked great on stage, too.

But it was never really a career that she was cut out for. Fairport's sound was getting heavier, too. While Judy's voice was great for the early, more folkie stuff, the sound of the band was starting to overwhelm her vocals. As the band's approach got more rock-y, Judy no longer really fitted in. She knew there were times when she was struggling, and so did the rest of us. We felt it wasn't working out with Judy. She wasn't bringing enough to the performance. There were times when her presence was beginning to dictate how we played. That's not the way it should be in a band. So we decided to cut our losses. Ashley took her out for a walk and sat down with her on a park bench and said, "Here's your hat; what's your hurry?" He was the only one with the bottle to do it, partly because he was older than the rest of us, but also because he'd known her as a near neighbour for longer than the rest of us.

ASHLEY: It was difficult and sad. Contrary to some reports, Judy was definitely not asked to leave to make way for Sandy. Her voice wasn't strong enough for the band's heavier sound and was suffering as a result.

JUDY: It was like something out of a Sixties spy movie. Ashley called and asked me to meet him on the bench by the bus stop in Muswell Hill. We sat at opposite ends of the bench. That's where he told me the news.

SIMON: It was his first experience of being a hatchet man – something he's had to do on countless occasions since. The amazing thing is – if you think of the vast number of people who have been through various versions of The Albion Band,

and remember that it has always been his decision that some-one should move on – he has handled the whole thing so skilfully that he has always maintained good relations with all of those people.

Judy's singing of 'I Don't Know Where I Stand', Joni Mitchell's song of betrayal, took on an added bitterness in performances between that park bench conversation and her *'et tu, Ashley'* in Rome's Palazzo Dello Sport. Strangely, it was the first song from the early repertoire to survive into the set with Sandy. She can be heard sing-ing it on a BBC session recorded on 28 May, 1968, for John Peel – ex-actly a week after she joined the band. It was the only song from the band's new album, which hit the shops on 1 June, the day before the session was broadcast.

ASHLEY: For a short time, we were an all-male band again. There is a recording of Leonard Cohen's 'Suzanne' with Iain taking the vocal. After Sandy joined, it became a duet. That was an iconic version, and is one of the things we never got round to recording for release that I was particularly pleased – and proud – to be able to include in the *Heyday* collection.

SIMON: It was actually a few weeks before it dawned on us that Judy had made more of an impression on the audiences than we thought. When we went back to play gigs that we'd done with her, people were asking, "Where's the girl gone?", "What's happened to the chick singer?" We realised then we'd established ourselves as a band with a female lead vocalist, so bowed to the inevitable. We had to find another one. We advertised for a new singer, inviting people to auditions. We also asked around to see if anyone had any suggestions.

Heather Wood was a part of The Young Tradition, alongside Peter Bellamy and Royston Wood. Although they performed *a capella* and sang almost entirely traditional material, they had an attitude that appealed to a rock audience. What's more, they were visually remarkable, dressed in King's Road finery, fashionable in a way cer-tainly not expected of folk acts.

HEATHER WOOD: I was one of many people asked about singing with Fairport. I don't think it was even put as strongly as join-ing the band… perhaps it was like the situation with Swarb, a guest appearance that might turn into membership if things worked out. Although YT broke up a few months later, at the time I would not have considered leaving it. No hard feelings, though, and our paths crossed after that. Simon and Ashley played on the album I did with Royston later.

Heather was also a guest during Fairport's set at Cropredy in 1997, their 30th anniversary gig during which eight female vocalists joined the band on stage.

Hello, Love

Sandy Denny's impact on Fairport is inestimable. As late as the Noughties, there were people going to see Fairport on their American tour who thought she was still in the band. Her arrival ushered in their most remarkable period. Inevitably, a lot of people have claimed to have had a hand in persuading her to go along to Fairport's audition; the myth also has it that she turned up expect-ing them to play so she could decide.

SANDY: It was definitely Heather Wood. She told me there was a group looking for a girl singer.

SIMON: We auditioned about a dozen girls. Some played guitar; some just sang. If there's anything worse than going to an audition, it's holding one. By the end we thought we were never going to find the right person. It was both embar-rassing and difficult. You have to remember that we were still young, but we were a band with an album to our credit, a con-tract with Island, and already quite a reputation. Then Sandy appeared. Joe Boyd was at least partially responsible for put-ting her name forward.

RICHARD: None of us had heard her sing before that day. Our paths had never crossed. I knew her name from seeing it in *Melody Maker*.

ASHLEY: She sang 'You Never Wanted Me' – which was to become part of Fairport's repertoire for a few months – and we all just knew. I don't think we even discussed it. There certainly wasn't any delaying tactic like "we'll give you a call" or "could you just go out of the room while we talk about it". One song and she was in. One of the best decisions Fairport ever made.

For the first time, and not the last, Fairport were faced with the situation of releasing a new album when their current line-up no longer matched that on the disc. In a worst-case scenario, this can render tracks on the latest release redundant as far as live performance is concerned.

Fairport Convention

Polydor
June 1968

SIDE 1:

'Time Will Show the Wiser'
'I Don't Know Where I Stand'
'If (Stomp)'
'Decameron'
'Jack O'Diamonds'
'Portfolio'

SIDE 2:

'Chelsea Morning'
'Sun Shade'
'The Lobster'
'It's Alright Ma, It's Only
    Witchcraft'
'One Sure Thing'
'M1 Breakdown'

A year and five days after the band was formed, Fairport released their debut LP. It included 12 tracks, seven of which were written by the band. Setting a pattern that would run right through their career, the album included an obscure Dylan track – a setting of a Dylan poem from the sleeve of *Another Side of Bob Dylan* by the actor and would-be rock star Ben Carruthers. The song 'Jack O'Diamonds' was another that would carry over into the repertoire with Sandy Denny. 'A sophisticated kind of folk-rock' was how *Record Mirror*'s review summed up the release.

SIMON: No one in the band was entirely happy with the first LP. It tried so hard to show everything that we could do, that it ended up not being representative of what we *did* do.

ASHLEY: I think it tried too hard. There was a sense of pulling in too many directions at once. Over the following year, I discovered how vital it is that an album works as a whole. That would become my philosophy with every record I was to make after *Liege & Lief*. The first album, though, is just a collection of tracks. When you look at what we were playing live at the time, there was lots of much stronger material that we could have included in it but didn't.

RICHARD: Ashley encouraged us all to write. Sometimes it felt like he was setting us homework. I am glad he did: perhaps without his guiding push, Fairport's songwriters might never have got started. The songs on the first album, though, are mainly juvenilia and I think they were all joint compositions.

The seven songs from the band on the first album include the instrumentals which close each side. The other five tracks, all by American writers, overshadow them in both performance and quality of writing.

RICHARD: Only 'Time Will Show the Wiser' really survived as a Fairport song from that first album. It's one that we'd been playing since our early days and it sounds more played-in than a lot of the other tracks. Some were studio creations, as I think their titles might suggest.

Fairport's debut single didn't make it on to the album, though its B-side, written by Iain Matthews and Richard Thompson, did.

RICHARD: I don't think you could fairly call any of us songwriters at the time of the first album. Bands wrote their own songs because they were expected to do so. Like most people who are interested in music, I had written some songs when I was at school. They were joint compositions with my friends Paul and Andrew, who were part of the gang who sang backing vocals on 'Meet on the Ledge'.

'Decameron' was the earliest Richard Thompson song to have been officially released. Written with Paul Ghosh and Andrew Horvitch, it is prime evidence for anyone wishing to categorise him as a doom and gloom songsmith – a man who, in Patrick Humphries' memorable phrase, "makes Leonard Cohen sound like Barry Manilow". It certainly is a despondent world – no colours where the children play, blood running cold, and pragmatically if bathetically, 'no stamps… on the morning mail'.

But *this* is to miss the point of why the song, slight though it may be, is significant. This piece of schoolboy writing embodies the timelessness of Richard's work. As he would again countless times in later songs, he portrays a world that seems to coexist in several time frames.

Stamps on the morning mail – the postman with the underpayment slip – is very Sixties. The song's visions of decay – arms growing old, blood running cold – reminds us that in a world where his contemporaries were writing musical space odysseys, twee post-Romantic verse, or psychedelic meanderings, young Richard 'saw the skull beneath the skin'.

The title takes us back to Italy in the Middle Ages. Boccaccio's *Decameron* of c1350 (the title is from the Greek for 'ten days') is built around a tale of half a dozen nobles who escape an outbreak of plague in Florence and pass their time in voluntary Florentine quarantine recounting risqué ribaldry. Hints of that journal of the plague year appear in Richard's song – the white crosses on the door, the arms growing cold, or 'the white truck ring[ing]' (a modern ambulance?). The structure and a couple of the stories were the inspiration for Chaucer's *Canterbury Tales*.

The other four Fairport originals on the LP are each credited to band members ('The Lobster' also acknowledges the 20th-century scholar and poet George Painter). Ashley Hutchings is credited as co-author on four of the songs.

ASHLEY: My involvement was more in the way of suggesting themes and encouraging the writing process.

Every member of the band received a composer credit on at least one track ("We'd *all* be making songs," as Richard put it in the penultimate track on their next LP). Each side ended with a brief instrumental – Judy Dyble and Tyger Hutchings' 'Portfolio', and a track the title of which mixed bluegrass terminology and British motorways. Given the events that were to follow in May 1969, a closing track called 'M1 Breakdown' would prove sadly ominous for a studio throwaway.

Turn Turn Turn Again

16 JANUARY, 1969
SOUND TECHNIQUES STUDIO, CHELSEA

As they entered their third year, Fairport were optimistic. 'Meet on the Ledge', which everyone had predicted would be a hit single, had got lost in the Christmas chart rush, but the band was not disheartened. Sandy Denny had turned out to be an asset, being not only a great vocalist but also a stunning songwriter; Richard Thompson's songwriting was also flourishing; and, despite relying on some chestnuts for radio sessions, they were in the process of abandoning their old 'West Coast' repertoire.

Within days of releasing their second album, they were hard at work on their third and their reputation was spreading. The mainstream music press, which had tended to either ignore or dismiss them, now found them a worthwhile subject for both features and gossip items: in October 1968, *Melody Maker*'s gossip columnist The Raver saw fit to list what Simon had received on his 18th birthday – 'a jigsaw, two pounds of bulb fibre, and a dust-pan and brush'!

Fairport began recording their third long player with two songs, one a cover of a very obscure and long Dylan number ('Percy's Song'), the other an original by Simon Nicol. As a title – nothing at all to do with the content of his song – Simon chose the headline from an early review of a Fairport gig, 'A Shattering Live Experience'.

SIMON: In the early days, we were very conscious of having had a speedy elevation from amateur status to professional. It's the way it happened back then: you'd be playing venues around London and someone would come along with an offer to pluck you from relative obscurity. It could be a manager (or someone calling himself a manager), or someone from a record company. In our case it was Joe Boyd, who was both.

48

It all happened very quickly. Suddenly we were doing lots of BBC Radio sessions. We were also getting consistent copy in the music press. Some of it was no more than 'Who's on Where'; some of it was news about the band; some of it was reviews. Because we were an unknown quantity to most of the reviewers, they were rather at a loss as to what to say about us. Hence the cursory reviews. Pete Frame did us a large favour by making us the main feature in what was intended to be the magazine of the new rock scene.

One of the reviews, early on, had picked up on the idea that we were, as a turn, 'A SHATTERING LIVE EXPERIENCE'. It stood out to me because it was the headline of the article; it wasn't just buried in the text. It was, obviously, a glowing review of a concert performance somewhere and at that point in the band's existence I had not ruled out the idea of songsmithery.

The phrase stuck in my head as something that might prove a starting point for a song. I cobbled together what I now feel is a very juvenile piece of work, and ended up using that as the title. In the end, it didn't apply to the band, but instead to an encounter of a romantic nature, which turned out to be 'a shattering live experience'.

A press report at the time suggested Simon's song was being considered as a potential single.

SIMON: I wouldn't set too much store by that. Having a hit single was important at the time. Everyone asked what your next single was going to be and responses could be pretty random. You never said, "I have no idea."

Singles were still at the heart of the record industry as the Sixties came to an end. Not even the increased sales and significance of albums had changed the attitude of the industry. Certain genres – significantly jazz and folk – were exempt from this way of thinking, but pop, rock, country and soul still had not reached the moment when, in Pete Townshend's words, they "liberated rock from the three-minute song". Singles were the only way to secure regular airplay on Radio 1, which was the only British radio station to play current pop music. However, airplay helped sales, and singles success often also secured an appearance on the BBC Television show

Top of the Pops – which was an exposure that for many acts proved to be career-changing.

RICHARD: It wasn't cool to admit it, but everyone secretly wanted to be on *Top of the Pops*.

Screened early enough in the evening to be accessible to even the youngest pop fans, the show (which started in 1964) was skilfully programmed to have a mass audience appeal. Because of its policy of only playing records going up the charts, each week it included the biggest names in pop, rising new stars, middle-of-the-road singers ('for the mums'), and go-go dancers and camera angles perilously low in the era of the mini-skirt ('for the dads').

SIMON: For most young people, watching *Top of the Pops* was a weekly ritual. Many of the people we knew from bands watched it, too. We all claimed to be doing it for a laugh – especially when someone we knew was appearing – but deep down, even the coolest players had a hankering.

RICHARD: Let's face it – if it was good enough for Hendrix, Cream, The Beatles, The Stones and Fleetwood Mac, who was really likely to decline?

The single was, therefore, hugely important, and yet bands had long been in the habit of recording album-only material. Radio 1 still predominantly played records that complied with its three-minute format slots. At least one record company adopted the policy of marking studio logs to indicate tracks that did not fit the singles mould: the letters NAS (not a single) could clearly be applied to Fairport's epic version of Dylan's modern tragic ballad, scheduled to be recorded the same day as Simon Nicol's single contender.

SANDY: There's no denying that having a hit was important. Ashley, in particular, always wanted the best for his band, and in the late Sixties that really meant having a hit record.

ASHLEY: A hit record increased your profile with both the record company and the public who, if nothing else, got to see you on *Top of the Pops* – not that that did us much good when it finally happened.

SIMON: Certainly Island Records liked its artists to have success in the singles chart. They turned a number of acts you might think of as album-based into hit-makers.

Island may have a reputation as the label that brought the bands of London's late Sixties underground scene to a wider public, but its roots were in Jamaica's reggae culture where the most important format was not the album but the seven-inch single – the one-sided seven-inch single at that. The first hit that Island created was Millie's 'My Boy Lollipop', which was then followed by a string of hits from The Spencer Davis Group.

SIMON: My not-very-good song might have been considered a single. I really can't remember, which alone tells you how significant the idea was. But so was every song we recorded that was under three minutes long. In the end, it didn't even make the album.

The fact that there is no record of a finished Island version of 'A Shattering Live Experience', together with its failure to appear on any expanded CD reissue, suggests the band may never have recorded it.

IAIN MATTHEWS: A lot of songs fell by the wayside so far as Fairport were concerned, when I left the band. That was when we were recording *Unhalfbricking*. Mainly, of course, they were the songs where I had sung lead. They wouldn't have been appropriate given I was no longer part of the group. I recorded some on my solo albums, and a lot of what might have been included came out eventually on the compilation of BBC sessions that Ashley put together.

Among the many cover versions of American songs featuring on *Heyday* is a live recording of 'A Shattering Live Experience'. That album also includes the BBC version of 'Percy's Song'. Dylan had recorded it for his third album, but it was not released at the time. Possibly based on the real experience of someone Dylan knew (though this is much debated and remains unconfirmed), the song uses the narrative structure of the traditional ballad (specifically 'The Two Sisters'). Dylan's version is long and can feel repetitious. The version on *Unhalfbricking*, on the other hand, uses an extended crescendo arrangement to mask the incessant refrain and highlight the narrative development.

The song begins with the most folkie of arrangements, *a capella* harmony vocals reminiscent of the Copper Family or, more recently, The Watersons or The Young Tradition. The recording features Iain Matthews' last appearance on a Fairport studio album: the layered harmonies are all the better for it. Iain's voice doubles Sandy's lead on the verse line, while the whole chorus remains on the refrain. As the song proceeds, instruments join the harmonious chorus. At first, a simple acoustic guitar and drums, then bass – a spare rhythm section. As the narrative progresses, Richard's electric dulcimer and lead guitar fill the sound out. Yet the dynamics are subtler than a developing crescendo: everything falls away, leaving just drums and dulcimer. From that moment on, after a sudden deep rolling explosion, Martin's drumming becomes richer and increasingly inventive, mirroring the growing, frustrated anger of the lyric.

It's an important recording, not least because it created a template for the way Fairport would approach traditional ballads later in the year. It's a restructuring of the song itself by means of an arrangement that expands and complements the meaning of the lyrics. As folk-rock became more and more their focus (and they were inventing the genre), they applied the technique of creating a setting for the songs based on electric instruments and a group of players, just as they had with this ballad. Over the decades, countless bands have used Fairport's template to create their own music based on traditional song. More significantly, Fairport's new approach would have a direct influence on many of the biggest names on the folk scene.

Most Dylan biographers agree that 'Percy's Song' was inspired by events surrounding a doorman by that name at a club where Dylan performed. Following an auto accident, Percy was given a severe sentence for causing the death of his passengers by reckless driving. Dylan's song omits two key facts in Percy's conviction: alcohol and possibly marijuana were involved, but no other vehicle. As they began their third album, Fairport could not have known that an incident on 11 May, 1969, would make the content of this song tragically and specifically relevant to them.

SIMON: Although we'd been playing 'Percy's Song' live for a while, the album featuring it wasn't even out. It was finished and mixed, but circumstances overtook events and the accident occurred before the release date. No doubt the irony flashed through everybody's brain in the months after the accident, but no one mentioned it. Perhaps political correctness has made us all more aware of, and responsive to, such things these days.

I suppose today one might go back and think about replacing the song, but that wasn't something we ever considered at the time. It was never raised by anyone else either. Also, today it is easier to replace a track or restructure an album even at that late a stage; back then, it was a much more complex process. We had lost our drummer (Martin); neither Richard nor Ashley were in a fit state physically to go back into the studio.

SANDY: I doubt if any of us would have been up to it mentally. Actually, the demands of replacing the song would have been more heartless than just leaving it as it was.

ASHLEY: At that point, we were in too much of a haze to even think clearly about whether Fairport should continue. Things were at the stage where it is the record company's decision as to whether or not one releases the album. I've never even considered our replacing the track. Including a recording without Martin would have been a terrible thing to do.

SIMON: The final factor would have been that we didn't have anything to replace it with anyway. It's a long song and would have required either something similarly epic or a couple of other songs to take its place. There was nothing else finished and in the can.

Unhalfbricking

Island
July 1969

SIDE 1:

'Genesis Hall'
'Si Tu Dois Partir'
'Autopsy'
'A Sailor's Life'

SIDE 2:

'Cajun Woman'
'Who Knows Where the
    Time Goes?'
'Percy's Song'
'Million Dollar Bash'

Given the regular changes in line-up that were a key factor in Fairport's early history, it might seem odd to single out any one release as a cusp album. However, the description fits *Unhalfbricking* well. It embodies the band's developing musical and lyrical styles, bringing exotic terms and places into the lexicon of British folk music.

Few who bought the album at the time were likely to have known what 'Cajun' meant. Even the biggest-selling pocket dictionary of the time offered as its prime definition: 'an American style of cooking which involves excessive use of hot spices'. Only those familiar with the precise details of organised squats and sit-ins in London would have got the point of the title 'Genesis Hall'. Even today, few realise that the building it celebrates is now a part of the footprint of the Centrepoint development, that it was a real place in London, or that the song's opening lines refer to the disquiet felt by Richard's policeman father, who found himself in the position of having to take shelters away from the homeless. Richard's use of the expression 'rides with your sheriffs' is more evocative of Robin Hood than the star-spangled lawmen of TV westerns. It conjures up Guy of Gisborne more than Wyatt Earp. Here was the first glimmer of Richard's potential – one of the finest modern writers of folk song, a key contributor to the folk repertoire. The song's chorus, 'helpless and slow / And you don't have anywhere to go', reflects a resignation, a fatalism, even a sense of inevitability that would be a key aspect of songs like 'Sloth', 'Night Comes In', and 'Dimming of the Day'. Regularly revived, 'Genesis Hall' would become a vital element in Fairport's post-1980 repertoire – they have so far released over half a dozen versions on live albums.

In total contrast, Richard's other song on *Unhalfbricking* ventures much further afield, not just south of the river but South of the Mason-Dixon line. At the time, Cajun music was virtually unknown in Britain which, while it had embraced other forms of American roots music as far back as the skiffle era – with New Orleans jazz, blues, old-timey and country being familiar to most music fans – more minority forms remained a closed book. Not many in this country had discovered the delights of Belton Richard, the Kershaw Brothers, or the Savoy Family. Much in the manner of Dylan's *The Basement Tapes*, which Fairport had certainly heard, and the newly released debut by The Band, Richard's 'Cajun Woman' embraced a rarer aspect of the rich musical heritage of the USA.

That Fairport were aware of *The Basement Tapes* is supported by one of the three Dylan tunes on this album coming from the 14-track demo then circulating among musicians in the UK. While it barely scratched the surface of a huge repository of music Dylan had created but not released, it had already proved a rich seam: among the songs covered and made popular by other artists were 'The Mighty Quinn', 'This Wheel's on Fire', 'You Ain't Goin' Nowhere', and 'I Shall Be Released'. Fairport opted to create a version of 'Million Dollar Bash'.

Though there is no earthly way Fairport could have been aware of it, each Dylan track they chose – and three Dylan songs is a pretty high quotient for an album with just eight songs – would have a singular resonance with events about to overtake Fairport.

The Basement Tapes had been created at the Big Pink, a rambling old house in upstate New York, by Dylan and The Band as he recovered from a motorcycle accident and reflected on his life and career before returning to his traditional roots on *John Wesley Harding*. Similarly, Fairport would find themselves living in each other's pockets in an artificial, isolated, but creatively conducive environment as they reflected upon their next step after a serious vehicle accident; opting for a direction which involved a completely fresh approach to the roots of traditional English music.

'Si Tu Dois Partir' was Manfred Mann's fairly recent hit 'If You Gotta Go, Go Now', in Gallic disguise. Musically, it could well have been from the same repertoire as Richard's 'Cajun Woman'. Though Dylan had recorded the former three times for release, aside from a brief, almost accidental appearance as a single in the Netherlands, his original version had remained unheard. Fairport wanted a lead fiddle and picked Dave Swarbrick as the ideal session man. As it turned out, he would prove perfect for the 'Sailor's Life' experiment. And although Dave was to become the key figure in shaping Fairport over the next ten years, he was hardly an obvious choice for a jokey, rough-hewn, sing-along in a cod-American-roots style.

While 'Percy's Song' benefits from one of Fairport's best-ever arrangements, inexorably building towards a catastrophic climax, neither of the other Dylan songs could be said to be musically tight or significantly arranged: the aim was to achieve the effect of an informal, in-the-studio sing-along and both did just that. Fairport were not the only group taking pains to suggest they didn't take themselves too seriously in the studio; other artists who included similar disposable delights were Cream, The Stones, The Kinks, Small Faces, The Who and The Beatles.

'Million Dollar Bash', with its ragged chorus of studio mates, would later acquire another level of significance for Fairport, Ashley Hutchings reviving it twice at Cropredy with rewritten words referring precisely to Fairport's history. Both performances happened to be on occasions when the Festival was being recorded for release; so the words gained currency among anyone who bought those Cropredy souvenir releases. They are part of an informal collection of songs in which Fairport musically updated its own history.

ASHLEY: The release of those rewritten versions is quite special to me because of the composer credit. I'd always wanted to see 'Dylan-stroke-Hutchings'.

SIMON: What you do in your own time is your own business.

Unhalfbricking – the Final Recording Session

9 APRIL, 1969
SOUND TECHNIQUES STUDIO, CHELSEA

When Sandy Denny stepped up to the microphone for a second attempt at recording one of her old songs, she knew that she had to create something special. They had decided not to use the version from the previous day, and with three other recordings of the song potentially about to become available – including one on which she had sung – it was crucial that Sandy get this just right.

Most rock bands have their 'classic' songs. Fairport's would have to include 'Matty Groves', 'Meet on the Ledge', 'Genesis Hall', 'John Gaudie' and, as it would turn out, this song.

SIMON: I clearly remember the first time I heard 'Who Knows Where the Times Goes?' It was just after Sandy had joined the band. I went to visit her flat in Gloucester Road. It was a sunny Saturday afternoon. The windows were open. She just sat there and sang me the song. It was a simple, understated performance; basically, she was asking, somewhat nervously, "What do you think of this?" I thought, "That's very nice. We'll have that one."

It is one of those perfect memories – hearing that song for the first time, sitting on her bed, just Sandy and her guitar. The song has remained very special since that day.

RICHARD: I heard that Judy Collins had recorded one of Sandy's songs. One day when I was visiting her flat, I asked her about it. She said something about its being a song I wouldn't have heard. Then she picked up her guitar and played it!

ASHLEY: Sandy seemed self-confident and brash, but she wasn't. She was actually quite fragile. Where that showed most was in her attitude to her songwriting. With Fairport's first line-up, I was used to having to encourage people to write. With Sandy, it was a matter of persuading her to show us things she'd written. I suspect a lot of wonderful Sandy songs remain unplayed and unheard because she was just too nervous to let them out into the world.

SIMON: She was actually quite slow at putting the song forward – perhaps because she'd already recorded it with The Strawbs. In any case, it missed out on her first album with Fairport, *What We Did on Our Holidays*, but it was certainly one of several highlights on *Unhalfbricking*. That was a strong album – Sandy's greatest song, three Dylan songs including our only hit single (he said with only a hint of irony), Richard's 'Genesis Hall' and, of course, 'A Sailor's Life'.

Sandy's reluctance to put the song forward for Fairport may have been because when she first recorded the song solo, in Copenhagen in July 1967, it was intended for inclusion on a new Strawbs' album *All Our Own Work*. For various reasons, however, that album didn't come out until 1973. But as far as Sandy was concerned, in late 1968, the Strawbs version of her song was simply awaiting release.

'Who Knows Where the Time Goes?' soon developed a life of its own, however, and when Sandy's demo version found its way to Judy Collins, she made it the title track of her 1968 album release.

Sandy's performance of 'Who Knows' with Fairport at a BBC recording session on 4 February, 1969 – the first since Iain Matthews' decision to leave the band – was to be the first of a great many recordings of the song. The session was broadcast on 9 February, 1968, as part of *Symonds on Sunday*, and Lonnie Donegan was listening. He was so impressed with 'Who Knows' that he recorded a version for his next album *Lonniepops: Lonnie Donegan Today* (1970), having released it as the B-side of a single ('My Lovely Juanita') before that, in 1969.

'Who Knows Where the Time Goes?' was the last track to be recorded for *Unhalfbricking*, and was also Martin Lamble's final recording session with Fairport. It remains his memorial.

JOE BOYD: I was convinced, that spring of 1969, that we had recorded Fairport's breakthrough album. They had become a great band and they knew it. No other British rock guitarist played with Richard's sophistication.

The title *Unhalfbricking* came from a word game called Ghosts that the band played to alleviate the boredom of long journeys to and from gigs. The idea was to add syllables or letters to an existing word, until a new word was created that could no longer be extended. This particular word was Sandy Denny's creation. Appropriately, it is her parents who feature on the cover, standing in front of a wall which might be described as representing the title – half-brick, half-fence. Beyond it is the band, lounging in the summer sunshine. They look like bystanders who have accidentally been caught in a family snapshot. The effect is enhanced by the fact that neither the band's name nor the album title appear on the cover: it is quite simply a 12 × 12 image of a quintessential English scene.

The title, though, has a sense of incompleteness implicit in both the negative 'un' and the diminishing 'half'. Iain Matthews left the band not long after recording had begun, taking with him the band's penchant for cover versions of little-known American recordings, less evident in their released official albums than in their setlists from the period, their choice of songs for numerous radio sessions, and the tracklist for their bootleg-that-became-official – *Heyday*.

While their first two albums had included guest musicians on back-up vocals, *Unhalfbricking* featured a guest playing an unmissable and crucial lead instrument. Dave Swarbrick's violin soon became the irreplaceable element of Fairport's sound, which had previously been dominated by Richard's guitar and Sandy's vocal. It was there after both of them had left the band – the element that would require a replacement when eventually the band decided to continue working without Swarb.

By the time *Unhalfbricking* was finished, the guest fiddle player was considering an offer to join the band full-time. His credentials doubled the folk influence of Sandy Denny. As work on the album was completed, Fairport Convention were faced with a Robert Frost-like choice of direction. They could either continue with an eclectic approach, incorporating whatever styles and genres they chose; or, with the talent now being displayed by the band's songwriters, they could elect to become an act which featured entirely self-penned material; *or*, they could focus on cover versions of unfamiliar material, which had been a Fairport USP up to this point.

Certainly, the tracks on their third album embraced a surprising range of musical approaches – folk, rock, novelty, comedy, protest, ballad (in both musical definitions of the term), progressive (a very new definition in music's lexicon), and pop.

Like many of their contemporaries, they too had the option of becoming a band that maintained its profile through regular chart appearances. *Unhalfbricking* was, after all, the LP that included Fairport's only hit. And then there was the option of further developing their highly original approach to English folk song.

Ultimately, for reasons not obvious at the time, they would opt for the road less travelled.

Si Tu Dois Partir

This is the recording by which Fairport are most widely known, thanks to the fact that it is their only chart hit (albeit a small one, peaking at 21 in the UK charts). It led to their notable *TOTP* appearance on 14 August, 1969. Subsequently, the song has represented Fairport on a number of compilations – rock hits of the later Sixties, one-hit wonders, folk-rock classics and, most widely, cover versions of Dylan songs. Many of these factors led to the song being the *only* Fairport track available in the libraries of local British radio stations when the band resumed touring in the mid-Eighties and turned to the new network of stations for publicity.

PEGGY: It could get frustrating, especially as we were careful to send our new stuff out to stations. With a few exceptions, they were only interested in hits, so an album on an independent label from a folk-rock group wouldn't get much of a look-in.

SIMON: Of course, by that point, I was the only person in the band who had had anything to do with the recording. Even then, it was far from typical.

Fairport would record a cover version in 2004, having performed the song on their Winter Tour for a couple of years. That new recording found Fairport sampling themselves in order to recreate the serendipitous percussion break on the original from 35 years ago. Briefly, drummer Martin Lamble, who had died a couple of months before the original single had been released in 1969, was reinstated as a working member of Fairport Convention. It is ironic that the track should have come to represent Fairport. At the time, and indeed at any point in the band's career, it was so left-field as to be almost irrelevant.

ASHLEY: When Island decided to release 'Si Tu Dois Partir', we were already thinking about our new direction. We were engrossed in developing British folk-rock. Without being immodest, it's fair to say we were in the process of creating an album that has since come to be regarded as a classic. As a result, when the single charted and we were asked to be on *Top of the Pops*, we didn't take it entirely seriously.

The band that appeared on screen that Thursday night in 1969, was not a Fairport that their fans would have recognised. Dave Mattacks was making his debut with them, miming on a washboard to the percussion of his late predecessor. Roadie Steve Sparks sat stage left, closest to the camera, playing a triangle (which Trevor Lucas had played on the recording). Richard Thompson sat centre stage with vocal mic, playing the melodeon. Dave Swarbrick hunched stage right behind Sandy, who stood in the centre with a hand-held mic. Swarbrick would have been the most familiar face to TV viewers, thanks to several television appearances with the Ian Campbell Folk Group and Martin Carthy. Ashley dug out 'the onion', the huge Perspex double bass filled with fairy lights that had appeared on the band's very first publicity shot. Having mimed this with a legitimate bow at the rehearsal, for the recording he stroked the strings with a baguette. This was only part of the Gallic flavour of the performance – there were striped shirts, berets, and onion strings in abundance.

ASHLEY: We tried to be eccentric and just came across as being silly, and looked as if we were trying too hard. Anyone who already knew the band and saw that appearance was probably confused – it was a long way from our normal style, and at least three people on screen would not have been known to them.

The video recording of Fairport's appearance was unfortunately wiped, and only a few photographs of the event exist, one of which graced the cover of the 'very semi-official' bootleg *A Chronicle of Sorts* (1995). Unfortunately, though, they had all been taken during the run-through: no photography was permitted during the actual recording of BBC television programmes.

SANDY: Swarb and I had done some telly in the past and were pretty cool about it. The rest of the group were very nervous. Between the rehearsal and the recording, as we waited in the dressing room, people were coming up with ideas on how to make our 'big chance' more memorable.

So Fairport, a band currently masterminding a revolution in rock music, came across as little more than a novelty act. To be fair, the recording itself had been something of a joke – 'a folkie, Cajun Skiffle Dylan cover in classroom French' – as rock writer Chris Welch succinctly described it. Its story begins with a playful exchange between Sandy and members of their regular audience at a gig.

RICHARD: Middle Earth was the place. Sandy enjoyed talking to the audience… not making announcements through the PA but actually holding two-way conversations. It was all quite informal back then. One night, the topic of Dylan in French came up and a group of two or three French speakers contributed to the translation after the set.

SIMON: "Translation" is probably a little generous. It was an approximation in very much O-Level-standard French. It was a joke, which simply got carried on and made it to the studio.

SANDY: The song's melody was well-known because it had been a big hit for Manfred Mann. People liked it – for the time, it was quite risqué. More importantly, the words were relatively simple and so within the French vocabulary of all involved. *N'est-ce pas?*

ASHLEY: It says a lot about Fairport in 1969. We were going through so many changes. It is natural and right to focus on the accident, but that tends to overshadow the fact that lots of organic changes were happening anyway – American songs disappearing from the repertoire; Richard emerging as a songwriter; Sandy bringing in her own thing. Then you had the whole folk element, too. So you had something playful and fairly trivial like 'Si Tu Dois Partir' on the one hand, and on the other the first experiments with full-blown folk-rock in the shape of 'A Sailor's Life'. The great thing was that both those aspects could make it as far as the studio and on to vinyl – on the same record!

Fairport had aimed for a different sound on their recording of the Dylan song. Richard had played accordion; Martin Lamble had applied his drumsticks to the back of a stack of plastic chairs, which had toppled as if on cue (and exactly on the beat) at the end of his percussion break; Simon had played fiddle ("very uncertainly and low in the mix") on previous Fairport recordings, but because the fiddle was to have a greater prominence, Dave Swarbrick had been brought in. It would not be stretching things too far to say that without this novelty track, Fairport may not have made it far into the Seventies, when Swarb was to become the driving force behind the band.

The Flying Burrito Brothers recorded their breakneck version of 'If You Gotta Go' around the same time as Fairport, and the two bands have a lot in common: Pete Frame, who developed his 'rock family tree' specifically to chronicle the vagaries of Fairport's many line-ups, also applied the approach to documenting the history of The Burritos and the band from which they sprang, The Byrds; and as Fairport were taking English folk music and fusing it with electric rock, the Burritos were doing the same with American country music.

The two bands' paths would cross on a number of occasions. When Fairport played the Troubadour in Los Angeles, supporting Rick Nelson in 1970, his band included several Burritos' members (his set included his version of 'If You Gotta Go'); and when Richard Thompson's friend Marc Ellington recorded the album *Rains/Reins of Changes* in 1971, his backing band consisted of members of Fairport (RT, Peggy, DM, Sandy, Iain Matthews, plus Gerry Conway and Trevor Lucas who had yet to become full-time Fairport members) and the Burritos' Sneaky Pete Kleinow and Chris Hillman.

SANDY: Marc Ellington made his album at the same time as I was recording *Sandy*. We used the same backing musicians. It was an astounding set of players.

PEGGY: When Beth Nielsen Chapman appeared at Cropredy, she wanted to do 'Bushes and Briars' from that album. I'd always thought the amazing solo was Richard with Sneaky Pete on pedal steel, so I asked P J Wright to come and play with us on that number. Richard asked what he was there for. When I explained, Richard just said, "Oh no – that solo's all me. I can do it live." It shows what an unbelievably good player he is.

Like most bands of the era, Fairport released a number of singles in the course of the late Sixties and early Seventies. Fans, their record company, reviewers and disc jockeys happily predicted chart success for songs like 'Meet on the Ledge' and 'Now Be Thankful', only to be consistently proven wrong. The band's genre-defying, quasi-French version of an abandoned Dylan song remains their only entry in the *Guinness Book of Hit Singles*.

In the process of recording *Unhalfbricking*, Fairport continued to gig most nights, and when they weren't playing live they were recording sessions for the BBC. Nights off were certainly a luxury. So much for their original scheme – not yet two years old – of working just three nights a week. The music press regularly kept fans up to date with events surrounding the band. Island felt confident that 'Si Tu Dois Partir' would be a hit, albeit one with a lot of novelty appeal, and that this would further extend the band's reputation. But what might have been will always remain a matter of conjecture. The events that occurred around midnight on 11 May, 1969, changed the future for Fairport, forever.

11 MAY, 1969
MOTHERS
HIGH STREET, ERDINGTON, BIRMINGHAM

That night, Fairport had played their second booking at the venue in just over a month.

SIMON: We were travelling back from a gig at Mothers in Birmingham. It was a venue we played quite regularly. Eclection, the band which included Sandy's boyfriend Trevor Lucas, was also playing in Birmingham, and she travelled back to London with him, so wasn't in the van with the rest of us.

Gary Boyle, Eclection's guitarist and today one of the world's most respected jazz players, offered the pair a lift back to London in his car, which was a more comfortable option than the front seat of a poorly heated Ford Transit.

GARY BOYLE: Trevor and Sandy snuggled up on the back seat so

I just kept my eyes on the road and ignored them. Being capable of maintaining a higher speed, we were a fair way further down the road than Fairport. I dropped them off in London and headed back to my own pad. Next day, I got a phone call telling me what had happened to Fairport. There was a real sense of community in bands at the time, and we all felt moved by it. In a way, it felt like an accident that had been waiting to happen to someone.

SIMON: Nowadays there is a greater awareness of the need for safety, but back then it was more free and easy. This was before the days of Health and Safety, when if you wanted to start putting on gigs you could, and it was relatively easy to find people willing, indeed eager, to play and, equally importantly, to come and listen. Every college would have a Friday night and a Saturday night gig. Every pub with a big enough room above or to the side would put live music on – there had been folk and jazz clubs for years, but the late Sixties added rock bands to that menu; in lots of places, it was every night. You can see that when you look at the gigs pages of old copies of *Melody Maker*: a venue would take out an ad to list what was on every night of the week.

SANDY: There were lots and lots of bands travelling up and down the country. Lots. We all knew each other and you'd bump into people at motorway service stations.

The Blue Boar Services at Watford Gap was a small, family-run business that had become famous after *Rave* magazine published an article citing the number of rock acts that stopped there. It was named after the petrol station the family had run nearby since the late Forties, but differed from many motorway services in that it had a transport café as well as the usual self-service cafeteria and restaurant. *Rave* used the American term 'truck-stop' to describe it. It was a preferred stop-off point for lorry drivers heading north, Oxford students trying to thumb a lift, bands returning from gigs or TV work in the Midlands, and bikers taking the motorway circuit out of London.

These days, the same service area is a useful reference point for M1 travellers on the lookout for the exit to head west to Cropredy.

SANDY: My song 'No End' began as something about those early days with Fairport, being a band on the road. Not on tour, which is a different and more organised thing: that's something that came later. It was all new to me. On the folk scene, you'd go somewhere to play and you could go by public transport because all you had to take with you was your instrument. Bert Jansch famously didn't even bother with that – he just borrowed one when he got there. Playing a folk club is very unpressured, almost a social event. Afterwards, you can always find a floor to crash on or someone will offer you a bed for the night – occasionally, of course, it was their bed so you had to be careful. Next day, you could sleep in, have a late breakfast, and head off home or to wherever your next booking was. All my time with Fairport, I kind of felt I was observing a very different process, from the outside. I didn't have to think about instruments and equipment, I just had to get there and sing. To be honest, I've never really been much of a band person.

SIMON: Everything was relatively cheaper: you could pay 25 quid and get a van that worked – at least some of the time. Of course, this was before the days of seat belt regulations and MOT. Add to that a road system that was pretty primitive and the fact that many of the vehicles were not in the best state of repair; it was an accident waiting to happen.

SANDY: We were young, and sometimes, the young are less careful than they should be. People were often tired: they'd have played a concert somewhere, having travelled from London, then packed everything up and headed back. It was like that night after night. Sometimes people were not in a fit state to be driving for other reasons, like drink or drugs or emotional upset. Very often, they were in some rust bucket they'd bought cheap and didn't maintain properly.

SIMON: The Fairport van was a heavy-duty Transit built for neither comfort nor speed. It wasn't shall-we-say the most road-worthy of vehicles. Harvey Bramham, our roadie, was driving and was so tired he fell asleep at the wheel. He had complained about feeling unwell, and we had stopped for a while at Watford Gap for some fresh air. I had a headache and went to sleep in the back of the van, lying down beside the equipment. That's the last thing I remember before the accident.

Just north of Scratchwood Services, as the vehicle veered across the road, Richard Thompson tried to grab the wheel. The Transit hit the side barrier and somersaulted down an embankment.

SIMON: After the crash, I was the only one left inside the vehicle. That was the reason I escaped relatively uninjured. In fact, there was nothing left in the vehicle apart from me. That was the first thing that struck me when I came to. Everyone else had gone out either through the doors or windows. The PA and all the kit had gone out through the back doors. I woke up as the van was somersaulting. Somehow or other, I avoided being ejected. As a result, I was only concussed and had a few bits of glass in me, but that was all.

ASHLEY: We were scattered all over the field. Richard was out cold, I think. My face was bleeding so badly I couldn't see.

In a field beside the M1 lay the remnants of the band and their guitars, drums, and amplifiers, scattered everywhere. Harvey was in a daze, staggering around. Richard lay some distance away. Ashley tried to figure out what had happened, too shocked to realise the severity of his own injuries. There were two others, now very still. Jeannie Franklyn who was Richard's girlfriend, and Martin Lamble who almost exactly two years prior to that had put himself forward as Fairport's drummer. Both were dead.

Jeannie Franklyn was a clothes designer. Her flamboyant fashions appealed to the peacock mentality of rock's more image-conscious acts, and her designs had been bought by members of Jefferson Airplane and The Doors as well as Jimi Hendrix and Eric Clapton. An American who became a significant King's Road figure, she was known as Jeannie the Tailor. Jack Bruce dedicated his first album, *Songs for a Tailor*, to her. Among the British acts to be attracted to her colourful costumery were The Young Tradition and Peter Bellamy. A member of that trio had nicknamed her Lady Franklyn, after the folksong correctly known as 'Lady Franklin's Lament', though sometimes referred to as 'Lord Franklin'.

SIMON: Martin Lamble will always be 19 in my mind. I simply cannot bring him up to date, or in any way imagine what might have been if circumstances had been different. I have no idea where he might have been today, or even whether he would have remained a musician. I don't know whether we would have remained working together, or for how long.

Obviously it could have been any one of us that died in the crash. For someone of that age to die so unnecessarily is a real tragedy. When it's someone you could change places with, it does bring home just how fragile life is. Although I had lost my Dad when I was 14, losing a contemporary just a few years later was my first true awareness of my own mortality.

Martin's playing on *Unhalfbricking* demonstrates a wit and inventiveness that belie his age. His image is caught forever in semi-silhouette, laughing at the breakfast table with the rest of the band, on the rear of the album sleeve.

ASHLEY: Martin was a great drummer but, no pun intended, unconventional. It's frightening when one listens to the recordings he did with Fairport and you remember how young he was and how little experience he had had as a drummer. In some ways he was making it up as he went along, and traditional concerns like having to be the one that kept time didn't necessarily impact on his playing.

Unhalfbricking received lavish praise upon its release. John Peel said, "It is an LP that you will want to hear daily for a very long time." Fairport were more and more in demand on the live circuit and their bookings diary was rapidly filling – many of the gigs that they were forced to cancel because of the accident became tribute or benefit nights for the band.

SUNDAY 25 MAY, 1969
THE ROUNDHOUSE, LONDON

A fortnight after the accident, one of the capital's most prestigious rock venues hosted a night paying tribute to Martin Lamble and Fairport. Artists appearing included Pink Floyd, The Pretty Things,

Family, Eclection, Blossom Toes, The Deviants, John and Beverley Martyn, and Martin Carthy and Dave Swarbrick. All the performers appeared for free, and all proceeds were donated to Fairport. Though they were unable to appear themselves, the event was organised by Soft Machine (the band with which Ric Sanders would first perform professionally in the mid-Seventies).

Other acts who played benefit gigs or supported Fairport in other ways include The Beatles, The Stones, Jethro Tull and The Kinks. Perhaps the most high-profile memorial to Martin is the fact that the accident was one of the incidents cited by name in Parliament when it was debating the importance of making the wearing of seat belts compulsory.

At the time, Fairport's manager, Joe Boyd, was in the final stages of negotiating their first American tour, which would have taken in The Fillmore and allowed Fairport to make their US debut at the Newport Folk Festival. Since he was in the States concluding those negotiations, it was left to Anthea Joseph at the Witchseason offices to issue the official statement, which read: 'Those poor children. We are all in a state of shock because this tragedy is so unbelievable.'

Everything was on hold. The question for Fairport was clearly: "What next?" Should they give up, or should they try to pick up the pieces and carry on?

SANDY: I remember someone coming round to tell me what had happened. They didn't want me to find out by seeing it in the papers. I was shocked, of course. I didn't really know how to deal with it. Martin's death was a tragedy. He was probably the member of the band I'd got to know least – I think he may have been a bit scared of me. I just wanted to get away from it. Joe Boyd suggested going to America.

Amid a busy schedule of gigs, radio sessions, and album recording, Sandy had continued to play solo gigs after joining Fairport. She asked to not be billed as 'Sandy Denny of Fairport Convention' when appearing solo.

SANDY: I love to play in front of an audience. There is no better feeling. Nobody knew what would happen to Fairport – and I'd only been in the group for something like a year. I didn't have the same kind of loyalty to Fairport as did its other

69

members. Iain had already decided to leave and work on his solo career. In all that uncertainty, naturally I was prepared to do some work in America.

SIMON: I went to see Ashley in hospital. He'd had his face fairly well broken; his cheekbone and his forehead were shattered. He looked pretty hideous after they put him together. Facial wounds are very prone to exaggerated swellings and there's no denying his were pretty severe. That's one of the reasons they don't give people in that situation mirrors.

   I was totally shocked when I saw him. I remember feeling physically sick. It was an absolute shock to see someone I regarded as a kind of mentor in such a state. Equally, to see how quickly both he and Richard healed was also astonishing. That healing was physical, of course. There were deeper scars for all of us.

The accident received coverage in the music press, naturally, but also in national papers. Radio 1's *Newsbeat* led with the story.

SIMON: The shock of a big crash touched more people directly…the bands, of course, and the concert organisers, but also parents who were concerned about their teenage sons and daughters. The thing about Fairport was that we hadn't reached a level of fame that would make us seem different from the thousands of kids, amateurs and professionals alike, who were risking their lives every time they went out to play. It was inevitable that something like that would happen. As it turned out, it was us that it happened to. It was symptomatic of the high-risk enterprise we were all involved in.

In the immediate aftermath of the accident, disc jockeys in clubs and bands on stage paid tribute to Fairport and empathised with their loss. I was in the String o'Beads in Bradford and distinctly remember the DJ taking a break from playing his imported rock singles before introducing that night's live guest – The Crazy World of Arthur Brown. He told us what had happened to Fairport and asked us for a minute's silence. Clubbers, many of us in an enhanced state of giddiness, suddenly stopped, stood still, and were silent. Those of us who had been to see Fairport at their Bradford gig exchanged incredulous glances. Then, as the minute ended, the strains of 'Meet on the Ledge' came through the speakers. Tears flowed and we joined the chorus. As we sang, Arthur Brown came on stage, took up the refrain, and encouraged us to continue to sing as the record faded away.

Before bringing his band on, he told us that several members of Fairport were still in hospital. He added that he hoped they would be able to find a way to carry on.

SIMON: After the accident, no one put any pressure on us. I am still grateful for that. The record company and the management company were both very sympathetic to us as individuals. We were their wounded charges and I would say there was a degree of responsibility being felt. Joe Boyd and Anthea Joseph couldn't have been kinder to us or less demanding. They said, "Just do what you need to do, and we'll decide what to do about the band when you've all got yourselves recovered and Martin has been safely laid to rest."

When we decided that we would carry on, they were encouraging, but they never pushed for that to happen. In a way, everyone, including the band, was surprised when we finally made our decision.

However, whatever happened, there was some unfinished business – *Unhalfbricking* was completed and awaiting the final stages of its production.

SIMON: I was involved in the mastering of the album, which took place at a studio in LA. I was over there as part of the recuperation process, getting over the accident. I had very little in the way of physical injury, so I was able to take a break. Joe Boyd flew me over to Los Angeles. I went along to the mastering suite and heard the record in its finished form right the way through for the first time. It was surreal: I was in a strange place, extremely American – listening to something fundamentally English. It was a tentative step on the road that eventually saw me working as both performer and producer with the band.

Simon may have escaped the potential inquisition of the press and the public in the UK, but his experience in America, which he was visiting for the first time, was lonely and alienating.

SIMON: There was the strangeness of hearing Martin play in the knowledge he was no longer with us. Then as now, I had a vivid mental image of him in the drum booth playing a stack of chairs. Because of the accident, the rest of the band were not there to hear it with me either. It was a solitary experience. We did not know what was going to happen, how we would be together, whether we would play music together again. Everyone had their own decision to make, and most were not in a state to do so.

SANDY: I needed to get away. I wanted to avoid the questions from friends and from the music press. I didn't want to become Fairport's spokesperson. So I went to America.

SIMON: Sandy, Richard and I appeared together on stage at The Troubador in LA – it was billed as a Sandy gig with us accompanying her. She could have decided to leave the band at that point and simply resume her solo career: the fact that she did a couple of solo appearances may have been a catalyst in our decision to carry on before we lost her.

SANDY: Describing it coldly now makes it sound like emotional blackmail, but it certainly wasn't. They just made it clear that if I left, Fairport couldn't play any more. They'd already been through that when I joined. Most of the old repertoire from the first album had been dumped in favour of new material. If I left, history would repeat itself.

Sandy's joining had coincided with the band's move to a new label, and Island Records, two albums in, would be less than delighted to have a band incapable of properly representing their most recent product. Little did they realise this was to become 'normal' for Fairport. In all their time with Island, the band released only two albums with the same line-up.

ASHLEY: I was well-known in pre-Fairport days for getting bands together. There were several names we used regularly

– Dr K's Blues Band, The Ethnic Shuffle Orchestra and so on – but they were more an indication of the sound you could expect to hear rather than the line-up on stage. Fairport were intended to be the first band with a permanent line-up: as it turned out, they seemed to inherit that shifting sands approach to being a band. You know, the dunes may be different, the sand may have moved, but it's still the Sahara.

The start of the Seventies would see a traumatic fragmentation of Fairport. Ashley, Sandy, and Richard held their positions – like loyal troops at a threatened outpost – until things stabilised but, whether they knew it or not, they were biding their time.

ASHLEY: Richard had lost his girlfriend. When people write or talk about Fairport's history, they naturally discuss the accident. They always remember the fact that Martin died. A lot of people overlook Jeannie's death because she wasn't part of the band, but she was an enormous loss.

The two Richard Thompson originals which found their way on to *Liege & Lief*, Fairport's next album ('Farewell, Farewell' and 'Crazy Man Michael'), are about coping with loss and the burden of guilt and responsibility. The first clearly makes reference to Jeannie with lines about never cutting the cloth.

CHRIS: 'Farewell, Farewell' was the most surprising choice to come out of the poll for songs to record for *By Popular Request* (2012). I think for Simon in particular, it was still painful.

SIMON: 'Farewell, Farewell' is still raw and painful. Despite all the songs we have revived over the years, that is one Fairport have avoided. I don't think Richard has ever done it either.

It took 33 years before, by popular request, they returned to the song on the album recorded to mark their 45th anniversary.

SIMON: That was a surprise. Not because it's not a great song – it is, but because it shows how Fairport's fans remember things. Outside a couple of Cropredy performances, it was a song we hadn't done since 1969.

PEGGY: Chris came up with a great arrangement of the song which gave us a different approach.

With absolute respect for both the tone and the layered meaning of the song, Chris took the bold step of having it begin with *a capella* harmonised vocals – never an approach associated with Fairport – and then used a flute accompaniment to set it apart from the distinctive violin part which enhanced the original.

SIMON: The body can recover from physical damage over time; mental hurt is less obvious and less readily repaired. That is the thing to remember. The trauma of the crash and discovering that Martin and Jeannie hadn't made it created scars of a different kind – ones which are in many ways far more permanent. It's probably true to say that no one who was in that crash has ever fully recovered from it.

We were all lucky. Young human bodies are incredibly resilient and robust. Months later, you wouldn't have known that anything untoward had happened to us – at least not from outward appearances. So, if you survive the incident, your body will heal very well – as, of course, did the band.

JOE BOYD: For a band to get the kind of publicity that Fairport had received, they'd normally have had to do something horrendous. The last big music business story in the papers at the time had been The Stones' drugs bust, for example. Everything that was being written about Fairport was totally sympathetic.

Even when Harvey Bramham was sent to prison for causing death by careless driving, the papers did not seize the opportunity to resurrect the story with a negative twist.

JOE BOYD: I am sure the band were aware that they were in the public eye, but the only way that influenced them was in the knowledge that they would have to reach a quick decision. Initially it was as simple as, "Do we carry on or not?" If they had decided not to, Island would probably still have released the album and that would have been the end of things. They decided to carry on. When they then came to the difficult, detailed part of *how* to carry on, they made decisions which permanently affected the face of rock music.

That might sound like a grand statement, but it's true. Fairport had received some coverage prior to the accident, but it had been half-hearted. John Peel used his influence to persuade *Disc and Music Echo* to feature Fairport in one of their band profile questionnaires. Most of the questions were pretty banal – age, favourite food, current rave, instruments played. Fairport's band profile was the last thing to be published about them before the accident. In the section labelled 'previous occupation', Fairport had an interesting set of answers – stained-glass designer, nurse, printer, cinema projectionist. Martin Lamble had written simply, 'child'.

ASHLEY: The album was finished and our American record company A&M were taking a serious interest in the band. It was a disorientating experience for Simon, but I think he was the only person in the group who was emotionally up to the task at the time.

The album had strong links to the States – enough in fact to make A&M get behind it. They changed the cover to a curious antique image of elephants and circus performers, presumably with the idea that it was more in keeping with the artwork used by West Coast bands.

Joe Boyd was still in negotiations with A&M at the time of the release, and having three members of the band with him was a decided advantage.

JOE BOYD: It was a very strange time… stranger than you could imagine. Any decision about the future of Fairport would have been difficult. They were young and still pretty shy, lacking in confidence. They had always relied on Ashley to make decisions and negotiate on behalf of the band. He was very much their leader. You might have expected Sandy, as the group's singer, to take on that role, but at the time she was very clearly unwilling to do so. I believe, if she had, things might have turned out differently.

SIMON: Even with a finished album released, we had to decide first whether the band could continue…not just whether we were able to but whether we *wanted* to. Swarb had already been asked whether he would like to join, but hadn't yet played live with us at that point.

SANDY: I know there was generally a feeling among the boys in the band that Fairport should continue. I discussed it with various friends outside the band. I was actually very slow coming to a final decision. I don't think to this day anyone in Fairport realises how late in the day I made my final decision.

I considered joining Eclection who were having their own problems at the time. The main thing in favour of that was being able to be with Trevor. I think it was Anne Briggs who finally said I ought to carry on. She said, "You have to. Those boys need you. They'd be lost without you."

SWARB: When they put to me the idea of my joining the band, someone asked "Do you sing?" When you've worked with Iain and Lorna and Martin, that's not something you actually think about. Sandy at that point was very obviously Fairport's lead vocalist. Simon used to make the joke, given the band's reputation of changing line-ups, of referring to her as "the ir-replaceable Sandy Denny".

SANDY: Actually, it wasn't that. They could always get a new singer. They could have got someone else. It was more the point that Annie felt they needed looking after, someone to mother them. It was very typical of Annie's way of thinking. It was also very persuasive.

The most difficult thing to deal with, if Fairport were to continue, was the matter of finding a new drummer.

ASHLEY: We chose someone who was almost the polar oppo-site of Martin. But holding auditions, which are not pleas-ant at the best of times, could hardly have taken place under worse conditions.

Dave Mattacks had been keeping strict tempo with ballroom dance bands for the preceding couple of years and was looking for a change of direction. Fairport Convention were an unknown quantity to him, and he may not even have been aware of the precise reason they were auditioning for a new drummer. In 1997, when the band was celebrating its 30th anniversary, Fairport invited fans to send in their memories of 'the first time I saw Fairport'. DM wrote, as part of his programme notes, 'The first time I saw them – Simon, Richard, and Ashley, actually – was in the back-room of a pub in Chiswick mid-'69. I was auditioning to join; I got the job.'

DM's assimilation into Fairport was made somewhat smoother by several factors. In effect, he and Swarb were joining the band together; and Fairport, as part of their recovery process, were about to go into an intense period of rehearsal. Old material was dropped, which meant that Dave did not have the task of learning Martin's old drum parts – apart from 'Si Tu Dois Partir' for the *Top of the Pops* appearance.

Unhalfbricking – Release

Unhalfbricking was released at the end of July 1969. It went straight into the LP charts, where it stayed for eight weeks, peaking at number six. Above it, in the NME album [LP] chart of 30 August, 1969, were the soundtrack to *2001: A Space Odyssey*, two country albums (Jim Reeves' *According to My Heart* and *Johnny Cash at San Quentin*), *From Elvis in Memphis* and, at number one for the fourth of its six weeks, *Stand Up* by Jethro Tull – a band that would over time contain the occasional membership of a large percentage of Fairport's later line-ups.

ASHLEY: If you look at Fairport's diary, you'll see that we did very little to promote *Unhalfbricking*. There was some radio work, but that was as much a way of earning some money. Certainly, there were no live gigs where we featured 'tracks from our latest LP'.

At times of crisis, it is a natural tendency to seek the security of the familiar, to return to one's roots. A lot of bands did that at the end of the Sixties. Fairport did it more extremely than most.

RICHARD: In the Sixties, you could hear any kind of music

on most nights in London. The London scene was very eclectic – so someone would listen to folk music alongside
everything else that was going on – blues, pop, underground,
strange things from America's West Coast, traditional and
modern jazz, jug band music. Folk music was part of all that.
Someone might be in a folk club one night who had been
at Middle Earth the night before and on the following night
was dancing to Motown in a discotheque or listening to John
Mayall at The 100 Club.

Most cities in the late Sixties had a thriving music scene, with different clubs offering a wide range of music in the course of a week. In
London, there were rock clubs like Middle Earth and UFO. The 100
Club in Oxford Street had been around since 1942 and prided itself
on its open-minded music policy that embraced jazz, blues, rock
and folk. The Marquee Club had been providing a home for blues
and guitar-based rock since its opening night in 1964 which featured The Yardbirds, Long John Baldry and Sonny Boy Williamson.
Folk was particularly well-catered for; a leaflet called 'Tradition
by Tube' from 1969 lists over a hundred venues accessible via the
Underground – The Troubador and Cecil Sharp House head the list
which also takes in Bungies, Les Cousins, The Black Bull (Barnet),
The Partisan (Soho), The Marquis (Paddington), The Empress of
Russia, The Fox (Islington), Dingles, The Herga, The Dungeon at
Tower Bridge, The Half Moon in Putney, The Enterprise (Chalk
Farm), Peanuts in Liverpool Street (a hotbed of CND activity), and
The Brentwood Castle. Many of these clubs advertised alongside
rock venues in the emerging underground press.

RICHARD: Although Fairport had played on the underground
    rock scene, where we would have heard people like Hendrix
    or the Floyd, most of us would go and listen to other kinds of
    music. On a night when we weren't playing, you might have
    spotted Simon, Ashley or me in a folk club or a jazz club or
    listening to a visiting blues player. We took in a lot of influ-
    ences and if you look at those early albums, you can easily
    spot influences. 'Cajun Woman', for example, has pretty
    transparent musical roots.

Sandy and Swarb had both come to Fairport via the folk scene.

Ashley, typically, plunged headlong into the pool of tradition and began a rapid course of self-education. Richard's connection to the tradition went deeper.

RICHARD: My songs have a lot to do with traditional lyrics. My father was Scottish and loved music. He had jazz records, so I heard great guitarists like Django Reinhardt and Les Paul, but there was also traditional music. I grew up with that, reading border ballads or the songs of Robbie Burns, hearing Scottish folk songs. When I started to write, that folk background came out in the way I wrote. It wasn't deliberate, it just happened. A lot of folk songs are about tragedy: look at a song like 'Matty Groves' – a plotline Shakespeare would have been proud of. If you look at Scottish folk music, a lot of it deals with loss in different forms.

At the point where, in terms of the accepted measure of commercial success in rock and pop, Fairport Convention were at their most successful, they had moved on from the music that put them in the charts. While the album and single made their nominal dent in the charts, Fairport were closeted away in idyllic Hampshire preparing *Liege & Lief*, which would redefine them as the 'world's great folk-rock band'. At the same time, Fairport played a small number of gigs.

SANDY: We were playing *Liege & Lief*, but we did very few gigs. Mainly we played at places we knew well, places we felt comfortable in.

ASHLEY: Obviously there were gigs which had to be cancelled after the accident. There were places that were particularly supportive. Going back when we were able to was a way of saying thank you to people for their support.

14 OCTOBER, 1969
CIVIC HALL, DUNSTABLE

One of the select gigs that Fairport decided to play was a benefit concert. In April 1969, *ZigZag* had been launched as an alternative music publication promising 'depth and insight' and a guarantee to cover bands that mainstream music papers like *Melody Maker* and *NME* tended not to feature. It described itself as 'The Rock Magazine', but its first issue had Sandy on the cover and a major article about Fairport as its main feature. Back in 1969, when *ZigZag* first appeared, there was nothing like it. At two shillings an issue, it was not a cheap read and, despite its good intentions and high quality music journalism, by October it was struggling.

PETE FRAME: Without the concert that Fairport played in October 1969, the magazine would certainly have folded and I would have gone back to my day job.

ASHLEY: We owed a debt of gratitude to everyone who had supported us that summer. We set out with the intention of repaying it. Making Fairport continue was one way. The *ZigZag* benefit was probably the most tangible.

Having played Dunstable on 14 October, the band travelled up to Glasgow for a gig at Green's Playhouse the following day, before returning direct to London to begin work on the LP. Appetites were whetted. Much had been promised. Finally the time had arrived to start recording.

CHAPTER THREE

Liege & Lief

This Fairport album stands out as their defining achievement. *Melody Maker*, *Rolling Stone*, *Mojo*, *Uncut*, and *Q* have included it in their lists of essential albums, as have many folk magazines including *Folk Roots*, *Living Tradition*, *Sing Out!*, and *English Dance and Song*. On 5 January, 2006, Radio 2 made *Liege & Lief* 'The Most Influential Folk Album of All Time', as voted by listeners.

Released at the very end of the Sixties, it ranked alongside contemporary releases like *Let It Bleed*, *Abbey Road*, Frank Zappa's *Hot Rats*, *The Band*, *Led Zeppelin II*, and *Bridge Over Troubled Water*.

The period between 11 May and 2 November, 1969, proved to be the single most influential and creative six months in Fairport's long and varied career. On both dates the band played the same venue in Birmingham, but the sets they played on each occasion, and the musicians who played them, were significantly different. Both evenings concluded with journeys back to London that were traumatic and could easily have brought about the end of the band. The first trauma required immediate and drastic action, the second would take 38 years to set to rights.

6 JULY, 1969

Ashley, Richard and Simon meet in Sandy's new home at 92 Chipstead Street, just off the King's Road, near Parson's Green

Underground Station. The tone is set by Sandy's announcement that she already had a solo gig at Les Cousins at the start of August. News had come through that Island had scheduled *Unhalfbricking* for release in late July, and that they had chosen 'Si Tu Dois Partir' to be the single from it. That was out of the band's hands. They were free to participate in publicity for it through press interviews, if they felt up to it. Live gigs and even radio were out of the question at the moment.

SIMON: I wonder how many times in the band's career we'd gathered together and decided to 'give it a go' and see what happens. It was almost like letting the Fates decide.

RICHARD: We were all pretty much in a state of shock. We were expected to make some decisions. But the pros and cons seemed evenly balanced.

SIMON: The press had already assumed we would continue. In a way, the decision had been made for us.

RICHARD: Obviously, the first thing that had to happen was finding a replacement for Martin. Actually, 'replacement' is the wrong word – a new drummer, a different drum.

Dave Mattacks didn't replace Martin when he took over the drummer's stool in Fairport. Everything the band had done up till that point was about to be abandoned, and many of the songs that had been the staple of their repertoire would not be played again for over a decade. They had moved on from the cover versions of other people's songs. Their original material simply had too many painful associations.

Although outside DM's frame of reference – at the time more *Come Dancing* than 'Come All Ye' – Fairport were a far-from-unattractive career prospect. They were an established act, very much in the public eye (even if for tragic reasons); and they included some of the most respected musicians on the scene at the time, with serious established management and a record deal. There was an album and a single about to be released, and they had a list of postponed bookings that could be taken up whenever they wished.

DM: Even if things hadn't worked out in the long term, joining the band would have made sense. I wanted a break
from something that had become rigid and repetitious, and
Fairport certainly provided it.

SWARB: As I remember it, I had decided I would join Fairport
once my commitments with Martin Carthy were out of the
way. When the time came, Fairport's continued existence
was still uncertain, and three-fourths of the band were in
America. Even when they did come back, I didn't join straight
away. They used a session player for some radio work, though
I was able to do the *Top of the Pops* appearance. I tend to think
of my time as a full-time Fairporter beginning with the rehearsals that led to *Liege & Lief*.

ASHLEY: We didn't go to Farley Chamberlayne to make a folk-
rock album, we went to decide what to do next. *Liege & Lief*
grew out of that. Fortunately, it was exactly the kind of music I
wanted to play and the kind I have continued to play ever since.

Farley Chamberlayne

To allow them time and space to regenerate the band, assimilate
two new members, and explore further the possibilities of merging
folk and rock that they had already begun, Island Records secreted
them in a mansion in the quiet village of Farley Chamberlayne, in
Hampshire.

ASHLEY: Idyllic – that was the word. Vaughan Williams used
it to describe some of his settings of traditional tunes – 'an
English idyll'. The peace, tranquillity, and lack of pressure –
after everything that had gone before, and not just the accident – was incredible. It was welcome. It was needed. It was
restorative.

RICHARD: At the time it felt like 'natural magic', something
about the place that would help put everything right.

SANDY: I think it was DM who pointed out that the place and the band had the same initials. Sometimes I wonder if it was more than just coincidence.

SIMON: A lot has been said about the Farley Chamberlayne experience. I can honestly say that, despite all the research and experimentation and all that, the thing that was uppermost in my mind was to use the time to ensure Fairport could continue. Maybe it's my rhythm guitarist's mentality – keeping it steady, on track and, so far as possible, harmoniously in tune.

Ashley was developing what would become his lifelong academic and artistic interest in English traditions and traditional music. Richard was consolidating his talent for writing darkly English songs, informed by the tradition. Sandy was feeling the restrictions of being a songwriter forced into the role of a lead vocalist – and also realising how much she missed Trevor Lucas, whose professional commitments kept him away from the Hampshire village. Dave Swarbrick was discovering and reinventing the electric violin. Dave Mattacks was defining an entire new genre of drumming.

SIMON: Farley Chamberlayne was absolutely crucial to the band's next stage of existence. It was such a pleasant environment. It meant that in terms of getting to know each other, living together, working together, playing and simply getting the next album together, everything could be condensed. It was a very concentrated period of activity, and yet it was also unpressured. It was a happy summer. It was absolutely idyllic. I cannot tell you how fortunate we were to have found ourselves there. It was an idyll: a beautiful Queen Anne house, in fabulously quiet countryside. It had everything you wanted in terms of distraction: you could walk in any direction and just see more and more beautiful things. You could explore the house, which even had rambling cellars and amazing lofts. It was packed with family treasures which, I am pleased to say, we treated with a respect not normally associated with young rock bands.

At the foot of the stairs in Simon's current home in Chipping Norton hangs a photograph taken at Farley Chamberlayne. It shows Richard, with what Marc Ellington once described as his "fairy music hair". He is sitting, relaxed, on an old-fashioned swing, made from a piece of board and a couple of ropes – a snapshot of a perfect, idyllic memory.

ASHLEY: My happiest memories are of those days, working on *Liege & Lief*.

SIMON: Everybody in the band could tell you happy stories about our times there. Often, it was simple things – being able to break off whenever we wanted to, and take the dog for a walk or play football. Using the swing which hung from the branch of an ancient tree – that particularly appealed to Richard. Being able to leave all the instruments set up, and come in and play whenever we wanted to.

ASHLEY: In the big downstairs room we set our instruments up in a circle, so everyone could see what everyone else was playing. DM had his kit with his back to the window; Simon to his left, then me on bass; Swarb to my left, Sandy next to him, and finally, completing the circle, Richard between Sandy and DM's drum-kit.

SANDY: Folk clubs have singarounds, where everyone sits in a circle, someone leads off a song or a tune and gradually everyone joins in. I suspect everyone in the room, with the exception of Mattacks, would have come across that concept at some point. I don't think we did it consciously, but it certainly felt right when we started doing folk songs.

ASHLEY: It wasn't a purist thing. We didn't just play traditional songs. There might have been the odd country song or a Dylan song. I remember doing 'We Need a Whole Lot More of Jesus (and a Lot Less Rock 'n' roll)', which Swarb and Richard liked. We did some *Basement Tapes* stuff, too, and I think we were attuned to the spirit of *Big Pink*.

SANDY: We'd do some rock 'n' roll things, too – the sort of songs we ended up doing on *Rock On*, which developed in a way similar to *Liege & Lief*. That was light relief. All work and no play and all that.

ASHLEY: We always returned to the *Liege & Lief* music. To me, it became the reason for Fairport still existing.

RICHARD: I think at Farley Chamberlayne we were still deciding what to do. We weren't rehearsing a precise set of songs for the album. We were experimenting, then returning to familiar territory, and maybe using that to inform the new things we were trying.

ASHLEY: It's impossible to explain what it was like to work on *Liege & Lief*. It was such concentrated work. It was the six of us, in one room, working together with a single purpose. There was determination. There was a real sense of purpose and urgency. Up till then, it had been, "I've got or written or found this song. Would you like to hear it?" All pretty informal and rather random. *Liege & Lief* changed that.

JULY – NOVEMBER 1969
LIEGE & LIEF

ASHLEY: We had no idea how radical what we were planning to do was. I cannot honestly say how we would have responded had someone told us.

The period between their motorway accident in May and the completion of *Liege & Lief* in November was one of huge decisions, massive reconstruction and an enormous learning curve. A fresh start was needed.

SIMON: Tragedy creates a sense of distance. It is how we cope with things that are unbearable. *Unhalfbricking*, and everything that went with it, felt oddly more than the proximate past. The album came out and we did various things connected with it, but we all knew it was a matter of tying up loose ends.

ASHLEY: *Liege & Lief* was the last in a trilogy of albums Fairport made that year. It's the band's Triple Crown, and those albums represent something few artists in any area of music ever achieve.

The most significant aspect of their work at the time was the creation of an entirely original approach to traditional British music. It began with two tracks on *Holidays*, 'Nottamun Town' and 'She Moves Through the Fair'. The latter, while not actually a traditional song, was regarded as such by singers of folk songs. *Unhalfbricking* included only one traditional tune, 'A Sailor's Life', but Fairport's approach rewrote the book on how a traditional ballad could be performed. *Liege & Lief*, which was in effect a concept album, undeniably demonstrated that 'A Sailor's Life' was no mere flash in the pan.

ASHLEY: We were conscious that we were heading down a route we had already embarked upon, and by doing so we were creating something new and original.

SIMON: A lot has been said about the innovation that was going on – how we were inventing a new genre and so on. I really was not aware of that: we didn't speak about it in those terms. I was more concerned with the immediate, urgent, issue of simply rebuilding the band.

RICHARD: It was a retreat, in both senses of the word – an escape from the world and a considered step back in order to go forward. There were two new people to integrate into the band, and the rest of us needed to get the measure of each other again.

SWARB: It was wonderful. No outside pressure, lots of sharing of ideas, playing with Richard, magnificent surroundings.

SANDY: There's a saying, 'sing like no one's listening'. That's what the band was able to do at Farley Chamberlayne. That was where I really found my own voice for the first time.

SIMON: It took all the pressure off. We were together but, equally, we could escape each other easily if we needed to. There was space to work, either individually or as a unit. There were places to relax and to study in. If we'd tried to go straight back on the road, I think things would have boiled to the surface and we'd have ended up screaming at each other.

The music we made there was very therapeutic. It's amazing that it produced an album that today everyone regards as a classic; at the time, what it did for our wellbeing as individuals was beyond measure.

Of course, Fairport were by no means the first to recast traditional music in a new context.

At the turn of the 20th century, English composers had reworked borrowed melodies into classical music. In some instances, they had collected the songs on cylinder, which had preserved some of the earliest recordings of English traditional singers. Decades later at Cecil Sharp House, singers like Martin Carthy, The Watersons, Anne Briggs, and The Young Tradition would listen intently to those recordings for inspiration and repertoire. Joining them, in July 1969 Ashley Hutchings donned his ex-BBC Bakelite headphones to sample, for the first time, their arcane delights.

SIMON: It is quite odd when you think about it. These people we perceive of as being straightlaced traditionalists were actually into new technology. A mechanical recording device would have been an absolute mystery to 99 per cent of the population back in 1908.

ASHLEY: It is amazing that *because* people like Cecil Sharp recorded what they heard rather than just writing it down, we can still hear things like Joseph Taylor singing 'Creeping Jane'. It's the sound of English music from before the First World War, when so much of our culture died in the trenches.

In May 1937, British jazz saxophonist Buddy Featherstonhaugh directed Ye Olde English Swynge Band at recording sessions which produced trad jazz versions of the likes of 'John Peel', 'Early One Morning', and 'Widdicombe Fair'. Kathleen Ferrier popularised songs like 'Blow the Wind Southerly' and 'Dance To Your Daddy'. Skiffle, in the Fifties, added teenbeat to timeless tunes from the American tradition, many of which had developed out of an earlier English tradition. When Dave Pegg recorded 'Donegan's Gone' with P J Wright, he was paying tribute to one of the first folk-rockers.

PEGGY: Lonnie was always a great entertainer. It's fair to say he was a pioneer of folk-rock, of course, but without him and skiffle, it's hard also to imagine English pop music at all. Cliff, The Beatles, The Stones, and many more all started out playing skiffle.

By 1969, a number of traditional songs had been recast as pop and become hits – Anthony Newley's 'Strawberry Fair', The Animals' 'House of the Rising Sun', Paul Simon's 'Scarborough Fair', and 'Widdicombe Fair' as reimagined by The Nashville Teens, for instance. Bill Oddie even rendered 'On Ilkla Moor Baht'at' in the style of Joe Cocker, on the radio – eventually releasing it as a single in 1970. These, however, were one-offs. The songs just happened to be authorless.

Shirley Collins was the first singer of the English folk revival to explore the potential of traditional songs in other musical contexts. In the Fifties, she played folk as skiffle while part of Alan Lomax's group The Ramblers. In 1960, she was part of a project to create an LP of modern songs based on traditional models, anticipating one of the approaches employed on *Liege & Lief*, ultimately recording an oddity called 'Space Girl'. The song had been written by Ewan MacColl in 1952, and would be revived by Eliza Carthy on the second *Imagined Village* CD in 2010. In 1964, Shirley teamed up with guitarist Davey Graham to record *Folk Roots: New Routes*, an album of traditional songs with jazz accompaniment, which included the version of 'Nottamun Town' that was to inspire Fairport's recording. In 1969, *Anthems in Eden* featured a suite of songs designed to recount a relationship. Like *Sergeant Pepper* and *Babbacombe Lee*, the suite appeared as a continuous track, occupying side 1 of the LP with no gaps to separate songs. The whole piece was accompanied by a consort of medieval instruments. In 1971, Shirley embraced folk-rock with *No Roses*. Produced by Ashley Hutchings, the album features an all-star backing band which included two-thirds of the Fairport line-up that had recorded *Liege & Lief* (minus Sandy and Swarb): it is one of the few records that pose a serious challenge to Fairport's *Liege & Lief* for the title of greatest folk-rock album of all time.

Fairport's early forays into folk music saw them linked with folkier acts than they had been used to. At the Royal Festival Hall, they had been part of a 'Pop Meets Folk' event on 24 March, 1969. John

Peel, the host of the show, introduced them as "The band that more than any other spans the gap between the two styles of music we are sharing tonight – the ever-surprising and always wonderful Fairport Convention."

ASHLEY: No one thought about it at the time, but with hindsight, given everything that had happened to us that summer, folk music was a very natural place to turn to.

SANDY: There's something secure and permanent about folk songs, especially the real old ones. They are survivors. They make me think of medieval castles, still standing and so full of the echoes of history, distant and recent. Folk songs can be a great comfort in all kinds of situations. That's why I'll never stop singing them. My best friends were folkies – Annie Briggs, Jackson [C Frank], John Renbourn, Heather Wood.

For Ashley, English folk music was a new discovery. He approached it with the unremitting zeal of the born-again.

ASHLEY: I found myself more and more drawn to English traditional music. Iain Matthews had been very into American music, and had liked the West Coast feel of the early band. After he left, he formed Southern Comfort – so he was developing country-rock at the same time as Fairport were creating folk-rock. Dave Swarbrick was one of the folk scene's biggest stars, of course, and his duo with Martin Carthy was a top of the bill act.

SWARB: When I agreed to join Fairport – this was before the accident – I had no idea what they were about to evolve into. I just loved playing with Richard – such an inspiring musician.

As folk became more important in Fairport's repertoire, Swarb's musical background acquired significance. Fairport explored the potential of folk-rock and thereby defined the band's long-term identity; meanwhile, its individual members were unwittingly shaping their own futures.

Fly Me To The Moon

SIMON: For me, 20 July, 1969, is an enduring memory. We all went out into the garden on a warm summer's evening and looked at the moon, just as Neil Armstrong was walking down the ladder. We really felt part of something historic that was happening. I think a few bars of 'Fly Me to the Moon' were played when we went back inside. I suppose it was science fiction becoming reality and that, of course, connects to the magical, fantastic world of the songs we were discovering.

'Fly Me to the Moon' was still being played at the first recording sessions, featuring Sandy on piano (an instrument she doesn't play at all on the released LP), as was another American songbook standard, 'The Lady Is a Tramp'. Fairport recorded a version of it, with Richard Thompson providing some very hip vocals, for a John Peel radio session on 27 September, 1969. They also recorded a majestic version of 'The Ballad of Easy Rider' and, maintaining their fondness for little-known songs by American singer-songwriters, Richard Farina's 'The Quiet Joys of Brotherhood', set to the Irish tune 'My Lagan Love'. Along with a version of 'Sir Patrick Spens', all of these would be dropped when the final running order was drawn up. Had they been included, it would have made for a rather different and certainly less iconic album.

SIMON: Because as a band we had always dared to be different, it was exciting to work on something that led us into previously uncharted territory. We could all go there together – rather like Armstrong, Aldrin and Collins.

ASHLEY: It was very exciting playing that music. Every morning I would wake up looking forward to what new sounds we would create that day. We were making music that no one had ever made before.

RICHARD: It wasn't one big decision. It was a lot of decisions of different sizes. What sort of band should we be? How do you incorporate the fiddle as lead instrument in a rock band? What songs should we play? What should remain from the old repertoire?

ASHLEY: Absolutely nothing carried over. That's the really odd thing. Not the traditional songs we were already playing. Not the songs we had played live but not recorded. Not even the original songs people in the band had written – and there were already several that have since become classics.

Gone were the Dylan covers, which he has described as some of the best-recorded versions of his songs. Gone were the songs by Joni Mitchell and Leonard Cohen, whose compositions Fairport had been among the first to perform and record. Gone were Richard's earlier songs ('Genesis Hall', 'Cajun Woman', 'Meet on the Ledge'); Sandy's songs ('Who Knows Where the Time Goes', 'Fotheringay', and several new songs that would surface after she left the band); and even that rare, unreleased Simon Nicol song – 'A Shattering Live Experience'.

SWARB: Having an entirely new repertoire created more of a level playing field. We all approached the songs from the same distance.

GERRY: That's rare. Normally, if you join an established band, you're told "Here's the setlist. Learn it."

ASHLEY: We shook the dust from our shoes and moved on. It was the ultimate fresh start.

Talk at length to any of the participants in the creation of *Liege & Lief* at Farley Chamberlayne and you'll discover an amazing array of explanations about the album's *raison d'être*. Some members thought the album was carving out a new direction; others believed it was a one-off concept album; still others thought the album was about providing new rock settings for old songs; while the song-writers (in the main) believed its focus lay in rewriting and updating old songs with new words. *Liege & Lief* did all those things, of course, and more. It was the spectacular flowering of all Fairport's work over the preceding two years. It was a step that was, at the same time, both absolutely logical and totally unpredictable.

SIMON: I don't think there had been any conscious mission statement, as it were. To a large extent, it was a chance to get to know each other. There was also what today would be called reconstructive therapy going on. Those of us who had been involved in the accident had to find ways of dealing with it. For Ashley, that meant a lot of intellectual exercise. I appreciated and benefited from the tranquillity and the sheer beauty of the place. Richard's songwriting developed: his songs echoed with the loss of his girlfriend Jeannie.

Of all the albums in Fairport's back catalogue, *Liege & Lief* holds the unique distinction of having had every single track revived and adapted for inclusion in the Winter Tour sets of Fairport's later incarnations.

SWARB: At Farley, I was certainly the one most familiar with the music. I'd already recorded some of the songs: I'd done 'Reynardine' with Bert Lloyd, and it was on the newest album with Carthy; I had also played on Luke Kelly's version of 'The Deserter'. The set of tunes was one I was already playing; I wrote the tunes for 'Tam Lin' and 'Crazy Man Michael'. The tune at the end of 'Matty Groves' came from Martin.

SANDY: Not everything worked out. Not every song we played was meant to be for the album. I think Richard and I both wrote things that were either not ready in time or not suitable. In the end, we focused on a shortlist, really working out how we were going to do them. Not all of those made it on to *Liege & Lief*, but I think they all found a home somewhere – in Fairport, on one of my albums, or Richard's, or as part of one of Ashley's projects.

Returning to London, Fairport recorded a session for John Peel's *Top Gear* on BBC Radio 1. Five tracks were recorded for later transmission, including 'Reynardine', 'Tam Lin', and the 'Lark in the Morning' medley. With the release of the album three months away, Peel used the recording "to let those of you who couldn't make it have a taste of a groundbreaking concert". He re-broadcast the recordings at Christmas to tie in with the album's release. His Christmas programme was produced to resemble a party: Sandy was one of the guests – talking about the album, complaining that the booze had run out at Peel's party, and keeping tight-lipped about the fact that she would have left the band by the time her recorded interview was broadcast.

SANDY: The Festival Hall concert was nerve-wracking. The audience was full of folkies, many of whom were friends. We really didn't know how they would take it.

Three years prior to that, British audiences had booed Bob Dylan for 'going electric'. Famously, a loud cry of "Judas!" had rung out at Manchester Free Trade Hall. In Birmingham, after they had sat admiringly through the acoustic first set, as soon as Dylan came on with an electric guitar, the rest of the Ian Campbell Folk Group had walked out in obvious protest, only Dave Swarbrick remaining in his seat. At every gig, fans of Dylan's 'folk style' jeered, and many later complained vociferously to D A Pennebaker's documentary cameras. "It's not what we came to hear," said one, "it's not folk music, it's just loud rubbish."

SWARB: Sandy and I were from the English folk scene. We knew that certain pockets were resistant to change. As far back as when I was playing with Beryl Marriott, I was accused of jazzing things up. We honestly had no idea what kind of reception we would receive.

ASHLEY: We were very confident in what we had achieved. We believed in it. We thought it was a valid thing to do. Swarb's involvement added to its credibility, too. However, not only were we unsure as to how the folk community would take it, we didn't know whether our old fans would go along with it either. So far, they'd maybe heard a couple of trad arr things as part of a set which included Dylan songs, songwriter material, and original songs from the band. In our sets to date, most of our fans would certainly have heard a few things they were familiar with. The *Liege & Lief* set wasn't like that, though. It broke the cardinal rule of not playing a whole evening of songs entirely new to the audience. While today one is familiar with the likes of 'The Deserter' and 'Matty', it's hard to imagine how strange those songs must have seemed to an audience not raised on folk music, hearing them for the very first time.

RICHARD: Spare a thought for the chap who'd bought a ticket
because he'd seen us on *Top of the Pops* and whose knowledge
of Fairport was limited to 'Si Tu Dois Partir' – because it had
been a hit. There we were with songs about shape-shifting
Scotsmen and murderous cuckolds. When you look at what
folk songs are actually about, you'd think they were from another planet. We were playing the medieval equivalent of
'Flying Saucers Rock 'n' roll'.

WEDNESDAY 24 SEPTEMBER, 1969
THE ROYAL FESTIVAL HALL

The advertised screening of the film *Swan Lake* had been relocated,
to make way for a 'folk concert'.

Fairport were supported by a very nervous Nick Drake – barely
able to communicate with the audience and seemingly determined
to get offstage as quickly as possible – followed on stage by John
and Beverley Martyn, recently married and yet to release a recording as a duo. Then Fairport took to the stage to unveil their new
music.

'Come All Ye' was a natural starting point – a welcome, an introduction, a mission statement, and an assured return. As each musician was introduced, a surge of applause rose from the audience
as if to greet their return. Sandy made the line about the high notes
coming "from you and me" very inclusive, with a sweeping gesture
that took in the entire audience. It was as if she was inviting everyone to join in on songs they had never heard before – certainly not
in their current form. Unlike a typical folk set, there wasn't a single
chorus in sight after that first number.

'Reynardine' followed, causing an immediate mood change, as
the sound of the instruments drifted from the stage like mist over
moorland. Then 'Sir Patrick Spens', the first of four songs played
that night which didn't make the album, the last of which brought
Swarb to the vocal mic for a curious version of an old American
hymn. The two big ballads at the heart of the set – 'Tam Lin' and
'Matty Groves' – may well have been familiar to the audience. They
would not, however, have expected the rock punctuation that divided the flow of the narrative or the extended instrumental that
concluded each song. The announcement that "the next song was

written by Richard" brought a cheer. Clearly there were Fairport fans in the audience, though anyone expecting 'Meet on the Ledge' was instead regaled with a tale of murder, magic and talking ravens. As expected, afterwards, opinions were divided.

ASHLEY: It's one of the great delights of my life that today I am *so* accepted by the folk community that I have been given awards for my contribution to folk music. Back then, I was just the bass player in a rock band with the temerity to play traditional music – and not simply folk songs, but big ballads.

SWARB: Some folkies had only just got used to the idea of accompanying folk songs on an acoustic guitar. There was definitely a feeling that big ballads deserved to be sung unaccompanied. Any other approach detracted from the storyline, or something.

Doubts were expressed. But, on the whole, those among whom folk-rock was not well-received saw it as a topic for constructive debate rather than downright disapproval. Some, however, surprised even the band with their enthusiasm. Both Swarb and Sandy recalled being accosted by Bert Lloyd afterwards.

SANDY: A L Lloyd was a hugely important and respected figure. He'd been around since the Fifties. He was immensely knowledgeable, had written books, edited collections of songs, and made loads of albums. He came straight up to me – and there was I thinking "Oh God, what's he going to say?" – and with that giggly voice he had when he was excited about something, he said, "That's the most exciting thing I've heard in years."

SWARB: Bert – whom I knew quite well because I'd recorded with him several times – shook me by the hand and said, "Well done, my boy." He'd found 'Reynardine' particularly thrilling.

Swarb had recorded an acoustic version of 'Reynardine' with Bert, but the band did not know that his version had been adapted (for which we might read rewritten) by Bert to make it fit more closely

96

with his theory that the song was the preservation of an English vampire legend.

In the meantime, Fairport continued to try out their new material on live audiences. They played Croydon's Fairfield Halls on 10 October, and four days later were the headline act at the benefit gig for *ZigZag* where, for eight shillings you could spend your Tuesday evening listening to Soft Cloud, Mighty Baby, and Fairport – all creatively lit by Optic Nerve's lightshow. The same day, 14 October, *Rolling Stone* published an in-depth article titled 'Fairport Convention: Beginning to Continue'. Over three pages, they offered a serious and perceptive overview of the relationship between folk and rock in the context of the 'experimentation carried out by Fairport Convention in a mansion in rural England'. Every member of the band was given equal prominence. In his first-ever interview as a member of Fairport, Dave Mattacks explained how his jazz background influenced what he would bring to the band, as well as discussing drumming techniques within a wide frame of reference that ranged from John Coltrane to The Byrds via Blood, Sweat & Tears.

That article not only heightened and increased the sense of anticipation preceding the new album, it also had a key role in raising Fairport's profile in the States where – minus Sandy and Ashley – they would tour for the first time in 1970.

SANDY: I think the Englishness of the whole enterprise appealed to *Rolling Stone*. Still, it was an American-run magazine, and to feature a band who hadn't had any success in the States was very unusual.

16 OCTOBER TO 1 NOVEMBER, 1969
SOUND TECHNIQUES STUDIO, CHELSEA

Fairport carefully transformed their vision of traditional music into a permanent reality. Recording at Sound Techniques Studio on four-track, they aimed to lay down two songs a day. 'The Deserter' and 'Farewell, Farewell' were the first songs to be recorded on 16 October, 1969; three days later, they cut 'Crazy Man Michael'.

There was a certain serendipity to the day when Richard, recording a song inspired at least in part by the loss of his previous girlfriend, met the woman who was to become his first wife. During a break in the recording sessions, the group bumped into a session singer who had been recording the vocal for a new Kellogg's TV commercial (the 'pour out the sunshine' ad). She was Linda Peters who, in the years to come, would become Sandy's close friend, Mrs Richard Thompson, a member of The Albion Band, a Fairport guest at Cropredy, guest vocalist on Simon Nicol's first solo album, and a singing legend in her own right, once identified by The Everly Brothers thus: "Aren't you the 'Dimming of the Day' woman?"

'Reynardine' was completed three days later, on 22 October.

Today, completing a classic album over a few days seems preposterous, but although The Beatles were allowed the luxury of months to make an album, every other UK act was given restricted studio time, and was expected to arrive rehearsed and ready to record within that block of precious time. *What We Did on Our Holidays* was recorded over five days; *Unhalfbricking* in four. Even by the exacting standards of the time, Fairport were professional and productive to an astounding level.

They took time out from recording to perform live in Manchester and Redcar on the weekend of 25 and 26 October, the gigs setting them up for what would be the final session to produce tracks for the album. Productively, the last session on 29 October secured four tracks: 'Come All Ye', 'Tam Lin', and 'Matty Groves', which they had already started work on, and the 'Lark in the Morning' medley – the last track to be recorded. A version of 'Sir Patrick Spens', recorded on 1 November, was not used on the album, though Fairport would return to it for their next LP. 'Ballad of Easy Rider' and 'Quiet Joys of Brotherhood' were also set to one side.

'Matty Groves', which was recorded in sections – the instrumental coda being edited on to the ballad – proved the most problematic. The band would return to it on three separate occasions. Overdubs and mixing for the album were done at Olympic Studios, which had eight-track facilities.

Release

Reviews of *Liege & Lief* were mixed and uncertain. Rock reviewers found themselves on unfamiliar musical territory; folk reviewers seemed unsure which way to jump. *Rolling Stone*, having given the album a big build-up, complained that it was 'worthy enough of quiet admiration but a little boring'. *Disc* found it 'less accessible and memorable than their previous albums'. *Record Mirror* praised the group's 'courage in tackling revered folk songs' and admired Sandy's vocals, but still found it, 'a bit self-indulgent at times'. *Sounds* felt that these were 'the most magnetic versions [of folk songs] yet conceived'. Only Karl Dallas, writing in *Melody Maker*, saw both the point and the potential of the album: he declared it 'beautiful listening' and 'worth the money for the second side alone'. He would go on to write regularly on the subject of folk-rock, beginning his first piece: 'Fairport Convention may have seen their latest album as a one-off project. In fact, they have turned the oldest genre of popular music completely on its head.'

The Sunday Times described the album as 'original, inventive, exciting and utterly British'.

While reviews were uncertain – and views have been revised since – the music press were united in their respect and admiration for the strength Fairport had shown, and for the quality and musicianship of the latest line-up. Sandy Denny topped several polls as Britain's best female singer.

Liege & Lief

Island
December 1969

SIDE 1:

'Come All Ye'
'Reynardine'
'Matty Groves'
'Farewell, Farewell'

SIDE 2:

'The Deserter'
'Medley'
'Tam Lin'
'Crazy Man Michael'

Even the look of *Liege & Lief* confirmed it was special – folk musicologist Bob Pegg (no relation) had been hired to devise an illustrated guide to folk traditions inside the gatefold. Packaged in a violet-tinted gatefold sleeve, its front cover had small portraits of each individual band member: it had the look of a Victorian family album, an effect enhanced by the overall design. The stark minia-ture monochrome portraits emphasised, as did the opening song, that this was a group of distinct individuals. The cover images, like the songs on the LP, seemed to have been preserved from a dif-ferent era.

The rear featured a strange and evocative carved head, some-thing Swarb had acquired in Scandinavia.

Inside the gatefold were what looked like a collection of infor-mational postcards, several of which had been drawn especially by Bob Pegg. One might have expected these illustrated boxes to speak of the songs or the band, but instead they reflected differ-ent aspects of the traditions by which the album had been inspired. Here were the great song collectors (Child and Sharp), a source singer, a broadside seller, and several obscure customs (the Furry Man, Pace Egging, the Padstow 'Oss').

Clearly, Island's design and marketing departments were put-ting their weight behind the band's new release. Its first three albums, though attractive and intriguing, had been single-sleeved and lacking in supporting information. The sleeve notes of those albums told us little more than the names of the band members, and where and by whom each album had been recorded. *Liege &
Lief* subverted that trend with a wealth of academic information: *objets trouvés*, curious survivals and relics, the carved head (which Ashley believes was found wrapped in an old sack that preserved it from rotting), the photos which have the look of casual snapshots from an era when photographic portraiture tended to be necessarily formal, and the gatefold postcards – each featuring iconic survivals.

ASHLEY: Farley Chamberlayne has rambling attics, which I liked to explore. Lots of things had been abandoned up there and, while we were very respectful of the main body of the house, one or two unsecured items were liberated from for-gotten recesses. One of those was the strange little postcard of a gravestone, which is reproduced inside *Liege & Lief*: that was what sparked the whole idea of a set of cards with infor-mation on a few folk traditions.

The advertisements for the release – full page in all the music press – offered still more information. This was, we were told 'The first (lit-erally) British Folk Rock album'. The album's eight tracks not only drew on various strands and genres of English folk music, but also created a template for a variety of approaches. Herein were big ballads, broadside ballads, folk songs, dance tunes and original songs in a consciously traditional style. Moreover, all were played on entirely electric instruments. Over four decades on, it is almost impossible to appreciate how refreshingly radical this was.

The album incorporated several approaches to music that had developed on the rock scene. There was the steadily building instrumental framework constructed around the lyrics of the song, which was very much part of the approach of British blues revival bands. The brooding atmospherics of 'Reynardine' are reminiscent of the musical soundscapes created by early prog rock bands like King Crimson. The use of a song as a springboard for extended instrumental improvisation was already familiar through bands from Cream to the Grateful Dead. Massive, magical, traditional ballads were driven along by a driving rhythm section and punctuated by terse articulate instrumental statements – precisely the approach The Stones were developing for their new longer songs. While the LP introduced a whole new audience to the big ballads, side one closed with a pop ballad, described by *Frendz* magazine as being 'as perfect a pop production as McCartney's 'Yesterday''. Like The Beatles' song, it is an understated jewel in an unusual but entirely appropriate setting. As for the jigs and reels, the most succinct review simply said, 'they are what we would have heard if John Mayall's Bluesbreakers had been born Irish'.

'Come All Ye' is the only composition jointly credited to Ashley Hutchings and Sandy Denny. Ashley had shared composer credits with Richard, Iain and Judy on the first album where his role, as he explains today, was "to encourage their talents and suggest subjects and styles for songs". Sandy was already established as a songwriter, and one suspects Ashley was guiding her towards this totally perfect opener. It is also the only song on the album on which Sandy has a composer credit.

There could have been other Sandy songs on the album, because she had been writing during the band's time at Farley Chamberlayne. 'Pond and the Stream' and 'Winter Winds' were certainly written by this point. 'Tam Lin' and 'Matty Groves' had originally both concluded with an extended instrumental featuring Richard's guitar and Swarb's fiddle in the style established by 'A Sailor's Life'. Only 'Matty' retained it on the album, though. 'Tam

Lin', of all the songs on the LP, was the one with which listeners might already have been familiar as it had been included in a large number of anthologies of English verse (despite the fact it is actually Scottish).

SANDY: When we were picking traditional songs, I was seen as the person most likely to make suggestions. I knew 'Tam Lin' because a lot of my folk-club repertoire comprised Scottish songs. The version I was most familiar with was the one Alex Campbell sometimes sang.

'The Deserter' should really be called 'The New Deserter' to differentiate it from an older song with the same title and a very different story line. To further confuse matters, Simon Nicol recorded a more modern song with the same title for his second solo album, and that eventually made it into Fairport's set.

SWARB: 'The Deserter' and 'Reynardine' were the two songs I suggested to, and taught, the band. 'The Deserter' is very clearly a Victorian song, which at one point I was told might be too modern for the album!

The *Liege & Lief* 'Deserter' is a broadside reworking of the 'Man / Maid Freed From the Gallows', with a hint of 'The Honest Labourer'. The song's hero habitually abandons his post, only to find himself repeatedly captured and brought back into service; martially caught and court-martialled. One failed attempt sees him sentenced to a serious lashing ('three hundred and three'), the next to be shot. Then along comes Prince Albert, a *deus ex machina*, with a reprieve to truly stretch credulity. The way the band's arrangement surges in response to the storyline and Sandy's vocal rides it like an assured surfer lends validity to a narrative twist, which might otherwise be the album's one weak spot.

Ballad number 81 in Francis Child's collection of *The English and Scottish Popular Ballads* tells the story of Little Musgrave and Lady Barnard. The story dates from the 16th century. When the song migrated to America, as often happened, names were changed and Little Musgrave became Matty Groves. A subsequent development changed the whole thing into the murder ballad 'Shady Grove', the tune of which Fairport used for their recording.

SIMON: Does it really matter that this one version seems to have overtaken all others? I don't think so. Whatever you do to a folk song, it remains inviolate. The source material is always going to be there, for anyone who wants to go back to it. 'Matty Groves' is a great chorus song, even if it breaks all the rules about what a chorus song should be.

SANDY: When I rejoined Fairport, I had to learn 'Matty Groves', because Fairport were still doing it and people in the audience would expect me to do it. It felt like a lot of them knew it better than I did.

SIMON: There's footage, which has cropped up on YouTube, of us playing a version of it at the Cambridge Folk Festival. If you listen to it – and bear in mind it was not a specifically Fairport crowd, as we merely stood in because Linda Thompson had to cancel at short notice – you'll see I could have stopped singing and let the crowd do the song: they sing it loud and word perfect. They are all singing from beat one, all 19 verses and no chorus.

The album includes two Richard Thompson co-compositions, so highly regarded that when Fairport asked fans to vote for their favourite Fairport songs to be re-recorded for an album marking their 45th anniversary, both made it into the top 10. 'Farewell, Farewell' borrows the tune from Andy Irvine's version of 'Willy O'Winsbury', and is a perfect coming together of Fairport talent, with Richard's moving, poetic words supported by the understated and assured backing from the rhythm section. Sandy's rich, empathetic vocal and Swarb's blissfully ascending fiddle add to the beauty of the recording.

'Crazy Man Michael' was the first collaboration between Richard Thompson and Dave Swarbrick. Richard had the words, intended originally for a traditional tune, and Swarb had an original tune, which suited them better. The song is a haunting reworking of 'Polly Vaughn', a short ballad in which a young man out hunting shoots his girlfriend whom he 'mistook… for a swan'. Also known as 'The Shooting of His Dear', the song is allegedly based on a real event – though it must be one of the most bizarre defences ever offered in a murder case. The ballad's elements of magic and metamorphosis famously inspired Tchaikovsky. In Richard's version, the silent swan is replaced by a shape-shifting raven with coal-black eyes and a curious ability to talk.

'Crazy Man Michael' may have been based on tradition, but its content was too personal and painful for Richard to consider playing it until well into the following century. He recorded a version for the box set *RT* because no other recording of it by him existed at the time. Fairport revived the song in 2004, and it has remained a regular part of their repertoire ever since. It is the most covered song from both *Liege & Lief* as well as from the Fairport canon in general. It is sung in folk clubs in the UK as though it were part of the tradition, a further reflection of the impact of the album.

RICHARD: That's good: I like the fact it's being sung as trad arr
    In a way, that's a great compliment. It's a very emotional song.
    I myself didn't sing it for decades. Firstly, it's a difficult song
    melodically to sing, and I wanted to find a way to modify the
    melody slightly. Plus it's about Fairport's car crash back in '69:
    there's nothing in it directly about what happened. You could
    look at it circumspectly and say, "This is about losing my girl-
    friend," but at the time I was in hospital and I just began by
    writing a story, just enjoying the process of putting down a
    story. It emerged that it was about stuff close to home. It is nice,
    given all that, to be able to get close to the traditional model.
        At that time, because we had all got so close to the tradition,
    there were a few archaisms creeping in. These days I'd want
    to appear more consciously contemporary, but still retain
    the roots. It's all about cadence. Because the tune changed as
    well: we started out with 'The Bonnie House of Airlie' as the
    tune, before Swarb's tune threw it further back somehow. It's
    the better for it and it changes the pattern of the lyric.

Richard's starting point – of which not a vestige remains – is a bothy ballad describing an ancient dispute between Clan Argyle and Clan Airlie. It climaxes with a raid on the house of Airlie and the gang rape of the lady of the house 'on the bowlin' green O'Airlie'.

As the LP's closing track, 'Crazy Man Michael' – the only 100 per cent original composition on the set – points the way forward, though no one at the time had any idea where Fairport would go next, or with whom.

Finally, *Liege & Lief* includes Fairport's first-ever set of jigs and reels: 'The Lark in the Morning' medley. This was unlike anything rock fans – Fairport's target audience – had heard before. Alongside reinventing and validating the genre of folk-rock, Fairport were creating its first sub-genre. The idea of playing high-octane tune sets is now a *sine qua non* of every folk-rock act, and has even become one of the tricks up the sleeve of mainstream rockers.

Dave Swarbrick was used to playing set piece medleys. He knew the session approach of Irish musicians in South London and the North East.

SWARB: I'd always played tune sets, sitting in on sessions, playing in Beryl Marriott's group and then with Ian Campbell and later Martin. To me, it's one of the ingredients of live folk music. I wasn't thinking I'd invented some new dimension of rock, all we were doing was what I'd always done, except on electrically amplified instruments.

Though Swarb's album from 1968, *Rags, Reels & Airs*, would furnish many of the tunes that appeared in Fairport's sets through the Seventies, in this case he dug further back to a favourite set he had played with Beryl Marriott's Ceilidh Band. By way of acknowledging its origins, Beryl would be invited to join Fairport on stage at Cropredy to perform. With Ric, Chris and Swarb on fiddles, and Ashley and Maart swelling the ranks, the 'Medley' had the benefit of being a real Fairport big band performance. It has proven to be durable and far-reaching, with musicians around the world taking to performing it.

Years later in 2003, while at New York's Old Songs Festival, Ric and Chris were walking around the Altamont fairground checking out morning workshops when they came upon a fiddle session – about 30 players representing a vast array of American traditional styles from Celtic to bluegrass, all playing together – and stood to one side, unnoticed. When the assembled throng moved naturally on to the 'Lark in the Morning' set, a look of delight and pride came over their faces. Out came their fiddles, the other players thrilled to find themselves joined by the two fiddlers from the band that had first recorded it.

RIC: It was definitely a touch of things coming full circle. I'd learned those tunes from the Fairport album – that and Swarb's *Rags, Reels & Airs* influenced everybody. Here we were on the other side of the Atlantic, playing along with people who learned them in the same way. It's one of those moments which make you realise why Fairport are important. Swarb was seriously ill at the time and I remember thinking as we played, "This one's for you, Swarby."

2 NOVEMBER, 1969
MOTHERS, BIRMINGHAM

Sunday evening. Though they did not know it, this was to be the final live gig played by the *Liege & Lief* line-up. In what was a traumatic booking, they returned to the club they had played on the night of their crash. In the audience, celebrating his 22nd birthday, was the bass player with the Ian Campbell Folk Group. This was his first encounter with Fairport Convention. He was therefore unaware of just how different the set he was hearing was from the one the group had played in the same venue six months earlier. That afternoon, he had earned a few extra quid as a session player on an album by The Couriers, but tonight he intended to relax and enjoy his birthday. His name is Dave Pegg.

PEGGY: I'd gone to the gig because I knew Swarb was playing with Fairport now. We'd overlapped slightly in the Campbell Group and I was interested to see what he was up to. I was surprised that I already knew quite a lot of the music from more traddy sources, and was particularly impressed by the tightness of the rhythm section, Ashley and DM. I went with Harvey Andrews, who didn't like it because they were too loud, but I loved it.

ASHLEY: In the six months between those two gigs at Mothers, so much had changed. There were the obvious things, such as DM being Martin's replacement; Swarb now a full-time member of the band; and the change in repertoire – playing the folk-rock set whereas before it had been more American-influenced. But those were the superficial changes.

RICHARD: We'd done a lot of growing up in a very short space of time. It was a rapid maturing process.

SIMON: What had happened had made us very aware of our mortality. Not many people of our age have the kind of experience that makes you realise how fragile, how tenuous, life is. That applied to us as individuals; it also applied to our band. We had invested time, energy and careers in making Fairport our full-time career.

ASHLEY: I suppose you could say we eased ourselves back into performing live. You have to remember that, quite apart from all the music being new – to us as well as to the audience – we also had two new members.

SANDY: We were all nervous. We all had our own reasons for that. I had no idea how Fairport's audience would react to listening to narrative songs with 30 odd verses.

RICHARD: Apart from those couple of gigs with Sandy in the States, we hadn't played in public for nearly half a year. We weren't out of practice because we had played every day at Farley, but returning to the stage after time off always gives you butterflies.

PEGGY: I'd never seen Fairport before that night, but like everyone else I was aware of the significance of that gig. It must have taken a lot of courage to go back there – a lot of ghosts… one in particular.

DM: It was strange joining Fairport. It was different from anything I'd done before. The circumstances were the worst possible, of course. They did their best to make me welcome and include me, but that night things felt strained – not with me particularly, just among the band.

SANDY: That was the night we really had to confront the fact that Martin was no longer with us.

Fairport included all the songs from *Liege & Lief*. Just over a week later, Ashley decided to leave the band. Dave Swarbrick rang Peggy and invited him to audition as Fairport's bass player. At the same time, Sandy announced she, too, was going her own way. *Melody Maker* broke the news in the edition published on 22 November: 'Sandy and Ashley have quit to pursue solo careers and Fairport will cease performing.' The Birmingham gig had been traumatic for everyone. Any jubilation at the triumph of the music they had invented – which that night received its most enthusiastic reception to date – was muted by darker, more reflective thoughts. The journey home was conducted in almost complete silence. Sandy was in tears most of the way.

SANDY: Everything seemed to come to a head. The things I wanted to do with my life – personally and professionally – didn't fit in with staying with Fairport. But I loved the band and all the guys in it. I loved making music with them. In fact, I continued to record with them right through my career – if you just read the credits on my solo albums, it's obvious. But that night, it got on top of me. The emotion of the gig, the long cold journey back. Wanting to be with Trevor. I told them I didn't want to do the American tour we had planned. I didn't even want to go to Denmark where we were booked to play on the radio.

SIMON: She didn't exactly resign. When we went to pick her up to go to the airport, she simply wasn't there.

ASHLEY: Eventually, she was tracked down and was put on the next available flight to join us. It was obvious that we could not continue with a lead singer who was so determined not to be part of the band.

The broadcast from Copenhagen on 7 December was Ashley and Sandy's last performance with Fairport (at least for the time being). They played 'The Deserter', 'Matty Groves', and 'Crazy Man Michael'. The brief introductions to the songs were significant. Ashley carefully explained that 'Michael' was "one of the few songs we play that isn't from the folk repertoire". Sandy introduced 'Matty' by pointing out that it was "a song about a woman whose loyalties are divided between a sense of duty and the man she loves". Like Lady Barnard, Sandy was about to opt for the latter.

SANDY: It had all been very fraught and traumatic. No one really knew what was going to happen next. I certainly didn't fancy the idea of being in a band where it would be hard to have my own songs played because the band was more about traditional songs and instrumentals. I had several songs which could have been included on *Liege & Lief*, but I knew it wasn't worth putting them forward. Added to that, I wanted to be able to spend more time with Trevor.

Sandy played a solo gig at Les Cousins in December. She opened her set with one of those songs which she could have put forward for *Liege & Lief* – her tribute to her friend Anne Briggs: 'The Pond and the Stream'. The rest of the set featured traditional songs and the work of singer-songwriters. Her only acknowledgement of the newly released Fairport album was the inclusion of a version of 'Crazy Man Michael'.

Even with Sandy gone, it was obvious that Richard's rapidly developing songwriting talent, particularly in partnership with Swarb, would make it impossible to maintain a purely folk-rock approach within the band. Ashley had the commitment of the newly enlightened and for him it was all or nothing. He left and began a quest to find and ultimately create bands with which this would be possible.

The struggles, trauma and emotional defibrillation which had gone into keeping Fairport alive and creating a groundbreaking album seemed wasted as the group's founder and then its award-winning lead singer went their separate ways. After two years and four albums, it looked as if Fairport might end up going the same way as so many Sixties bands. However, they didn't: against all odds, they did what they did best and what they would continue to do for 45 years. At the end of their greatest year, Fairport 'began to continue'.

CHRIS: Keeping the garden – that's right, that's what Fairport do – tend what others have planted, add a few new ones where appropriate, even do the occasional bit of weeding!

JOE BOYD: Simply surviving against all the odds – and there have been lots of times when the tables seemed really stacked against them – is obviously one of Fairport's great achievements. You could think of lots more – the success of Cropredy Festival, the number of musicians the band has nurtured over the years, the astounding musicianship, which has been their hallmark since the very first time I saw them. But all that aside, it finally comes down to the fact that in the second half of 1969, Fairport Convention – a bunch of kids from North London who liked American rock music – did the impossible: they made folk fashionable.

Some have claimed that after the accident Fairport retreated to the past to avoid the present. Instead, they found their future.

AUGUST 10, 2007
HOME FIELD, CROPREDY

It's Friday evening. The weather is cool but dry. Fairport Convention is about to take to the stage. Normally, you'd find Dave Pegg in the wings, checking the position of his bass on stage, just a little restive. Tonight, though, he is nowhere to be seen.

With a sense of occasion, Peggy strolls past the back stage security guard and out into the field, finding himself a good spot from which to see the stage with its huge cyclorama screen, and with easy access to the bar. Peggy, the band's bass player and the person most responsible for its continued existence, was on his way to watch Fairport Convention.

PEGGY: The thought of having a night off while Fairport played at Cropredy had a definite appeal. It was a bit like skipping school. I was determined to enjoy the set as a punter…a total contrast to how things normally are for me at Cropredy. It was a Fairport highlight for everyone, of course, but for me, watching those guys play *Liege & Lief* was particularly emotional. They were bloody marvellous, of course.

The line-up of Fairport that is about to perform is in effect the one that existed just before Peggy joined. Richard Thompson and Simon Nicol on guitars, Dave Swarbrick on fiddle, Ashley Hutchings on bass, Dave Mattacks on drums and, standing in for the late Sandy Denny, Chris While. For the first time ever, they are about to play the whole of *Liege & Lief*, in sequence. In recent months, Fairport's album, released at the end of 1969, had been feted by both the BBC and their old record company for its unique influence and accumulated sales. It was a dream line-up which few had expected to see play together again: Dave Swarbrick had been seriously ill and his increasingly infrequent live appearances had been in a wheelchair, accompanied by an oxygen tank – yet here he was, clad in a red shirt, revelling in prancing around the stage, fit (one might suggest) as a fiddle. Dave Mattacks, now resident in Boston, Massachusetts, and normally preferring to consign Fairport to his past, was also up there.

DM: I'd taken some time out from Fairport: I hadn't been to Cropredy for a few years. I was glad to return for this, though. That line-up, that particular configuration of musicians, made only one album. It was right that all the surviving members should get together to play it one last time.

SIMON: Chris While had the hardest job. We were all aware of Sandy's absence more than usual on that occasion.

CHRIS WHILE: As a female singer, you can never join Fairport on stage at Cropredy without a very real sense that Sandy is somehow there with you. That night I really needed her there, holding my hand.

PEGGY: Chris did such a great job. She didn't try to impersonate Sandy, but she really captured her spirit. It's hard to think of anyone else who could have done that.

SIMON: Lots of ladies have joined us at Cropredy to sing Sandy's songs. But it is always that, singing Sandy's songs, very much like when I sing 'Time Goes'. It's only ever for a couple of songs. In 2008, we even had a sequence of great girl singers doing a Sandy song each. This was different, though. Chris was on stage for the full set. She was the only person to sing lead vocals. She was performing what most people would agree is the band's greatest album.

ASHLEY: It really was music without a safety net. If things didn't work, there was nowhere to go. There was no get out. There was tension in the air born of the audience's anticipation. This was an event, an occasion, a genuine first, a unique moment. What we were about to receive (for which we were indeed truly thankful) was the ultimate Fairport feast.

PEGGY: It was very emotional to return to that body of work. Swarb in particular found it difficult.

SWARB: It was more than the just eight songs. It was the album… the way it came about… Sandy. Six months of all our lives.

SIMON: People have described that set as 'historic'. And it was!

Who knows where the time goes? We are about to be transported back to 1969, in effect to an event that, despite the claims of some, has never actually happened before. Cropredy can sometimes become a time machine carrying 20,000 people back to a particular place. Ashley has once more stepped back to his role as bandleader. He glances from side to side, checking each musician is in place. Finally, Chris…a nod…an exchange of smiles, and they're off.

Sandy, Richard, Simon, Ashley, Swarb and DM. For most fans, this was the greatest of all Fairport line-ups. Astonishingly, it existed for less than six months, hardly played in public and did only one UK radio broadcast. And made just one album

As he had 38 years earlier, Dave Pegg, glass in hand, watches Fairport perform. As they reached the final song 'Crazy Man Michael', he smiles broadly and says, "Brilliant, just brilliant. Wasn't that brilliant."

Then he adds, allowing history to repeat itself as it so often has for Fairport Convention: "Well, I suppose I'd better go and join Fairport now."

CHAPTER FOUR

Inns and Outs – 1970

In the idyllic setting of Farley Chamberlayne, Fairport had discovered not only a new music, but a new way of making that music. Working together, relaxing together, living together, Fairport could operate as a true musical co-operative. As they ended their Farley Chamberlayne experience, plans were already being laid for perpetuating it, for getting back to being the self-contained collective they'd always been. However, Swarb lived in Milford Haven...

SIMON: At the far point of Wales, with, in those days, very limited road and rail connections. For a non-driving professional musician, we felt Swarb had made a bizarre choice. But then, after Fairport broke up, he moved to Aberdeenshire, thereby outdoing even himself!

SWARB: I was keen on moving back to be closer to the band. If I was going to be a proper member of Fairport, that was more or less essential.

First, however, Fairport had to deal with the decision of Sandy and Ashley to leave the band.

SIMON: I think we had seen it coming with Sandy. She had become increasingly unhappy – not particularly with Fairport, but with the way her life seemed to be going.

One issue for Sandy was the fact that while she was topping polls in music magazines as the nation's best female vocalist, she had no way of taking advantage of that accolade.

RICHARD: The news that Tyger had also decided to quit was more serious. He was the band's founder and leader. We all looked up to him. I think the impact of the accident hit him a little later than it did the rest of us.

Ashley had taken the longest to recover after the accident. His initial approach to dealing with it had been to thrust himself into the task of making sure Fairport continued.

ASHLEY: Why did I leave Fairport? It's a big question and one I don't truly know the answer to. There were all kinds of reasons, but I know mentally I just couldn't continue.

After he left, Ashley toyed with the idea of joining Bob Pegg's group Mr Fox (a name partly inspired by the song 'Reynardine'), out of which came his song 'Kitty Come Down the Lane'. He then considered joining the Irish folk group Sweeney's Men, whose version of 'Willy O'Winsbury' had furnished the tune for 'Farewell, Farewell'. Ultimately, though, he stayed true to his new love and formed the essentially English and determinedly traditional Steeleye Span.

It's fair to say that with Fairport clearly set to continue, and *Liege & Lief* already receiving acclaim, Ashley's immediate job was done. His role as bandleader had been relinquished, partly because he was not in a position to fulfil it when the big decisions had to be made. As his entire career has shown, he is, by nature, a man who needs to set himself new challenges.

SIMON: In theory, we could have continued without a lead singer, but there was no way we could continue without a bass player.

Auditioning and interviewing new band members was something Fairport had done too often. No one relished the idea of trying to find Ashley's replacement. Dave Swarbrick, asserting his authority in the band for the first time, had a way around the problem.

SIMON: Swarb was very insistent. We hadn't even finalised the wording for an ad in *Melody Maker*, so we agreed to listen to this guy just to shut Swarb up.

RICHARD: That was Dave Pegg. So far as we were aware, he was the bass player with Ian Campbell's group – another folkie. He also played upright bass – and, of course, Ashley was an electric bass player.

Although Swarb and Peggy had both been members of the Campbell group, there was very little overlap. Swarb left as Peggy joined. Peggy's ability to play mandolin and therefore cover part of what Swarb had done within the group was part of the reason he was recruited.

IAN CAMPBELL: Everybody thinks of Peggy as a bass player, but he also plays the guitar and the mandolin. It's always good to have individuals in a group who can help provide different textures in the sound.

The only Campbell line-up to feature both Peggy and Swarb is a spin-off from an educational TV programme for a budget record label, on the sleeve of which Peggy is shown playing his mandolin. At the time, nobody in Fairport was aware of Peggy's rock roots.

SIMON: We had our doubts about Peggy. It seemed like we were adding another folkie to the group and, given the direction we were heading in, that seemed like a step too far. Then he arrived, and he not only played Ashley's parts perfectly, he played them better.

SWARB: …The sound of collective jaws dropping. Both Richard and I stopped playing at different times to just listen to him. I knew he was good, but I had never realised just how good.

Peggy ended up being more than Fairport's bass player, of course. A decade later, he would become the band's saviour.

SIMON: Simple fact: without Dave and Chris Pegg, there would be no Fairport Convention today. There are dozens of reasons why that is true, but they kept the ship afloat and turned us into a financially viable proposition. They also, it has to be said, invented the business model that made that possible.

Peggy's journey to his rehearsal was anything but indicative of great entrepreneurial skill.

PEGGY: I had two auditions that day – Fairport and The Foundations. I was working my way through bands beginning with F. Seriously, I'd seen Fairport a couple of days earlier, liked what they were doing, and already sort of knew Swarb. He insisted I come down to audition. I borrowed a van to get to London from Birmingham, and it had something mechanically wrong with it. It was only really capable of making left turns, so I had to plan my route with that in mind.

The audition took place in a small rehearsal room in a Kensington basement. At the end of the audition, Peggy was asked when he could start.

DM: From day one, Peggy was a delight to play with. As part of a rhythm section, he knew exactly what he was doing. He's a melodic player and does a lot more than just keep time. But he keeps time perfectly.

SIMON: Peggy is a great storyteller and, after the audition – we had already started running through a few things when he arrived late (not a good way to get a job) – he started talking about the bands he had played with. We quickly realised that despite the fact he was coming to us from the Campbell Folk Group, his background was in rock music.

PEGGY: Playing rock, becoming more Progressive (big P), then finding more security playing folk. That was my Sixties story and it's also Fairport's. Our paths crossed at just the right time. The list of people I'd played with was a bit like the list of people who had been in their band.

Peggy's list includes Robert Plant, John Bonham, Jimmy Cliff, Diz Disley, Tony Cox, Cozy Powell and Steve Gibbons. He had switched from lead guitar to bass when Roger Hill joined a band called The Uglys, whom Peggy also played with.

PEGGY: Roger was one of the true guitar heroes of Brum. Steve Gibbons, then leader of The Uglys, really wanted him in the group when the chance came up. He suggested I switch to bass if I wanted to keep my job, so I have a lot to thank him for.

Peggy applied his lead guitarist sensibilities to the bass. As a lead guitarist, he knew what he expected of a bass player; as a bass player, he knew how to incorporate melodic lines and phrases into his playing. He still sometimes plays lead guitar and is credited on a number of recordings, including: Ashley Hutchings' 'The Electric Guitar Is King', tracks from his two live birthday releases, the odd Cropredy recording, his *Cocktail Cowboy* album, and more (uncredited) Fairport tracks than you might at first imagine.

Peggy's diary for December 1969, the month following his 'audition for Fairport', shows how busy he was at the time. As bass player with the Campbells, he was gigging almost every evening – including a radio session in Belgium – and shared the stage with Martin Carthy, Bridget St John, the Strawbs and Magna Carta. Day times were often occupied by recording sessions with Diz Disley, Tony Cox and Phil Picket, among others. His appointment to Fairport was formally announced on 20 December, in *Melody Maker*: 'Dave Pegg of the Ian Campbell Folk Group replaces 'Tyger' Hutchings'. A week later, Dave Pegg's diary reads: 'Started rehearsing with Fairport Convention.'

Those initial rehearsals were spent selecting material from Fairport's existing set. Beginning with a traditional number left over from *Liege & Lief* – 'Sir Patrick Spens' – the band had to decide what old material should be retained, and who should sing it.

SIMON: I don't think we decided to not appoint a new singer. We simply didn't look for one. Sandy was irreplaceable. Those of us who had been through that audition process couldn't face having to do it again.

SWARB: We did consider some quite well-known folkies as possible singers. There have been lots of rumours about who it
could have been, but I don't think anyone was seriously considered beyond the tossing-ideas-around stage.

The success of *Liege & Lief* encouraged folkies to 'go electric' – as
can be seen with Mr Fox, The Dransfields, Magna Carta and John
Martyn. Ashley built up Steeleye Span using singers who were
well-established on the folk scene: Terry Woods from Sweeney's
Men and his wife Gay who was a solo singer, and Tim Hart and
Maddy Prior who had already released two albums and were rapidly becoming the must-see double act on the folk scene.

Among those who have been rumoured – and in some cases
have claimed – to have been invited to be Fairport's singer at that
stage are Bert Lloyd (the source of several Fairport songs and guest
reader on *Babbacombe Lee*), Bob Davenport (from whom Swarb
learned 'Hexhamshire Lass'), Peter Bellamy (with whom Swarb
recorded on several occasions, most notably on *The Transports*),
Martin Carthy (who eventually took the primrose path of folk-rock
and joined Steeleye Span – twice), Mike Waterson (who recorded
one of the great folk-rock albums *Bright Phoebus* which included
'Rubber Band', a Fairport single in 1979), and singer-songwriter
Allan Taylor. The list does not feature female singers.

SWARB: I think Trevor Lucas might have been in the running,
but he had decided to form Fotheringay with Sandy.

SIMON: The subject matter of some of the songs on *Liege & Lief*
was too close to home for anyone to feel comfortable singing them. So we ended up preserving the traditional songs –
'Matty Groves', 'Tam Lin', 'The Deserter' – and virtually drew
lots to decide who'd have to sing them. It was between Swarb,
Richard and, to a lesser extent, myself. We'd all sung lead with
Fairport in the past, on stage at least, but that is not the same
as thinking of yourself as lead singer. Just like I had played
fiddle on a couple of recordings but would never list myself as
one of Fairport's fiddle players – different league and all that.

Despite having formally left the band, Peggy honoured one last
commitment with the Ian Campbell Group, at their 1969 Hogmanay

party at the Jug O'Punch in Digbeth Civic Hall. Swarb went with him, an ex-member appearing as a special guest. Although most of the evening was given over to Ian Campbell and friends, one of the support acts was the mysteriously named Purple Phlange. They were a one-off group consisting of Peggy, Harvey Andrews, Brian Clark, Andy Smith, Geoff Bodenham and Cozy Powell. They played covers of Buddy Holly songs – giving a foretaste perhaps of later Fairport offshoots The GPs and The Dylan Project. After sets from Bob Davenport and Diz Disley, whom Swarb and Peggy joined on stage for a couple of rags, the Campbells began their set.

PEGGY: It would be wrong to say I was bored with folk, but I was excited about playing something rockier again with Fairport. I told Swarb how pleased I'd been to have a bass guitar and not the huge, cumbersome, upright, double bass to lug around. Swarb suggested I smash up the double bass at the end of the gig as a kind of ceremonial farewell.

Swarb has what some describe as 'an impish sense of humour'. More than one member of Fairport has said that sometimes he doesn't know where to draw the line. Old Year's Night in 1969 was one of them.

PEGGY: We came offstage and headed for the bar. Swarb collared me and said, "Well, are you going to do it then?"
    "What?"
    "Execute your double bass!"
    I was fairly refreshed by this point in the evening, and it seemed like a good idea at the time. So I went on stage and jumped up and down on it. As it lay in bits beneath my feet, I noticed the shocked expressions on the faces of the rest of the group. Then Swarb calmly reminded me that, "it's only the interval".
    He has continued to exert a positive and supportive influence on my life ever since.

Another influence that Swarb had was in the choice of place Fairport would live together in for the next 14 months. After sharing a rented – and rather grand – house had proved fruitful, Fairport decided to continue doing so on a more permanent basis.

SIMON: It was a bizarre thing to do. But with Swarb having chosen to put himself down the end of this utterly inaccessible peninsula, it meant that he was always several hundred miles from wherever he might want to be. Swarb of course has never driven; heaven forfend that he ever would. He would represent a bit of a challenge for the rest of us on the roads. Wherever his gig was then, he would need to be driven at least a couple of hundred miles before he even started going towards the gig.

And it simply wasn't working with him living down there. Don't forget that it was less than a year since we were able to drive back to London – or out of the centre depending on where the gig was – and within a few short miles drop off every band member. The same applied in reverse for gathering the band together to set off. We had remained, in effect, quite a local band in terms of personnel.

Swarb's location was one of the key factors for finding somewhere at least central where we could live together. On top of which, Dave Pegg and his wife Chris wanted to move down from Birmingham, for much the same reasons. Dave Mattacks was living in Haywards Heath (a town in Sussex, two-thirds of the way from London to Brighton). I was in a flat in Primrose Hill.

The day after Peggy's bass-smashing farewell to acoustic folk – 1 January – is traditionally a time for new beginnings. It may not be the best time for house-hunting. Nevertheless, trying to turn Fairport's dream of a permanent communal base into a reality, that is exactly what the band's new manager Robin Gee and Simon Nicol were doing.

SIMON: Robin and I started cruising estate agents and looking in newspapers for a new base for the band. Somehow we ended up outside a disused pub in North Hertfordshire: The

Angel in Little Hadham, which was to become another piece in the jigsaw of Fairport legend.

It was a typically cold, dull, grey, drizzly-on-the-point-of-sleety kind of English winter's day. A shut-down, empty village outside Bishop's Stortford was probably the last place on earth you'd want to be. The pub had been out of commission for six months; it was stark, bare, uncared for, and utterly un-inviting. It was unpleasant, dirty, cold. The windows rattled; some of them were broken. It was, in short, a totally unsuitable prospect for a shared habitation. So we jumped straight back in the van and drove back to London.

We phoned round the band to tell them, "That's not going to work, but we've got a couple more to look at tomorrow." We spoke to everyone but Swarb; there was no reply at his place. Then Robin got a call from him to say he was on his way; he had everything in a removal van; he'd spoken to the owner of The Angel and would be arriving tomorrow, with fiddles, family, bags, baggage, and other paraphernalia.

So that was it, really. It was settled. Against our better judgement, The Angel was to be our new home.

Swarb and his then-wife Birgitte and her daughter Sys, who was about five or six at the time, were about to move into somewhere they hadn't seen. It was a real case of them buying a pig in a poke.

So, we made do and mended, quite literally in the latter case. It was at least big enough for everyone to have a family bedroom each. The Peggs had two bedrooms because Stephanie was a toddler by then – that's her in the gatefold photo of *Full House*, a shot taken just behind The Angel.

It was fairly basic. I would certainly never do it again. But, against the odds, at the time, it was the right thing for the band to do.

Two Fairport albums grew out of The Angel. Both had titles inspired by the band's home. *Angel Delight* was the more obvious reference. The other, *Full House*, deliberately reflected their domestic situation.

RICHARD: It was a hand with five kings. Maybe that should have rung alarm bells.

The new line-up made their live debut playing some stuff from *Liege & Lief*, some new songs – including early versions of 'Sloth' and 'Walk Awhile' which no one knew the words to – a couple of country songs, Dylan's 'Country Pie', and some audience requests.

Most of those requests came from Sandy and Trevor who had turned up to support the band. One was for 'Yellow Bird', an old Harry Belafonte number, miles from anything Fairport had ever done and probably inspired by the fact Swarb was sporting a bright lemon shirt.

SANDY: There was no ill feeling. Mutual respect has always been a big aspect of Fairport. I was there at the first gig they played without me. It should have felt weird, but I suddenly found myself acting like a fan rather than an ex-member of the band. I stopped worrying about whether they would suddenly invite me up on stage, which I'd said I didn't want to do.

Lots of people were shouting out requests. Old songs they didn't do any more. Someone kept shouting for 'Meet on the Ledge' – it could have been Karl [Dallas] – and I knew there was no way they would want to play that. So I started shouting out silly requests – Dylan songs, old rock 'n' roll songs, anything. One of the wackiest was the Harry Belafonte song, and bloody hell, they played it.

Not only that, but they kept it in the set and played it whenever they had time to fill (the song appeared on the first version of their *Live at the Troubadour* LP). Despite her earlier reservations, Sandy joined them on stage for a couple of ragged rock 'n' roll covers as an encore.

Fairport continued to hone their new set at large-scale gigs in the provinces. By now, Fairport were a big-enough act to sell out Liverpool Philharmonic and Manchester Free Trade Hall, before returning to London for the official launch gig of 'the new, all-male Fairport Convention'. Lurid green posters, with the name of the band spelt out in bright yellow broken branches, appeared all over the city.

On 14 February, 1970, Fairport played the Royal Festival Hall in London. "Happy Valentine's Day: we are Fairport Convention and we are here to steal your daughters," yelled Swarb by way of introduction to the standing-room-only crowd. They launched straight into 'Walk Awhile', which ran straight into 'Dirty Linen' – by which point the audience were dancing in the aisles.

Karl Dallas raved about the gig in his *Melody Maker* review, with just one caveat: 'A pity they seem to have jettisoned so much of their old material. Someone shouted at the encore for 'Meet on the Ledge' and I agreed with them.' It would be nine years before Fairport would honour that request.

For the next two months, Fairport gigged extensively, mainly in the South and the Midlands. March, however, offered some variety with a gig in Zurich, supporting Deep Purple, and a BBC TV appearance on the seemingly unlikely *Disco 2* programme. Two more BBC radio sessions were recorded on 20 and 21 April. They knew they would be out of the country for a couple of months and wanted to stay in the public consciousness. In the main, they performed the songs that would appear on their next album – 'Walk Awhile', 'Doctor of Physick', 'Sir Patrick Spens', 'Flatback Caper' – and a couple released on later albums, 'Poor Will and the Jolly Hangman', and Dylan's 'Open the Door, Homer'.

In the midst of all this live work, Fairport also found time to go into the Sound Techniques Studio to lay down backing tracks for their fifth album. At Dave Pegg's first recording session with them, they recorded 'Walk Awhile'.

PEGGY: It's a song that keeps coming in and out of the repertoire. It's a great opening number and it gives everyone a chance to sing a verse.

SIMON: That was where the all-male Fairport really started. We rest it from time to time and it keeps coming back. I think it's been played most years at Cropredy.

CHRIS: I love 'Walk Awhile'. It has everything going for it – great tune, amazing riff, catchy chorus, verses that give everyone a chance. It's high impact in terms of the audience, and it gives us all a chance to warm up.

RIC: As an opening number, it can be ragged; it doesn't matter if it goes a bit wrong, because the way it's structured you can pull it back on track in seconds.

On 23 April, 1970, Fairport played the Roundhouse as a part of the Pop Proms, which had shifted from the Royal Albert Hall where it had been the previous year (Fairport had missed that gig due to the accident). The night was dedicated to 'a night of English folk-rock'. Fairport headlined a bill featuring Matthews' Southern Comfort (who apologised for not playing much folk-rock, but opened with 'Blood Red Roses' and ended with their version of Joni Mitchell's 'Woodstock') and Fotheringay (who delivered a spellbinding version of 'Banks of the Nile' and "an old traditional song we collected from an American source singer Charles Edward Berry" – 'Memphis Tennessee'). Despite those highlights, Fairport stole the show. An *Oz* magazine reviewer wrote: 'Fairport definitely proved they are not only the first but also the greatest folk-rock band. Their set was mainly traditional – or so it seemed that way. But it was as exciting and loud as any rock band you care to name, including The Who.' Fairport raised a few eyebrows that night by delivering the world premiere of the extremely bawdy 'Bonny Black Hare', introducing it with: "This is what folklorists called a *single entendre* song."

America

A week after the Pop Proms gig, Fairport played the first date of their American tour. Four consecutive nights at the Fillmore West in San Francisco were followed by a week-long booking at Los Angeles' Troubadour Club, to which they would return on their second visit to America in 1970. While they were in LA, the band spent some time in the studio.

SIMON: *Full House* might seem like a very English album but, oddly, a lot of it was recorded in America. We continued work on it at the Gold Star studios in LA, where Phil Spector made all his classic records with The Crystals and The Ronettes. We went in and tried recording an electric version of a Napoleonic ballad lasting 11 minutes. It was a long way from 'Da Doo Ron Ron'.

The US tour included a number of free concerts at universities.

SIMON: Those gigs were important in building up a fan base. We still get fans coming up to us who first saw us as students, when they couldn't afford to pay to go to gigs but came to see us because we agreed to play without an entrance fee.

They played at the Boston Tea Party, a small folk venue on 7 and 8 June, 1970, and while in the area they met with several musicians from the (American) Cambridge folk scene, who had been influential in the early Sixties. One of the prime movers was Eric Anderson, a songwriter whose work a younger, more innocent version of Fairport had once respectfully covered.

ERIC ANDERSON: When Fairport came to town in 1970, they created quite a stir. It was a major event. We'd all been bowled over by what they were doing with folk music. I suppose we responded to them in much the same way as they had reacted to The Band. The most amazing thing was the way they seemed to know so many of the songs we'd written.

SWARB: I was very depressed in Boston. It was the end of quite an exhausting few weeks. I wrote a tune to capture the mood, which was called something like 'Sad Little Boston Tune'. Richard came up with some words for it. They turned it round into 'feeling down but knowing it's going to get better', and it became 'Now Be Thankful'.

The tour that began at the Fillmore West took Fairport across the country and ended with two nights at the Fillmore East on 10 and 11 June. The *Village Voice* reviewer wrote about 'epic ballads and traditional dance tunes brought to life electrically by a rock 'n' roll Baron Frankenstein', before going on to liken Fairport favourably to both the Grateful Dead and The Band.

SIMON: We stayed at the Chelsea Hotel on West 23rd. We went to Vanguard Studios and recorded the vocals on to the backing tracks from London. So *Full House* was recorded half in Chelsea, England, and half in Chelsea, New York.

RICHARD: We were confident as musicians, but very reluctant vocalists. That, in a way, was what 'Sloth' was all about.

SWARB: It's one reason why the album, which was quite short, had two long instrumentals – about ten and a half minutes or a third of the LP.

PEGGY: 'Sloth' is something like ten minutes long and has only three verses.

RICHARD: I was never happy with the vocals on *Full House*. It was all a bit too tentative. We pulled one track at the last minute, after the sleeve had been done!

FRIDAY 10 JULY, 1970
SPINNING DISC, HIGH STREET, OXFORD

The chap who ran the shop was a big folk fan. *Full House* had just arrived and he took the opportunity to fill his display with the sleeve, showing off its gatefold (featuring the band looking chilled as opposed to cool, at the back of The Angel, with Robodog and little Steph Pegg). The shop window also had various items of Island publicity material. At eye level, fastened to one panel of the Georgian framed windows – which had been consciously remodelled to be 12 inches square – was the back of the sleeve and, to its right in the next frame, a note saying 'Read this * it's REALLY funny'. It was a blown-up clipping from John Peel's column in *DISC*: 'Stroll into your local record shop and read the sleeve notes by Richard S. Thompson. I have no idea what, if anything, they are all about, but there is a fine madness about them.'

Full House

Island
July 1970

SIDE 1:	SIDE 2:
'Walk Awhile'	'Sir Patrick Spens'
'Dirty Linen'	'Flatback Caper'
'Sloth'	'Doctor of Physick'
	'Flowers of the Forest'

This was a *revised* tracklisting, after Richard Thompson vetoed the inclusion of 'Poor Will and the Jolly Hangman'. The CD reissue restored the original running order (as printed on the first 1,000 copies of the album) and added some key tracks recorded as part of the same sessions. The CD version (released October 2001) added 'Now Be Thankful' (*single*), 'Sir B McKenzie's Daughter's Lament for the 77th Mounted Lancers Retreat from the Straits of Loch Knombe in the Year of Our Lord 1727, on the Occasion of the Announcement of Her Marriage to the Laird of Kinleakie', 'Bonny Bunch of Roses' and 'Now Be Thankful' (*stereo*).

First impressions on hearing the album were that while the music it contained was excellent, it was a little short at just under 32 minutes and only seven tracks. Of those tracks, 'Walk Awhile' has remained a Fairport classic, as has 'Sloth'. Richard's cryptic tale of interpersonal conflict proved to be a great Fairport survivor, despite being developed to highlight the instrumental inventiveness of a particular line-up.

PEGGY: As Fairport went through various changes in the Seventies, 'Sloth' always stayed in the set. Even the short-lived line-ups – with Roger and Tom in '72; and Dan, Bob and Roger in '76 – played it. The mid-Seventies line-up with Sandy did a great version, too. We played it as a three-piece acoustic group; Swarb and Simon played it as a duo; Richard has included it in his solo set. We were still playing it with the last line-up on the Farewell Tour.

SIMON: You can only play so many long songs in a set, otherwise people feel cheated or bored. 'Matty' with its ancillary
bits is always pretty epic. We have various other long songs,
too. One is aware that audiences may have diminishing attention spans.

PEGGY (interrupting):   Long songs play havoc with your blad-
der. That's why I like 'The Hiring Fair' – I can pop offstage for
the first bit and then come back where the bass comes in.

In the second decade of the 21st century, long songs, warmly wel-
comed at Cropredy, often have to battle for a place during the
Winter Tour. The later Fairport revival of the epic 'Tam Lin' had
surprisingly limited outings, for instance. At one stage, 'The Hiring
Fair' and 'Who Knows Where the Time Goes' jostled for a place in
the set each night. The members of the current line-up continue to
have a soft spot for 'Sloth'.

RIC: It is great. Like a jazz thing, each player has a chance to
head off into the stratosphere, be really inventive, and then
return to where they left to hand it on to the next player. It
reminds me of the kind of playing that Coltrane and Miles
Davis used to do. It's a paradoxical combination of freedom
and tight structure. When we play it at Cropredy, I love to be
able to sit back and see where Richard or Swarb or Jerry or
Peggy take it. It's always thrilling.

Playing Away

Throughout 1970, Fairport departed Little Hadham for an astonishing array of venues across the UK and overseas. The year proved to
be a period of intense musical creativity, of ancient songs reworked
and modern songs invented.

SIMON: When we were all living at The Angel, gigging was even
easier: we all clattered back to the yard and we were home.
All you then had to do was stumble back into your own living
space in the house. The next morning we piled into the van
and headed off to wherever the gig was. I wouldn't want to

live that commune-based life today, but at the time it was a huge practical advantage, not to mention the creative bonus of all being together. You could bang on somebody's door and say, "Here's a new musical idea." You didn't have to make an appointment to try things out.

In 2012, with the exception of Gerry Conway, all the members of Fairport still live within a 15-mile radius. For years, Woodworm Studios, adjacent to Dave and Chris Pegg's home, which also housed the band's offices, was the hub of our activities and we could all be there within minutes. Our current offices are in Chipping Norton, where I live, and the same applies.

PEGGY: Forty-odd years later, I spend a lot of time at my place in Brittany and am aware of being out of the loop sometimes. But I still have a house in Banbury, so when Fairport are functioning – whether it's playing live or recording or preparing for Cropredy – I am back at the heart of things.

RIC: Fairport Central has always been 'drop-in-able'. Of course, recent advances in communications make that less necessary. You don't have to see somebody to play them your new tune, you can email them an MP3.

Back in 1970, Fairport's gigs ranged from small clubs to huge festivals. These included the Bath Festival, which was rapidly becoming the biggest in the UK. (1970 was also the year of the first Glastonbury Fayre – Fairport would be one of the headline acts the following year.) On a much smaller scale, there was the Maidstone Fiesta, which was filmed for Stanley Baxter's Oakhill productions. Supported by Matthews' Southern Comfort, Fairport were featured in the summer sunshine playing the *Liege & Lief* 'Medley', 'Sir Patrick Spens', and 'Now Be Thankful', plus an impromptu version of 'Star Spangled Banner', Hendrix-style, when the departure of a military helicopter interrupted proceedings. Fairport's appearance at Maidstone Fiesta was later released as a B-movie, and just as they had in 1968, they became the support act to Pink Floyd when it was paired in British cinemas with *Live at Pompeii*.

Six days later, Fairport played what they would describe as "the most convenient gig we've ever done" – at a fete in Little Hadham.

They were second on the bill to TV presenter Judith Chalmers who presented Peggy with a pair of socks for winning the best ankle competition. A small event, it was a precursor of the Cropredy village fete, which evolved into the Cropredy Festival and without which, it is fair to say, Fairport Convention would not exist today.

The Krumlin Festival in the Yorkshire Pennines has now passed into legend, if only because the event was so badly planned, the site so remote, and the resources so restricted that when bad weather arrived, the place became something of a disaster area. Fairport were one of the few bands to perform before the gales and torrential rain stopped play. The event was one of the first professional ventures of the late Jeremy Beadle, who would come to be renowned for the TV programme *Game for a Laugh* (1981–85), on which he played practical jokes on the unsuspecting public. Among the people Fairport hooked up with at Krumlin was local songwriter Bob Pegg of the band Mr Fox, who was inspired by the bizarre events of the Festival to write a song titled 'The Last Dance'.

Over 50 acts were booked to appear, but very few did. The Friday evening was intended to provide entertainment for those arriving and setting up camp for the weekend. Backstage squabbles resulted in the event starting three hours late, by which time rain had set in, causing regular interruptions to performances and forcing what audience there was to find cover. Acts scheduled to appear included Elton John, The Humblebums, Groundhogs, and The Pretty Things. The planned 'all night folk and blues jam' failed to materialise.

Next day, those who emerged from their tents or arrived on foot – roads were at a standstill for miles around as no one had considered the logistics of so much traffic hitting the narrow lanes of the upper Pennines – faced a sea of mud. The large flat plastic sheet covering the stage, meanwhile, was already sagging under the weight of water. Fairport shared the bill with Pentangle, Fotheringay, Ralph McTell, bluesman Champion Jack Dupree, who was living locally at the time, Graham Bond with Alexis Korner, Alan Price, Manfred Mann Chapter III, and The Who. The Sunday was totally written off, though one dreads to think how the small stage and limited access might have coped with The Mike Westbrook Orchestra, Quintessence, Steamhammer, Yes and Ginger Baker's Airforce – not to mention Mungo Jerry and Taste.

SIMON: There was a lot of confusion, and what can only be described as the spirit of the First World War trenches. You know, "We're all in this together and somehow we'll get through it, chaps." Friendships were forged – we got to know Ralph and Danny Thompson better.

The confusion was such that even today no one is certain which bands actually appeared. Photographic evidence suggests that Ralph, Pentangle, Fairport and a few local acts made it to the stage. The weather broke part way through the Saturday. Tents and marquees were flattened. The police declared it a disaster area and proceeded to start evacuation. Speculation abounded about the organisers, and wild rumours spread: supposedly, one organiser had run off with carrier bags full of money; another was found wandering the moors days later, a victim of exposure; while another was helping the police with their enquiries. One supposed organiser was found in the pub denying all involvement. It was whispered that the site was haunted. None of it true.

RICHARD: They were carting away the audience suffering from exposure, everyone was dressed in those bin liner things. It was great fun. For some reason or other, everyone was totally legless backstage. We all got very silly. We were playing 'Bonny Bunch of Roses', but Simon was playing an Indian raga in a different key. He was in his own world, sitting cross-legged in front of his amp. So we had to sort of kick him, and unplug him. But he carried on playing those ragas.

Simon opened Fairport's set at 5.00 pm on the Saturday by telling the assembled crowds that they had been in the beer tent since 2.00 pm. The band cut short his rambling words of welcome by launching straight into 'Walk Awhile' at about 50 per cent faster than its normal speed, running straight into a medley at the time referred to as 'Tunes My Mother Taught Me', but today better known as 'Sir B McKenzie'. At the end, Swarb and Richard jointly addressed the jigging crowd: "You look like you could do with a bit of warming up… A bit of internal heat should help dry you out. Our next song, with no irony intended, is called 'Now Be Thankful'."

PEGGY: It has gone down as one of the worst gigs of all time: badly organised, battered by some of the worst weather ever, illegal ticket sales, no one getting paid. If Little Hadham was what we wanted Cropredy to be, albeit small-scale, Krumlin was what we wanted to avoid writ large.

America: The Return

At the end of August 1970, Fairport were in America, their second visit that year. The tour opened with two nights at the Fillmore East in New York on 28 and 29 August, before heading to Philadelphia, to play the Folk Festival. A semi-official history of the Philadelphia Folk Festival cites Fairport's closing set that year as one of the all-time highlights.

SWARB: The Festival has a strict no encores rule, which they broke because there was such a demand for us to go back on. There were about 25,000 people watching, and half of them were dancing throughout our set.

The performance – recorded, broadcast, and quite heavily boot-legged – was a perfect summation of the band at the time: 'Walk Awhile', 'Dirty Linen', 'Staines Morris', the *Liege & Lief* 'Medley', 'Sloth', 'Banks of Sweet Primroses', 'Sir Patrick Spens', and 'Jenny's Chickens / Mason's Apron'.

SWARB: The recording captures that line-up at its best. We were confident, fresh, and pleased with what we were doing. I think everyone who plays on it has a favourite track. [Swarb would one day request this version of 'The Medley' be in-cluded in his box-set, *Swarb!*]

After playing two venues on the East Coast, they flew across the USA to repeat the process in the West with three nights at the Fillmore in San Francisco. They followed this with a six-night stint at the LA Troubadour, which has passed into legend.

SIMON: In fact, most of the stories are true. Let's start with the most famous one. They gave us a tab on the Tuesday and said, "Just help yourselves to the bar. We'll write everything down, and we can sort it out at the end of the week." You need to understand we were there for six nights – a Tuesday to a Sunday. We did two shows on the Tuesday, Wednesday, and Thursday, and three shows on the Friday, Saturday, and Sunday. That's a lot of shows, and they were all full sets. We were alternating with another group – Rick Nelson and His Band. We'd open and close the night, the other band would do a set in the middle.

It was all highly convivial. Because it was Rick Nelson's birthday during the week – I recall he was 30 – lots of people came down to celebrate. They were showbiz-y people, of course. Ozzie and Harriet were there [Rick's parents – he'd become famous after appearing on their hugely popular TV show]. We simply took advantage of the atmosphere. We stayed on late after the show, chatting up waitresses and generally carrying on.

By the last night, we had exceeded our fee on our bar bill. That night, Rick Nelson's band had finished their last set and were getting ready to go home, packing their stuff up as we were preparing to go back on. We were all saying our goodbyes...shaking hands and so on. The bass player, who I think went on to become one of The Eagles, came over to me and said, "I've really enjoyed listening to you guys, but, take my tip, you could really do with a bit more pizzazz, stagecraft, you know – showmanship."

"Like this?" I replied, taking my trousers off. The joke carried on as these things do, and I ended up playing our last set at the Troubadour in just my underwear. Apparently, the sight of my legs was enough to make the owner waive our bar bill. So although we did spend more than we had earned, we still got paid. And we all lived happily ever after, and all because of the sight of Nicol's knees.

RICK NELSON: My previous season at the Troubadour had been recorded for a live album, and one cut from that – a version of Dylan's 'She Belongs to Me' – had become a hit. I was also writing songs and we were working on a style that fused rock and American traditional music. Then I find myself sharing the bill with these five English guys who have done exactly that with rock and English folk. They were an inspiration, and it encouraged me to head down that line and create The Stone Canyon Band.

Fairport's very new and very different style of music, together with their very unshowbiz-like approach to presenting it, made them an act to be seen during their stay in LA.

RICHARD: You'd look round the audience, and half the faces there were people who made you think you ought to be paying to see *them*.

SIMON: It was during that same season that we persuaded Linda Ronstadt to get up out of the crowd and sing a song with us. The Troubadour was a fairly hip place to be, very much a place to be seen at. I think some nights the audience spent more time looking at each other than at the band on stage. So on any night, in the crowd, you might have a Hollywood star and entourage, TV people over from Burbank, and some famous names from the emerging LA rock scene. Linda, I think, already had quite a reputation as a singer.

As a member of The Stone Poneys, Linda had already scored a Top 20 hit with 'Different Drum' by Mike Nesmith, and had launched a solo career off the back of this, appearing on national TV as a guest on Johnny Cash's top-rated weekly show. The appearance made headlines when she revealed that she tended not to wear knickers, prompting June Carter to step in and put a veto on that if she was on stage with her husband, Johnny.

Incidentally, it was at the Troubadour a year later that Linda would recruit the members of her new backing band, all of whom played regularly at the club in a number of short-lived line-ups: Randy Meisner, Glenn Frey, Bernie Leadon and Don Henley split with Linda after three months to become The Eagles.

SIMON: She was an admirer of the band – in particular of Richard's playing, I think. So, during a break, we asked her whether she would like to join us on stage for a couple of numbers. She replied that she'd like to, but didn't know our songs. One of us said, "That's all right, we know all of yours." We ended up on stage together doing a couple of her songs, and 'Silver Threads and Golden Needles'.

She was in something of a wind-up mood. While I was playing, she proceeded to tease me by rubbing her bare foot up and down my legs. In other circumstances, that would have been a most enjoyable experience. On that occasion, let's just say it was memorable! I recall everyone sitting at her table being very amused.

Linda was not the only surprise guest during Fairport's LA sojourns. Odetta sang with them on a different occasion. Equally legendary is an extended jam session with members of Led Zeppelin, who knew the band through Dave Pegg.

PEGGY: Singers wanted to sing with us because we were a great backing band.

RICHARD: I wonder if sometimes they heard us and took pity. You know, "Great backing, chaps, shame about the lead vocals."

ASHLEY: A lot of it was because of Richard. Everyone wanted a chance to play with him – Hendrix, Clapton, Jimmy Page, lots of American players, too. I sometimes wonder if we took him too much for granted; he's always been so unassuming. I think we still do. I can't imagine asking Eric to play pennywhistle on a version of 'Telstar'!

SIMON: Peggy, being a very sociable chap by nature, seemed to know everybody. When I eventually left Fairport, Peggy and Swarb turned to the huge pool of Birmingham musicians they knew as one source for a replacement. If our paths crossed, we could easily end up jamming with some of Peggy's mates: in a way, it was a return to what used to happen in the London clubs earlier in our career. It was informal and fun. Those jam sessions have passed into legend, but inviting someone from the audience to join you on stage was not unusual.

Unfortunately, none of these legendary events was captured on tape.

PEGGY: Or let's just say if by chance it had been, Zeppelin's manager Peter Grant would have made very sure the tapes ended up in his safe-keeping. The details of the night with Zeppelin are lost in an alcoholic haze: Richard and Jimmy playing together, Planty on vocals, Bonzo pounding DM's kit. We played things we all knew – 'Hey Joe', some rock 'n' roll, simple blues – the kind of thing Robert would later sing with us as a Cropredy guest.

Over the years, the event has trailed clouds of imagined glory and legend has attached itself to an event which few witnessed. Among the songs it has been claimed they played are 'Mystery Train', 'Morning Dew' and 'Banks of Sweet Primroses'. Joe Boyd recalls Jimmy Page "trying to keep up with Richard" on a set of jigs and reels.

RICHARD: That night ended in a drinking competition, with Peggy taking on John Bonham and Janis Joplin. That's Olympic-standard alcohol intake. Peggy won. Bonzo ended up missing a couple of Zeppelin gigs; Peggy was back on stage with Fairport the following night.

Fairport's record company did capture a couple of nights' performances from the Troubadour sessions, released as *Live at the Troubadour* and *House Full* seven years later. It was a budget release, issued when Fairport left Island Records.

Back Home

The British *Full House* tour, which began on 7 October, 1970, at the Royal Albert Hall, was Fairport's first 'proper' UK tour. With barely a night off, they gigged up and down the country right through to 12 December at Exeter University.

SWARB: We'd seen in the States how people went about touring, and adopted the same approach. It's the way most bands were developing. They were moving away from the idea of getting a booking, heading off to do individual gigs, and always returning to base.

Fairport adopted what would become the standard rock tour approach to being on the road. As the headline act, they were expected to appear after a support act – usually someone trying to reach a wider audience. However, Fairport gave this approach their own unique twist by joining the support act on stage for the final number in their set: this was soon revised so that Fairport took the stage *with* the support act, and then remained on stage to play the second part of the first half of the evening's entertainment.

Partly as a result of 'supporting the support', there have been a large number of albums by other artists on which Fairport appear as guest musicians performing the song (or songs) on which they had provided live backing. The first of these, from the *Full House* era, was Allan Taylor's *Sometimes*.

DM, Peggy and Swarb are credited, and are best heard on 'Tudor Bop', an instrumental Allan had played with them on stage during the tour.

As their *Full House* tour began, rumours circulated that a bootleg of unreleased material was about to come out. It was to be a double LP, possibly called *The Chronicle*, featuring tracks by all five line-ups of the band. In an interview at the time, Swarb revealed plans for what would be the next official release: "It will probably be a double album, possibly live, or perhaps one live album and a studio album of new stuff. We are writing a lot at the moment. We've also added some more traditional material. People will hear a lot of things by us on the tour that we haven't played before."

SIMON (from the stage): Here's one you won't have heard before: in fact, it's quite possibly one I haven't heard before either.

PEGGY: We were keen on getting something live out, because Fairport always have been and always will be, essentially, a live act. That's where we're at our best. It's one reason we have released so many live albums.

There was a real sense of anticipation as the full-house audience awaited the arrival of Fairport. I'd been able to grab a brief interview for a University magazine by gatecrashing the soundcheck. DM was setting up his kit; Richard and Simon were round the corner at the local music shop, not the first and far from the last to succumb to the blandishments of Russell Acott's window display. "Rich and Si have gone window-shopping for Fenders," Peggy told me. "You can talk to us if you like. DM doesn't like talking." So I ended up 'interviewing' Peggy and Swarb. Both were still keen on the idea of recording Fairport live.

SWARB: There are some live recordings we made in the States. The trouble is, they are mainly songs we've already released. There are some new traditional songs, some rock 'n' roll which Richard enjoys playing, and a couple of comedy numbers. Not the right material for an album. What we might do is record the next album live in the studio in front of an invited audience.

PEGGY: We work best when we are playing to people. We need that kind of feedback. I don't think we could ever be one of those groups who spend weeks in the studio perfecting cymbal overdubs.

The Oxford gig that night attracted a largely student audience, most knowing roughly what to expect. *Full House* had been out since July. The house lights dimmed and the five members of Fairport took the stage. Swarb said, "Right, lads, side one, track one," and led off into a straight play-through of the album – with a detour at the end of side one, and bonus tracks to close the set.

Starting the album with a song that 'sampled' 'Bonaparte's Retreat' would have made a great musical joke if Fairport had retained the album's planned closing track, 'Bonny Bunch of Roses'. Like the other lost track from the album, 'Poor Will and the Jolly Hangman', which had several references in the sleeve notes, it would have given the album a greater sense of cohesion.

This was a very different Fairport to the one I had seen 18

months earlier. The repertoire now included lots of traditional songs where once there had been American singer-songwriter material, and their own work was stronger. There was more emphasis on instrumental prowess, demonstrated in the jam at the end of 'Matty Groves', an extended double solo in 'Poor Will and the Jolly Hangman', 'Sloth' and four instrumentals – two on *Full House*, plus the *Liege & Lief* 'Medley', and ("renamed for one night only") 'Bridge Over the River Isis'. The following year, the same song would become 'Bridge Over the River Cherwell', its usual *nom de clef* at Cropredy. The band was, of course, all male. This, in itself, was unusual in folk-rock where most of the emerging bands had followed the model of Fairport and Pentangle by having a female lead vocalist.

Asked about Sandy's departure earlier, Swarb replied: "It makes dressing rooms easier; you don't have one band member with a room to herself while the rest of us have to share."

RICHARD: People still expected Sandy to be with us. It's not like today when people keep up to date with the latest information. There was, of course, no website where you could check details. I gather Fairport were still being asked well into the Nineties where Sandy was, which shows a spectacular level of unawareness when you think about it.

Speak to any member or ex-member of Fairport Convention about the band's history and at some point you'll hear an ironic tale that illustrates the band's "studious avoidance of the constraints of commercial success", as Richard Thompson once described it.

It may be the *Top of the Pops* appearance that reversed the upward progress of their only hit. It may be the contract with Phonogram, which resulted in Fairport being paid to *not* make any more albums for them. It may be the fact that of all the acts signed to Island in the late Sixties, Fairport were one of the best known and least commercially viable.

There is, however, another side to the story. Along the way, there have been some unusual attempts to broaden the band's fan base. There were two separate occasions in 1970 when a teen pop magazine (*Jackie*) featured full-page pin-ups of the *Full House* line-up looking, to be blunt, more than a little dishevelled. Or as Swarb put it: "How many young girls were permanently traumatised by that?"

However, it would take a stellar leap of the imagination to think of these as 'Fairport – the boy band years.'

SIMON: Fairport as a boy band! It has been said, but apart from the gender of the line-up and the fact we are a band, there is no further advantage in that line of thought. I don't think we ever qualified as a boy band. We'd always been conscious of the fact that there was a lady in the van. Not the *Lady in the Van* in the Alan Bennett sense. But if you're brought up in a certain middle-class way, having a girl with you makes a lot of difference in so many ways. You behave more decently, I suppose. You don't spit out of the window – things like that.

I hesitate to use the word liberating, but certainly the all-male line-up – the three Daves, Richard and I – did feel different. At the time, and looking back on it, we were just a bunch of chaps, touring the country, playing music round the world. At least that's how it felt.

As for *Jackie* magazine, it has always been a mystery to me how they got around to doing an article on us. We were hardly typical of the sort of act they featured. At the time, the only publications interested in Fairport – probably the only ones who had heard of us – were *Melody Maker*, *Disc* and the NME.

The year 1970 got off to a shaky start for Fairport, but the new boys found their feet quickly. All of the band were getting used to the fact that the burden of lead vocals was now being spread.

RICHARD: Nobody was leaping up and down to say they wanted to sing. We kept only a few songs from our earlier setlist. I think it was a case of "If I do this, then you have got to do that." Swarb agreed to do 'Tam Lin', a song he'd always loved; I drew the short straw and got 'Matty', until it got passed on to Simon.

PEGGY: The instrumentals helped. They filled time. The one that became 'Sir B McKenzie' went through all manner of variations. I bet if you got together all the performances of that, you wouldn't find two the same – different lengths, different tunes, different order. 'Sloth' was designed to stretch out, and gave everyone a chance for a solo. Sometimes we'd just play a tune like 'Mason's Apron' and it would go on and on, getting faster and faster. Those were the days when high-speed playing was very much the thing – everyone was talking about Alvin Lee's performance in the *Woodstock* film.

All seemed set fair for 1971...but this being Fairport, the New Year brought another body-blow departure and another accident, "a hole in the wall where a lorry came in".

Despite not having settled on a format – studio album, live set, studio recording with invited audience – Fairport were clearly thinking ahead to their next album as the new decade began. They had established a foothold in America and, for the first time, were about to release an album with the same line-up as their previous album. They had also overcome the problem of being a group without a lead vocalist. Fairport had its own sound, which was new and unique.

31 DECEMBER, 1970
LITTLE HADHAM

Exactly a year prior to that, Dave Pegg had been on stage with the Ian Campbell Folk Group at the Jug O'Punch, playing his last gig with them. He was a working but not famous musician. The ICFG were at the top of their trade, but Fairport were in a different league.

PEGGY: Anyone who thinks folk and folk-rock are the same thing couldn't be more wrong. They have a lot in common, sure, but the differences are considerable: the venues, the way you are treated, the circles you move in, the audiences and their reactions, the pay scales, the sort of venues you play, even the musicians you mix and play with. I think it was always a problem for Sandy; she wanted to be in a world with the approach of folk and the acclaim of rock.

The perks are better, too. No folk act ever had a rider to make sure they were properly catered for at gigs. Very few had roadies. The whole sex and drugs and rock 'n' roll thing was different. Folkies may have had the odd old hippy smoking dope, but that and a lot more were common in the world of rock. And who ever heard of a folk groupie?

The genre Fairport had invented was officially acknowledged at the Pop Proms and elsewhere: *The Times*, for example, published a lengthy article by Karl Dallas which put the new music in context and documented its blossoming, concluding that, 'It is linked very definitely and organically with its origins: the fads of yesteryear did not endure so long.' Fairport had developed their repertoire to be based more on sing-able folk songs than daunting big ballads. The Swarbrick/Thompson partnership was turning out songs at a prolific rate. Even the imposed communal experience of Angel-dwelling had worked out, despite misgivings in several quarters.

JOHN PEEL: 1970 was the end of an era. The Beatles and Simon & Garfunkel split. Dylan seemed to have lost it. Jimi, Janis and Jim Morrison all died within weeks of each other. Woodstock had turned to Altamont. There were some hopes for a brighter future, though: underground acts, like Tyrannosaurus Rex, breaking through; serious rock bands emerging in the wake of Zeppelin and Yes; a whole new generation of singer-song-writers, led by people like James Taylor and Ralph McTell; and English music from Fairport Convention, who were at their peak, and the many bands that branched off from them.

In 1970, *Full House* was joined in racks containing 'folk-rock' albums including *Fotheringay*, *Hark! The Village Wait* by Steeleye Span, Matthews' Southern Comfort's *Later That Same Year*, and Trader Horne's *Morning Way*. A number of similar bands like Trees, Mr Fox, Magna Carta, Dando Shaft and the JSD Band were playing live across the country. Folk-rock was here to stay.

Open The Door, Richard

It's a simple statement that cannot convey what must have been a shock for Peggy. Written clearly, among the chronological gig lists that wind through the pages of his scrapbook, are the words 'Ritchie quit band'. They were written on Sunday 24 January, 1971, at The Angel, Little Hadham.

SIMON: Richard was a huge loss. I think, aside from Martin, it was the departure we felt most. His playing had always been

142

a crucial part of Fairport's sound. He was the group's song-writer. He was the strongest singer in the group. His departure meant I was the last remaining member who had been on Fairport's first three albums.

ASHLEY: When I heard Richard was leaving, I thought it would be the body blow that downed Fairport and it made me sad. But they – we – had achieved so much. Fairport's legacy would certainly continue. Richard had always been Fairport's unique selling point, quite simply the best guitar player around.

Of course, once I knew he was at a loose end, I invited him to join some of my projects. He has been an active participant in various Albion activities over the years as a result. As, of course, have many other members and ex-members of Fairport.

Among the Ashley Hutchings' projects Richard became involved in, in the years after quitting Fairport – alongside appearing regularly with Linda as part of the live Albion Band – were *No Roses*, *Morris On* and, as a writer, the first Albion Band album *Battle of the Field*, which included two of his songs. He also began work on his debut solo album *Henry the Human Fly*.

SIMON: I've been asked before whether Richard's first LP included things that should have been on the next Fairport album. We have performed songs from it, of course, and even recorded our own version of 'Poor Ditching Boy', but I am sure Richard didn't take anything with him when he left Fairport. If you look at the album following his departure, you can see there are several Thompson/Swarbrick songs on it.

RICHARD: It was a totally amicable split. I carried on sharing the house until a runaway truck came down the hill and we blew!

20 FEBRUARY, 1971
THE ANGEL, LITTLE HADHAM

SIMON: We had come back from a gig at the Big Apple in
Brighton. It was a Saturday night going into Sunday morning. We'd got home in the small hours, switched the van off,
made sure everything was secure, and gone to bed. The next
thing I remember is my then-wife waking me up, sitting up
in bed in horror. She was shaking me and asking, "What the
hell was that?" I am a deep sleeper and it hadn't woken me up,
but the expression on her face made it clear something pretty
horrendous had just taken place.

The house was situated at the bottom of a half-mile,
straight, downhill road, which took a sharp turn at the
bottom, a left-hander into a sharp S-bend. We were in direct
line of fire should anyone have the misfortune to fall asleep at
the wheel on the hill. That's exactly what happened to the unfortunate Dutch truck driver who was hurrying to catch the
ferry out of Harwich in the early morning. His co-driver was
sleeping. He fell asleep. He didn't apply the brakes and didn't
make the turn.

As a result, the lorry ploughed into the front of The Angel,
ending up in Dave Swarbrick's bedroom. Fortunately for us,
the truck was empty. Otherwise, the sheer weight of it would
have taken it right through the house. The chimney-stack collapsed on to the cab, and the driver was killed.

The room where the lorry ended up had been my room
since we moved in, but two weeks earlier, Swarb had negotiated a swap. He had rearranged the room to suit himself: he
had a large antique bed, which fitted only on the far side of
the room furthest from the outside wall. The front axle of the
truck ended up exactly where my bed used to be.

When the fire brigade arrived, Swarb was sitting up in
bed – shocked, naturally, but totally uninjured – listening
to the moans of the co-driver. What was astonishing was
that the room was completely full of rubble, bricks from the
front wall, which had completely collapsed, and the chimney-stack which had fallen on top of that, but there was not
one single brick on Swarb's bed. The bricks in the room were
up to the level of his bed, all around him. Aside from his

bed, everything in the room was completely destroyed. Hard to believe there isn't somebody up there, looking after that little person.

SWARB: I suppose I have Paul Simon to thank for it. I had been booked to play a session with him. It never came off, but I still got paid. I regarded the money as a bonus and bought a huge antique bed, which wouldn't fit in my room, so Simon and his wife agreed to swap. Their bed had always been below the window where the lorry came through.

PEGGY: Tragically, the driver died instantly. We were lucky that none of us was injured. The building was rendered unsafe and uninhabitable, of course. Richard's precious record collection was destroyed, as was Swarb's most valuable instrument, an 18th-century fiddle.

SIMON: Richard was still living at The Angel, but he was away on the night of the crash. In London, I think – probably playing a session somewhere. It was a good thing because his room was directly above Swarb's, where the lorry punched a hole.

PEGGY: Richard's stuff was hanging out of the building…his bed, his hi-fi, everything. We were trying to figure out how to try and salvage things for him when we became aware of all these oblong bits of paper blowing out from the room. They were cheques from sessions and royalties. Richard never had a bank account: he was a bit useless with money. There must have been a small fortune in uncashed cheques!

Fairport were forced to find alternative living conditions. The Angel, however, survives and still stands, repaired and renovated at the bottom of the hill by the River Ash in Little Hadham. Last time it changed hands, it was for a little under a million pounds.

The band adopted a 'show-must-go on' approach. Revived by a bottle of salvaged poteen and fed on sausage and bacon donated by the local butcher, the night after their front wall was gone they played The Greyhound in Croydon which was, according to Simon, the worst gig they ever did.

They commemorated the tragedy in song, making it the conclusion to a communally composed ditty about their life together, 'Angel Delight', which became the title track of their next album and would remain a part of their regular repertoire, off and on.

SIMON: We'd already started work on the next album. We had a pretty full diary of gigs, too. We fit the recording sessions around that.

One of those gigs was at the regular Implosion event at the Roundhouse on 28 February, 1971. This would be the first time London fans would see Fairport without Richard. They played familiar material from *Liege & Lief* and *Full House*, but also brought in some new stuff, including 'Bridge Over the River Fleet', 'Sickness and Diseases', 'Banks of Sweet Primroses' and, freshly minted, the first public performance of 'Angel Delight' which, Simon explained, offered "an update on our recent history and a curtailed experiment in communal existence". They also debuted two heroic ballads, which would open the new album; 'Sir William Gower' and 'Lord Marlborough'.

The second week in March was set aside to complete the new release, whose contents were revealed to a wider audience via consecutive radio sessions recorded for *Folk On 1* and *Night Ride* on 15 and 18 March. *Angel Delight* was scheduled for release in June. Island's advertising campaign treated it very much as a collection of songs, with adverts that listed all tracks, and comments by the band. The latter may not have been up to Richard Thompson's standard of copy, but gave a flavour of what to expect. The ad appeared to coincide with the release of the LP on 19 June, but its differing sequence of tracks revealed how last-minute the running order had proved.

The album was dominated by traditional material – four songs and two instrumental sets. The advert described the graphically bawdy 'Bonny Black Hare' as 'one for the Tom Jones fans'. Each side ended with a song bequeathed to the band by Richard upon his departure.

SWARB: They were the last things we wrote together. Fairport had already been playing them before Richard left, and so he left them with us. I think 'Journeyman's Grace' is one of the best Fairport songs.

The remaining tracks comprised the title song and 'Wizard of the Worldly Game', a rarely performed collaboration between Swarb and Simon.

SIMON: 'Wizard' was as much about me getting to grips with the electric lead guitar as anything. The song also introduced keyboards played by DM, a talent of his which is underrated.

PEGGY: 'Angel Delight' is about the whole experience of being at The Angel – not just the band but roadies and engineers. Everybody put something in, writing comments on other people. It was just a bit of fun, and we rounded it off with the destruction of The Angel. It has the same plot structure as *Star Wars*, actually!

Aided by an extensive, full-page advertising campaign and a two-song plug on *Top of the Pops'* short-lived album slot, *Angel Delight* went to number eight in the LP charts.

SIMON: Following news of the crash – which appeared in all the papers – many assumed the ruin on the cover was what remained of The Angel. In fact, it was a long-abandoned workers' cottage in Furneux Pelham.

Before the album came out, Fairport spent a fortnight touring Hungary, inspiring Peggy to write 'Hungarian Rhapsody'.

PEGGY: That's really 'Angel Delight II'. We'd been effectively made homeless, so a fortnight overseas with everything taken care of seemed like a good idea. This was the era of glam-rock and camp pop stars. Let's say a boozy load of scruffy folkies who walked on stage in their street gear was not what was expected!

While at The Angel, Fairport had become very much a part of the community of Little Hadham. After the crash, villagers rallied round to offer sustenance and support. Having had a taste of English rural life, it was only natural that their enforced move should seek a similar environment. They decamped to the Cotswolds.

The Oxfordshire village of Cropredy is now so closely associated with Fairport Convention that even the Virgin Trains Windowgazer Guide included it as a spot to look out for as the trains passed:

> 'The village, thought to take its name from the Old English "crop" meaning "hill" and "ridig" meaning "stream" is now famous for the folk music festival founded by Fairport Convention.'

SIMON: When Richard left Fairport, there suddenly was this big hole in the sound we made: I had to develop a new approach that would allow me to fill that hole without trying to emulate what he had done, which would have been beyond me technically and spiritually. I don't have that free-thinking imagination he has musically. I simply had to make a sound to complement the other instruments, and round it out. That meant going out and buying a completely different guitar and finding a way of co-operating with it to make that noise. For the same reasons, I was forced to sing more.

Angel Delight had Simon taking lead vocals for an entire song for the first time, on 'Sir William Gower'. Curiously, it's one they have never returned to.

SIMON: The rest of the band were incredibly supportive. I had my doubts about both my singing abilities and my guitar playing. Richard was already a legend in his own lief-time [*sic*] so far as playing lead guitar was concerned. There was no way I could replace him, but I had to find a way to fill out the guitar sound with one guitar, where previously there had been two, one of which had been played by Richard Thompson.

Swarb and Richard had become the voices of Fairport after Sandy left, and Iain before that. Suddenly you found yourself with that heritage behind you and you knew you had a lot of expectations to live up to.

Both Peggy and Swarb really encouraged me. They were helpful and honest. Of course, I don't know what they might have said behind my back, but so far as I am aware there never was any conversation about finding a replacement to bring into the band because we weren't cutting it without Richard.

PEGGY: In all my time in Fairport, I don't believe we've ever thought in terms of replacing someone. If someone leaves, there is a gap and that means a chance to bring in someone new, or not. When Richard left, we didn't look for another lead guitarist because we knew Simon had the skill as a player for us to make it as a four-piece. The struggles we had after *Simon* left are the best evidence for that statement.

With *Angel Delight* in the shops, and a major US tour supporting Traffic lined up for October 1971, Fairport wasted no time in proceeding with their next album, which was to be a total contrast. Instead of a collection of individual songs, it was a concept album, which told the story of John Babbacombe Lee, the man they couldn't hang.

Ironically, given the turn events were about to take, Fairport's seventh album was the first to feature exactly the same line-up as their previous release. Already renowned for their metamorphic membership, Fairport found themselves reading reviews which speculated as to whether 'Fairport Convention, who seem to change band members as often as they change T-shirts, have finally settled on a stable permanent line-up' (*FRIENDZ*, issue 1, October 1971).

No Hanging Around

On 23 February, 1885, John Lee, convicted (perhaps wrongly) of murdering Miss Emma Keyes of Babbacombe, had his death sentence commuted to life imprisonment, after the gallows set for his execution at Exeter Gaol refused to work – three times. Swarb, on his endless hunt for antiques and pre-owned bargains, had discovered a few bound copies of *Lloyd's Weekly News* in a secondhand shop in Ware. In it, he read the story of the thrice-failed hanging. At the turn of the century, Lee had been the subject of magazine articles, books, a play and three films. Swarb decided the story would be a good topic for a song. It quickly evolved into a whole album, for which the rest of the band was co-opted to write tunes and lyrics.

PEGGY: Swarb became quite obsessed with getting the story told, and we were working to a very tight time-frame. It had to be planned out, written, rehearsed, recorded and mixed before we headed off to America.

SIMON: *Babbacombe Lee* was very much the burr under Dave Swarbrick's saddle: he was a man inspired, fired up by the idea. I don't know whether it was because it suddenly gave life to this urban myth of 'the man they couldn't hang' – three strikes and you're let off the gallows – but there it was, the story made real, a first-person narrative. He set to with gusto and it quickly spilled over into a sequence of ideas, linking this young man's whole life story together. All the source material was coming from Swarb, and he and Dave Pegg wrote some of the songs together, but I wasn't involved in that. Then, for some reason I genuinely cannot recall, the idea of an external point of view came up, and it was a very short step from creating something using these old newspapers as source material to me writing a song in which contemporaries read those newspapers at the time.

The song, 'Breakfast in Mayfair' is Simon's only lead vocal on the album, and also features a rare lead guitar solo from him. Sandy chose to sing 'Breakfast' when the album was re-recorded for a BBC TV documentary.

SIMON: It fitted really nicely, and takes a step back from the main narrative. It's a chance to take stock of what has gone on so far. It's set in Mayfair because it is a long way from Babbacombe: I had a mental image of these leisured toffs sitting around tutting over their breakfast marmalade, kedgeree and devilled kidneys about the state of the lives of the poor.

I remember writing it – partly because it came easily and was done in one go, sitting in an undecorated room in my house in Islip in Northamptonshire. We were then in the process of doing the house up, and because it had stood empty for a very long time, everything had been stripped down to the bare plaster and the floorboards. There was one 25 by 15-foot room, from which we'd removed the floor as well as underpinned the main load-bearing wall. I had a wheelbarrow with which I had been bringing in cobblestone-sized pieces of rock to fill the floor up. I was taking a break from this and had gone into a room on the top floor, out of the way of the main renovations, essentially for a break. The song just came to me there and then, and really didn't take long to do.

Swarb became something of an expert on John Lee, developing his own conspiracy theory as to why the gallows failed to function. The folk-opera that he had created inspired a BBC TV documentary in which he appeared as an authority on the subject.

With Swarb and Peggy taking on most of the composing duties, Simon happily took on the role of producer.

SIMON: That was the first album where I got a formal 'hands-on' credit. However, that was a kind of reciprocity because Swarbrick had put so much time and effort into developing and creating the material, it was a way of 'balancing the budget' if you will.

One big difference, though, is that the producer's job isn't finished when you record the final note. In a way, it just begins then. *Babbacombe Lee* has to be listened to very much as a whole. That meant part of my job as producer was putting together all the bits of the puzzle – the songs, the tunes, the sections of spoken word – in a way that made them cohesive.

It was an economical process in a way: there was, as I recall, nothing left over. We recorded exactly what Swarbrick had written, and knew from the outset what the album was going to be like. My decisions in the final stages were about what space to leave between tracks, if any... and so on.

As it turned out, this made it seem like a *fait accompli* to the rest of the band – the overall sound, the way I ran tracks together, whereas *Angel Delight* was more a collection of individual tracks. You feel more able to go back and change elements when each track stands alone.

Even though Simon was the producer, there is one recording from that session which he had absolutely nothing to do with. With every letter accounted for and many lines too obscene to see the light of day, an alternative take of the album's one traditional song – 'Sailor's Alphabet' – was created.

MARTIN CARTHY: 'The Naughty Sailor's Alphabet' – that's a real skeleton in the closet. I know it is circulated among Fairport fans in bootleg form: a warning to all about committing to tape things that seem like a good idea at the time.

SIMON: It was another late night lock-in at the studio. For some reason I wasn't there; and for some reason Martin Carthy was. The revised version was something that Martin and Swarbrick and Pegg cooked up.

SWARB: Martin Carthy, Peggy and I were sitting together one evening when the album was being finished. We rewrote the words together and, as we got drunker, it got ruder. It was a good joke, but afterwards took on a life of its own.

SIMON: I believe it was John Wood who facilitated the record-ing of it – in fact, they just dug out the existing tape of the backing track and put these obscene lyrics they'd concocted over it.

'Sailor's Alphabet' was the only traditional song on the album. Had Fairport gone ahead with an album of entirely original material, aside from a couple of incidental tunes, it would have raised a few eyebrows, perhaps because that wasn't what people expected of them. 'Sailor's Alphabet', nevertheless, is the section of the folk-op-era Swarb remains least happy with.

SWARB: It may have been because we were running out of time or inspiration, but I think we cheated a little with the section that deals with John Lee's time at sea – a couple of tunes and a so-so folk song. We should have written something.

'Sailor's Alphabet', which had come to Fairport via Bert Lloyd who appears on the album, is normally associated with the Norfolk singer and fisherman Sam Larner. It is a kind of 'completion game' song, in which each singer in turn has to add to what has gone before. It's a musical slant on Ghosts, the game that created the word 'unhalfbricking'.
Sometimes it is an accumulating list (most familiarly used in 'The 12 Days of Christmas'); in this case, it is a steady alphabeti-cal progression through nautical terminology. So Swarb, Peggy and

Martin worked their inebriated way through the process but supplied obscenities and scatology instead.

> Y, we might wonder, was it ever written
> And X, the certificate it should be given.

According to Dave Pegg, the original plan had been to remove the legit version of the track from the roughly assembled master-tape and replace it with their bawdy parody. The proper version would then have been secreted away, much to Simon's chagrin when he came to work on sequencing the album. The incident is an example of the contrast between the sense of devilment in the approach of certain band members and Simon's sometimes overly-serious, meticulous approach to producing what he considered to be an album more weighty than previous projects. The desire to see his reaction got the better of this particular scheme.

SIMON: They felt a need to witness the moment of panic first hand. As I understand it – and this is based on what I was told years later, as I was in no mood for explanations at the time – I was supposed to play through the album and happen upon this quite clearly unreleasable version of 'Sailor's Alphabet'. A degree of panic would have been inevitable.

Both Swarb and Peggy attended the playback. Peggy was encouraging me to play the track and, when I did, those ill-suppressed Pegg giggles gave the game away immediately. I certainly did not share their amusement. They were beside themselves, seized up with the giggles. They were so pleased with their efforts.

Suffice it to say that, despite the vast amount of rare and unreleased Fairport material that has surfaced on authorised releases over the years, this is one recording they have both individually and collectively vetoed.

PEGGY: We're proud of Fairport's family appeal. You can see that in the Cropredy crowd. There are people who now come along with their kids because their parents had once brought them as kids. It would be wrong to put out something as filthy as that. When we included the April Fool's Day tape

on a Cropredy CD, we put a parental guidance warning on it –
and that was just because of Swarb swearing. If anyone really
wants to hear that version of 'Sailor's Alphabet', they'll find a
way of getting their hands on it.

SWARB: It was funny at the time. But it's long ago and far away.
As a recording, it has no bearing on Fairport or on any of the
participants, even if how and why it happened is significant
in other ways.

Simon can enjoy, and indeed perpetrate, a prank as readily as
the next man. Despite the unmitigated smut, the verbal dexter-
ity in rewriting the words might normally have appealed to him: a
dysphemism for every letter of the alphabet takes some doing. But
Simon was under pressure as producer, and knew he was facing an
absolute deadline as the band headed off for an American tour.

There he was, confronted by two of his band-mates who had
time enough to rewrite and re-record the vocals for an entire track:
it was an aggravating situation and added impetus to his inevitable
departure from the ranks of Fairport Convention. He was beginning to feel like the outsider in the band that he had formed.

SIMON: The rest of the band finished recording their parts and
had a few days off to unwind and prepare for America, but
my job was really only just beginning. It was a tight schedule.
John Wood and I finished the mixing somewhere between
three and four in the morning and I had about two hours' kip,
before flying to America. The tapes followed me over, about
ten days later.

In the end, I wasn't best pleased with the reaction of the
rest of the band to my efforts. I was fairly wrung out by the
time they got to hear it. What with one thing and another, I
didn't enjoy that tour. That was when I decided it was time for
me to leave Fairport.

Keen to widen their audience in the States, Fairport's tour supporting Traffic would take them to cities and areas they had not played
previously, and give them access to a different audience. Fittingly,
Traffic's setlist featured one of the all-time great folk-rock arrangements inspired by Fairport, their version of 'John Barleycorn',
which Steve Winwood had learned from Mike Waterson.

When the acetate of *Babbacombe Lee* arrived in the States, the
band was less than enthusiastic about Simon's production work,
and let him know what they thought. So it was that he found himself physically and mentally drained, on stage with people whose
respect he felt he had lost, in front of an audience who were not
there to see Fairport.

SIMON: Just over halfway through the tour, in the middle of
'Sloth', I suddenly felt like I wasn't in the band any more and
asked myself, "Why am I doing this?"

Right after the show, I told the others that I wanted out. I
didn't know what I wanted to do – I just wanted to get away
and try something different. I'd been a part of Fairport for
four years, and my attempt to find a new role for myself as
producer had met with (shall we say) a less than favourable
reaction. At the age of 20, four years is a long time – 20 per
cent of your life, and in effect all of your adult life thus far. I
was the last of the original Fairport left – the others had all
come and gone. I needed a break. Despite all that had happened, I suppose production was an option, though I wasn't
consciously thinking that at the time.

A major part of Simon's job had been to make sure the sequence of
tracks worked, musically and logically. It proved invaluable experience and helped develop one of his less-celebrated skills – that of
putting things in order so that they worked to their best effect, be
they two sides of an LP, the running order of 16 or more tracks on a
CD, or a setlist to be played live.

On the inner gatefold of the sleeve of *Babbacombe Lee*, there is
a drawing of Fairport with Simon shown standing apart from 'the
three Daves'. It unknowingly reflected a problem within the band.

SIMON: I wanted to go then and there, really. However, we had the rest of the tour to complete, and there was an English tour booked immediately afterwards.

SWARB: We knew *Babbacombe Lee* would be a difficult sell. Simon was a key part of it, and we couldn't go out and play it without him.

A tour was one thing. It would sell the album to Fairport fans and give those who already owned it a chance to see the whole thing live. A TV appearance would have reached an even wider audience, however, the only official recording of the next, short-lived line-up of Fairport is an appearance on *The Old Grey Whistle Test*. Swarb had other plans, though, and there was talk of the album making a great TV programme.

PEGGY: Somehow Swarb managed to sell the idea of turning the album into a TV special to Melvyn Bragg. That would have been great publicity but it came far too late. I don't think anyone had thought of the concept before then, though.

The idea of a TV plug for a new long-playing release wasn't entirely original. The Beatles had considered it for *Sergeant Pepper* as well as for the album that eventually appeared as *Let It Be*. Neither venture got beyond the rushes stage, although Paul McCartney later made a TV show based around one of his releases with Wings. *Babbacombe Lee* did eventually make it to television in 1976, but although the programme featured Fairport performing most of the original songs from the album, it was more about the man and his life than about the LP.

Island Records presented *Babbacombe Lee* in an elaborate gatefold sleeve, and included an insert reproducing the sections of *Lloyd's Weekly News* that had inspired Swarb. There was also a retrospective sticker campaign, bearing the legend 'Don't Hang Babbacombe Lee'.

SWARB: We didn't play it on the American tour, and our plan had been to promote it with a complete performance in the first concert of the British tour. It was going to be what they used to call a 'happening', with sound effects and a programme designed like a Victorian newspaper. Yet if Simon pulled out, all that simply wouldn't be possible.

PEGGY: Simon was the last of the few. If he left, we didn't know what would happen. There might not even be a Fairport. So we did the only thing we could, and appealed to Simon's better nature.

SIMON: Chris Blackwell, the boss of Island Records, was with us on the American tour – because of Traffic, I should explain – and was obviously concerned our new album be promoted. He also wanted the band to complete the UK tour. That would obviously be difficult to do as a trio. He persuaded me it would be in everybody's best interest if I stayed on.

The concept demanded that Fairport play the album in its entirety.

SIMON: It was an unusual idea. We'd do the first half – the old stuff, have an interval, then come back and do the whole of *Babbacombe Lee*. That was a true challenge. It did feel like you were putting on a bit of a show, rather than just trotting through the songs.

The original live version of *Babbacombe Lee* was, by latter day standards, something of a multimedia event. We had a programme that resembled a newspaper – so from the moment you took your seat you were being sucked into the atmosphere. To replicate the way the album worked, we also had spoken passages on tape and these were played in.

Busted

The *Babbacombe Lee* tour reached Van Dyke's Club, Plymouth – a long-standing favourite Fairport venue – on 25 November, 1971. Acting on a tip-off, the drug squad raided the gig with the intention of targeting certain individuals in the audience. Part way through the raid, one of those pre-recorded sections nearly landed Fairport in deep trouble.

SIMON: It's one of Swarbrick's favourite stories. It was obvious that the police weren't particularly interested in the band on stage; Fairport may have been world-class drinkers and certain band members were virtual chain smokers, but we never acquired a reputation for a fondness for other stimulants.

PEGGY: Everyone had to stand where they were, hands raised, while the police went round and checked everything. We were up on stage, exchanging reassuring glances and feeling rather stupid.

SIMON: Then someone by accident triggered one of the voice inserts and Philip Sterling-Wall was intoning Lee's sentence through the speaker… "John Lee: you have been found guilty, and the sentence of this court upon you…", etc. I am sure the police had no idea about the content of the show, and gave us some very suspicious looks.

PEGGY: That was it. The gig was cancelled.

SIMON: The story raises a smile in retrospect – at the time, it was a lot of very stern faces looking at a lot of worried ones.

SWARB: The police decided to check our instrument cases. Somehow, a lump of a certain substance had found its way into my fiddle case. It was nearly arrest and prosecution but we managed to convince them it was rosin rather than resin.

This particular story has grown in the telling, and several variants have planted themselves in the consciousness of individual band members. Inevitably, one gets a different version of the story depending on who is narrating it and when.

PEGGY: Of course, I would not want to go on record implying that any member of Fairport past or present would ever consider the use of illegal artificial stimulants. Any such suggestions are like the story of 'Lucy in the Sky with Diamonds' – purely coincidental…or circumstantial…whatever the word is.

When Free Reed [Fairport's online store] decided that the box for the four-CD set *Swarb!* be a representation of his fiddle case, inside and out, Swarb was very keen that it should include a small piece of 'dope'.

SWARB: Just a reference for those who know the story to smile about.

The 'bust' added extra interest to the tour for a music press who circled like vultures over what they clearly saw as the bones of a once-great band. *New Musical Express* broke the news of Simon's departure in connection with the drugs bust, in the 11 December, 1971, edition. The headline screamed, 'NME was right – Nicol IS leaving Fairport.'

The tour had been scheduled to end at the University of Essex on 11 December, 1971. However, not all the advertised gigs took place, and Simon recalls his last gig on the tour as being in Dublin on 4 December. So it was that the NME announcement and story, which treated his departure as a kind of betrayal, ran on the 11th. He was the last of the original line-up to quit, but there was no reason for seeing his departure as any more heinous than that of Ashley or Richard or, for that matter, Iain or Sandy. Simon has always maintained that a good band is not defined by its membership and should always be more than the sum of its parts.

SIMON: I don't see it as really breaking the chain that leads back to the early days from where we are now. It's accepted in every other field of endeavour that someone can take time out and return without things changing. I believe Fairport are like that in a way that is not true of many other bands, certainly not in the field of rock music. Of course, Fairport are not unduly encumbered by hits, or songs that are particularly associated with a certain era or moment in the commercial sunshine. There are some obvious songs which, if not included, would make audiences feel cheated; but audiences want to hear Fairport play them and are not concerned by the fact that only one person currently on stage happened to have been on the original recording. The songs belong to Fairport, whoever the members of Fairport happen to be at the time.

After the departure of the last remaining original member, Simon Nicol, in November 1971, attempts to sustain the band saw the arrival and departure of three different members in three different line-ups over ten months. The disintegration of Fairport Convention immediately prior to starting work on the *Rosie* LP marked the end of an almost desperate period of attempting to keep the good ship Fairport afloat.

An audit of the comings and goings within the band during its first six years of its existence took place at Island Records. With no new Fairport product to release, Island put together a lavish, two-LP chronological 'story-so-far'. Pete Frame's family tree, on the sleeve of *The History of Fairport Convention*, proved that Fairport were one of the most mutable bands on the planet. (A later Tree produced for *The History of The Byrds* proved Fairport were not without American counterparts.)

By May 1973, with the brief chart appearance of the *Rosie* album, Fairport had been in existence for exactly six years, and had seen 12 musicians come and go in that time.

Soon after Simon's departure, Dave Mattacks left Fairport for the first time, in February 1972. The man who had invented folk-rock drumming was in demand as a session player and "A permanent offer from The Albion Band came at a point when I was particularly pissed off with the way things were going with Fairport."

PEGGY: DM is truly one of the world's great drummers: he has the distinction of being the only person to join and leave Fairport three times!

There followed a series of short-lived Fairport line-ups, before the group that appears on the sleeve of *Rosie* and features subsequently on *Nine* finally came into being. While nothing by these line-ups was released at the time, various tracks, both live and in the studio, have surfaced on archivist releases and compilations since the turn of the century.

Roger Hill had been recruited by Peggy as a direct substitute for Simon. They had worked together in The Uglys and The Exception. He remained a member of Fairport until June 1972. His subsequent career involved playing country rock with Raymond Froggatt and trad jazz with Chris Barber.

Tom Farnall joined Fairport in March 1972, as Dave Mattacks' replacement. Like DM, he had a background in dance bands, but found the various demands of being a Fairport member too much of a strain. He confessed at the time: "I really never was a big fan of folk music."

David Rea, a Canadian, had been recruited by Swarb, who had befriended him during a folk package tour in the mid-Sixties and had whisked him straight into the studio upon arrival in this country to join Fairport at The Manor in an attempt to record their urgently required album. Previously, Rea had worked with Leslie West's heavy metal conglomerate Mountain. If that reads like an appointment doomed to failure, you will not be surprised to learn that his residency in Fairport lasted less than six weeks.

CHAPTER FIVE

History of...

Both *Rosie* (1973) and the dreadfully titled *Gottle O'Geer* (1976) are best described as transitional albums. Each arose out of a time when the band struggled to create a viable live line-up. Each consists of tracks from a range of sources, including some not originally intended for a Fairport album. Each comes from a time when Fairport were essentially reduced to just 'the two Daves' – Pegg and Swarbrick – although they both give the impression of featuring an existing band. And each features an extensive list of 'guest musicians' – six and 12 respectively. The second album saw the band briefly dropping the second half of their name.

The albums act as quotation marks around the three years and eight months when founder member Simon Nicol was no longer a member of the band. His departure not only confirmed a generally held view that Fairport had a constantly changing line-up, it also inspired a career-defining moment for a journalist.

PETE FRAME: Those who play in rock bands are not the same as pop stars. Fans have a different, more serious kind of interest in them. In most cases – though by no means all – rock bands are bigger than their individual members. With the endless comings and goings in lots of rock bands, I found myself constantly checking who was in a band when (and indeed *who* was in which band when). I thought it would be a good thing if there were a simple way of doing this. I realised I was not the only person who would find that interesting. Hence the rock genealogy, or family tree.

The 1972 New Year's issue of *ZigZag* featured the first rock family tree; it catalogued the changing personnel of Fairport Convention.

PETE FRAME: They were a natural first choice. I'd admired Fairport since their earliest days. They were also very approachable, which makes gathering precise information like dates and previous careers easier. Needless to say, they'd been through more than their share of band members.

So it was that the groundbreaking family tree became, in a very simplified but also slightly extended form, the front cover of Fairport's next – compilation – album.

PETE FRAME: As it turned out, Fairport also proved a very good choice because their history made it clear that what was needed was not just a timeline but a whole 'roots and branches' thing. There weren't many other bands around who could be traced as the source of so many acts that had found fame in their own right.

The list of offshoot bands in that primordial pictography of personnel included Giles, Giles and Fripp (and hence King Crimson), Matthews' Southern Comfort, Fotheringay, Ashley's Albion Band, and Trader Horne. The Tree also gave account of some key folk acts and a small slice of the Birmingham rock scene of the late Sixties. Pete's subsequent family trees highlighted bands that represented, similarly, the trunk of a 'many-branchéd blooming': The Byrds, John Mayall's Bluesbreakers, and Alexis Korner's Blues Incorporated. Eventually, his collected family trees would become the subject of four large-format books.

Pete later returned to Fairport to create the impressive genealogy that accompanied Fairport's *unConventional* box set, detailing the origins and destinations of members of 21 different Fairport line-ups. When Pete published his first Fairport Tree it ended with 'Fairport 6' and was titled, 'Sorting Out the Fairport Confusion'. While Fairport were not the only rock band to regularly change membership, few had changed line-up with every release. After the apparent consistency of *Angel Delight* (1971) and *Babbacombe Lee* (1971), the band was in disarray. Between the end of 1971, when Simon left, and August 1972, Fairport went through four different line-ups in which six new members joined and, in most cases, rapidly left. Album projects were begun and abandoned. An album was virtually completed at Richard Branson's new Manor Studios and then totally scrapped.

Nevertheless, Island Records released *History of Fairport Convention* in spring 1972. Sequenced chronologically, it provided a balanced overview of their career to date with a well-chosen selection of tracks. For contractual reasons, the first album was omitted, but the set included the hard-to-find single 'Now Be Thankful' and an early version of the instrumental set that would eventually appear on *Rosie*. Elegantly packaged, it included a high-quality book with photos of the band's various members.

There have been several retrospective compilations of Fairport's career since, of variable quality, but that first remains a definitive example of the approach.

SWARB: They could have called it *Fairport – The Simon Nicol Years*, because that is what it summarised. We didn't think he'd be coming back.

PEGGY: The band wasn't heavily involved in putting the LP together. In fact, there was no one left in the band who could fairly claim to have a proper overview of that period. We were pretty desperately trying to work on our future at the time.

A year had passed since Fairport had released an album and Island Records were worried. Money was being invested in studio time and nothing was thought suitable for release.

SWARB: It was frustrating. We spent more time rehearsing and recording than performing.

In the meantime, Peggy's former band-mate Roger Hill had stepped in to fulfil Simon's role.

PEGGY: Roger Hill had been playing since the early Sixties; his band had even supported The Beatles. He was a revered guitarist in Birmingham. When we left The Uglys, he and I formed a group called The Exception, which was the first band Robert Plant recorded with – playing tambourine.

Fairport continued to take up bookings, playing their recent repertoire, and made an appearance on *The Old Grey Whistle Test* playing songs from *Babbacombe Lee*. The line-up existed for a couple of months until, following a gig at Birmingham's Jug O'Punch, Dave Mattacks resigned.

PEGGY: When DM quit we needed a drummer. I knew Tom Farnell from my Brumbeat days and asked if he'd like to join.

Dave Pegg, Fairport's second bass player, had securely taken on the mantle of his predecessor, recruiting members for the band. Dave Swarbrick put on a brave face in an interview with *Melody Maker* headlined 'Lovesongs from Swarb'. He claimed, somewhat disingenuously, that the band was making an album of love songs, "One of them is a slow love song, one is a humorous love song, and one is an instrumental." Peggy told another interviewer, "We are thinking of giving up folk music and concentrating on our own songs."

From Far Away

The band returned to America in March of 1972. Most of the gigs were at colleges, including one with The Kinks. In Philadelphia, they played with Lindisfarne. In LA, they supported King Crimson and were rewarded with an enthusiastic standing ovation from a crowd of hardcore Crimson fans that a reviewer described as 'pleasantly surprised by the latest edition of Fairport'. Other gigs saw them sharing the stage with the Mahavishnu Orchestra and Sea Train. During the tour, 'Sloth' developed into an even longer *tour de force*: they played highlights from *Babbacombe Lee*, 'Walk Awhile', 'Matty Groves', 'Sir Patrick Spens' and – "by way of bringing Dylan back under our wing" – 'Country Pie'.

At the end of the tour, Peggy was interviewed by Jerry Gilbert for *Sounds*. He told him: "Last night we did a gig with David Rea and Happy & Artie Traum. We might try to get these people to England with us."

A two-week tour of the UK that April and May saw them return to the Jug O'Punch to celebrate its tenth anniversary, as well as play gigs to support two favourite venues which were facing closure due to financial pressures – London's Roundhouse and Van Dyke's in Plymouth.

JOHN PEEL: The early Seventies were a hard time for bands who depended on gigging rather than record sales. A lot of venues were closing down and funding was drying up on the college circuit. The music business was changing and glam rock saw people leap from being virtual unknowns to stars who would only play major venues for large sums of money. It all became very showbiz.

For a band like Fairport Convention, there were fewer and fewer convenient venues. On stage, although some Fairport standards re-mained, the new songs seemed like try-outs and the sets became increasingly instrumental. Swarb frequently dipped back to the tunes that the band knew from Ian Campbell's group: 'Tail Toddle', 'Haste to the Wedding', 'Hen's March'. The fact that one new tune was an instrumental called 'Scotland' featuring Roger, Peggy, and Swarb on acoustic guitars was a foretaste of what was to come from the band.

PEGGY: We all bought Martin guitars in the States – three big, beautiful ones – and as a result started doing more acous-tic stuff and writing things for acoustic guitars. That is a big factor in the sound of *Rosie*.

Rosalind Russell, writing in *Disc*, declared Faiport to be 'an all Brummies band'. They had exchanged their North London roots for the Midlands, Muswell Hill for Cropredy, which was now the effective home of the band. In May 1972, they toured Sweden play-ing for the first time with Steve Tilston who, years later, would not only furnish the band with several songs that would become audi-ence favourites, but would also write 'Over the Next Hill' in tribute to them (the title track of a Fairport album in 2004).

Things were not running smoothly, though, and after three months with the band, Roger announced he was leaving. He played his final gig as a member of Fairport on 16 June at St Edmund's Hall,

Oxford's smallest college. Shortly after that he joined the Chris Barber Band. Then Fairport, that most English of bands, made the shock announcement that they were recruiting a non-Brit.

SWARB: We tried various musicians at the time, trying to find a way to make Fairport work. Some were friends of Peggy from the Birmingham rock scene. David Rea was someone I knew – and the only Canadian to join Fairport.

Swarb had known David Rea since 1966, when David had toured as guitarist with Gordon Lightfoot and Ian & Sylvia. They had toured with the Ian Campbell Folk Group, during which time he and Swarb had struck up a friendship. He had been on hand to jam with Fairport during their seasons at the LA Troubadour. A good friend of Felix Pappalardi, he had worked with Mountain and written one of their best-known songs 'Mississippi Queen'. A respected guitarist, singer and composer, he seemed just what Fairport were looking for.

DAVID REA: I joined Fairport as a replacement for Richard Thompson [sic] and found it difficult to fill his shoes. I have been privileged to play with many fine musicians but none finer than Fairport.

Eager to have something in the record shops, especially after some rather premature plugging by Swarb, the band headed for Richard Branson's newly opened Manor Studios in rural Oxfordshire. Designed as a haven for bands that wanted to closet themselves away and focus on the music, its appeal to Fairport could be summed up in four words – local and surprisingly cheap.

The recording didn't work out, however. Listening to the tapes today, one feels that a lot of what went down was little more than rehearsal. There are songs that would eventually become more fully realised on *Rosie*; there is a rather good Swarbrick original called 'Sad Song', which would have made it on to the next Fairport album had it not made the album seem like too much of a Swarbrick showcase. Dave Rea had taught the band one of his best-known songs, 'Maverick Child', the title track from an album he had released in 1970; and there were several instrumentals. The line-up at this point spent most of its time rehearsing and recording, "when we weren't drinking".

Dave was with Fairport less then two months – June and July of 1972. This created the strange anomaly of the music press still printing interviews about his joining the band (he had been singularly keen to talk to the press) when he had actually left.

So *History of Fairport Convention* became the 'next' release. As Swarb pointed out, "Purely on a business level, something new was needed in the shops to earn money." With Fairport currently not attracting any kind of new audience, *History* was clearly aimed at their existing fans. As subsequent expanded CD reissues show, there was at that point a lot of unreleased material that might have been included to make it more appealing to Fairport's hardcore fans. Island could have included previously unavailable material such as a version of 'Suzanne' which was the only recording by the all-male line-up between the departure of Judy and the arrival of Sandy; outtakes from all three of their 1969 releases, including their magnificent version of 'Ballad of Easy Rider' from the *Liege & Lief* sessions; live recordings from the LA Troubadour; 'Bonny Bunch of Roses'; and a couple of B-sides to long-deleted singles. Quite a few of which were to emerge on the first Richard Thompson retrospective (*guitar/vocal*) four years later.

Also Starring…

Although Fairport were not creating Convention releases, various members and ex-members could be heard on a raft of different releases in 1972. Ashley's Steeleye Span had released (and re-released) three albums, while releases by Al Stewart, Mike Heron and Nick Drake all featured various Fairporters. Sandy Denny released her second solo album, the sublime *Sandy*, in September 1972. Richard Thompson featured throughout it, while Swarb appeared on 'Quiet Joys of Brotherhood', a song originally recorded for *Liege & Lief*.

Iain Matthews released three solo albums with contributions from Richard Thompson and, in April 1972, the highly praised plainsong album, *In Search of Amelia Earhart*. Richard began his solo career that same month with *Henry the Human Fly*, which is a natural extension of *Full House* and includes songs that Fairport would later adopt.

No Roses, the folk-rock album by the most respected female singer of the folk revival, Shirley Collins, had been released in

October 1971. Masterminded by her husband Ashley Hutchings, it used 26 backing musicians including Richard, Simon, Ashley and DM. The backing on the album's closing track, 'Poor Murdered Woman', was effectively Fairport '69 reconvened. It was the first album to use Ashley's Albion Band, the album being credited to Shirley Collins and The Albion Country Band.

In 1972, Ashley worked with squeezebox maestro John Kirkpatrick to create *Morris On*, giving folk-rock its first real sub-genre, Morris-rock. Richard, DM, and Barry Dransfield completed the album's five-piece band. That year, Ashley also produced an album of original songs by Lal and Mike Waterson, two of the country's most respected unaccompanied traditional singers, with Martin Carthy. *Bright Phoebus* is a left-field, folk-rock masterpiece, presenting contemporary songs by traditional performers. Richard, Ashley and DM played throughout.

John Kirkpatrick's *Jump at the Sun* (1972), also included Richard and Ashley on a version of 'Widow of Westmoreland's Daughter', a bawdy ballad later adopted by Fairport. Richard Thompson's friend Marc Ellington released *Restoration*, with backing provided by DM and Simon, among others. Various Fairport members would make notable contributions to Ellington's string of albums through the early Seventies. In 1971, he had been the support act at Little Hadham's fete.

The Not-So-Wild Bunch

On 27 November, 1971, at London's Rainbow, as one of the first gigs to feature Fairport's latest line-up headed towards the closing number, Sandy Denny and Trevor Lucas walked on stage. With nothing rehearsed and a band unfamiliar with most of the music from Sandy's Fairport era, they fell back on the common ground of most rock musicians of the time – old rock 'n' roll songs.

PEGGY: Playing rock 'n' roll from the Fifties is always pretty safe ground so far as audience response goes. It's something you all share. Plus there's the novelty of the music not being what the audience expect you to play.

So successful was the jam that it was repeated in the unlikely setting of Cecil Sharp House, the temple of folk tradition, six days later. It inspired Trevor Lucas to book time at the newly opened Manor Studios to try and reproduce on vinyl what they had achieved (to be released as *Rock On* by The Bunch in 1972).

TREVOR: Partly, it was a chance to show my skills as a producer. That's one reason why a lot of the tracks have little production touches. I came up with the idea on that night at The Rainbow. Fairport were then going through some difficult times, and the album – which began with Sandy and me joining the Fairport line-up then in place – ended up with us playing with ex-members and the rest of Fotheringay.

Simon was not included in the project.

SIMON: I believe one of the reasons that album got made was as a way of putting Richard Branson's new studio at The Manor, Oxfordshire, through its paces. It's something of an oddity really. There's no tangible reason why I wasn't involved. I wasn't really around when they were getting the thing together, which happened very rapidly. Of course, as I was slightly younger than the rest of them, most of the songs were before my time (to borrow a phrase). I don't suppose my mindset at the time would have been right for recording an album which was in its approach informal and light-hearted, and thought of as a musical *cul-de-sac*. I was available to work on the various albums people from Fairport were making at the time. I simply wasn't involved in any of them.

PEGGY: Fairport itself weren't involved in The Bunch because we were too busy trying to get the band together. We still think of it as a Fairport thing, though, because it involved so many of our mates who had recently left the band. I haven't checked but I'd say most of the songs from it have been revived at Cropredy since. At one point Fairport had Gerry's 'Let There Be Drums' in the set for a couple of years.

Gerry's version of Sandy Nelson's prime piece of percussive pop was included as a 45-rpm cardboard disc attached to the cover of the original album – a design feature that upped the production cost of the record considerably. The disc was easily damaged, and if you stored it in the album's pre-cut retainer it became frayed and scratched. Original copies with a playable version of the disc are therefore quite valuable.

A glance down the 12 tracks on the album shows why it is so readily regarded as an Fairport artefact: Sandy sings five tracks, including a duet with Linda Thompson that has since been included on Fairport compilations; Richard is lead vocalist on four; Trevor sings 'Don't Be Cruel'; even Ashley Hutchings turned up to provide vocals on a version of Chuck Berry's 'Nadine'. Richard Thompson and Jerry Donahue were the album's two lead guitarists.

The album title, *Rock On*, almost seemed like a response to Ashley's *Morris On*. It's fair to say that without Fairport, none of those folk-rock albums would have existed – at least not in the form we know them. It's also true to say that Fairport created a lot of competition in the commercial market.

PEGGY: Putting my 'record company boss' hat on, I can tell you that bringing out a record in the face of such close competition is never a good idea. It's an even worse idea to *not* bring something out.

SWARB: It looked bad. Everybody who had been in Fairport seemed to be making great records and we were getting nowhere. We gave interviews and promised new albums that simply never got made.

PEGGY: Fairport still got a lot of press coverage, but too often it was a piece in the news pages announcing another change of line-up.

Oh, Rosie

Fairport Convention were in disarray. Four gigs at the start of August, 1972, saw Dave Hill return briefly to help them out. It was with just such an approach in mind that plans were hatched for what was now essentially a two-man group to call in friends to help record the songs they had been rehearsing. Calls went out to Sandy, Richard, Ralph McTell and Gerry Conway who all agreed to help them make a start: the resulting track would be a Fairport classic. Work began on *Rosie* with the title track: it was the fourth time they had attempted to record it.

PEGGY: By that point, Fairport had been reduced to just Swarb and me. We'd tried recording an album and it hadn't worked. Essentially, the band had fallen apart around us. We talked about an album with just the two of us, but there was a feeling that if there wasn't a new Fairport album soon, that would be it so far as Fairport were concerned.

'Rosie' was re-recorded with Richard Thompson on guitar, Gerry Conway on drums, and Sandy and Linda Thompson providing backing vocals.

PEGGY: Richard wasn't available for the rest of the sessions. He was working with Ashley on various things and was gigging quite a lot. In any case, I don't think he would have wanted to be part of Fairport.

Three other previously abandoned tracks were then reworked. 'Me With You', 'Matthew, Mark, Luke and John', and 'My Girl' were all rescued from the Manor sessions and re-recorded. Ralph McTell provided some ragtime guitar for a multi-tracked vocal by 'The Swarbrick Brothers – David, Cyril and Eric' on 'Me With You'.

PEGGY: 'My Girl' was recorded by just Swarb and me, and so is a taste of how the album might have sounded without a few mates to help us along.

'Matthew, Mark, Luke and John' was credited to all five members of the *Full House* line-up.

RICHARD: Possibly it was something that began at The Angel. There had been a lot of team-writing and a lot of songs had ended up being abandoned. I really don't have any recollection of writing that, though.

Simon and DM draw similar blanks. The song did, as Richard suggests, start life at The Angel in the form of a poem by Fairport roadie Dave Martin. Swarb and Peggy saw its potential as a song and adapted it; Peggy then wrote some additional words and the tune.

PEGGY: It had been forgotten about. We were hunting for songs for the album from as far back as the Manor session with Dave Rea, and so I dug it out and reworked it.

Trevor, who had shown his production skills with The Bunch and Sandy Denny's solo albums, was brought in as producer but was soon providing harmony vocals and guitar. They then turned their attention to a song that featured Dave Pegg as composer and lead singer. Peggy's 'Hungarian Rhapsody' harked back to an eastern European tour in the days when Simon had been in the band.

PEGGY: Allowing for a little exaggeration and poetic licence, everything in the song was true. We had been booked to tour Hungary in May 1971. Glam rock was big in the UK then and the promoters had expected something like that. It was like The Beatles in Hamburg with the audience shouting '*Mach Schau*'.

The mix of the song betrays the budget constraints the band were facing towards the end of recording *Rosie*. The massed voices shouting, "We're only here for the beer" (the tagline for Double Diamond at the time) are not properly integrated, while the chorus at the end of the song is messed up by Trevor who sings "drinking our goulash and eating our wine", before declaring: "I cocked it up."

PEGGY: Those rough edges are in keeping with the song. It's not the greatest vocal ever to appear on a Fairport track but Trevor decided to leave it in.

Trevor was convinced that if Fairport were to be a viable concern, they needed a lead guitarist.

TREVOR: I've always been a rhythm player, quite happy to strum along, probably best kept low in the mix. I'm certainly no Simon Nicol. As for playing a lead line…at the first Fairport sessions I did, that was all down to Peggy.

Trevor made a long distance phone call to Paris where his old band-mate Jerry Donahue was playing in Johnny Halliday's band.

JERRY DONAHUE: When we started recording at Sound Techniques, it was going to be an album credited to 'Dave Swarbrick, Dave Pegg and friends'. Then their manager, Philip Sterling-Wall, told Trevor Lucas and me that they had decided to release under the name Fairport and followed that up by asking if we would like to come on board full-time.

The band still hadn't got a drummer, though. Aside from Gerry Conway on *Rosie* (his first recording with Fairport, whom he would eventually join in March 1998), Timi Donald had played on all the tracks. He had no interest in joining Fairport full-time, however. Certainly he did not want to go on the road with them. The band, on the other hand, had gigs lined up.

JERRY DONAHUE: Our first gig was in Duisberg, Germany (16 September, 1972), with Tom Farnell sitting in on drums, just before he left. DM filled in for the next two gigs and was then persuaded to join full-time.

Tom Farnell had never been comfortable within Fairport, having no interest in folk music. He was not involved in plans for the new LP. The German gig was a one-off overseas booking. DM joined them for gigs at Doncaster Top Rank and Newcastle Poly.

SWARB: Eventually, we recruited Trevor Lucas and then Jerry Donahue who had together been two-fifths of Sandy's band, Fotheringay. DM rejoined and that became our next line-up. It's what's usually called the *Nine* line-up, after the album we made.

DM: I didn't simply 'rejoin Fairport'. I was asked to play on *Rosie* and then agreed to come back into the band. There are three drummers on the album.

The first tracks recorded by the new Fairport line-up were instrumentals; 'Peggy's Pub', and a medley of two traditional tunes – 'Hen's March' and 'The Four-Poster Bed' – both of which had appeared on Swarb's solo album *Rags, Reels & Airs* (1967). Both tunes in the medley are onomatopoeic, simulating clucking chickens and creaking bedsprings. The second track is undergirded by DM's inventive percussion. As a foretaste of Fairport's future, a rough mix of the track was used as the final track on *History of*, where the set of tunes is almost a minute shorter than the version finally included on *Rosie*. Next they turned their attention to a Swarb original, 'Furs and Feathers'.

SWARB: The introduction to 'Furs and Feathers' – the one that fades in – is very Trevor. It's quite obviously his guitar style.

To represent the new line-up, two Trevor Lucas songs were taken from the abandoned second Fotheringay album.

TREVOR: I'd been asked to join Fairport full-time before we finished recording *Rosie*. It was felt that I shouldn't be just the rhythm guitarist on the album, as obviously I would sing on stage. We had two months to record the album and both time and the budget were running out: the obvious solution was to use a couple of songs we'd recorded for the second Fotheringay album whose release had now been permanently cancelled. Sandy had already used a couple of tracks from it on her first album. She doesn't appear on the two tracks we used for *Rosie*, though.

Peggy replaced Pat Donaldson's bass part, and Swarb overdubbed fiddle and harmony vocals. Since he was already on the album, the drum parts recorded by Fotheringay's Gerry Conway were left intact.

GERRY: That meant I played on three tracks on the album.

As did DM and Timi; three drummers played on three tracks each.
    The album that emerged from / after the chaos of Fairport in 1972 proved their least satisfying to date. Its title track 'Rosie' has since become a classic, but the rest of the album is now largely ignored by the band and most of its fans. The title track has been recorded live on a number of occasions, and returned to the Fairport setlist with an assured vocal from Chris Leslie, who had incidentally performed

it alongside Swarb in his post-Fairport band Whippersnapper. In 1997, when Fairport marked their 20th anniversary with a chrono-logical two-night set, they played three tracks from *Rosie* (the title song plus 'Hen's March' and a version of 'Me With You'). 'Rosie' was one of 15 songs picked by fans to feature on *By Popular Request*, the re-recorded 'best of' produced to mark the band's 45th anniversary.

CHRIS: There were live recordings of me singing 'Rosie', so people could hear it if they wanted to. It is a great compli-ment that they also felt they wanted to own a proper studio version of that performance.

Most reviewers agreed that the LP had several strong tracks, but the general feeling was that the album didn't hang together. One review unkindly noted, 'it sounds less like an album than *History of* which features half-a-dozen different line-ups recorded over five years'.

SWARB: If *Rosie* didn't end up sounding like a Fairport album, it's because it didn't begin as one. It started out as a solo album but Chris Blackwell had other ideas.

The album's distinctive sleeve design was distinctly low budget, compared to previous, increasingly lavish packaging. A single slip-cover, it had no inserts and depicted a wall decorated with slightly tacky paper on which hung – in carved frames that curiously an-ticipated the woodwork which would one day adorn Woodworm Studios – portraits of 'the current Fairport'. One reviewer likened it to 'a kind of suburban pastiche of *Liege & Lief*'s classic artwork'.

   The band only just existed in this form at this stage, and they cer-tainly were not the group who had made most of the LP.

Five Into Nine

Although they had already played a few gigs, Fairport's new line-up was officially announced in October: Swarbrick, Pegg, Lucas, Donahue and Mattacks. The announcement conveniently coin-cided with publicity and reviews for *History of*, which concluded with the first released track from the new line-up. To promote the

February release of the new album, Fairport embarked on a massive UK tour from January through March 1973, opening each night with 'Rosie'. 'Matthew, Mark' was greatly extended with a searing guitar solo; and 'Sloth' remained in the set, with the shared vocals of Swarb and Trevor complementing each other. Where once Fairport had focused on Dylan obscurities, they now included two of his singles, 'Country Pie' and 'George Jackson' – the latter a personal favourite of Trevor's. 'I Don't Believe You' was added towards the end of the tour. There were plenty of jigs and reels including a closing set designed "to totally knacker those of you who want to carry on dancing". They ended with Buddy Holly's 'That'll Be the Day', one of the songs Trevor had produced for The Bunch.

JERRY DONAHUE: There were some jibes from fans and reviewers, who coined the phrase 'Fotheringport Confusion'. It is fair to note, especially after Sandy joined again, that the line-up was closer to Fotheringay than to any previous version of Fairport. I should point out, though, that the music that line-up of Fairport made was quite different from what either Fotheringay or Fairport had done in the past.

This quintet would be the nucleus of Fairport over the next two years.

TREVOR: You'd normally say "a band made a record"; in the case of *Rosie*, the record made the band. But it wasn't *all* that the band was. It's a sort of patchwork album, separate things stitched together. We were determined to make the next album one that really represented who Fairport now were.

SWARB: After *Rosie*, we had to make a proper Fairport record on which all of the band played on all the tracks.

That album was *Nine*. When asked about the title, Swarb once replied, "It's what the German actress said to the bishop." Fairport's ninth LP is still reckoned to be one of their best. It's less a return to form than a fresh start.

TREVOR: You'd have thought some of the band's fans had been on a desert island for a few years. They were shouting for

'Meet on the Ledge' and 'Walk Awhile'. We were a different band from the one that had made those records.

SWARB: Maybe *Babbacombe Lee* lost us some fans. *Rosie* certainly didn't do us any favours. Neither of those had much for the more folkie fans.

PEGGY: There was a real sense of diminishing returns at the time.

SANDY: There were a lot of us [folk-rockers] touring, often at the same time. Our biggest audience in the UK were students, and so we tended to tour in term-time. You'd see a list of gigs and it would be Fairport one week and then Fotheringay or me solo, or Richard and Linda, or Steeleye or The Albions. Student grants only stretch so far. People used to tell you they'd had to pick which gigs they really wanted to see.

In 1973, Fairport turned their fortunes around and were booked on *The Old Grey Whistle Test* on 17 April. The line-up produced three albums which, while not on a par with the high standard of their 1969 trilogy, still endure as remarkable and enjoyable albums: *Nine*, *Live* and *Rising for the Moon*. The release of the first of those showed the band meant business, and their record company was taking them seriously once more. Not only did it see Fairport return to a gatefold sleeve, there was even a promotional video, shot in Cropredy, to support its release.

SWARB: We had a proper lead singer in Trevor. We had an amazing lead guitarist in Jerry – something we knew we had lacked since Richard left. DM was back on drums and that is always a good thing.

PEGGY: The *Nine* line-up was great. Fairport were really back on form. The icing on the cake was when Sandy decided to come back into the band.

Brilliancy, August 1972

'Schubert didn't quite make it,
but Fairport have just completed their ninth.'

The advertising copy was confident. Fairport were slightly less so as they began work on their new album, with a new band. They spent three months working on the album, fitting sessions between regular gigs in the UK. The first track they recorded was an instrumental written by their new guitarist, Jerry Donahue.

JERRY: Fairport had a reputation for instrumentals but, even when Richard had been in the band, they had usually been built around Swarb's fiddle playing and based on traditional tunes. My guitar-led piece was different. We had planned to record it live and drop in the second solo. It ended up with lots of overdubs – Swarb's multiple fiddle, mandolins from Swarb and Peggy, DM adding clavinet.

That tune, 'Tokyo', became the closing track on side one of *Nine*, while Tokyo was to be their first port of call on a world tour designed to promote the new band. In a way almost typical of Fairport, even as they embarked on the tour to promote their newest release, Sandy Denny's guest appearances and subsequent return began to overshadow the band she was rejoining. Similarly, Sandy's songs began to ease out the material from their latest LP.

TREVOR: The *Nine* line-up came about by accident. I was producing *Rosie* and providing some acoustic guitar. Then Jerry was asked to the sessions because Richard wasn't available. We were asked if we wanted to join when Swarb and Peggy were taking a break. DM was playing sessions and sitting in on gigs when Jerry mentioned that he should come back to the band, and he jumped at the idea. Sandy was with us on tour, and it seemed silly to have her sitting in the wings and not on stage; once she was singing with us, it made sense for her to rejoin, too. So that was it – two existing members, two new recruits, two people returning to the band – half Fairport and half Fotheringay, with Sandy as the common area of that particular Venn diagram.

While the early Seventies line-ups of Fairport had received some media exposure, including appearances on *Folk On 1* and *The Old Grey Whistle Test*, they had not recorded a Peel session since 1970. On 20 February, 1973, they were invited back. They included one track from the about-to-be-released *Rosie*, the revamped extended version of 'Matthew, Mark' with its emphasis on the guitar solo. Two tracks were from *Nine*, scheduled for release that October, each track giving prominence to the band's new members – Jerry's 'Tokyo' and Trevor's 'Possibly Parsons Green'.

Nine

Island
October 1973

SIDE 1:	SIDE 2:
'Hexhamshire Lass'	'Bring 'em Down'
'Polly on the Shore'	'Big William'
'Brilliancy Medley' /	'Pleasure and Pain'
'Cherokee Shuffle'	'Possibly Parsons Green'
'To Althea From Prison'	
'Tokyo'	

The album has an unusual structure, reflecting the direction the band was taking. Side one feels like a folk-rock album, featuring two settings of traditional songs, a trad arr medley, a setting of a 17th-century poem, and an instrumental. The opening song, 'Hexhamshire Lass', even had a source credit 'from the singing of Bob Davenport' – just as one would find on the album of a hard-core revival singer like Peter Bellamy or Martin Carthy.

The next song, as Trevor was to explain to the Cropredy audience ten years later, "is called 'Polly on the Shore', the story of a pirate and his parrot". Though not credited, traditional singer Pop Maynard was the source of the song, which had been collected from him by Peter Kennedy in 1955. There exists a version of it on the 1969 album *Prince Heathen* by Martin Carthy and Dave Swarbrick, but the setting and original tune used by Fairport came from Peggy.

Some folklorists, including Bert Lloyd, trace the song back to the same originating story as that of 'A Sailor's Life', told from the point of view of the male protagonist. When Fairport reintroduced 'Polly' into their repertoire, Chris Leslie opened it with a verse from 'A Sailor's Life' played on a Native American flute. Peggy's understated arrangement follows a structure similar to Fairport's remodelling of 'A Sailor's Life' – enhancing the words of the song and leading to a coda in which the story is retold.

These two songs, together with a trad arr instrumental, make this the most folkie opening of any Fairport album. 'Polly on the Shore' is one of the most durable Fairport songs, but it was almost not recorded by them. As pioneers of folk-rock, Fairport naturally avoided recording versions of songs that other folk-rock acts had got to first. This was growing more difficult on a weekly basis.

While pre-Fairport, English trad and British beat had been oil and water, by 1973 there were many bands and solo artists who were direct branches of the Fairport trunk, with some making the choice to be folk-rock acts, just as once they might have decided to be a blues band or a rock 'n' roll group. Furthermore, many mainstream acts, inspired by Fairport, were also making folk part of their repertoire. Led Zeppelin, open in their admiration of Fairport, were one example; while Thin Lizzy would have their first hit in 1972, taking that old chestnut 'Whiskey in the Jar' into the Top Ten Singles Chart.

One of the many new bands that drew their inspiration from Fairport were Trees. Not to be left out of what was seen as 'the next big thing', CBS had signed them as their token English folk-rock act. Their second, and final, album *On the Shore* not only included a version of 'Polly on the Shore', but took its title from it.

Undeterred by the prior existence of folk-rock versions of 'Polly', Peggy turned it into the perfect showcase for the talents of each individual member of the new Fairport. There is a remarkable live recording of it made at the Sydney Opera House on 26 January, 1974, by which point Sandy was about to rejoin the band, broadening Fairport's possibilities and repertoire immensely. Trevor was, by then, hankering to introduce more of his own choice of material into their set, which meant that songs without an obvious role for Sandy were most in jeopardy.

PEGGY: 'Polly on the Shore' really suited Trev's voice, and he
    nailed it on *Nine*. We'd stopped playing it before he left the

band because there had been so much new stuff coming out of the band. Then when he left, there was simply no one who felt up to tackling it.

It was, however, one of the songs Trevor would choose to do when rejoining Fairport at Cropredy 1982, and again when he returned in 1985 – his final appearance with Fairport.

SIMON: 'Polly on the Shore' is an example of one of the songs from Fairport's past we were uncertain about returning to. I think it was mostly about my confidence in tackling it. Trevor's mighty vocal performance is quite an act to follow, unless your name happens to be Ralph McTell. There are things you know our audience would love to hear Fairport doing, but the band had to feel ready for it.

Like Peggy, Swarb provided a tune for a set of existing words. 'To Althea From Prison' was written by the Cavalier poet Richard Lovelace in 1642, while incarcerated in the Gatehouse prison. Famous for its aphorism 'Stone walls do not a prison make,' it is an interesting companion piece to *Babbacombe Lee*'s 'Cell Song'. Side one of *Nine*, then, was mostly traditional.

TREVOR: There was no masterplan behind *Nine*. There have been various theories: traditional side / composed side; old Fairport / new Fairport; even English / American (which ob-viously I take *great* exception to!). I cannot say we thought of the songs in those terms. It's just the order in which the tracks sounded best.

If side one of *Nine* is folk-rock in approach, firmly rooted in the kind of music Fairport had made at the start of the Seventies, side two is all about the songs that did not draw their inspiration from British folk music. Although Swarb and Trevor sing two each of the side's four songs, the composer credits are dominated by the latter, almost as if an attempt is being made to establish him in the contin-uing line of Fairport songwriters. Of the four songs, the last is the most interesting. Its title, 'Possibly Parsons Green', betrays a direct Dylan influence (Trevor instigating the reintroduction of a number of Dylan songs into the Fairport set). The song is so close to Sandy's

obliquely autobiographical style as to seem almost a pastiche –
Parsons Green being where Trevor and Sandy were then living. The
flat was suburban and relatively small, its space further reduced by
Sandy's Steinway – which took up a third of the living room – and
the large amount of paper, the working notes of two professional
songwriters. Whereas Sandy's songs of the time tended to idealise
her relationships, Trevor's point of view in 'Parsons Green' is both
cynical and impatient.

'Pleasure and Pain', which Trevor had always wanted as the
band's 'singalong song', was usually introduced with a cheeky
drugs reference to explain the line about 'mixing the reds along
with the blues'. A chance remark from co-writer Swarb might be a
clue to its real meaning:

SWARB: Trev was always known as Long Red. He was a happy-
go-lucky sort of chap, and used to find it difficult when Sandy
got depressed. In a lot of ways, they were not well-suited.

PEGGY: We'd not played much live, particularly not in London,
throughout 1972. We had spent lots of time rehearsing but
the truth is we were embarrassed. With the *Nine* line-up, it
was different. Everything worked on a personal level as well
as on a musical and professional one. We knew we were
making great music.

Fairport were on the road (or ferry or aeroplane) for most of 1973.
They played over 100 gigs, did several sessions for radio, were on TV,
and recorded two albums – their own and Sandy's. The year began
with a brief visit to New Zealand, a trip made possible by funding from The Great Ngaruawahia Festival. Immediately upon their
return to the UK, they began a tour that started at Mile End's prestigious Sundown Rock venue and ran through February.

On 17 April, they appeared on BBC's *Old Grey Whistle Test*, playing an unplugged version of 'Brilliancy Medley', with Swarb in-
explicably wearing a large black Mexican sombrero. Peggy played
mandolin while DM deserted the drum stool to play bass. As was
his wont at the time, his T-shirt was imprinted with a statement –
'bored stiff'; previously, we'd had 'miming'. Most of April was spent
touring the UK, including a gig – at The Howff, London, on 23
April – four cuts from which would later appear on the expanded

CD reissue of *Nine*. The gig was recorded for transmission on BBC radio.

In May, Fairport went global. Booked to accompany Sandy on the album she was recording at A&M's studios in LA, they played two gigs at UCLA; for the first, on 9 May, they were Sandy's backing band. The next day at noon, they performed as Fairport at the foot of Janss Steps, the famous original entrance to the University. On 11 May, they travelled south to appear on KPRI, San Diego. 'Capri', as the station was known, had, barely a month earlier, shifted to an AOR format – a direction Fairport were about to follow. Just four days later, they were on Trevor's home turf, playing gigs in Perth, Adelaide, Melbourne and Sydney. Though some have claimed the last of these was at the Opera House, in fact they played the State Theatre, but would move on to bigger things in seven months' time. This was Fairport's first visit to Australia, though they had played the Festival in New Zealand at the start of the year.

16 MAY, 1973
PERTH CONCERT HALL, AUSTRALIA

PEGGY: The band has a strong following in Australia. Fans there have even released live albums of the band that include some really strong material. There were those who had known about us before, but a lot of support dates from that first tour with the *Nine* line-up.

MARTIN CARTHY: I toured Australia with Swarb years later, and he and Fairport were held in incredibly high esteem. One place we went to had a huge photo of them hanging behind the bar. Unfortunately, for reasons that might be obvious, Swarb had absolutely no recollection of ever having played there.

SWARB: We knew we had a big fan base there. It was a chance for us to meet them and for Trevor to visit home. I fell in love with the place and eventually moved out there. That's why I wrote a tune called 'My Heart's in New South Wales'.

PEGGY: That was a kind of paid holiday. One particular memory is of meeting Barry Crocker whom we all knew because he had played Barry McKenzie in the film [*The Adventures of Barry McKenzie*], a real Fairport favourite at the time.

Barry McKenzie was an uncouth, fictional, Australian archetype invented by Barry Humphries (better known in his guise as Dame Edna Everage), and his misadventures featured each week in *Private Eye*. 'Sir B McKenzie' is Fairport's tribute to him.

TREVOR: It was great to play with the band on home turf. I think the only downside to the whole event was the journey home when we ended up stranded in Fiji Airport for about six hours.

After a round-the-world trip lasting a month, the band could have been forgiven for wanting some time off, even though they had tried to see it as a working holiday. June, however, brought a tour of Holland, a festival in Denmark, and UK gigs from Ayr to Brighton.

Like An Old-Fashioned Waltz

After a five-year romance that had seen its share of ups and downs, separations (enforced and voluntary), and musical collaborations, Trevor Lucas married Sandy Denny on 20 September, 1973, at Fulham register office. One newspaper ran a story under the headline, 'Fairport Convention singer marries', and they were referring to Sandy – who had not been in the band since 1969 – and not Trevor, who had been a band member for a year.

SANDY: Yes, Trevor finally decided to make an honest woman of me. Sadly, it didn't work the other way round.

Photos of the wedding, taken by a freelance press photographer who'd been notified of the forthcoming nuptials by Trevor, appeared in the press. Never shy of self-promotion, he figured the marriage of two Fairport stars would be good publicity. Looking less than formal, he wore a red rose on the lapel of his suit jacket and an open-necked red check shirt. Sandy, more dressed for the occasion, wore a dark floral Laura Ashley dress with a plunging neckline.

The wedding took place the day after Fairport had finished a fragmentary tour which had begun in June and involved detours from UK gigs to take in festivals in Roskilde, Denmark, and Helsinki, Finland. The flat that Sandy and Trevor shared in Parsons Green had become something of a base for Fairport in the preceding couple of weeks – just the kind of thing you need when you are preparing for a wedding. At the start of September, the band had radio sessions with both Bob Harris and John Peel. The night before the wedding, Fairport played the Lyceum in London. Only two songs had survived from the old days – 'Sloth' and 'Dirty Linen'. For their encore, they invited Sandy on stage to sing 'Down in the Flood'.

Swarb had put that gig at risk when, on 7 September, he had climbed on a chair to see over the heads of the standing audience as The Stones played the Empire Pool, Wembley.

SWARB: I had wanted to see them playing 'You Can't Always Get What You Want', lost my balance, knackered my knee, and ended up in hospital with the whole of my left leg in plaster.

He had moved on from thinking about *Nine* and so the interviews he gave after the mishap did little to plug the album. With Trevor newly wed and Swarb distracted and dislocated, it fell to Peggy to provide press interviews to promote the album. He did so from his semi-detached home in Birmingham. Although *Nine* looks like the first Fairport product of the Cropredy era (the gatefold photos are from a small outdoor performance there), at that point only Swarb had taken up residence in the village. The business acumen Peggy displayed, realising that his band-mates were wasting valuable column inches which could be put to good promotional use, was indicative of the invaluable support he was to give Fairport in the Cropredy era. As he told an interviewer at the time, "It's a line-up I really believe in. It works really well both in the studio and on stage. We had a bad year but everything is now back on track in Fairport-land."

The previous year, of course, there had been four different versions of Fairport, and they had averaged less than three gigs a month. In 1973, they were working almost non-stop and enjoying it. As the year drew to a close, Fairport found that – having been virtually bankrupted – they were now a viable going concern. Which was both a good and bad thing for their recently re-joined singer.

SANDY: [1973] was a sad year in many ways. Either I was away
gigging or Trevor was off with Fairport. We just didn't seem
to see each other. Then Island put back the release date of the
album.

"The album" being *Like an Old-Fashioned Waltz*. Speaking about it
three years later, Sandy observed: "It's a solo album, but one I associate very much with Fairport. It's not just that some of the songs
relate to the band indirectly. Fairport were my backing band on a
lot of the album. By the time it came out, I was touring with them
and playing several of the songs from it live as part of Fairport's set."
These songs include the album's title track and 'Solo', the opening
track of *Waltz*. According to Sandy, it was considered the album's
title track. Dave Pegg has frequently cited it as a favourite session.

PEGGY: It was just Sandy, DM and me. Richard was going to
put the lead guitar on later.

The released version of 'Solo' credits neither Peggy nor Richard, but
states it was recorded in Los Angeles and London. As he would
with the rest of the album, Trevor filled the track with more overdubs and harmonies than were originally planned. There are recordings of Sandy performing the song with Fairport at Ebbets
Field, Denver, during a three-night stint at the start of November
1974: she introduces it by saying, "This is off an album of mine, but
as Fairport played on the original track, it is really a Fairport song."
She had already adapted the words and now sang: "I've always kept
a unicorn and I *hardly ever* sing out of tune"; the final chorus is
semi-spoken and addressed directly to members of the band.

Island had originally scheduled Sandy's album for release in
October 1973, the same month as *Nine*. Sandy had started arrang-
ing gigs and radio appearances to promote *Waltz*. Then the label
had a change of policy, which would also directly affect Fairport.
The label were concentrating on new acts like Roxy Music and Bob
Marley who could sell far more records in the lucrative pre-Christ-
mas period.

So the release of *Waltz* was delayed until June 1974, and when it
made it to the shops it was in direct conflict with the *Live Convention*
on which Sandy had featured heavily. Understandably, she was unhappy with the way her career was being handled.

SANDY: I felt disillusioned. Fairport were off on a major tour, taking them around the world. I saw no point in gigging. I'd be stuck at home without Trevor. I decided to go with them.

In December 1973, Fairport played warm-up gigs in London – at the Rainbow and Fairfield Halls – and Sandy went along. It was only natural that she came on as a surprise for the encore. Speculation that she had rejoined the band was either wishful thinking at the time, or retrospective deduction.

PEGGY: She and Trevor were newlyweds, after all.

SIMON: There is a phrase: 'What goes on the road, stays on the road'. A lot of rock wives have to live with that, but Sandy had seen it from both sides.

SWARB: Trevor thought of himself as pretty much unattached when he was on tour. I think, now they were married, Sandy hoped to keep him in check. Not that she wasn't missing him horribly, of course.

SANDY: It was ironic, really. One of my main reasons for leaving Fairport in the first place was that I had wanted to be able to spend more time with Trevor. We'd formed our band Fotheringay, but when that didn't work out, I'd followed a solo career, with Trevor producing. Then he was asked to join Fairport. So I ended up back in the band for exactly the same reason as I had left it.

PEGGY: It certainly wasn't a case of asking Sandy to rejoin the band, plain and simple. I think we'd got used to being a band without a girl singer. In fact, I had never been in the band when they had had a female vocalist. I knew Sandy through playing with her on her albums and on stage; I obviously had a great deal of respect and affection for her – we all did. She was at the first gigs we did with the new line-up, and it seemed silly not to ask her on stage for a guest spot. That was happening off and on for about a year. Then when we headed off on a tour that took in the Far East, Australia and the USA, Sandy decided to come with us. The tour started in Japan. It seemed stupid her sitting there in the wings while we played. So I said: "You are going to come on and join us for a couple?"

Knowing that the situation would repeat itself every night, Fairport accepted Sandy back into the band. Swarb was uncertain about it, however, fearing that having Sandy back would erode his position. The record company were of course delighted, given Sandy had been the lead singer on their three best-selling albums. Suddenly, the idea of a live album seemed an attractive project for Island.

For a band with such a reputation for live performances, it is remarkable that no live Fairport material had yet been released, especially as quite a lot had been recorded up till that point. The tour moved from Tokyo to New Zealand and then on to Australia, where on 25 and 26 January, 1974, Fairport played Sydney Opera House (at last). The prestigious venue had then been open for slightly over three months and was understandably choosy about whom it allowed to perform on its stage. Folk music – particularly traditional English music – was acceptable. Fairport dressed for the occasion in suits (though Peggy wore dungarees – 'traditional Australian dress', apparently). DM's T-shirt informed us that 'You're only as good as your last gig', while Sandy wore a black sequinned evening dress and looked suitably elegant. They played 20 numbers in all, including five instrumentals. 'Sloth' stretched out for a dozen minutes, matched by a new extended version of 'Bring 'em Down'. Almost all the new album was played, but after 'To Althea' came a moving rendition of 'Cell Song', accompanied on the piano by DM. The band were on top form and Island Records were recording it. Sandy sang on six numbers, introduced as a special guest. She was, however, on stage throughout providing piano accompaniment and harmony vocals

SWARB: Sandy still hadn't decided whether she wanted to give up her solo career. And, to be fair, we hadn't actually reached a decision as to whether we wanted her in the band.

TREVOR: She was still a guest. She was not properly a member of Fairport at that point. The live album blurs the distinction.

PEGGY: We hadn't had time to rehearse. Everything else in the set we'd been playing together for a year and we were good at, really good – the way you can only be when you play together a lot. Sandy's songs were only possible because we were so used to playing together.

Fans had waited for a recording of Fairport in concert and when it arrived it was good, but not as good as it could have been. Certainly it was unrepresentative. The album presents Trevor Lucas as rhythm guitarist adding occasional harmony vocals, when on the night he had been a commanding lead vocalist.

Fairport Live Convention (renamed *A Moveable Feast* in the States) shows Island trying to find a commercial niche for Fairport to occupy. Obviously, any band would want to be successful, and both Sandy and Trevor craved success and were likely to accede to any plan that looked like making them commercially viable. It was, however, to bring about a major change in direction for the band.

Recordings made on the next leg of the tour, at the Troubadour in LA, could not be used because money was running out and Fairport could not afford to pay for them. Sandy's material was stronger by that time, being both more played-in and properly rehearsed, as can be heard on the tracks that subsequently appeared on Sandy box sets and reissues.

Fairport's residency at the Troubadour ran from 28 January to 3 February, 1974. It may not have acquired the legendary status of their seasons at the same venue at the start of the decade, but it did prompt the *LA Times* to liken Sandy's rejoining the band to a reunion of Lennon and McCartney.

The band returned to the UK that February, and on Valentine's Day NME confirmed the rumours it had been repeating since the start of the year – that Sandy had rejoined Fairport Convention. Soon after, the band were busy once again as one tour followed another during 1974. Scandinavia was followed by a tour of the eastern seaboard of America, before a long journey as far west as Denver. On their return to the UK, they had several gigs before 7 July, and an appearance at the Pop Proms at Olympia. Their diary for June reflects a fad of the time – three appearances at local festivals put on for residents of a particular borough. Right after the tour, Fairport returned to the BBC's studios to record that John Peel session, where Sandy introduced "a new song I've written which I hope will be on our next LP". It was 'Rising for the Moon'.

While one BBC recording at the time anticipated Fairport's future, another definitely looked back at the past. Inspired by Fairport's seventh album, Melvyn Bragg had decided to make a documentary about John 'Babbacombe' Lee, and on 24 September, 1974, Fairport filmed their contribution to Bragg's film in a dark, vaulted building. It remains the most atmospheric footage of Fairport ever shot. As the scene opens, a camera tracks through the intimidating edifice before discovering Fairport mid-song. The film returns to the band throughout the programme, using them to punctuate and expand the narrative. The current line-up, of course, was not the line-up that had made the original album. Simon joined the band for the programme, although Sandy sang 'Breakfast in Mayfair'. Swarb was also shown at home in Cropedy, talking about *Babbacombe Lee*. Screening of the show was scheduled for early in the following year.

On The Telly Again

According to the *Radio Times'* listing for 9.05 pm of 1 February, 1975, the BBC series *2nd House* was to air *The Man They Couldn't Hang*. On page 14 of the magazine, facing a full-page reproduction of *The Police News* dated 6 December, 1884, was the headline 'Unhung, drawn and chronicled'. In those days, the *Radio Times* dealt exclusively with BBC programmes. That particular issue ran a full-page article on the John Lee case, featuring photos of Lee and Swarb alongside a background piece on the programme, the historical event, the album, and Fairport. Captions quoted Fairport's lyrics. In case readers were forgetful of, or unfamiliar with, Fairport, the article assured them that Swarb 'might be familiar from his recent appearance in *Far From the Madding Crowd*'. John Schlesinger's 1967 film, based on Thomas Hardy's novel, had had Swarb appearing as a fiddler in a couple of sequences. Trevor Lucas was heard on the soundtrack, and briefly seen on screen, singing three traditional songs. In addition to a unique version of the *Babbacombe Lee* songs, Fairport also supplied some new material for the BBC film in the form of incidental music, including familiar tunes to accompany clips from an Australian film based on the event that had been made in 1912. In fact, excerpts from two silent movies about Lee – the original 1912 movie and its more successful 1921 remake – were included in Bragg's documentary.

There was also a new song, 'Lament for a Poor Man's Son', which plays behind the closing credits.

SWARB: The new song wasn't an outtake that we hadn't been
able to fit on the original LP; I wrote it for the documentary.
So far as I know, Fairport have never played it live, though it
is on the CD version of the LP as a bonus track.

Martin Carthy was engaged to perform a contemporary broadside
ballad about the case outside the prison where Lee's failed execution had taken place. Swarb appeared throughout the programme;
credited as the driving force behind the album that had inspired
the programme, he was treated as an authority on the subject. He
shared with the audience the original bound magazine editions
that he'd found, speaking knowledgeably and with passion about
John Lee.

   In the course of the programme, Swarb came up with an elegant conspiracy theory about the murder involving a frame-up,
freemasonry, a sex scandal, and the royal family. "I think someone
else committed the murder. Lee was caught up as witness to a love
affair," was his stated conclusion.

   The documentary renewed interest in the story, and Swarb was
sought out for a couple of press interviews. When pressured as to
why the gallows failed to work – a question that no one has yet
satisfactorily answered – he suggested: "It could just have been a
ropey hangman."

   The documentary provided invaluable exposure for Fairport.
Unfortunately, a repeat of the programme scheduled for 21 June
was cancelled at short notice. With that, the possibility of new audience interest generated by word of mouth or reviews was lost.
The repeat was to have been a slightly edited version of the show,
trimmed to fit a shorter time slot. That remains the only surviving
version of the programme.

   Naturally, the documentary created a demand for Fairport's
album. Unfortunately, a shortage of vinyl and the prohibitive cost
of the elaborate packaging meant that it was 'temporarily out of
print', as Island's catalogue put it.

SWARB: It was a case of 'John Lee – the album you couldn't buy'.

Fairport did not see the original transmission. They were in
Holland that night, on the Van Speyk Show on KRO-TV, as part of
a tour of the Netherlands and Scandinavia. They played 'Rising for

the Moon', 'One More Chance' and 'White Dress'. All three songs would appear on the next Fairport album, which they had begun recording before heading off to fulfil their European commitments.

That album is unlike any other Fairport record in that it clearly tries to reflect contemporaneous music tastes and fashions, following the trend rather than creating it. It was the first Fairport LP not to include a traditional song.

AOR

The mid-Seventies marked a period of massive change and re-alignment for the music business. Its biggest acts turned over money at a phenomenal rate, with enormous sales and unparalleled levels of excess on and off stage. Bands who, like Fairport, had been travelling Britain in old Transits only half a dozen years prior to that were now traversing the States in customised luxury jet airliners – their names emblazoned on the side. The bands that played rock music, that is, and *not* folk-rock.

In America, AM radio stations played pop music. Higher quality FM stations, once the province of classical music, had moved in the late Sixties into playing rock. Now those stations, taken over by conglomerates, were being switched to what was called AOR – that's Adult (or Album) Orientated Rock – later renamed Adult Contemporary. The radio format became a music genre, as bands tailored their music to match radio station needs.

Many of Fairport's former contemporaries did so successfully. Jefferson Airplane became Jefferson Starship and then just Starship, who built a city on rock 'n' roll. Guitar-based blues band Fleetwood Mac moved to the West Coast and became platinum album-sellers. Al Stewart abandoned Soho bedsits, French prophets and Russian generals and decided it was the year of the cat. The Bee Gees began jive-talking with slick harmonic smoothness before being swallowed up by the polycephalic monster of disco and Hollywood.

The Eagles, whose members had befriended Fairport in LA, took American folk music – country, old timey and cowboy ballads – and remodelled them for a hip young audience. With huge sales of both albums and singles, they achieved what The Band and, for that matter, Fairport had been unable to do by updating roots music. Dire Straits were the leaders of the first generation of bands born to play that sound; one of the earliest reviews of the band dismissed their 'sub-Dylan vocals and guitar playing that comes over like a poor man's Richard Thompson'. The sound of AOR was to become the sound of CD – smooth, slick, musically dexterous and bland. The US music scene seemed in little need of a band playing electric versions of 18-verse tales of lust, adultery, revenge and murder.

PEGGY: I think everyone was aware that change in music was imminent. It felt like a last chance. With Sandy back in the band, the record company was prepared to support us. We really wanted to get it right.

SWARB: The words 'baby' and 'bathwater' spring to mind whenever I think of that era of Fairport.

Still touring heavily – the BBC shoot for the John Lee programme was followed immediately by a month-long tour of the States that had begun in Washington, DC and ended in San Francisco, three days before they were to begin a month-long tour of the UK – Fairport knew they had to start on a new album as soon as they came off the road. It was not the best time to have to record; constant playing may have resulted in a very-together band, but that is in many ways an unimportant factor in the multi-track environment of a modern studio. After gigging for the best part of three months, bodies are tired and voices have suffered strain.

PEGGY: I think all of us wondered how long it would last with Sandy. But, apart from the live album, there was nothing that thousands of people who had come to see the latest version of Fairport could buy.

SWARB: It would be fair to say that Sandy's second stint as a Fairport member divides into two parts. The first was the live work. That was great: a real band, working together, all mates. Good times. Fans were overjoyed to see Sandy back with us – it gave us a chance to revive some older songs that we hadn't done in a while. Sandy and Trevor together made a great frontline team.
     Then we recorded the album and the band took a break, but things had by then started to fall apart.

194

The tours that followed were accompanied by the sound of Fairport fragmenting.

JERRY: There were a lot of egos clashing, lots of people who felt they had different claims on the band – Swarb and Peggy from the old Fairport versus Sandy and Trevor. It wasn't actually like that on the surface – we all got on – but there were different undercurrents. Then there was the songwriting. Swarb had become Fairport's writer by default, but Sandy had originally joined as an established writer; Trevor was writing stuff, too, and he was angling to get that on.

SANDY: I saw an article that talked about AOR acts tending to produce introspective work…songs about themselves and the inner workings of a band. *Rumours* is the obvious example, but also Joni Mitchell's songs, or Crosby, Stills and Nash, or *Hotel California*. *Rising for the Moon* fits right into that state of mind – you don't have to dig too deep to find which songs were inspired by relationships within the band. It happened in our live sets, too; a song like 'Solo' fitted well into Fairport, partly because it was very obviously about band members past and present.

During their American tour, Fairport had become aware of the changes taking shape in American radio. Britain, too, was undergoing a radio revolution. Since starting in 1922, British radio had always been controlled exclusively by the BBC. Briefly, it had been challenged by offshore pop music stations like Caroline and Radio London, those 'pirate' stations that were destroyed by the new laws which came into force within days of Fairport's first gig. As a sop to those who had lost their beloved pop and rock pirates, the BBC offered Radio 1, which would, of course, be hugely important in Fairport's early years.

There was, however, a feeling that it was wrong that the BBC should have total dominance of the airwaves. In 1973, the first British Independent Local Radio station went on air. The coming of commercial radio to Britain meant that artists no longer had to rely on the BBC for publicity and promotion. Whereas a BBC station might easily decide you were 'not our kind of artist' – which was a comment on the BBC playlist panel's approval sheet alongside the single 'Rosie' – commercial stations were far more interested in what was happening locally. Initially centred on providing major cities (Manchester, Liverpool, Birmingham, Newcastle, Swansea and Glasgow) with their own radio stations, the plan was that eventually every town and city would have its own radio station. In the Eighties, Fairport's network of friends and fans in these new stations, many of which included a folk show in their required roster of specialist music programming, enabled the band to publicise Cropredy, tour dates and, ultimately, album releases in a way that simply would not have been possible had the BBC retained its monopoly.

Initially, though, no one was sure quite what these new stations would sound like. There was no point in their being chart-based and simply competing with Radio 1 – whose presenters were stars in their own right, featuring regularly on TV as well as radio, and whose output of non-stop pop was not interrupted by commercial breaks. The 'Oldies' stations – today known as 'Gold' or 'Magic' – were totally unfamiliar in the UK. Other American formats such as all-talk or specialist music were simply too niche for Britain's limited radio audience who, in any case, would have found the approach too alien. Many at the time thought that AOR would be the way to go for Britain's radio stations.

BOB HARRIS: Shows like *Whistle Test* had shown there was an audience out there for music that didn't come straight from hit singles. Albums had, after all, been outselling seven-inch vinyl in the UK since 1967. A lot of people hoped that commercial radio would find a way to cater for that audience.

In many ways, Fairport were ahead of the game in 1975, tailoring their next album for a British radio market that unfortunately would not emerge for a quarter of a century.

SANDY: [speaking about her final album *Rendezvous* in a radio interview]: This time we've deliberately included some things you'll be able to play, even a couple of familiar oldies, like the Elton John song which is coming out as a single. It's something we started doing with my last album with Fairport – making it more radio-friendly.

JERRY: When we began planning *Rising for the Moon*, Trevor suggested we bring in what he called "a proper producer". At the time, he said he didn't want to divide his attention. In fact, I think he was keen to find a way to a hit.

Sandy's description of the album as "radio-friendly" is valid. Not only does its smoother sound make it more suitable for general airplay, but only its final track – the majestic, eight-minute 'One More Chance' – fails to comply with timings demanded by most UK radio stations of the era. Despite *Radio Times*' description of Swarb as Fairport's songwriter-in-chief, he was to contribute only three songs to the album: the cod-country-stomp 'Night-time Girl', 'Let It Go' written with Sandy and Peggy, and 'White Dress', a romantic wedding waltz, which Sandy sings.

RALPH MCTELL: That was the start of my long and happy association with Fairport. Swarb agreed to let me rewrite it, and I recorded it as a tribute to Sandy. It's a lovely song.

There are two Trevor Lucas songs, 'Iron Lion' and 'Restless', the latter first recorded for the unreleased second Fotheringay album. Like the other Lucas originals on that set, 'Restless' had once been redubbed for possible inclusion in *Rosie*. The remaining six songs are by Sandy.

JERRY: It was Trevor who suggested we use Glyn Johns as producer.

PEGGY: Glyn Johns was very much "a proper producer". He had worked with some of the biggest names in rock. I was pleased because I was keen for Fairport to go in a more rock 'n' roll direction.

Among the acts Glyn Johns had produced or engineered albums for were The Stones, The Who, the Steve Miller Band, The Beatles, Led Zeppelin, Eric Clapton, Family, Wings and, perhaps most significantly, The Eagles. In an interview with the BBC, he revealed that the offer to produce Fairport Convention hadn't exactly stirred his imagination.

GLYN JOHNS: It seemed to me a side of folk music that I'd never
  really liked.

One reason why Trevor and Peggy considered him a proper producer was that he was fully involved in the production process.
The first thing he did, while still considering whether to take on
the project or not, was to meet with the band and get them to play
everything they had available for the planned record, not just the
list of what they planned to include.

JERRY: Often, you turn up to recording sessions with the songs
  you want to do and in effect say, "Here are the songs, now
  record them."

Johns, like Joe Boyd many years earlier, was immediately impressed
by the band's musicianship and cohesion as a group. He decided to
record them, and set about helping them select the songs, which
ultimately he would sequence to create a cohesive album. Of the
things they had available, all traditional material and cover versions were immediately ditched. This was to be a genuinely original Fairport album.

  The first recording sessions took place in December 1974 at
Olympic Studios. They recorded 'Rising for the Moon', 'Restless',
'White Dress', 'One More Chance', 'Dawn' and 'Tears' – which was
released as a B-side. The band then broke off the recording process to go on tour. Their new producer was less than pleased with
the arrangement, feeling it showed a lack of commitment to the
album. He was even *less* pleased when they returned to reveal they
would have to find a new drummer. Dave Mattacks had achieved a
first, becoming the only member of Fairport to leave the band twice.
Fairport's first choice of replacement, Gerry Conway, had already
recorded with them and had been Fotheringay's drummer: unfortunately, he had to turn the band down as he had just signed up to
tour with Cat Stevens (his time would come, though, when DM
completed his hat-trick of Fairport resignations in March, 1998).
According to Peggy, 32 drummers were auditioned before the group
eventually ended up with a shortlist comprising the band's roadie
Paul Warren (who had stepped in when DM left so that gigs were
not cancelled), Pete York who had once been in the Spencer Davis
Group, and Bruce Rowland. Rowland had been drummer with Joe

Cocker's Grease Band and Ronnie Lane's Slim Chance, both of whose albums had been produced by Glyn Johns, who had recommended him to the group.

The band returned to Olympic Studios to complete the album, but headed off in April for yet another tour of Australia and New Zealand.

The sleeve of *Rising for the Moon*, a painting of the band, is another 'Fairport around the table' image. The illustration was designed so that the drummer had his back to us, disguising the fact that the person occupying the drummer's stool had changed during the course of the recording.

In *Rising for the Moon*, Island felt they finally had a marketable Fairport Convention album. Its radio-friendly tracklist meant pluggers had an easier job than they would have had with an album of high-octane instrumentals, extended tracks and traditional electric-folk. The plug sheet directed Heads of Music to 'White Dress' and 'Stranger to Himself' with a slightly cautious proviso: "This LP may not include any obvious chart material but we are confident it has a couple of great turntable hits." It was aimed at programmers on commercial radio stations up and down the country, whose policy was to find strong material for airplay regardless of whether it fitted in with the sales charts that shaped Radio 1's playlist at the time.

The record label threw a dinner reception on Wednesday 4 June at the Meridian Restaurant, lasting from 6.00 pm to 10.00 pm, for the press. It was an opportunity to eat well, drink heartily, hear Fairport's new album, meet the band, and head home with an armful of promotional goodies. The venue was handy for Sandy and Trevor, as it was just round the corner from the flat where they then lived. They were, however, about to move from sw3 to rural Oxfordshire and the village of Byfield, neighbouring Cropredy, where Sandy would live for the rest of her short life.

Rising for the Moon was launched with a concert at the Royal Albert Hall on 10 June, 1975 where, before introducing the new album, they set things up with a string of Fairport oldies that was effectively a potted history of the band to date. 'John the Gun', 'Hexhamshire Lass', 'Brilliancy Medley', 'Sloth', 'Rosie', 'Walk Awhile', 'Tam Lin', 'Who Knows Where the Time Goes' and – most surprisingly, bringing a whoop of delight from the audience – 'Mr Lacey'. In a move which unwittingly anticipated the negative reactions that would ultimately destroy this line-up, Sandy offered an overview of her solo recordings: 'Quiet Joys of Brotherhood', 'It'll Take a Long Time' (both of which had become part of Fairport's live set), 'Listen, Listen' and – performed solo – the world premiere of 'No More Sad Refrains'.

Reviews of *Rising for the Moon* were not all favourable. The album's excellent production was deemed too slick. Similarly, others complained they missed 'Fairport's usual rough edges', while the strong tracklist was regarded as being too dominated by Sandy's songs. Colin Irwin wrote in *Melody Maker*: 'It would be easy to mistake the whole thing as a record of Sandy Denny with backing musicians.' Even the positive reviews managed to include a reference to Fairport's reputation for not being able to maintain the band's line-up from one album to the next. Which, of course, they couldn't.

One can understand why the six members approached what was described as a summer break with heavy hearts. Time off, for Fairport, was normally interpreted as time to do something else. Peggy joined DM and John Kirkpatrick playing with Richard and Linda Thompson. Gigs at the Queen Elizabeth Hall and Cambridge Folk Festival led to a UK tour in November, recordings from which would be released as an album in 2007. Peggy also joined Swarb and Simon on several of the dates they were playing as an acoustic duo. Sandy spent the time settling into her new home, but most days was working on ideas for what would be her next and final solo album, *Rendezvous*.

SANDY: I had a lot of songs and, when I began, I was writing things for the next Fairport album. Some of those weren't what I wanted to do once I left the band.

On 20 August, 1975, Fairport flew to America for a tour that would last five weeks. Sandy wasn't up to the pressure of touring and singing in front of a six-piece rock band. She had also been drinking a great deal. It had started to show in performances. In New York, she had put so much strain on her voice that she needed to be rushed to hospital.

PEGGY: Rifts were starting to appear. Swarb, Trevor and Sandy had regular bust-ups which occasionally reached the point of physical violence.

JERRY: It wasn't a Fairport tour, it was Fairport on tour. Sometimes, we'd be a support act. Some gigs were suddenly and mysteriously cancelled. All in all it didn't make for a happy atmosphere.

PEGGY: It started badly because we had been told we'd be doing press interviews during the first week and then nothing was arranged. We were sitting around in LA with nothing to do.

Inevitably, dissatisfaction led to squabbles and fallings out. Sandy became increasingly insecure and was often depressed. The fractures in her marriage to Trevor had begun to widen. The band played their final American gig in Providence, Rhode Island, on 3 October. Three days later, they began a month-long UK tour, which was to reveal a different problem. The sound of *Rising for the Moon* might have appealed to American audiences, but in Britain fans who turned up to see Fairport felt they were being short-changed. On several occasions, the band was greeted with shouts of "We paid to see Fairport, not bloody Fotheringay."

At one gig, someone in the audience threw a can on to the stage. Trevor stopped proceedings dead by threatening to "deck anybody else that throws something at my wife". While seldom this hostile, the atmosphere was often not good. Jerry Donahue was the first to throw in the towel, announcing at the end of the tour that he had simply had enough and was returning to the States.

PEGGY: The mid-Seventies were really great. Until things started to go wrong.

They gigged continuously until internal strain, external pressure, and the sheer irritation of living in each other's pockets shattered the band of six. They left behind a very good, if untypical, album in *Rising for the Moon* (June, 1975). Very much a work of its time, it also sits outside the general pattern of Fairport albums. It may have seemed like a new direction (smooth, glossy, not a trad arr tune or song in sight) but ended up being a dead end.

SANDY: Most of my songs are room songs, songs about being in a quiet and closed place and having time to think. 'Rising for the Moon' is definitely a road song: it's about being a musician. Everyone else gets up and prepares for the day. A musician gets up and prepares for going on stage at night. The fiddle riff that Swarb created always reminds me of the sound of the road under your wheels as you travel endless miles from gig to gig.

It's an album the band very seldom return to, even at Cropredy.

CHRIS: We put 'Rising for the Moon' back into the set and re-corded a new version of it [in 2010] for *Festival Bell*. It's a strong song that really drives along, and the fiddle part that Swarb created for it is a delight to play, especially with me and Ric together.

RIC: It's always seemed like an important part of Fairport's history and it was overlooked.

Dan Ar Braz, one of several musicians who would be brought in to try and keep Fairport going in the debacle that followed the dis-integration of the 1975 line-up, was to record 'Rising for the Moon' in 1990 at Woodworm Studios with Peggy on bass and Maart on piano.

DAN AR BRAZ: It is a beautiful song. When I played with Fairport, I had the privilege of meeting Sandy twice. Once she came with us to a gig in Cambridge. She spoke to me in French during the trip. When I recorded the song, I trans-lated one verse into French out of respect for the memory of that time with her.

Simon Nicol recalls the occasion, too:

SIMON: Just the other week someone showed me a photo of Fairport in a rock encyclopaedia. Peggy is very identifia-ble, as is Swarb. You can't see Bruce Rowland but there are Rototoms by the drumkit, so it was obviously him. Playing the fiddle is an unrecognisable guy with long hair. The person showing me the picture thought it was me, but actually it was Roger Burridge. It was a shot of the *Gottle O'Geer* line-up. They only played 12 gigs. Sandy and I actually went to one of them together – two ex-members turning up to see how the band was faring. It was a May Ball at St John's [College] Cambridge. Neither of us was invited to join the band on stage – and I don't think either of us had any desire to do so. In any case, while they were on stage, we drank the dressing room dry and would have been in no fit state to be called up for the encore.

Although I worked with Sandy during her first block of time in Fairport, I never worked with her on outside projects. By the time she rejoined, I was no longer part of Fairport. It was a brief working relationship, but we remained friends right up to her death. For much of that time, she was also a near neighbour, living just the other side of Banbury. We met up socially.

As had happened with Sandy's first 12 months as a member of Fairport, this era, too, was to be documented in a semi-official boot-leg. *The Airing Cupboard Tapes* were compiled, and amusingly an-notated, by Dave Mattacks. Using live recordings, the album docu-ments the period from the gig where Simon decided he wanted to leave Fairport to DM's departure. Since most of the tracks are live versions of songs Fairport had already released, the compilation did not have the same impact as *Heyday*. Nevertheless, it did preserve recordings of the group from a time when Sandy was clearly far more on form than she had been on the shaky *Fairport Live* recordings.

PEGGY: It had started out so well. Everyone had a great time. We made great music. By the end of 1975, though, it felt like the band was crumbling. There were lots of personal issues. It felt like there was always a row going on. DM is a quiet, or-derly man; it's hardly surprising he was the first to leave.

In December of 1975, a quarter-page ad appeared in the NME and other music papers which looked like a 'musicians wanted' insert. There was a fashion at the time, in the London alternative press, for designing job adverts that were deliberately obtuse and quirky. Their aim was to attract offbeat, creative people. This was a pas-tiche of one of them. Or was it? Headed 'VACANCIES For Name Band...(Yes, folks, you must be vacant to apply)', it included de-scriptions for half-a-dozen group members. Among them were an 'evil-looking spaced out fiddler', a 'bass player (must be able to consume 18 pints of beer per night)', and a 'husband and wife singing duo'. The 'long-established pop group' seeking this disparate lot of ne'er-do-wells was named as Fairport Prevention.

It was either caustically prescient or a coded message. The group was definitely breaking up.

JERRY: I yearned for anywhere where the rest of the band weren't. I'd known them for a long time. We were good friends. It was an awful situation.

Sandy's drinking was getting the better of her, making her depressed, erratic and irritable. Trevor seemed to spend half his time defending her and the other half arguing with her. Sandy and Trevor quickly reached a decision to quit Fairport, too. Trevor's exaggerated sense of self-importance was obvious in one of the reasons he would later give for quitting the band: "I'm a musician not a music teacher. I was sick of being in a band where you had to keep recruiting new members and teaching them all the songs." One by one the Fotheringay section of Fairport announced they would be going their separate ways, headed for Berkeley, Byfield, Brisbane or wherever.

History was repeating itself. Fairport, coping with the loss of a respected drummer, was faced with the departure of their lead guitarist, their lead singer, and their rhythm guitar and vocalist. Meantime, there were commitments to be fulfilled: between the departure of Jerry Donahue and Sandy and Trevor deciding to quit, Fairport had appeared on Dutch TV. Peggy played lead guitar and Arthur Cookson deputised on bass.

True to the pattern, Peggy and Swarb desperately tried to keep the band afloat. Peggy once again recruited friends from the Birmingham scene, while Swarb brought in folkie mates. Line-ups existed because there were obligations to fulfil – bookings and radio appearances – but they were going through the motions and new recruits lacked the commitment to make it through such hard times. The band changed membership on a regular basis. The music press could almost re-run their old Fairport stories and just change the names.

Seeing the band in danger of running aground, Swarb started another solo project, just as he had with the album that eventually became *Rosie*. Taking time out from Fairport, he played with the celebrated Breton harpist Alan Stivell. He had struck up a friendship with Stivell's guitarist Dan Ar Braz, and asked him whether he would be prepared to play with Fairport.

ALAN STIVELL: There has always been a strong musical tradition in Brittany, a heritage deeply rooted in its past. Everyone admired Fairport, and particularly Dave Swarbrick because he was a traditional musician expressing his talent through modern technology.

With Bruce Rowland taking a back seat, it was once again left to Peggy and Swarb to try and rescue something from the wreckage. As had happened after Simon's departure, there was another series of short-lived, unrecorded line-ups and a solo album made with guest musicians and packaged as a band release.

PEGGY: I asked Bob Brady, who had been playing keyboards with Wizzard.

Finally, Swarb recruited a young fiddler called Roger Burridge whom he had first met at the Sidmouth Folk Festival in 1969. Roger's father was a member of the old-school Dorset folk group The Yetties. Everyone who expressed doubts at Fairport's twin fiddle line-up when Chris Leslie joined years later had forgotten this short-lived and unrecorded version of the band.

CHAPTER SIX

Non-Convention

In 1976, Fairport Convention abbreviated their name. As Swarb saw it, "It had started to sound a bit Sixties, I suppose." With three new members breaking in and some difficult decisions to be made about repertoire, there was a lot of work to do. The band set aside six days from 15–21 March, most of April, and the first week of May to create a new Fairport. To add to the confusion, there were, in effect, two very different versions of Fairport – the new twin-fid-dled six-piece and a trio that was a drummer-less edition of the *Angel Delight* line-up. A tour booked through February and March featured Swarb and Peggy with Simon Nicol.

SIMON: I was still in The Albion Band, but wasn't sure whether I wanted to be part of the things they were about to do. This was around the time discussions were underway about the National Theatre. I had a gap in my schedule and so I was glad to help out.

PEGGY: Ideally, we wanted Simon back full-time, but at that point he wasn't available.

SWARB: I'm not sure whether that counts as a Fairport tour.

PEGGY: Sometimes we were billed as Fairport, because we'd announced we'd shortened the name. At other times we were

Fairport Convention. For some gigs, we renamed ourselves the Three Desperate Mortgages, which was at least honest!

An article in the Banbury local newspaper inadvertently summed up the Fairport Confusion at the time. Published on 22 May, 1976, it described the new line-up, which was about to head off on its first UK tour. The band was then in Germany, having played their debut gig at the Maidstone Technical College on 7 May: their support on the German tour had been Bert Jansch. A photo taken in their local pub showed the six-piece Fairport.

The greater part of the article was given over to an issue of local interest – the fact that Fairport had agreed to play at a fete in Cropredy to raise money for the village hall. The band would be Peggy, Swarb, Simon and Bruce Rowland – recruited at their producer's suggestion to replace Dave Mattacks.

SWARB: It was just a local fundraiser. They needed to raise money for the village hall. We had a link with the place because we used it for rehearsals.

The event took place at Prescote Manor – a local band playing locally. Other articles in the press referred to Fairport sharing the bill with 'the other Cropredy-based band, Cat's Cradle'.

PEGGY: As it turned out, the band that played that day was what would become the line-up we thought would be our last.

The newspaper also reviewed the new album *Gottle O'Geer*, which featured neither of the two line-ups mentioned in the article.

The six-piece version of Fairport lasted from 7 May, 1976 to 2 August, 1976. They made no official recordings, but can be heard on a session recorded for Capital Radio made two days before the band broke up.

PEGGY: After that, I think we were back in the studio with Simon.

Peggy's scrapbooks state that immediately after the line-up split, he, Swarb and Simon were 'finishing *Gottle O'Geer* at Hammersmith' for six days in August. It is, however, a rare slip in his meticulous record-keeping. That album was already in the shops – or more likely being returned from them as it hadn't sold – and those six days of recording mark the start of a new era for the band, as they began recording *The Bonny Bunch of Roses*.

Gottle O'Geer was released on 21 May, 1976, just ahead of Fairport's tour. However, the only connection the album had with the touring band was a photo of them on the back of the sleeve. None of the three new Fairport members appeared anywhere on the disc. Instead the album featured Swarb, Peggy and Bruce Rowland, with an extensive list of guest musicians and composers. Martin Carthy, Robert Palmer, Gallagher and Lyle, trumpeter Henry Lowther whose sister Claire had played on the first two Fairport albums, and Simon Nicol – who not only played electric guitar on the final track but also returned to the fold as producer – all appeared.

SWARB: That LP started out as a solo effort. I had lots of ideas and wanted to make it a mix of instrumental and vocal tracks. We started recording at Sawmill Studios in a nice, out-of-the-way, rustic setting.

SIMON: There's out of the way, and there's out of the way. It may be the only recording studio you have to get yourself and your equipment to by boat!

BRUCE: Initially I helped out with production and then Simon was brought in, basically because he knew what he was doing. It changed from being a Swarb to a Fairport album.

PEGGY: To be honest, it is a patchy album with a lot of filler. When you see something with a title like 'Cropredy Capers', you think it must be pretty important to the band. It was just a title for a tune we had knocked together in the studio.

SIMON: Before I became involved, Swarbrick was already working on his own project. He and Peggy went down to Fowey, Cornwall and worked on what was intended to be a Swarbrick solo album. You can still hear that on the tracks that have survived. I wasn't involved in the negotiations that steered it back to being a Fairport project, but I gather it was a decision made higher up at Island Records. No one seemed to know where to take it next, since it had already gone a fair way down a particular route. At that point, Bruce Rowland was in charge of the project, if anyone was. I was co-opted as a friendly face. Initially my role had been to do the engineering, but as it turned out, I played on it a little bit as well.

I became producer almost by default: I suppose it is because I was the one person involved who had any kind of track record as an actual producer. I also found myself absorbed back into the group. By the time the record was finished, we were already talking about forming a four-piece and going out gigging again. This began what, at the time, was the longest surviving secure line-up Fairport had ever had.

Rejoining Fairport was by no means an easy decision or a straightforward process. At the time, Simon was still a member of The Albion Band with Ashley Hutchings. For the rest of his career, his involvement with Fairport and The Albions would run in parallel, often involving careful juggling of his diary.

SIMON: *Gottle O'Geer* is probably the oddest and most confusing Fairport album. It's certainly the album to which we have returned least when reviving songs from the back catalogue.

There are disco-slanted takes on traditional tunes on this 11th Fairport studio album, alongside soft rock songs, a rare Sandy Denny number, a slice of folk-rap reminiscent of things Bob Pegg had done with Mr Fox, and yet another song-about-the-band from Dave Swarbrick. The sleeve contains a pointless cartoon of a depressed jester, which prompted one reviewer to begin his appraisal thus: 'Fairport – you're no fun any more…'

SWARB: We were making the best of a bad situation. As someone remarked, at least the fact that our name was different for that release meant we wouldn't have to include it in the Fairport *Convention* canon. There are too many things pulling in different directions on the album, and I think it's a shame that some good stuff got overlooked because the LP as a whole wasn't that good.

Swarb and Peggy had called in their mates and produced an album of threads and patches, a musical gallimaufry that almost broke the Trade Descriptions Act by being called a Fairport album. It would be their last studio album for Island Records.

Gottle O'Geer is important in Fairport's history however, because, like *Rosie*, it embodies the band's determination to continue in the face of adversity. Post-punk, many of the acts that had emerged from the same underground rock scene as Fairport had finally thrown in the towel. *Gottle O'Geer* laid the foundations for the version of Fairport that would see the decade out and provide a model for them when they reformed in the mid-Eighties. It was also the album that brought Simon Nicol back into the band, and there can be no doubt that without Simon's continuing presence on and off stage, the best of Dave Pegg's efforts would not have kept the ship afloat in the last two decades of the last century.

Phonogram and Pewit

Fairport had been signed to three major labels before creating Woodworm. They were Polydor, Island and Vertigo (which – rivals back in the Sixties and Seventies – would come to be part of the same company by 2012).

PEGGY: Back in the day, Island was an independent label. In 1977, Fairport had been with the label for nine years when they decided not to renew our contract.

Fairport had had a close bond with Island. Both Richard and Sandy would sign to the label upon leaving Fairport. Island would also release albums by Ashley Hutchings and Fotheringay. Today, the label regularly puts out compilations celebrating its folk-rock back catalogue, which includes Nick Drake, John Martyn, Amazing Blondel and the Incredible String Band. Although Fairport albums rank among the label's classics, Island's final Fairport output was unfortunate. After the Fairport studio release *Gottle O'Geer* – hardly their finest hour (or 42 minutes) – there came *Live at the LA Troubadour*. While there is a lot to enjoy on that set by the *Full House* line-up, it was released in some of the worst packaging ever inflicted upon a major act. As if to add insult to injury, it was released on the budget label HELP. It also needs to be said that not all the tracks were up to scratch: no one would list 'Yellow Bird' among essential Fairport recordings.

SIMON: That sleeve was put together by A&M, our record company in Los Angeles, who had done the odd thing before, including the alternative *Unhalfbricking* sleeve. They were certainly not as imaginative as the people at Island in the UK, and I think it would be fair to say they didn't care as much. They had had no contact with the band. They certainly had never seen us. We had never met them in the course of visiting the record company over there. They were big and corporate, whereas Island still functioned like a cottage industry in many respects. The structure of Island was a very flat pyramid: there were a couple of people at the top, with Chris Blackwell at the apex, but generally everyone just mingled together and shared ideas and job skills – it was very personal. A&M, on the other hand, very much followed the American model of clearly defined and confined departments.

   Live at the Troubadour just appeared one day. I couldn't make head nor tail of it. The sleeve gave you no impression as to what it was about, and I think for many people that somehow made the record less accessible. It didn't speak to you; it didn't tell you anything about the band that was on it. It left no visual impression on you, and it looked cheap and nasty.

The Round Dozen

In 1977, as Fairport completed its first decade, Island were no longer interested in a band it found difficult to promote.

PEGGY: Our album sales were dropping and we'd proved pretty conclusively that, unlike most rock acts on the label, we weren't capable of having hits.

Most labels have regular purges of their roster. As Island reviewed their catalogue in the post-punk era, there was no room for a group playing folk-rock alongside acts like Roxy Music and Bob Marley.

PEGGY: When you're as closely associated with one label as Fairport were with Island, sometimes it's hard to find someone else who will take you on.

In fact, they found a new home pretty quickly.

SIMON: Our manager at the time, Philippa Clare, got us a deal with Phonogram to record six albums for Vertigo. It's a matter on record that we only made two of them: the label paid us to *not* make the rest. That's a pretty good clue as to which direction your career is heading in!

Phonogram's prog rock label Vertigo's roster included Gentle Giant, Black Sabbath, Thin Lizzy and Status Quo. But there was room for music with a more rootsy approach. Like Fairport, Dr. Strangely Strange had, years earlier, moved from Island to Vertigo, and Magna Carta had released a string of critically acclaimed folk-based albums on the label. Iain Matthews also released his early albums on Vertigo.

Fairport still had enough clout to be able to tour not just the UK but also Australia successfully. So, in June 1977, Fairport flew south.

PEGGY: We were a little worried because Trevor – who had left the band in 1975 after the release of *Rising for the Moon* – had been our link to Australia. We were also going without Sandy of course. We were now a quartet, a smaller group than had toured Oz before.

They went down well. A couple of dates were recorded, though never released, and revealed a setlist which looked ahead to their new album and largely ignored the period after *Full House*. From that intervening period, only 'Limey's Lament' and 'Hexhamshire Lass' survived. There were four songs, including the epic title track, from their forthcoming album *The Bonny Bunch of Roses*. Five songs came from the *Full House* era. In a 13-song set, four were instrumental. Swarb even threw in his jokey version of Dylan's 'Country Pie'. More significantly for a band whose most recent releases had been dominated by original material, ten of the numbers were traditional.

SWARB: We'd tried going mainstream with Sandy and Trevor. It hadn't worked out. Now we were out on a limb. Vertigo wanted us to go back to being a more traditionally based group, which suited me fine.

The Bonny Bunch of Roses

Vertigo
July 1977

SIDE 1:

'Jams O'Donnells Jig'
'The Eynsham Poacher'
'Adieu, Adieu'
'The Bonny Bunch of Roses'

SIDE 2:

'Poor Ditching Boy'
'General Taylor'
'Run Johnny Run'
'Last Waltz'
'Royal Seleccion No. 13'

In many ways, *The Bonny Bunch of Roses* picks up where *Full House* had left off, its title track being one of the final recordings that had been made by that line-up.

SWARB: I was always sorry that 'Bonny Bunch' had spent so little time in Fairport's set. I was happy to go back to it. It also provided the album's cover.

SIMON: After a couple of frankly embarrassing record sleeves, it looked classy.

The front shows Napoleon in silhouette, clutching a bunch of red, white and blue roses: behind him, also in silhouette, staggers a single file of wounded soldiers.

SWARB: All those figures on the sleeve, including Boney, are actually me. I had great fun dressing up and striking poses.

The figures are set on a stark white background reminiscent of the Russian snows that ultimately defeated Napoleon's French

Revolutionary Army. Inside, the sleeve features individual band members against a background of the French Revolutionary standard.

SIMON: I wonder if John Tams minds that we pre-empted him with a sleeve that would have been great for the soundtrack of *Sharpe*?

The tracklist showed Fairport had gone back to the music they had been playing when Swarb and Peggy first joined.

SIMON: Aside from 'Bonny Bunch', the album had Richard's 'Poor Ditching Boy', which really sounds like it should be a traditional song. Swarb and I had played it as a duo, and it made sense to record it with the band.

PEGGY: Of course, we were looking to the future – just look at our optimistic, smiling faces on the sleeve. There are a lot of things about that album that looked further ahead than any of us could have foreseen. We did one of Ralph's songs. He would be important to us in the Eighties: writing songs for us, using Fairport as his studio band, and recording at Woodworm. There was a song called 'The Eynsham Poacher' which was quite local, with all of us living in and around Cropredy then. That came from John Leslie, Chris' brother: they were a duo and had appeared at one of the early Cropredy Festivals, and of course Chris was to play a really crucial part in Fairport's future.

SIMON: We were also laying the foundations of Fairport's new repertoire – the things we'd play over the following years and at those first Cropredy Festivals, though I think the Vertigo album had more songs with real staying power.

The album began and ended with instrumentals, a set of musical quote marks that would become more apparent when the album was released on CD. The first tune, composed by Peggy, would enjoy a new lease of life when he joined Jethro Tull and it was added to their repertoire.

PEGGY: 'Jams O'Donnells' got its name from a favourite book of the time by Flann O'Brien. It was something I really liked. Still quite a new composition when Fairport broke up and I had the chance to join Tull, it was the obvious choice when Ian asked if there was anything of mine I'd like them to play.

The other tune in the set, 'Royal Seleccion No. 13', was a medley of a few very well-known Scottish dance tunes. The title came from Bruce Rowland's favourite brand of cigar. The tunes included 'Haste to the Wedding' and 'Dashing White Sergeant' – which many Fairport fans would have recognised from Ashley Hutchings' album *The Compleat Dancing Master* (1974) – plus 'Toytown Parade', familiar to an entire generation as the 'Larry the Lamb' theme. Aside from 'Poor Ditching Boy' and Ralph's 'Run Johnny Run', the album included one other non-traditional song, Swarb's 'Last Waltz' ("That's one from my Engelbert Humperdinck period!").

Everything else on the album was traditional. 'General Taylor' is a sea shanty that, like the title track, had been a contender for *Full House* or its successor. 'Adieu, Adieu' had also been in Fairport's repertoire shortly after that and had been considered for *Rosie*. It was now revisited, with the 18th-century broadside given a new twist courtesy of a nicely-lifted lick from The Who's 'Happy Jack'.

PEGGY: Today, they'd no doubt just sample the original. To make it work, Bruce and I had to figure out what Entwistle and Moon were doing and duplicate it precisely.

SIMON: *Bonny Bunch* was, in a real sense, a fresh start. It does lean back to the point where Fairport's first period of real success had started to wind down. It also continues very naturally from the point where I left the band, not that the two are connected.

PEGGY: You could almost imagine *Bonny Bunch* as the follow-up to *Angel Delight* and *Babbacombe Lee*. It skips that period between *Rosie* and *Gottle O'Geer* when Sandy was in the band and Simon wasn't.

SWARB: That doesn't signify anything sinister because mostly the songs are traditional, but there isn't much on the *Bonny*

Bunch album that we couldn't have recorded in '72 or '73. We had already played, and in some cases recorded, several of those songs then.

Knowing what Island had in its archives, it is quite possible that Fairport were in fact pre-empting the release of a rag-bag compilation of outtakes.

PEGGY: We'd seen CBS delve into their archives when Dylan left them briefly for Asylum. The album called *Dylan* that came out then was a compilation of outtakes.

Bonny Bunch was well received by critics, who described Fairport as 'back on form' and 'back on track'. It didn't sell as well as hoped, however, an indication that Fairport's hardcore fan base was diminishing.

Telling Tales

At the end of October 1977, Fairport embarked on a six-week UK tour to promote the album. It was another tour where their most recent repertoire had to be dropped as the result of a change in line-up. Fortunately, though, they were able to revive some older material, including tracks from their first two albums of the decade. They were still playing large venues and the tour began at the Fairfield Halls in Croydon. At one gig, a banner hung from the balcony – placed there presumably by a fan displeased by the 'Fotheringport' era – declared 'Welcome back, Fairport!'

At the end of the year, Vertigo announced there would be a new Fairport single in 1978 – what was to be their version of Mike Waterson's 'Rubber Band' – only to cancel it. As part of their severance deal, the recording passed back to the band.

As 1978 began, Fairport had reason to feel confident. Their latest album may not have sold well, but fans had turned out to see them on tour. So, in February, they recorded their next album, making it two in a row with the same line-up, at the conveniently located Chipping Norton Studios.

SWARB: There was a lot of talk at the time about a four-piece

Fairport being the band's winning formula. They may have been right.

As if anticipating what was to be the inevitable, complete split between them, all four members of Fairport had booked extracurricular activities into their diaries. Mostly it was session work and non-Fairport live appearances, but Simon was also making use of the skills he had developed as a producer.

SIMON: I am not by nature a very forceful person. I know that is what a lot of bands are looking for in a producer. When I was invited to produce music for other bands – and probably Five Hand Reel was one of the first – I didn't know the people intimately, I hadn't worked with them. I usually didn't know the material they were playing. That was a big step away from what I had been used to.

You do end up being a referee in such a situation, particularly when you've got powerful personalities pulling together in a band. Five Hand Reel, for example, included three or four very powerful personalities, each of whom had his own ideas about how things should end up sounding.

So you become a diplomat – you have to be able to tell people when to back off, or when to try one more time, or simply keep coming up with new ideas. It is a very specialised skill to be a good producer, and involves a set of abilities that are more wide-ranging than people normally think. You have to be a man-manager, but you also have to be very musical.

All in all I did enjoy it, but I found it very challenging – and sometimes very draining, too.

Peggy, meantime, had set up another of those things he "files under 'hobbies that got out of hand'," a basic recording set-up at his home in Cropredy. When asked what it was like, he summed it up as "essentially a load of cables, a couple of reel-to-reel tapes, a mixing desk, and a large ashtray." This was the foundation of Woodworm Studios, though at the time Peggy had no vision of the state-of-the-art complex he would eventually own in Barford St Michael.

SWARB: There are pictures of Peggy's studios with big reel-to-reel machines perched on tables and cupboards. A couple of those were used to record the first Cropredy Festivals.

PEGGY: It was a matter of circumstances really. Adnams Brewery wanted Fairport to do the soundtrack for a promotional film – I can't think why they picked us! We decided it made sense to do it ourselves. We rigged up something using our sound equipment and then I kept adding bits.

The film ended up being used as a promotional video for the coastal resort of Southwold, where the brewery was based. It was called *In One End and Out the Other*.

PEGGY: The film was shown at Broughton Castle in 1981. The music was recorded by me in our little studio at Cropredy, and was written by myself and a chap called Arthur Conduit who was a double-glazing salesman in Banbury. It featured John and Chris Leslie – we all performed for free as we rated Adnams.

Fairport's next album, *Tipplers Tales*, came out in May 1978. The title and many of the tracks serve as a reminder that Fairport had channelled some of their recent energies into creating a soundtrack for a film about a brewery. Aside from three tunes by Peggy and an Allan Taylor song, everything on the album was credited as being trad arr Fairport. Swarb, who had been the band's composer since Richard Thompson's departure, contributed no new original songs. It was to be their last release for Vertigo.

Packaged in a rather unprepossessing 'modern art' sleeve, it seemed less impressive than its predecessor. Curiously, though, it would prove to be Fairport's source work when they began again.

PEGGY: The tunes we were playing live at the time the band called it a day were naturally mainly those from our latest release. You always have to plug the new record! We deliberately went further back to find things to play on the Farewell Tour, but essentially what was on *Tipplers* became our core repertoire in the early days of Cropredy.

SIMON: A lot of those songs have stood us in good stead, and are still very much a part of what Fairport do: 'Widow of Westmoreland', 'Three Drunken Maidens', 'Reynard the Fox' – which we later revived in a revised version courtesy of Chris Leslie – and even 'John Barleycorn' stayed with us for a very long time. Chances are you will always hear a couple of them at Cropredy.

When the band toured in 1978, reviewers were a lot less support-ive than they had been the previous year. Several spoke of perfor-mances that were 'lacklustre' or 'uncertain'; others spoke of Simon's lack of confidence as a singer – a surprising accusation given he had by then been providing lead vocals for both Fairport and The Albion Band since 1971.

SIMON: There were a lot of disappointments that year. I think uncertainty was inevitable. I had another brief bout of "Why bother?"

Then Swarb was told that he would have to stop playing with a loud electric band.

SWARB: My hearing had already suffered, and basically the spe-cialist said I had two choices – stop playing regularly with a loud electric band or go deaf.

Medically, he was already deaf in one ear. When an interviewer asked how this would affect him, he replied: "Well, if it's good enough for Brian Wilson and Phil Spector, I reckon I'll be all right. I might even go the whole hog and do a Beethoven."

When Vertigo terminated their contract, it really did seem like the end. For an act of Fairport's stature to not be signed to a major record company was almost unthinkable. Every Fairport cloud comes with its silver lining, though.

PEGGY: We had had a deal for six albums and we'd only made four. So they paid us off. We discovered Fairport could earn more from not making albums than from making them.

21 APRIL, 1978
ATKINSON-MORLEY HOSPITAL, WIMBLEDON

Four days after lapsing into a coma at a friend's home, Sandy Denny died peacefully in her sleep. She was 31. The circumstances of her death remain a matter of speculation. What is certain is that at the time of her death, family and doctors had been holding discussions about turning off her life support machine. As she had in life, in death Sandy went her own way in her own time.

She was to be remembered in song by many who had known her personally and many who had only known her through her music:- Dave Cousins, Dave Pegg, Dave Swarbrick, Iain Matthews, Paul Metsers, Kate Bush, Ocean Colour Scene, Thea Gilmore, and even the Spice Girls.

She spent the final years of her life at Byfield, the village that, every year, thousands of Fairport fans pass through just before they reach Cropredy. The two villages are only six miles apart.

Despite all that had happened to Fairport that year, Sandy's death overshadowed all else. Her passing was recorded in almost every national newspaper. *Melody Maker* dedicated its front page and two inside pages to her.

PEGGY: When I first joined Fairport, she had already left. She rejoined the band for a time, of course, was always a part of it. We all played on her solo albums. We had already been thinking about what might happen to Fairport: with Sandy gone, it felt like a piece of the jigsaw would always be missing.

So Long, Farewell

Without a record deal or a new album to promote, Fairport decided the best way to wrap things up would be with a big tour to give fans a chance "to come and say goodbye properly".

The tour began on 10 May at Cardiff's Sophia Gardens and ran through to a farewell gig on 4 August in Cropredy. There would be a live album recorded during the tour, with tracks taken from three nights in Birmingham, Southampton and Derby. Time was set aside on the tour to listen to the results and select appropriate tracks. It was eventually released by the band and not by Vertigo.

PEGGY: At the time, that was more than a disappointment, it was almost an insult. As it turned out, it was a good thing. We formed Woodworm Records as a result, so we could release it ourselves.

Woodworm would handle all things Fairport into the next millennium – record releases, tours, related projects like books, the two Fairport box sets, publicity, merchandising and, of course, Cropredy Festival. When the UK gigs came to an end, the Farewell Tour was booked for a couple more dates, in Europe.

SIMON: We had a couple of outstanding commitments after the big Cropredy Farewell gig, so typically Fairport retired and then headed for Belgium to play a couple more dates.

SWARB: It would have been nice to have gone to Australia where fans had been so supportive in the second half of the decade, but that was simply out of the question.

Farewell, Farewell

Woodworm Records, through Bear Records
September 1979
Reissued April 1980 as Simon's GAMA 1

SIDE 1:

    'Matty Groves' / 'High Road
       to Linton' / 'Orange
       Blossom Special'
    'John Lee'
    'Bridge Over the River Ash'
    'Sir Patrick Spens'

SIDE 2:

    'Mr Lacey'
    'Walk Awhile'
    'Bonny Black Hare'
    'Journeyman's Grace'
    'Meet on the Ledge'

Focusing on Fairport classics and oldies, the album of the Farewell Tour did not accurately reflect their set at the time, which included a large number of instrumentals – the CD reissue would add 'Dirty Linen', 'Flatback Caper' and 'Hen's March' – and several songs from their preceding studio albums. Ignoring *Unhalfbricking*, it only featured songs released by Fairport between late 1969 and 1971. Aside from the revised coda to 'Matty Groves', there was nothing one had not heard Fairport play on record before. Unfortunately, there was nothing here they played better than they had the first time round. It ended with a song Fairport had not played since 1969.

SIMON: It ['Meet on the Ledge'] was a natural for us to revive for that Farewell Tour – the lines about 'when my time is up' were obviously apposite. It also has a chorus you can easily sing along with. We believed that would be the last time the fans would see the band, so it was good that there was a song in the set that brought band and audience together.

RIC: It didn't matter that they hadn't played it for a decade; in many ways that increased its impact. 'Meet on the Ledge' has always been Fairport's anthem. Hearing them play it for what fans truly believed would be the last time was incredibly emotional. It's a great song because its words can mean so many different things.

The setlist for the Farewell Tour was a thoughtful one, and Simon, Swarb, Peggy and Bruce Rowland on drums didn't play safe. Songs were dusted off from the back catalogue that at least three-quarters of the band had never played. Here, too, was 'Bridge Over the River Ash', which deserved to be presented live on stage. Three tracks from *Angel Delight*, recorded with the Fairport line-up that most closely resembled the band in 1979, made it the most highly represented album on the set.

4 AUGUST, 1979
PEWIT FARM, CROPREDY

It was a wake, not a funeral. We turned up in the August sunshine to say one final goodbye to a band we had grown up with. There were friends and fans, ex-members and future members of the band, aspiring musicians, smartly dressed businessmen, dressed-down ex-hippies, some who had been old folkies when the band started and had kept the faith, some who had barely been born back then.

As directed, we made our way through the village – pausing for a double take on sighting The Brasenose Arms – and on to the Festival site: 'on Station Road, between the School and the Canal'. Those who had bought advance tickets (£2.50) went straight in; others paid £3.00 on the gate.

PEGGY: Of course, it wasn't called Cropredy Festival then. It was just Fairport's Farewell gig. It was in a field because Cropredy didn't have a venue big enough to fit everyone in.

The crowd waited, met old friends and made new ones, reminisced, chatted about Fairport. "When did you first see them?" "Which was the last album you bought?" "What's your favourite song?" "Have you ever met them?" There were some problems with the sound, which persisted into Bert Jansch's set (his group Conundrum had supported Fairport on their tour, and had subsequently been invited to play at the Farewell gig). Occasional electronic howls and whistles shrilled the air, momentarily terminating conversations. Four-thousand five-hundred people is a sizeable crowd, but the atmosphere was still intimate, friendly, tinged with sadness.

Meanwhile, in a galaxy far, far away (or so it seemed), Fairport Convention were at that moment the opening act at Knebworth, as specially invited guests of the headliners Led Zeppelin. They had been allowed to go on first so as to give them time to get to their own gig that evening.

Four o'clock came around and events got underway at Cropredy. Steve Ashley opened proceedings: he was an appropriate choice – members of Fairport had played on all his albums and, backed by Fairport, he would be one of the first acts to be released on Woodworm Records. With him on stage was a local fiddle player – his current stage partner, Chris Leslie.

CHRIS: I was the first musician to walk on stage. It truly was an honour. Ric was there too, of course, in the audience. So was, I believe, Maart. The future Fairport unwittingly gathered to bid farewell to the old Fairport.

Fairport arrived from Knebworth during Steve and Chris' set. A massive roar went up when Bruce and Peggy joined them for a couple of numbers. After Bert's Conundrum and a set from Earl

Okin, Fairport took to the stage. People had been turning up throughout the afternoon: Cropredy had been harder to find than some had imagined; others, relying on public transport, had discovered there was no frequent bus service; one fan, having somehow purchased tickets to Cropredy Station, discovered it had been closed down for 14 years and was only used as a starting point for pigeon races.

Fairport's set was pretty much the one they had played on tour. There were no ex-members turning up to play with the band for one last time. Ralph McTell joined them for 'Me With You'. Maddy Prior came on for one song, but anyone expecting either a tribute to Sandy or a Steeleye revival was disappointed: her choice was 'Mother and Child' from her solo album. There were surprises – 'Stagger Lee' and Loudon Wainwright's 'Red Guitar'. 'Matty' hit the floor for, we thought, the very last time. Simon led the massed choir of fans through 'Meet on the Ledge', sung with passion and sadness. We truly believed that might be the last time we ever heard Fairport sing it.

Their live album, unfortunately, was not ready for sale at the Festival; but in the middle of September, *Farewell, Farewell* arrived. It was a nostalgic collection of Fairport playing favourites. On closer inspection, the album omitted the large number of instrumentals played to flesh out the gig and included nothing recorded after 1971. It was as if Fairport were ignoring the years of chaos, disorganised gigs, and less-than-classic albums. In '79, Fairport were reaching back to what many fans described as 'the last real Fairport'.

14 AUGUST, 1982
HOME FARM, CROPREDY

As we travelled through the narrow country lanes that connect Cropredy to major Banbury roads, we noticed more organised signage to the site. Efficient and friendly stewards directed us to parking and camping fields (only a couple were needed back then) and explained how to get to the main Festival site. That was the first time most of us had set foot on the fields of Home Farm. It was time to ring some changes – 1982 would prove a groundbreaking year in many ways.

'Si Tu Dois Partir'. Fairport Convention rehearse for their
Top of the Pops appearance on 14 August, 1969 – the first
public performance of the *Liege & Lief* lineup

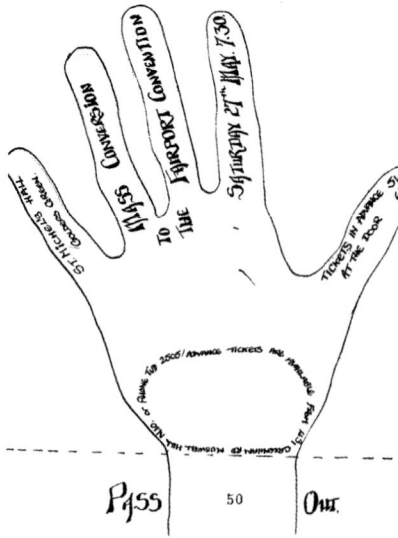

May 1967. Designed by Judy Dyble, the ticket for the very first
Fairport gig was an outline of Richard Thompson's hand

January 1968. Fishmongers' Hall was barely a mile
from Fairport. Gary Farr's album *Strange Fruit* featured
one of Richard Thompson's first recording sessions

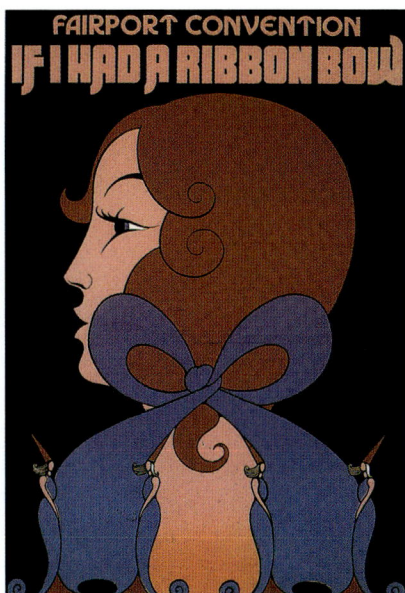

February 1968. The promotional poster for the band's debut single

University of Bradford Union
Cordially invites you
to spend an evening with

JOHN PEEL
and his friends—
Fairport Convention
Principal Edwards Magic Theatre
BRIGID ST. JOHN

Thursday 6th February 7.30 pm
Great Hall   Admission 6/-

February 1969. The author's first encounter with Fairport
on one of their early sorties into Yorkshire

1969. "Martin Lamble will always be nineteen in my mind" (Simon Nicol)

August 1969. Sandy and Trevor at her home in Chipstead Street

1970. The *Full House* lineup pose for PR photos.
L-R: Swarb, Peggy, Simon, DM, RT

1973. The *Rosie* lineup.
L-R: Jerry Donahue, DM, Peggy, Swarb, Trevor Lucas

17 April, 1973. An *Old Grey Whistle Test* appearance
to promote Fairport's forthcoming album *Nine*.
L-R: Trevor Lucas, DM, Jerry Donahue, Swarb, Peggy

January 1975. The World Tour featuring, L-R: Jerry Donahue,
Sandy Denny, Peggy, Trevor Lucas, DM, Swarb

1978. Fairport playing Cropredy Village Fete. L-R: Swarb, Peggy,
Simon. In 1979 it became the venue for their Farewell gig

𝓕AIRPORT CONVENTION

Invite you to their goodbye party to be held on the 4th August in their home village of Cropredy in Oxfordshire. The party begins at 3.00 p.m. with non-stop music and fun provided by many, many friends and colleagues; some billed and some to surprise you. We are insisting that we play as well.

For your refreshment there's Theakston's Ales or a drop of the hard stuff, or if you prefer wine we've even a wine bar. There are side shows, a re-enactment of the Battle of Cropredy performed we are reliably informed, by a cast of thousands, and ox roast, plenty of car parking space, so why not join us in making merry that occasion.

Entrance is by programme only and sorry to say, there is a restriction on the amount of people the village is capable of handling. If you fancy joining us admission is £2.50 . . . send a cheque or postal order made payable to Fairport Convention and address it to High Beech, Vicarage Gardens, Cropredy, Oxon. Please enclose a large stamped addressed envelope and we will then send you your commemorative programme plus directions.

If you can't make it along there, we would like to thank you for many magic moments and bid you all a fond farewell.

Adios,

**SWARB,
PEGGY,
SIMON,
BRUCE**

P.S Camping allowed

1979. The end of an era, the end of the band.
Fairport's formal invitation to the 'final' gig

Dear friends

We thought you might like to know that due to popular request Fairport Convention are having a re-union concert in Cropredy on Saturday August 30th

Special guests will be Ralph McTell and Richard and Linda Thompson, plus many of our favourite artists.

There will be camping facilities, a real ale bar and various food stalls

Tickets, which will be limited are £3.50 (£4 on the gate) Children under twelve are admitted free. T shirts will also be available but advance orders would be appreciated stating size

postal orders only, made payable to C. Pegg and a stamped addressed envelope to:

    WOODWORMS HILTON, CHAPEL ROW, CROPREDY, OXON OX17 1NS

    DAVE SWARBRICK, DAVE PEGG
    SIMON NICOL, BRUCE ROWLANDS.

1980. The typed letter sent out by the Peggs on behalf of Fairport, promoting the first Cropredy reunion

Reunited – Richard (electric lead), Simon (acoustic, rhythm)

1980. Peggy and Richard in a celebratory mood

1982. The band may only have existed for a couple of days
each year, but Fairport still needed planning meetings

1995. The band celebrate midsummer in Fairport fashion.
L-R: Maartin Allcock, Peggy, Simon, DM, Ric Sanders

2002. Fairport past and present at the BBC Radio 2 Folk Awards
show – with their Lifetime Achievement Award

2012. 'Meet on the Ledge' at Fairport's Cropredy Convention.
Backing vocals: Richard Thompson, Dave Swarbrick, Nigel Schofield

Cropredy capers: Ric Sanders and Chris Leslie

Dave Pegg

Gerry Conway

Simon Nicol

The crowd at Cropredy: See you next year!

PEGGY: We'd realised we couldn't just keep gathering every year, doing the same old thing. We had to find ways of making each year special.

CHRIS PEGG: I suppose that was the point where it dawned on us that Cropredy Festival was a going concern. If people had originally come for the novelty of seeing Fairport perform, that novelty would eventually wear off.

SWARB: We'd been through the experience of playing to gradually diminishing audiences. We didn't want to repeat the experience at Cropredy.

The Festival's growing popularity meant that we might have been facing a somewhat longer walk to the field than previously. Cropredy-goers are by now so familiar with the topography that it is hard to think back to what it had been like to encounter 'the field' for the first time. To refresh my memory, I looked back to what I had written at the time:

> 'The field is a steady slope from the Williamscote Road to a level area which ends with a stand of trees along the banks of the Cherwell, and beyond that the Oxford Canal. The lower flat area has enough space for a stage and backstage. The field is a natural amphitheatre with a clear view of the stage from all parts: its slope is enough to assist visibility but not so great as to make it awkward for walking. The fact the field has no direct exit to a road, but can be entered via adjoining fields makes security easier. In short, it's ideal.'

Flicking through the programme during one of the welcome breaks in the rain which fell over most of the two days, one could be forgiven for thinking this was a folk festival – Breton legend Dan Ar Braz (one of those blink-and-you'd-miss-him Fairport ex-members), Geordie troubadours Bob Fox and Stu Luckley (Bob would record *Dreams Never Leave You* with Fairport at Woodworm, in 2000), The Maddy Prior Band and Home Service—both offshoots of bands formed by Fairport's founder, Ashley Hutchings. The Maddy Prior Band had come out of Steeleye Span after they broke up. Home Service had developed from The Albion Band when

Ashley grew tired of leading the resident band at the National Theatre. Home Service, fronted by John Tams, would make a triumphant return in 2011; in 1982, the then line-up of The Albion Band was the day job of both Simon and DM.

Although the Festival was groundbreaking, it was still in electric folk mode. Dan Ar Braz played sets on both days. Captain Coco's Country Dance Band opened the proceedings on the Saturday. In those days, the audience could get right up to the apron of the stage, which was still made from scaffolding with a plastic canopy that kept off most of the rain. Large spotlights lit the band from the front, while the effects backline lighting consisted of a couple of dozen Fresnel spots. A ceilidh-style opening act was totally viable: with a caller on stage, sets would be formed in front of the stage where a kind of folk dancing took place.

Captain Coco was to make a number of Cropredy appearances. It was a *nom de jour* of various Fairporters and friends (including future member Chris Leslie), all wearing ping-pong clown heads, white and shiny with brightly coloured hair tufts. Extending as far as the eyebrows, they made an effective mask and disguised the identity of the players (until they referred to each other by name).

As had happened at the previous year's Broughton Castle Festival (the only Cropredy Festival not to take place at Cropredy), the event was recorded. It was issued on cassette the following May.

SIMON: I cannot say we thought that way at the time, but in hindsight, it was the year the focus of our attention shifted from the past to the future.

Ahead of Cropredy, well-timed to garner advance publicity for the Festival, in May 1982 an audio souvenir of the previous year's Cropredy set – *Moat on the Ledge* – was released. The title was a double reference: aside from the classic Fairport song (now established as Fairport's closing number), it also alluded to the venue of the previous year's festival, Broughton Castle. The sleeve showed Fairport in a rowing boat on the castle's moat during a break in rehearsals. It had been three years since Fairport had released the disappointing *Farewell, Farewell* LP, dismissed by *Melody Maker* thus: 'Little more than a ragged souvenir of the death-throes of a once great band.' Their new release proved a positive contrast to that.

The album's nine tracks showed the band in commanding form. Essentially featuring the *Full House* line-up augmented by Bruce Rowland, the LP also included guest appearances by Ralph McTell (on electric guitar) and Judy Dyble, making her first appearance on a new Fairport record in 14 years.

Judy sang 'Both Sides Now', originally recorded at Fairport's first session but never released. The album offered rarities as well as new versions of familiar Fairport fare. Here, alongside 'Matty Groves', 'Walk Awhile', 'Rosie' and the 'Brilliancy Medley' (played by Richard rather than Jerry) were 'Woman or a Man', an unreleased Richard Thompson song, Dylan's 'Country Pie', and a full on version of a Jerry Lee Lewis classic, 'High School Confidential'. It demonstrated the ability to amaze and surprise, which has become a hallmark of Cropredy. One review remarked, 'It feels more like an extension of *Full House* than Fairport's albums from the second half of the last decade'.

Even more significantly, it was WR001, the first release on Dave Pegg's Woodworm label.

PEGGY: We found out it was fairly easy to get a record pressed, and by using a live recording and selling only via mail order and later at gigs, we could keep both production and distribution costs down. Having our own label tied in with the studio, and became a service we were able to offer to anyone who recorded there – Woodworm 002 would be Steve Ashley's *Family Album*. At that stage, we hadn't thought of ever having a Fairport studio album to release. Then again, we hadn't thought of a lot of things – Cropredy becoming such a big event, Fairport reforming permanently, touring Britain and then the world. Really, it was just a hobby that got out of hand.

Following the break-up of Fairport, Peggy had accepted an invitation to join Jethro Tull, and 1982 had been spent recording and promoting their album *Broadsword and the Beast*. A return to touring with Fairport would be another first in '82. Their 'tour' of the Channel Islands consisted of Fort Regent in Jersey and Beau Sejour in Guernsey. It was the shortest tour possible in the remotest corner of the British Isles. The really significant first, though, was witnessed at Cropredy, with 'reConvening' stepped up a notch.

SWARB: We decided to revive *Babbacombe Lee* and play it in its entirety. It was to be a one-off event, and involved quite a lot of learning for a single performance. That does tend be the case with Cropredy.

PEGGY: It was a bit of a mad thing to do, especially as we were tempting fate by doing it on Friday the 13th.

SWARB: We got through it pretty much unscathed, though there were a couple of fluffs in 'Sailor's Alphabet'.

For Simon Nicol, things had come full circle.

SIMON: The *Babbacombe Lee* performance really was a case of 'it all comes round again'. It was the last thing I'd played with Fairport before I left. When I rejoined we had included a couple of bits from it, but it was good to play the whole thing again.

PEGGY: It made real sense when we'd booked Trevor and Jerry, because the *Nine* line-up had come after *Babbacombe Lee*. So it was that on the Friday night you got one line-up of the band, followed, on Saturday, by the next Fairport line-up playing (part of) a set that lasted in total four and a half hours. We played huge sets in those days – stronger bladders you know.

SIMON: There was a feeling that people were coming pretty much to see Fairport. The GPS set the previous year had gone down well. So, a unique chance to see *Babbacombe Lee* was clearly an audience draw.

The GPS were a scratch band who played covers of rock 'n' roll and country songs, with a couple of band originals thrown in. The group consisted of Richard Thompson, Ralph McTell, Dave Pegg and Dave Mattacks. GP, incidentally, was not a tribute to Gram Parsons but stood for Grazed Pontiffs, a reference to a recent assassination attempt on His Holiness.

DM: It certainly wasn't a name we planned on explaining if we did any Irish gigs!

PEGGY: We played a few gigs for fun, mostly stuff we all knew –
    or thought we knew. Cropredy 1982 was our biggest audience.
    We recorded it and it came out on CD a few years later.

Simon Withers later referred to the 1982 Festival as being akin to
"watching living history".

Simon Nicol opened the marathon set with Richard Thompson's
'Time to Ring Some Changes'. Fairport hadn't recorded it previously, although Simon had sung the song with The Albion Band
on *Rise Up Like the Sun* (1978), and with Swarb in the duo they had
formed to play folk clubs and festivals. Fairport's sets at the early
Cropredy Festivals had a sense of archaeology about them. At that
stage, the band had no current repertoire and so tended to start by
returning to their last touring set. Initially, the line-up on stage was
the one that had toured in the late Seventies and had made their
previous two studio albums. Little by little, like someone digging
through the strata of the band's history, they would delve further.

PEGGY: A lot of the early Cropredy sets comprised things we
    had played on the Farewell Tour, which had featured our most
    recent recordings as well as stuff we hadn't played for years.

Fairport reached back to *Angel Delight* for its title track and
'Journeyman's Grace'. Then Simon remarked: "Glad you liked that,
time to bring on the reinforcements." Peggy excused Simon for
"a tiddle break" and introduced "Long Red – Trevor Lucas, who's
flown over from Melbourne especially." Trev regaled the crowds
with a song about Australian marijuana-growing.

PEGGY: That was a request: it let us get Trev on to doing some-
    thing virtually solo. I thought it would go down well with
    the audience… and judging from the smells drifting from the
    crowd, I suspect it did.

Swarb then introduced Jerry Donahue, "all the way from Los
Angeles", who played his version of Jerry Reed's 'The Claw' to the
sound of collective jaws dropping. A live highlight during his touring days with Fairport, it had not yet been released at the time. To
many fans, therefore, it would have been like Trevor's song – entertaining if unfamiliar territory.

PEGGY: When the line-up with Trevor and Jerry reconvened at Cropredy, it was an event one genuinely felt had been worth waiting for. It set a standard for what we could and would achieve at the Festival in the future.

SIMON: I was offstage, watching. There they were. The *Nine* line-up on stage together for the first time in nearly a decade. It was something no one could have expected to see.

TREVOR: The cassette of the gig that came out didn't really show what we did. Understandably, it focused on things that hadn't been released before. In fact, we played a lot of the songs we had recorded on *Rosie* and *Nine*.

From *Rosie*, one had 'The Plainsman', 'Hen's March', and the album's title track. 'Iron Lion' was revived from *Rising for the Moon*. *Nine* was represented by 'The Hexhamshire Lass', 'Tokyo', 'Polly on the Shore', and 'Bring 'em Down'.
    That should have been enough to send any Fairport fan back to his tent feeling very contented. But it was only the interval. Fairport, who had not yet mastered the logistics required for the substantial changes of line-up that have become a crucial part of the Cropredy set, scheduled a break mid-set. The queues at bars and portaloos were at once impressive and frustrating.
    When we returned, two drum-kits and several ensuing songs benefited from the might of the combined percussion of Mattacks and Rowland, as they would 20-odd years on when Gerry and DM would join forces.

PEGGY: That was the first year without RT, who was in America. It made us pull our socks up and think what else we might offer the Copredy audience. The thought of having to fill four hours just by ourselves was pretty terrifying, not to say impossible.

Richard had split quite publicly and acrimoniously with his wife Linda at this point. She earned a very supportive cheer for making her return to stage work as Fairport introduced her as the first guest of the second half of that 1982 show. She sang 'Dimming of the Day' just as the sun went down. Cropredy can provide spectacular sunsets and that year – with its mixture of rain, lowering clouds and sunshine – provided one of the best as the water drops hanging from every surface glowed like liquid rubies. Linda stayed on for 'Genesis Hall' (the band's first performance of the song in 13 years) and 'Rosie', on which she had been one of the original backing singers.

Through the rest of the evening, Linda came and went from the stage with an entertaining randomness, teaming up with one-time Fairport manager Philippa Clare to provide bumps, grinds and girlie backing vocals on a couple of numbers. She came on to sing along to an epic 20-minute version of 'Sloth', bottle in hand. She ended the evening with an attempt to transform 'Matty Groves' into a duet.

Trevor and Jerry returned for a version of 'Lucky Old Sun', with Swarb providing some of the best harmonies he has ever sung.

It has since become regular practice to bring on guests from during the day to join Fairport. Part of the fun of Cropredy is trying to guess who among the day's performers might join the band during their set. Midge Ure scored a double whammy in 2008 when, having played the acoustic set immediately before Fairport, he not only returned but did so to perform Jethro Tull's 'Living in the Past'. In 1982, Dan Ar Braz performed what the setlist described as 'Dan's Blues' – actually a version of the Honeyboy Edwards' standard 'Love Me Tomorrow'. Then Bruce Lacey, who had provided 40 minutes of utter eccentricity that afternoon, came back on.

In what was one of his first major interviews since joining Fairport ten years earlier, Trevor Lucas summarised the band's approach to performing as "Guess the line-up – win a prize". No one would have won the prize for guessing who might join them at Cropredy in 1982.

Harbouring ambitions to be a professional singer, in August 1974 welterweight and middleweight wrestling champion Brian Maxine had inveigled Fairport Convention into acting as backing band on his latest album. So the *Nine* line-up, plus Sandy Denny and Linda Thompson providing backing vocals, had essentially made a country album with him. Jerry Donahue clearly enjoyed providing some Nashville-style picking while Swarb played some elegant old-timey fiddle, which was for some reason kept low in the mix. Entitled *A Ribbon of Stainless Steel*, it was released in the UK on Columbia Records, a subsidiary of EMI.

As Dan Ar Braz completed his song at Cropredy on 14 August, 1982, Brian Maxine ambled on stage, followed by Linda and Philippa. Supported on vocals by Trevor, he launched into a version of Dave Dudley's 'Six Days on the Road'. The song had become a part of Fairport's live set back in 1973, when the band had played sets peppered with interesting cover versions that never made it to disc. Among them were: a handful of rock 'n' roll classics; at least five Dylan covers; a couple of Antipodean folk songs; versions of several of Sandy's songs; and a couple of country standards.

As Maxine's song finished, Simon seemed to take stock of the stage around him, announcing: "This has got to be the biggest line-up of Fairport ever assembled." He was looking at a cross-section of Fairport's entire history: Simon, Judy, Swarb, Peggy and DM, Linda, Trevor, Jerry, Dan and Bruce. The audience was witnessing what was to become a regular annual event at Cropredy. Before long, the event's attendance would reach the legal maximum of 20,000 people.

Many of Cropredy first-timers in 1982 might have been surprised, as they passed through the village, to see The Brasenose Arms. The pub, named after the Oxford College, had featured on the rear of the gatefold sleeve of *Nine* – the band sitting on the parapet outside the 17th-century hostelry.

CHAPTER SEVEN

Over the Next Hill

Friday night, 9 August, 1985 – Cropredy Festival. Fairport are about to take to the stage. The programme announces this is the *Full House* line-up reconvened for a special one-off event. Saturday was to bring further surprises as both Trevor Lucas and Jerry Donahue would rejoin the band for the occasion. Those present enjoyed the rare treat of watching Richard and Jerry, Fairport's two legendary guitarists, playing together. They swapped lines on a lengthy instrumental known as 'The Big Duet' – designed entirely around their talents.

SIMON: *Full House* was the first album that we could return to and play with the original line-up. Anything before that would have required someone to 'stand-in' for Sandy and, of course, Martin Lamble.

Fairport would also play material from their three 1969 albums, together with a few tracks from Richard's solo albums. Guest vocalist Cathy Lesurf sang one of her own songs, 'My Feet are Set for Dancing', which had been included on Fairport's recent studio album *Gladys' Leap*, their first in seven years.

This sixth annual reunion had come in the wake of the band's first Winter Tour, which had opened with two local gigs on New Year's Eve and New Year's Day and run through to 27 January. It was a part of the promotion for the new, reborn Fairport Convention.

Their new studio album was the seventh for Peggy's Woodworm Records, and followed releases of recordings made at previous Cropredy reunion gigs.

What's surprising is that Fairport would not use Cropredy 1985 to promote *Gladys' Leap*.

SIMON: That was down to Dave Swarbrick. He had, by this point, moved up to Scotland, and while he was prepared to join Fairport for one day a year, he had no interest in reviving the band on a more permanent basis. When we played him the album, as a work in progress, he had been very disparaging of what he'd heard and had no interest in contributing to it. As a result, we had invited Ric Sanders to play on the album. Chris Leslie, who was local and already very much associated with Cropredy Festival and Fairport, might have seemed a more natural choice, but at the time he was a member of Swarb's new group Whippersnapper, who had appeared at the Festival that year.

PEGGY: We decided to release an album because it was time to stop being a band that got together once a year and become a proper functioning unit once more. Releasing a new studio album is obviously a significant part of that process. I was pleased it could be recorded at my studio and released on Woodworm Records.

DM: At that point, there were only three members of Fairport – Simon, Peggy and myself. There were guest musicians, however.

Also appearing on *Gladys' Leap* were Cropredy resident Harold Wells, providing the spoken introduction to Ralph McTell's 'Bird from the Mountain', Cathy Lesurf, Richard Thompson providing lead guitar on the final track, and Ric Sanders adding electric fiddle to three of the tracks.

RIC SANDERS: That album causes some confusion. To clear things up, I was not a member of Fairport at the time, I was simply brought in as a session player. Although I had worked with both Simon and DM in The Albion Band, it was

Peggy who had invited me to play. We went back a long way, through the association of our fathers who had both worked at the same school.

A gathering of over 10,000 hardcore fans who had travelled from across the British Isles and overseas primarily to see Fairport, whose two sets over two days dominated the weekend, might clearly seem a natural place to plug any new venture, let alone the full-time re-formation of the band and the release of their first studio album in years. Bizarrely, though, the Festival seemed resolutely to ignore these new developments. The cover of the programme depicted individual headshots of Fairport including Swarb. The programme said nothing about the new album, though it did carry a discreet plug for the forthcoming Winter Tour. Despite the two lengthy stints on stage, Fairport would include only one song from *Gladys' Leap* – the Cathy Lesurf song that had also been played the previous year.

SIMON: Swarb simply was not interested in playing songs from *Gladys*. He stamped his little foot and insisted we stuck to the old material. It wasn't worth having a stand-up fight over, because if he pulled out, we would have been left with only the new material and a three-piece band to play it, in effect. So the album was out and the opportunity to promote it was not available to us.

    At the time, I felt his attitude to the whole thing, particularly the recording, was unnecessarily negative. He seemed to me to be being a fool to himself by being so absolutely unprepared to have any association with it. Swarb is one of those people with whom you have to accept the fact that if he sets his mind against something, you are not going to change it.

Fairport were not in a position where they could have given Swarb a break to allow Ric to join them for some songs from the new album.

RIC: Before I finally joined Fairport in '85, I used to go to Cropredy each year. The problem, though, was that Cropredy clashed with the Edinburgh Festival, where I was usually working. If I had a gig there over the weekend, I would only be able to make the Friday at Cropredy. Usually, I'd be playing with Andy Cronshaw or Phil Neville. On Cropredy Saturday in 1985, I was in Edinburgh with Phil and (believe it or not) Julian Clary or, as he was known at the time, the Joan Collins Fan Club featuring Fanny the Wonderdog.

Fairport's only previous two-night stint at Cropredy had been three years earlier, in 1982, when they had devoted their Friday night set to playing *Babbacombe Lee* all the way through (as they would again when they returned to it 29 years later). In 1985, Fairport elected to reform the classic *Full House* line-up. They played songs from 1969 and 1970. Then on Saturday, they presented the *Nine* line-up, together with one-off aggregations only possible at Cropredy. Several songs were played on both nights – firstly in a version approximating to the original version; then, in what has come to be referred to as 'a Cropredy version'. Cropredy '85 did not provide Fairport with the chance to plug their latest LP, but it did set the precedent of creating totally valid new versions of classic material.

CHRIS: I don't think of that as turning us into some kind of Fairport tribute band. The people playing had either been in the band at the time it had originally played those songs, or had been fans of the band who had learned the songs through them. To me, it's closer to an oral tradition than a pop music cover.

RIC: The original version is in your mind, and sometimes it's tempting to recreate what Swarb had originally recorded, for example. It's much more exciting to say to yourself, "That's how *that* Fairport did it then, how would *this* Fairport do it now?"

GERRY: With a song like 'Who Knows Where the Time Goes', you might start quite close to the original, treating it with respect, handling it with kid gloves. But then you start to work on it, shape it, take possession of it. The fiddle duet that Chris and Ric have created for that song is not on the original version which is all rolling guitars, and is also nothing like what Swarb did with it when Sandy rejoined the band.

So, several songs we had heard in something close to their 'original form' on that Friday in 1985 were reinvented on the Saturday. These included two instrumentals ('Dirty Linen' and 'Sir B McKenzie'), 'Walk Awhile', 'Matty Groves' and, most surprisingly, 'Sloth'. Most of these appeared right at the end of the set as a kind of massive segue. Fairport have, over the years, created many surprising intros to 'Matty Groves', but that night's version – which had sprung off the back of an extended version of 'Sloth', which had in turn come straight out of 'Dirty Linen' – was exceptional.

PEGGY: From the point of view of someone on stage, it's hard to remember what happened in the set or why it happened. At Cropredy, we have a very definite finishing time. Everything on stage has to end by midnight. There have been lots of years when we have had to drop songs because we were over-running.

SIMON: I think in all the years Cropredy has been happening, there has been only one year when we ran short of material and had to add a song to the setlist.

PEGGY: What probably happened in '85 was that we were running a little behind schedule and decided to drop announcements to get back on track.

SIMON: I always keep an eye on the clock as the set nears its end. We have to play 'Matty', go offstage, and get back on in time to perform 'Meet on the Ledge' by midnight. This is pure conjecture, but I suspect with both Richard and Jerry playing, 'Sloth' might have stretched out a bit, and I then realised we had to start 'Matty' sharpish.

Since both Trevor and Jerry had joined Fairport that night (it was to be Trevor's last appearance), the band had taken the opportunity to feature songs from *Nine* and *Rising for the Moon*. As the old Fairport was being forced by Swarb to a final stand (the following year would be the first without him), plans were afoot to create a new working band.

SIMON: It was obvious Swarb was losing interest in Fairport, so virtually from the Farewell gig, Dave Pegg became in effect the band's manager. He and his wife Chris organised and managed the Festival. The studio and record company were Peggy's. That's the way it was to remain until they split up and the management structure of Fairport, for all kinds of reasons, changed. We have more to be grateful for to them than anyone realises – not least, for the very existence of Fairport in any form at all.

When it came to someone saying, "I think it's time Fairport made a proper record again," it was always Peggy who had the wherewithal and the drive to do it.

PEGGY: There were a lot of things to consider. *The Boot* and other live Cropredy releases had been on cassette: that meant they were cheaper and easier to produce and mail out. Obviously, we were going to have to put out a proper studio release on vinyl soon. We had to find material to include on it, because at Cropredy our setlist was oldies, plus things where we accompanied our guests.

SIMON: Finding songs was the first priority. As it turned out, we ended up with a really strong selection we hadn't done before, one of which would go on to be ranked alongside Fairport's classic material.

PEGGY: It wasn't deliberate, but *Gladys' Leap* would have only one traditional number on it. That's the last tune in the instrumental medley. Of course, as Fairport really only existed for a couple of nights a year at Cropredy, the album's tracklist was all material we hadn't played live.

DM: What we hadn't thought about was who Fairport were. After Bruce was no longer able to carry on drumming, I'd come back into the band. So essentially, Fairport were the four-piece from the *Babbacombe Lee* era, with Ric on fiddle instead of Swarb.

SIMON: In that gap where the band had had a lie down – between the Farewell gig in '79 and the release of *Gladys' Leap* in 1985 – Fairport had been getting increasingly busy. To start with, we had had a year off, between the Farewell gig and the first reunion. Then, one or two foreign festivals and a few gigs around New Year crept in. This was in response to demand: promoters were offering us money to do them, to be frank. I don't think we were actively going out looking for work as a band at that stage. So it built up and built up until we made the record. When we decided it was time for Fairport to make a record again, the band was a three-piece – rhythm guitar, bass and drums – with me left holding the baby in the vocals department.

This wasn't the only problem. For the first time in their history, Fairport faced creating an album without a songwriter in the band.

SIMON: When we reformed none of us considered himself a songwriter as such. In order to record *Gladys' Leap*, we had to go looking for material outside the band.

Gladys' Leap

Woodworm
July 1985

SIDE 1:

'How Many Times'
'Bird from the Mountain'
'Honour and Praise'
'The Hiring Fair'

SIDE 2:

'Instrumental Medley '85'
'My Feet are Set for Dancing'
'Wat Tyler'
'Head in a Sack'

The new Fairport album felt like a cottage industry product. Fans were delighted to have a new studio album after making do with 'official bootlegs' of live recordings and less-than-inspiring videos. Critics, too, were quick to honour and praise the new release. Derek Jewell in *The Sunday Times* called it 'unmissable', while Lawrence Heath in *Folk Roots* declared it 'vintage stuff' and described himself as being 'pleasantly stunned by the end result'.

The album's songwriters were mostly old friends. Simon knew both Cathy Lesurf and Dave Whetstone from his time with The

Albion Band in the early Eighties. Dave Whetstone's rocky 'Head in a Sack' featured Richard Thompson as the guest lead guitarist. Richard provided the song 'How Many Times', which he had recently played on his live solo acoustic album, *Small Town Romance*.

PEGGY: We liked Cathy's song and she had no plans to record it anywhere else. Richard's song was on an old demo tape he'd made in the very early days of Woodworm Studios. That was one of the ways having the studio fed into Fairport over the years. 'Honour and Praise' came the same way.

John Richards' 'Honour and Praise' is a stirring ballad of maritime prowess, recalling the days of British sea power and legendary privateers. It was a genre of contemporary song to which Fairport would regularly turn on future albums. Richards had been active on the Midlands rock scene since leading mod group the Echo Four. Having consistently reinvented himself, by the early Eighties he found himself in a pub rock band.

PEGGY: They were called Maurice and The Minors, and they booked studio time at Woodworm to record some demos, which might become an album. It was finally released the year after *Gladys' Leap* and was called *One Lady Owner*. I spotted the song and asked to have it for the new album Fairport were planning.

SIMON: Richards would later contribute 'The Deserter' to Fairport's repertoire, which came via my first solo LP (another Woodworm-recorded album).

Ralph McTell had always been a friend of Fairport. They had provided backing on several of his albums. He was, and remains, a Cropredy regular, whether he appears on stage or not. He wrote 'Bird from the Mountain' with Fairport in mind.

RALPH MCTELL: It's modelled on poaching songs, of which Fairport seem to have recorded a few.

Harold Wells, Fairport fan and local resident, was 65 in August 1985, and to mark his birthday Dave Pegg had organised a surprise party involving members of Fairport past and present who played at his home. He was the perfect choice as the song's narrator. Ralph McTell also contributed 'The Hiring Fair', co-written with DM, to *Gladys*, and it proved a popular addition to the catalogue.

DM: Although I was Fairport's drummer, I played the keyboards on some songs. 'The Hiring Fair' is one of them. Because I had worked on the melody and arrangement, Ralph was kind enough to give me credit as co-composer.

SIMON: I was delighted and flattered that 'The Hiring Fair' was one of the songs that fans selected for *By Popular Request*. I think everyone expected people to plump for songs by the pre-Cropredy Fairport, which is the repertoire most of the album draws on. It was reassuring to find some 'second phase' Fairport making the list, as well as quite a few recent songs that nearly made it.

'The Girl from the Hiring Fair' is one of Ralph McTell's greatest songs, and seems almost *in situ* at Cropredy, where the moon does indeed rise over the field on cue (these days via carefully timed back projection). Ralph would eventually release his own version on his album, *Bridge of Sighs* (1987), which was to feature an impressive array of Fairport members past and present in his backing band.

SIMON: It's the song I associate most closely with that second weekend in August. There is something about it that matches the atmosphere of Cropredy. It's also the song that, more than any other, was responsible for the rebirth of the band in '85. It's one of those very special songs that make you *want* to go and play it to people. It's about love in the open air – what's not to like?

RIC: It was the first thing I ever played with Fairport. They asked me down to the studio to add fiddle to some tracks and played 'The Hiring Fair', explaining what they wanted. Dave Mattacks had already created a great arrangement, but they asked – generously – if I had any ideas of my own.

PEGGY: I like it because it has a long intro, which gives me time to go offstage for a tiddle break! Seriously, it's a song close to Fairport's heart and stayed in both the full band and the acoustic set until the time we reintroduced 'Who Knows Where the Time Goes'. They are big, slow songs and there wasn't room for both. It does keep re-emerging, though, and is always great to play – especially at Cropredy. It's a song full of open spaces.

The band liked the song so much that Peggy created a slide show featuring photographs of his daughter taken in and around Barford St Michael amid amber fields of corn in golden, late-summer sunshine. It was a brief but fascinating return to the multimedia approach they had used when they took *Babbacombe Lee* on tour, and a forerunner of the live videos which now accompany several songs at Cropredy.

Ralph's third contribution was a historical epic that reached right back to the 14th century. In all of Fairport's repertoire, only 'Sir Patrick Spens' would delve further back than 'Wat Tyler', a song about the 14th-century Peasants' Revolt, the first uprising of working people in modern British history. It was very much in the public consciousness in the early Eighties, having just had its 600th anniversary celebrated.

SIMON: There was no real reason why Ralph McTell asked me to collaborate with him on writing it. It certainly didn't reflect our working relationship up to that point and, of course, Ralph has very seldom written in collaboration with anyone else. In fact, though we'd done a little bit of recording together, Ralph was much more of a social friend. For some reason, he got it into his head that I would be the right person to help him get a handle on some of the elements he wanted to include in this epic historical narrative about the lead characters in the story of the Peasants' Revolt.

   This was from a standing start. It was a really weird thing for him to come up with. I had no history of either scholarship or songwriting, which seemed to be the two things he required. Anyhow, when it comes to work, the only thing I turn down is my collar, so I pootled down to Barnes and we sat in his garden, surrounded by piles of books he had taken out of the library. He seemed to have got *anything* which related to the story: the characters involved, the period it happened in, even the larger timeline of events. We kicked it around for the afternoon, exchanging ideas, passing a guitar between us. The actual writing didn't take very long. It was finished in that one session; we didn't go back and change a line – so the exact song we wrote that afternoon is the very same we have been playing on the tour of 2012.

It feels good to have the song back in the repertoire again. I had something of a mental block about it because I was used to performing it with those massive powerchords on the keyboards that Maart Allcock used to play. So, after he left the band in '96, it was really only available to us if we were going to do it at Cropredy and he was going to join us on stage. It's lovely to be able to do it with the current line-up.

The song represents something which I have learned rather late in life, I suppose: even when a song – or your perception of it – is very clearly defined in your mind by the version originally recorded, it is still possible to convey the essence of the song in surroundings of a much smaller scale. Another example – again an epic Ralph McTell song – would be 'Red and Gold', which can work just as well as a duo piece as it does in a full-blown arrangement.

'Wat Tyler' is a great romping story and a great tale. That's what carries it beyond *how* you choose to tell the tale. Twice a year I still get cheques from Ralph's publishing company for 15 quid, 25 sometimes. There can't be many people who can boast that Wat Tyler still buys them the occasional curry!

The events behind the song, though complex, centre on one precise moment. On 13 June, 1381, an army of 30,000 peasants, led by Wat Tyler, descended on London from Canterbury, Rochester and Maidstone for two days of rioting, burning and looting. Richard II, all of 14 years of age then, insisted on addressing the mob personally, against the advice of his counsellors. William Walworth, the mayor of London, commonly known as 'the blond buffoon', mistook a friendly gesture on Tyler's part for a hostile approach on the monarch and attacked him with his sword. Tyler was taken to St Bartholomew's 'hospital for poor folks', from where the mayor had him dragged and beheaded in Smithfield, returning to the young king with 'poor Tyler's severed head upon a bloody pole'. Having lost its leader, the Peasants' Revolt then collapsed, though the king remained true to his word and implemented several of the changes he had agreed to.

That had been anarchy on a major scale.

Fairport may have missed the anniversary by a couple of years, but Ralph and Simon produced something that has remained chillingly contemporary. The revolt had been provoked by the imposition of a poll tax – a system of taxation the Conservative government was attempting to reintroduce even as Fairport performed the song in the late Eighties. Ralph and Simon's song spanned the six centuries that divided poll tax riots from Tyler to Thatcher. The riots that had preceded Tyler's execution centred around the trading and banking districts of Fleet Street. Flemish merchant bankers had been a particular focus of their anger, though the ensuing violence and looting greatly weakened any justification they may have claimed. There is an obvious parallel with the rioting that happened across the UK in 2011. The song made it clear that Fairport were still capable of creating an epic recording.

The instrumental track on *Gladys' Leap* – by now almost an essential part of any Fairport album – has the most unimaginative title from a band known for their inventive titles. Partly because this was their first tune set not to focus on Swarb and partly because it was Ric Sanders' first featured track with the band, it remained in the live set for many years. (It was always the tune set you couldn't remember the name of.) It consisted of three tunes – 'The Riverhead' (named after a mandolin), 'Gladys' Leap', and 'The Wise Maid' – the first two composed by Dave Pegg. Each of Fairport's three members, therefore, got a composer credit on the new LP. The last tune, the only traditional number, had been arranged by Simon and Peggy. The album set the pattern for the future whereby Fairport would generally go for songs from those working within the tradition, rather than drawing songs directly from it. There would be exceptions, of course, particularly when one considers the songs they chose to revive from their own back catalogue. But for this second phase of Fairport, music tended to be more trad-ish than trad arr.

One needs an Ordnance Survey map of the village of Cranham in Gloucestershire to source the album's title. The normal route of Cranham postwoman Gladys Hillier required she cross a local brook which flowed into the village. The crossing was an unfixed plank, which tended to be unstable. Rather than risk walking on a makeshift bridge that could prove treacherous, Gladys took to jumping the metre-wide gap. The spot became known as Gladys' Leap, and eventually local residents and ramblers persuaded Ordnance Survey to acknowledge this by naming the spot on their official maps of the area. *The Guardian* reported the event, which was where Peggy spotted it, writing his tune in tribute to this little touch of English eccentricity. Incidentally, the publicity which the spot achieved, not least through Fairport, led to the construction of a proper, stable footbridge, timber-built and with a sturdy hand-rail on either side. Which does rather defeat the point of the place. One is not surprised, however, to learn that during council discussions about the provision of the bridge, someone remarked: "The spot now attracts so many visitors, many of whom wish to emulate Gladys Hillier's leap, that without a bridge it represents a serious hazard to health and safety."

SIMON: A side effect of the album was that songwriters were encouraged to start sending us their stuff. Huw Williams was one of those and has been a fount of great songs, as you can see on both my solo albums. Maart, Peggy and Ric were all contributing instrumental material: that's one of the reasons our first album with that line-up was entirely free of vocals. That must have added to the impression that we were rather in need of songs. As the band's vocalist, most of them were sent to me.

In 1985, the first of three solid, long-lasting Fairport line-ups was to emerge. They were then a band, in the main, without internal conflicts (certainly without the massive ego-clashes one associates with certain periods of their history) and with no internal power struggles. Increasingly, Fairport's contribution at Cropredy would be a mixture of new material (from a recent or forthcoming album), a good slice of the Winter Tour set, some revivals from the back catalogue (often *en route* to the next Winter Tour), and songs determined by the presence of returning ex-members or special guests. Without losing sight of the past, and planning for the future, Fairport Convention were once more a band which thrived in the present.

Like Punk Never Happened

On 13 July, 1985, the world watched Live Aid, during which the best-known stars of rock music performed on an 18-hour 'global juke-box' broadcast around the world on television. The show revived careers and introduced virtual unknowns to whole new audiences.

JOHN PEEL: One thing about Live Aid was the way it carried on as if punk had never happened. There were current acts, many of whom had been on the Band Aid single, but mainly it served to remind people that all those rock bands from the Sixties and early Seventies were still going strong.

Musically, Live Aid emphasised the enduring popularity of rock's more senior citizens. Ask people whose performances they recalled and the list takes you back beyond the Summer of Punk that many had claimed destroyed the dinosaur bands of the mid-Seventies. Queen topped most lists but also there were McCartney, The Beach Boys, Led Zeppelin, David Bowie, Crosby, Stills and Nash, Neil Young, Status Quo – who opened proceedings, and – not necessarily for the best reasons, Bob Dylan, who concluded them.

On both sides of the Atlantic, artists of long standing were playing the 'what if' game of wondering what difference an appearance at the greatest rock event of all time would make to their career.

SIMON: There was no 'what if' so far as Fairport were concerned. On the day that Live Aid happened, there really wasn't a Fairport Convention, even though we had a brand new album ready for release.

That situation was to be rectified almost immediately, however, when Dave Pegg's mind turned to the future of Fairport. He had just finished work on *Gladys' Leap*, and the subject of live gigs had been broached with Ric in the knowledge that three separate ventures would be occupying Swarb's time over the coming months. Maartin Allcock had been on the folk scene for years, based mainly in and around Leeds. He was a particular fan of Fairport, always there when they played locally.

SIMON: I suppose Maart is the ultimate example of a hardcore fan. He used to skip school to see us when the band were in his area, and was always very polite – asking questions, offering to help move equipment, and so on. You'd often get someone like Maart saying, "Can I change your strings for you?" Peggy, in particular, would always be more than helpful to people like that, and if they had a genuine question, he would do his best to answer it. He would encourage that – and more to the point, encourage them. Maart, of course, acted on that advice and encouragement and became a full-time professional musician. Eventually, he ended up joining Fairport and being part of our longest-lasting line-up

MAART: The day after Live Aid, I got a call out of the blue from Peggy. He said they were thinking of reforming Fairport on a full-time basis, would I be interested in joining? I think he explained that Ric had been asked to join, because I would naturally have assumed that any plans for Fairport would somehow include Swarb. Of course, for both Ric and myself, joining Fairport was easier than joining most bands because we already knew all their best songs.

Prior to joining Fairport, Maart had been a significant player on the Yorkshire/Lancashire folk scene. He had been a member of Mike Harding's Brown Ale Cowboys; had spent two years with the final line-up of the Fairport-influenced Bully Wee Band; and was one half of a highly respected duo with Kieran Halpin. After joining Fairport, he would also join Peggy in his double life as a member of Jethro Tull.

With Cropredy out of the way, Fairport got on with the serious business of rehearsing the new line-up in September 1985. Part of the process was preparing songs from *Gladys' Leap* for their first public outing. In keeping with Fairport's established if fluid tradition, yet again the band playing tracks from the new album was not, to a man, the band that had appeared on it.

PEGGY: It was important to promote the album. Woodworm was a small label with very limited funds for publicity and distribution.

SIMON: The chances of anyone hearing anything from the new album on the radio were pretty slim.

Peggy did send review copies to press contacts and the broadcast media, but they were not accompanied by a standard press release. Instead, they arrived with a handwritten note from Dave Pegg: 'Enclosed is Fairport Convention's first studio LP since 1978, *Gladys' Leap* – we hope you'll enjoy it and play it!!' It went on to give details of how to buy it by mail order and to request, with a week to go, a 'free plug' for the upcoming Cropredy Festival. The letter then advised: 'We hope to do an extensive English tour in November / December to promote and play the music from this LP in your area. Thank you for your support of Fairport – in the past – and hopefully in the future.'

I was one of the people who responded to the offer of an interview with Fairport. In a lengthy conversation which covered most of the band's history, Peggy told me: "It was good to get together each year, play with old friends, take a trip down memory lane, and revive some old songs. But you can't just keep on doing that. We've had five years off from Fairport and we've all been busy with other projects. Now it's time to move forward. Fairport Convention are definitely back in business!"

What Peggy's handwritten note neglected to mention was Fairport's big news – the fact that *that* Fairport would be the first version of the band to tour without Dave Swarbrick in 16 years.

SIMON: We avoided the 'Swarb quits Fairport' headline. We'd had more than our share of that kind of headline over the years. It is very negative and backward-looking, when what you are trying to do is move forward optimistically. In any case, Swarb didn't leave; he chose to not join when we reformed.

22 NOVEMBER, 1985
EXETER

A new beginning. The first night of the first tour of the new line-up of Fairport – billed as the 'New Music from Old Friends' tour. It had been 11 years since Fairport had been more than a quartet. The fuller sound and variety of what they presented on stage showed they were a band with a real sense of purpose.

248

MAART: People had got used to Fairport reunions. We wanted them to know this was something different.

Visually, too, the band offered more than they had of late. Ric's athletic approach to fiddle playing was certainly a contrast to Swarb's. Maart's colourfully eccentric dress sense was nothing if not eye-catching. Simon Jones reviewed the Manchester performance two nights before the tour ended: 'A demented silhouette weaves and bobs around in strobe lights and laser effects, wringing electric cries from the violin. On the other side of the stage, another silhouette is doing similar tricks on the guitar. The music is loud, pounding, relentless and damn exciting.'

While the set included a lot of *Gladys' Leap*, there were the old favourites, too. They played 'Walk Awhile' and a version of 'Sloth' that seemed to get longer every night. 'Walk Awhile' served the same function as it had in 1970, giving the band's vocalists and instrumentalists a moment in the spotlight right at the start of the set.

CHRIS: 'Walk Awhile' has to be one of my favourite songs. Great words, great tune, great instrumental breaks. It's probably the best opening number ever written.

Continuing the precedent set at Cropredy, 'Matty Groves' was the final number and 'Meet on the Ledge' appeared as the encore. There was a certain shakiness to the tour, with publicity managing to insert an 'h' into Simon Nicol's surname and informing fans that Dave Pegg appeared 'by kind permission of Jethro Tull'. With greater accuracy, the tour programme announced: 'Fairport Convention [are] broadening their horizons while remaining true to their roots.' Originally planned as 31 dates, lasting until 18 January, the tour expanded to 44 as promoters and venues heard about how well it was going and decided to book the band.

MAART: I've known tours where you suddenly find a gig has been pulled. You find yourself at a loose end for a night. Of course, when that happens it puts a dent in the budget, too. To be on a tour where you'd ring the office to be told that yet another date had been added is pretty unheard of.

The extended tour left little time before Fairport flew to Australia.

RIC: It felt like the big time. Great reviews. Enthusiastic audiences. Promoters clamouring to put us on. Then we're on an aeroplane and it's a world tour.

The tour Down Under began on 21 February, 1986, at the Bussell Motor Inn Hotel, Bunbury, and included 21 dates. As Ric put it: "Even the venues sounded weirdly exotic. That looks like a bunch of random words." It was a month in all, in the Antipodes, allowing for nights off and travel time between gigs. Support act were The Bushwackers, a raucous Australian folk-rock band. In the early Eighties, their albums had been produced by Trevor Lucas, who had learned 'Marijuana, Australiana' from them.

TREVOR: They knew how to have a good time on stage and off, and they gave Fairport something to live up to. That was definitely good for Fairport who were turning into a loud rock band.

SIMON: Australia with the new band was a nervous moment. Fairport had remained big in Australia and there was a loyal fan base. Unlike in Britain, Fairport's popularity hadn't died off.

A gig on 12 March at the Canberra Workers' Club was recorded and released under the title *Here Live Tonight*. It revealed the band in fine form in front of a vociferously enthusiastic audience. A third of its tracks being instrumentals, the recording opens with a fast version of the *Liege & Lief* medley. Australian fans would also get a taste of the material from Fairport's next, very different album – which they were planning during spare time on the tour.

DM: Australia is a big place. You can have hours of travel between gigs. With the band all together, there was no escape. A lot of the conversation worked around to: "This seems to be going well, what are we going to do next?"

SIMON: Maart, Ric and Peggy were all writing tunes and we came to the decision to make our next album an all-instrumental.

Expletive Delighted!

On their return from Australia, the new line-up gathered at
Woodworm Studios for the first time to record the new album.
Sessions for the album took place during April and May of 1986.
It was scheduled for release that August, just in time for Cropredy.
However, Fairport fans wouldn't have to wait that long to acquire
new material from them. Joe Boyd's Hannibal label was then engaged in reissuing material that had been dropped from the Island
catalogue. One of these was the live Fairport album that had been
recorded in 1970. Somewhat unsatisfactory on its first issue, it was
now revamped: three tracks were dropped and replaced by different
songs, two of which had not been previously released by Fairport –
'Sir Patrick Spens', 'Staines Morris', and 'Battle of the Somme'. The
album was re-titled *House Full* (1986).

SIMON: In a way, it's annoying how record companies bring
    your past back to haunt you, especially when a band is trying
    to move forward and focus on new things. The Fairport fea-
    tured on that album is a long way from what the new line-up
    was all about. It'd been 16 years and a lot of water had flowed
    under that particular bridge.
        That said, it's a much better LP than was the first put to-
    gether from those sessions. It's a better selection of songs –
    far more representative of what we were about back then –
    and it looks like a Fairport album.

The 'Gladys' Leap World Tour' that had begun in London in
October 1985 kept Fairport on the road until January 18, when
they played the last gig of the tour at Sheffield's recently opened
Octagon Theatre. Just as Fairport finished that UK jaunt, Island
honoured Sandy Denny with a four-LP box set retrospective entitled *Who Knows Where the Time Goes?* A mix of 'best of' and previously unreleased material, it also included five previously unreleased Fairport tracks, three of which – including the title track
– had been recorded during the band's 1974 stint at the Troubadour
in LA. This would be the first of four Sandy sets to be released, each
making available rare Fairport material.
    Completists, however, did not need to delve into archival mate-
rial to find Fairport rarities. Two new recordings featuring the band

appeared on a charity album called *Where Would You Rather Be Tonight?* 'Quasi B Goode' was a song by comic poet Les Barker that Fairport had played on stage at Cropredy with John Benns. With the unlikely addition of Wurzel from Motörhead and Steeleye's Bob Johnson on guitars, they recorded the studio version early in the sessions for their new (1986) album. This unlikely fusion of Chuck Berry and Victor Hugo was released as a single.

PEGGY: Actually, despite being credited to Fairport, only DM, Ric and I played on it.

Another track on the same charity album ('The Electric Guitar Is King') – on which DM, Simon and Peggy appeared – was credited to Ashley Hutchings and friends. On that, Peggy played lead guitar. It would be the only studio recording to feature both of Fairport's bass players.

A third Fairport obscurity, recorded during the album sessions, was a track called 'The Mason's a Prune' (a neat, if unoriginal, play on words). It was recorded for the Ballad Opera *The Crab Wars*, by the Kipper Family. The album was a parody of Peter Bellamy's *The Transports* and Bellamy lent his seal of approval to the project by appearing as the town crier. Fairport repaid the honour by providing the instrumental for the silver edition re-recording of *The Transports*. Released in July 1986, that jokey rearrangement of 'The Mason's Apron' would be a true foretaste of Fairport's next album. (Incidentally, despite having been credited on the sleeve, Fairport's track was omitted when the album was reissued on CD.)

SIMON: In the early days of Fairport, those extra-curricular activities were an important part of our lives. It was good that we started off the second phase of Fairport's existence doing the same thing.

6 AUGUST, 1986
EXPLETIVE DELIGHTED!
WOODWORM

Fairport's all-instrumental album came out just in time for Cropredy. The rushed nature of its release was evident in a printing error in the track listing. Track four on side two was omitted: this was a version of 'The Gas Almost Works', a tune which John Kirkpatrick had written for his album *Going Spare*. It had been adopted by the Richard Thompson Band (which John joined), where Simon, Peggy and DM had become familiar with playing it. The other non-original tracks on the album were a version of the Irish tune 'Sigh Beg Sigh Mor' – which Simon had played with Swarb on stage and on *Swarbrick 2* – and 'Hanks For the Memory', a medley that Simon had christened when it was played at Cropredy 1985. Featuring the twinned Telecasters of Richard Thompson and Jerry Donahue, it was a medley of four classic early Sixties instrumentals played in the style of The Shadows, although only a couple of the tunes were actual Shadows' numbers. The medley consisted of 'Shazam', 'Pipeline', 'Apache' and 'Peter Gunn'.

PEGGY: It was a combination of nostalgia and a musical joke. They are iconic tunes, and hearing them has immediate associations for most of our audience.

Fairport's instrumentals, despite their titles, usually consisted of sets of existing tunes, played on the fiddle and sometimes the mandolin. They were to apply the same technique to rock 'n' roll tunes: rock-folk as opposed to folk-rock. 'Hanks For the Memory' was recorded as part of Cropredy 1985: Ric Sanders would add a fiddle part in 1986. All the other tracks were from within the band. Peggy's newer original material having been channelled towards his solo album in 1983, he contributed two tunes that had been recorded by the late Seventies version of Fairport. They were 'Jams O'Donnells Jig' and 'Bankruptured' which he was to take back into the studio in 2007, when recording on his album with P J Wright.

Maartin Allcock provided two tracks: 'Innstuck', which migrated into the Fairport acoustic repertoire; and 'The Cat on the Mixer / Three Left Feet', which Fairport had been featuring on their live set, and which had previously been released as the B-side of Tied Logs' version of 'Bluebell Polka'.

Ric Sanders provided the title track, 'The Rutland Reel / Sack the Juggler' – which had already become the new coda to 'Matty Groves' – and the album's classic, 'Portmeirion'.

RIC: We deliberately didn't try to do what Swarb had done. So we stayed away from sets of traditional tunes.

Swarb had set about making two largely instrumental albums during the Seventies with Fairport, only both had run aground. However, his series of six solo albums from the end of Fairport's first phase contained only one vocal track.

Original copies of Woodworm WR009 can be identified by a white sticker attached to the cover, showing the correction to the track's notes (i.e., the missing track four on side two mentioned above).

PEGGY: It was a combination of time and cost. We didn't spot the mistake in time. We knew we had to have the album out to reviewers and on sale at Cropredy. So the little white sticker it was.

This was not the only problem with the sleeve. One of several in-jokes on the sleeve went badly wrong.

PEGGY: We put on a little note saying, 'lyric sheet included'. As the album was entirely instrumental, it was meant to be funny. Apparently, Trade Descriptions demanded there be a lyric sheet. So anyone who complained got a blank piece of paper with the words 'lyric sheet' at the top.

Other jokes included the photo that had been taken at Woodworm. The impressive gold discs on the wall were for Jethro Tull albums; Simon is reading *The Spinners Song Book* – hardly a primary source for an instrumental or, for that matter, anything Fairport were likely to record.

The album's title was another joke – *Expletive Delighted!* (later adopted for the obsessively informative Fairport website run by Ian Rennie). Meanwhile, the album acknowledged Fairport's fan support groups: the UK Friends of Fairport; the Australian branch based in New South Wales; and the US Fairport Fanatics in Connecticut. It was these organisations that had helped maintain the link between Fairport and its audience and, now that the band was again active, would be a key factor in promoting the group and informing fans of its increasing activities.

Fairport were clearly in a playful mood, fired by the enthusiasm of a fresh start. Whereas most bands had a fairly normal approach to logo-ised merchandise (T-shirts, baseball caps, tour jackets and so on), Fairport came up with scanty panties, which were a small white triangle with appropriate fastenings and the name Fairport Convention hiding one's embarrassment. Naturally, band member and record company boss, Dave Pegg, felt obliged to pose in the studio with two young ladies wearing them – and nothing else – with the album sleeve standing in for a bra.

PEGGY: That's one for all those who tried to say 'knickers to Fairport Convention'.

Expletive Delighted! showed Fairport could overcome a great obstacle – the lack of a renowned songwriter.

PEGGY: The other impact of Swarb not being in the band was that we no longer had anyone with a long list of traditional songs to draw on.

Expletive Delighted! was the first of five albums produced by the line-up which would remain together until December 1996. So there they were, about to set off on a musical adventure, the members of Fairport sitting around yet another kitchen table, suitably adorned with a random selection of personal objects and fruit, lit by a central Tiffany lamp – an echo of a sleeve from 18 years earlier.

Milk Bars And Youth Clubs

Recording one's own history in song is by no means an original idea, and Fairport were to make their contribution to the genre in the form of the title track of their album released in November 1999: Chris Leslie's 'The Wood and the Wire'.

SIMON: That song explains perfectly why I have been doing the same job for the past 45 years. When Chris first showed me the words to 'The Wood and the Wire', it felt as if he had somehow opened up my skull, dipped into my brain soup, and pulled out a bunch of my own childhood memories.

Chris has a perceptive eye for detail, and his way of using those details in songs is immensely powerful and evocative. I *was* the little boy he writes about, captivated by the appeal of music... or, to be precise, of guitars. The shape, the look, the feel, everything about them – as well as what you could achieve with them. I knew I wanted to own one, to be able to play one. I have been lucky enough to spend my entire life so far earning a living from that particular bout of covetousness.

Simon Nicol acquired his first guitar when he was 11. Chris Leslie may have had in mind a high-street window in Banbury, but his words applied just as well to a store front in North London *circa* 1961.

CHRIS: There's a music shop in Banbury called One Man Band. It's deliberately old-school in its design. Any musician of a certain age who walks past it is certain to recall a similar window where once a musical instrument first caught their eye. That was the starting point of the song.

SIMON: I believe there still is a Les Aldrich music shop in Muswell Hill, but it is no longer in the same building as when I was a schoolboy. It used to be a double-fronted shop, on Fortis Green Road, which I had to pass on my way to school; so twice a day I looked at them. One window was full of brass, woodwind, cymbals and so on; the other was full of stringed instruments – fiddles, mandolins, ukuleles, cellos. Of course, there were guitars in that window too.

   I was 11 when my first guitar was finally released from the captivity of the shop that had been displaying it. When I was eight, I'd had two years of piano lessons, to which I had singularly failed to apply myself. Despite that failure, my parents finally agreed to get me a guitar. And so a fairly nasty but much-desired plywood Martin Coletti f-hole guitar was mine.

This, incidentally, was the same model as John Lennon's first 'serious' guitar.

SIMON: It proved pretty impossible to play especially as, at the time, I didn't know anybody who knew anything about setting up guitars. It was something of a miracle that I managed to overcome the physical discomfort of learning what I did learn on it – which was enough to make me realise it was never going to be the guitar for me. So I set my sights on getting a 12-string: at the time, I simply thought that was even more like a real guitar! This was before I had any real thoughts of being in a band; it was just that I knew I needed a better guitar. Given the sort of budget this would require, I decided that I was going to get one that was different in some way. I also liked the sound of a 12-string. I had figured out that if I couldn't master 12 strings, I could always take six off. You can't do that the other way round.

I found one in a music shop in Finchley. We used to go there sometimes from school, and hang around the music shop in the shopping centre. This was when I was 12 or maybe just 13.

With buying the guitar in mind, I got a summer job cleaning cars at a local garage. This was on a daily basis for a showroom in Muswell Hill. I saved up £40 and went and bought myself the guitar.

Like most children of the Fifties, Simon's social life centred around his local youth club. Once a week, it was a communal place to gather, to meet old friends and make new ones. It was somewhere out of the house, off the streets and in the warm. It was also a place to share and listen to music: in those distant pre-MP3, non-file-sharing, cassette-less days, the only way to share a new record with your friends was to play it to them.

The club Simon attended offered rather more, though. It was a place where local bands could play, even if performances sometimes amounted to little more than a rehearsal in front of an audience.

SIMON: The youth club I went to was attached to the Methodist Church in Muswell Hill. It was in a big old house called North Bank. It was just a Friday night thing: I never became involved in the Church's Sunday activities. Most of the people who went were between 12 and 18.

There was one room that had been knocked through and this was large enough to put on a small band. As often as not, there would be some kind of band playing in there every

Friday, and if there wasn't a band, or during the band breaks, we'd bring in singles we'd bought that week and listen to them on a Dansette.

ASHLEY: We were all under-age, and in those days pubs were pretty strict. You certainly couldn't have met up as a gang of friends in a pub. So we went to milk bars and youth clubs. The youth club in Muswell Hill was particularly good as it had a little live music scene going on. People who wanted to play and hear music went there.

One of the bands who played the youth club regularly was the other band from Muswell Hill that went on to find fame. They were called The Ravens, featuring brothers Ray and Dave Davies, and they were from the 'wrong' end of the neighbourhood.

SIMON: The members of Fairport Convention were generally nicely brought-up middle-class lads. We'd grown up in a semi-detached, Mock Tudor environment. My dad was a doctor; Richard's was a policeman – professional, pillar-of-society kind of jobs. On the other hand, the Davies family, Ray and Dave's folks, lived just down the road from me, but were much more rough and tumble; they lived in a very small terrace house. Their father was a frequent absentee. They were secondary modern kids, whereas we had been to grammar school with a view to moving into a career. Dave, in particular, had quite a reputation on the streets of Muswell Hill as a tough customer.

I went to the very first gig The Kinks did under their own name. They'd had a makeover. Their manager had changed their name from The Ravens to The Kinks. I'd seen them lots of times at my local youth club as The Ravens. They were a decent little amateur R&B band, playing mostly covers.

I do wish I had known Ray a little better, but he is something like five years older than me. When you're 15 and someone's 20, there's not a lot you can find in common. I'd still love to have him on at Cropredy; he'd be a top turn, but he deliberately spreads himself thin.

Ray Davies would be a perfect Cropredy guest because, like the band's songwriters from Denny to Leslie, he has a talent for creating narrative songs that are graphic and visual.

RAY DAVIES: Someone once said my songs are like "little movies for the ears". I like that. It's a good description; songs you can see as well as hear.

Canny Capers

While such songs may be based on some experience, they tend to be fictional. No band can claim to have had its history told, so frequently and in such detail in song, as Fairport. 'Cropredy Capers' is one of several tunes whose titles make direct reference to some aspect of Fairport's existence, for instance. They are, if you like, the soundtrack that accompanies the dialogue provided by the biographical songs. 'Canny Capers' alludes to the production company that handled all matters relating to Fairport's live work. 'The Bridge Over the River Ash' was named after the river that flowed past The Angel. 'The Bowman's Retreat' and, later, 'The Bowman's Return' are Ric Sanders' celebration of Chris Leslie's joining the band. Ric also celebrated Fairport's farewell gig (at Cropredy) by writing 'August 4' for his group 2nd Vision.

The most imposing song to be inspired by Fairport's home village, though, came from outside the band. In 1979, Ralph McTell was in Cropredy rehearsing with Fairport, working on the tracks that would become the album *Slide Away the Screen*. A conversation about the Battle of Cropredy Bridge made Ralph think it would be a suitable subject for a song for the band. 'Red and Gold' tells the story of 17th-century Cropredy villager, Will Timms, a bystander at the Battle of Cropredy Bridge. Working on the land, he cuts his hand, passes out, and on awakening sees a battle in action. It's a clever device because it allows the listener to share this detached, accidental act of witness. When Fairport perform the song at Cropredy, the audience is standing on the very ground where the battle's initial cavalry charge took place.

SIMON: Somewhere beneath your feet, deep in the ground, is the blood of that battle.

Ralph's choice of surname for his Cropredy villager is significant. Timms was the maiden name of Flora Thompson, the author of *Lark Rise to Candleford* (1945). The village which inspired Lark Rise is less than 20 miles from Cropredy. The novels were dramatised for a National Theatre production in 1979, with Ashley Hutchings' Albion Band providing the music. Ashley himself would write two songs telling the story of Fairport's formation, of course. One of them, 'Wings', appeared on Fairport's *Cropredy* box set. The other, 'Working Underground', was the opening track on Ashley's retrospective box set, *Burning Bright*.

ASHLEY: 'Wings' is about change and legacy. We were all kids when we started, and we had to grow up quickly. For Fairport, that meant *Liege & Lief* and the introduction of Swarb's 'flying fiddle strings'. 'Working Underground' is more complex, and was written as part of a project with Ernesto de Pascale.

Liege & Lief began with a song in which Sandy Denny introduced the band, 'Come All Ye'.

ASHLEY: Sandy began the song as a pastiche of the 'calling-on' songs that are a key part of the Morris and mumming traditions. They are songs that say, 'Here we are – now lend an ear.' She had a good chorus and tune and, I think, first verse. I added the verses about individual members. [Although] no one is named in 'Come All Ye', the song identifies the role of each person on the record (or on stage). It works for nearly every line-up, despite all the comings and goings.

Ironically, the first people to leave Fairport, almost at the same time as the album's release, were the two composers of 'Come All Ye' – Sandy and Ashley. The next but one line-up, after Richard had also left, would be celebrated in 'Angel Delight'. A description of life in the decommissioned pub that the group all lived in, it offered brief, slightly satirical portraits of all four group members and a couple of the people that worked with them.

PEGGY: It was a group effort. Everyone wrote verses about each other, and we kept all the best bits in.

'Angel Delight' is very specific about the people it portrays: Dave the drum, Pegg on the bass, Simon with his herb shampoo, not to mention the Mighty Glydd and John the Wood. The song is like a photo album – here are the embarrassing snapshots of your mates in awkward and unusual moments, here are brief descriptions of memorable incidents, here are arcane in-jokes. Years ahead of its time, 'Angel Delight' was Facebook for the ears. Within it, you can spot the neighbour's manicured garden (a stark contrast to the wilderness behind Fairport's residence), a peregrinating peacock that caused hassles for them, and the lorry hole which finally terminated their tenure.

Swarb would carry on providing thumbnail sketches of Fairport. In 'Rosie', he invites the lady in question to "settle down and listen to this band". The same album would include an instrumental, 'Peggy's Pub', assumed by fans to be an homage to The Angel.

PEGGY: The title is a play on words. Pub is a hostelry, but it's also short for publishing, which is one way to earn money in the rock business. Both are things I am fond of.

Given Sandy's penchant for writing obliquely personal songs, one would have expected her to have created something inspired by Fairport and its members.

SANDY: It's not quite right to say that I wrote songs about that time with Fairport. My songs draw inspiration from people and events, but can head off on their own. Fairport is certainly in there though, if you look closely enough.

Sandy wrote several songs relating to the band with which she is forever associated. Because of her oblique and sometimes consciously cryptic style, they are more poems than biography. And when she later rejoined Fairport, she put her reflections on the band into the songs she wrote.

SANDY: 'Rising for the Moon' is my response to being back on the road with a band. 'Stranger to Himself' is very much a song about Swarbrick. The first time I was in Fairport, I had barely time to get to know him; I was pretty much in awe of him because he had come with a great reputation from the folk scene. The second time I joined, I was around him a lot more. When you are on tour, you tend to live in each other's pockets a bit. I began to realise what a complex and odd character he was. Someone – it could have been Peggy – remarked that no one really knew who Swarb was; in fact, he doubted if he even knew himself. That's what inspired the song, which began as a series of images.

While Sandy's songs are 'about' the band, they don't advance the narrative in any actual sense.

PEGGY: There are lots of lines in Sandy's songs which strike a chord. They capture a moment you remember. A song like 'Solo' sounds like an anthem to Fairport and our famously flexible line-up. It's been played a lot at Cropredy over the years. Recording it is one of my favourite memories of Sandy.

CHRIS: The great thing about Sandy's songs is the way they are very personal – sometimes they have lines that only she really knew the significance of – yet at the same time universal, so we can all relate to them. Who could hear her sing that line about 'fickle friends all leaving' without thinking of someone you have known or, in Fairport's case, someone who has left the band and moved on. They've all 'gone solo'.

Dave Swarbrick's 'Our Band' (on *Gottle O'Geer*) was, he explains, "pretty optimistic. There wasn't really a Fairport at the time I wrote it. It's celebrating the *idea* of Fairport rather than the reality."

The three people working under the Fairport name when the album was made (Swarbrick, Pegg and Rowland) are joined on the track by pianist Nick Judd from Audience, whose playing dominates the song's brief two-minute existence, and Gallagher and Lyle. It's ironic that Fairport were recording songs about the band but having to bring in session players to make it possible – and, incidentally, sounding quite unlike Fairport a lot of the time.

Million Dollar Babies

The Five Seasons, Fairport's album from 1990, included a track called 'The Card Song'. Peggy had learned it when he was with the Ian Campbell Folk Group, who had recorded it for their album *New Impressions*. It is a game song in which singers are intended to improvise verses about other people in the room at the time, very much as Fairport had done on 'Angel Delight'. Peggy later rewrote it so that it name-checked several people closely associated with the band: Ralph May (or McTell as he is better known), Neil Cutts, John Jones, Tom Lynch, Doug Lake and Dave Glass. The 1997 Winter Tour programme would identify the people referred to and explain their Fairport connection.

In 1992 and 1997, for Fairport's 25th and 30th anniversaries, Ashley Hutchings would rewrite Dylan's 'Million Dollar Bash' so that it related to the events and participants of the current Festival. In effect, he was to take a song written in a basement near Woodstock, N.Y., and make it apply to a field near Woodstock, Oxon.

ASHLEY: I've always been fond of parody and it struck me as a nice tribute to Fairport and particularly to what Dave and Chris Pegg had achieved with the Cropredy Festival. It had been running for a dozen years when I did my first 'Million Dollar' rewrite.

Retaining some of Dylan's words and changing others to implicate the innocent, Ashley made the song feel like an improvisation based on the scene before him. Cropredy itself became the million dollar bash. That was in 1992, the 25th anniversary of the band. It was also a time to remember Trevor who, three years previously on 4 February, 1989, had died of a heart attack.

PEGGY: Three years after Trev died, we had Fairport's 25th anniversary and really wanted to remember him as part of it. Ralph McTell kindly offered to sing 'Polly' and he made a wonderful job of it. We included it on the CD of that year's Festival.

Five years later, Fairport celebrated their 30th anniversary with a two-night illustrated essay, put together by Ashley Hutchings. Part way through the first evening, just before bringing Swarb on stage, Ashley stepped up to the vocal mic. There, backed by some iridescent lead guitar-work from Richard, he took apart and reassembled Dylan's nonsense song. Despite an implication in the first verse about Dylan allegedly warning Ashley to lay off his song, the former's mad-hatter's tea party was neatly transplanted to suit current events. The band playing this version consisted of Ashley, Simon, Richard, DM and Vikki Clayton.

CHAPTER EIGHT

Cropredy

Cropredy, to any Fairport fan, indeed to most rock fans, is the location of an annual festival that *The Guardian* described, 'As much a part of an English summer as Wimbledon.' To local residents, it is simply 'the Fairport Festival'.

The release of *Gottle O'Geer* unfolded alongside certain developments in Fairport's home village – which not only transformed the band, but ensured its long-term existence.

Fairport and Cropredy are now inextricably linked. Fairport's Cropredy Convention takes over the village at the start of August each year, providing important revenue and social interaction. Several members of Fairport gravitated towards Cropredy in the mid-Seventies, beginning the band's long association with the village. It was where Dave Pegg first established Woodworm Studio and Records and then the management company that would handle the band's affairs for many years; where Swarb moved after a freight-truck took his Angel away; and where the band rehearsed.

The village has had, over the centuries, a curious ability to attract people with particular purposes. In medieval times, it had been the site of a shrine to St Fremund, the son of Offa of Mercia, which was claimed to have miraculous healing properties. In the 18th century, it housed the stores for the builders of the Oxford canal: anyone who has breakfasted with the canoe club during Cropredy Festival has eaten on this historic site. Once the canal was completed, Cropredy became the site of one of its toll stations.

Richard Crossman MP – whose diaries are considered essential reading for anyone attempting to understand British politics in the mid-
20th century – and his wife Anne had been keen supporters of this
village in which they lived. In 1976, two years after his death, Anne
decided to organise a garden fete as a fundraiser for local causes.
Fairport were not 'booked' in the normal sense of the word, they were
simply asked to appear as a personal favour. The event was decidedly
small-scale, and failed to cause much of a stir beyond the custom-
ary quiet of Cropredy. In an event that remains probably the least
publicised Fairport appearance since their very earliest days around
Fortis Green, promotion was limited to some mimeographed posters providing the date, venue, names of beneficiaries and attractions.
While some versions of this publicity mentioned Fairport, others
said no more than 'live music from local musicians'. It's a measure of
how small-scale the event was that those who required toilet facilities were allowed to use the downstairs loo in the house.

SIMON: Half the band at that time were villagers: the other two
     lived a very short distance away. We'd been using the village
     hall as a rehearsal space for some time. It seemed natural to
     give something back. It was very informal. I don't think I had
     even officially rejoined the band at that point. It was certainly
     one of my first gigs back as a part of the band.

SWARB: Don't ever tell Simon that that first Cropredy gig was
     really his audition!

Their 11th album *Gottle O'Geer* had been released two months earlier. Although they had dropped the second half of their name for
that LP, for this gig the 'Convention' was reinstated on the few posters that named them.
     The set included a few Fairport standards, some rock 'n' roll
crowd-pleasers, and a couple of tracks from their new album, including one of the very few performances of 'Cropredy Capers'.

DAVE PEGG: It had to be done. This was probably the only au-
     dience we would play to at the time who would understand

the title. I suspect if a recording of that performance existed –
and I know none does – it would sound nothing like the track
on the LP, which had been pretty much a studio creation.

With the band in some disarray, gigs had been limited of late.
Officially, the band was a six-piece and included Dan Ar Braz,
Roger Burridge and Bob Brady. The four-piece local band consisted of Daves Pegg and Swarbrick, drummer Bruce Rowland and
Simon Nicol – re-conscripted for the occasion. The line-up from
that garden fete would prove to be Fairport's most durable up until
the Eighties, and go on to make two studio albums, tour extensively, and survive for three years. Despite the legendary status of
their earlier line-ups, the longest lasting of them had survived less
than 18 months. That garden fete was the start of what could well
have been the last gasp of Fairport Convention. It would have been,
but for Cropredy Festival.

SIMON: We must have gone down well, because we were invited back the following year…or perhaps we were just cheap
and not too loud. Of course, those were pre-internet days,
so it was more difficult for word to get round. I won't flatter
myself by calling it a secret gig, but there were a few hardcore
fans around who would probably have travelled into deepest
Oxfordshire for a chance to see us in a more informal setting.
Word had got round by the *third* year, though, and I think the
number of people who turned up had by that time almost
doubled.

CHRIS: I remember being at one of the gigs at Prescote Manor. I
was desperate to be up on that stage. Of course, I didn't really
know the band then, but if someone had thrust a fiddle into
my hand…

In 1977, Fairport played for just under an hour, less than a third of
the time they normally spend on stage at Cropredy. However, that
second Cropredy appearance did establish a pattern that would
hold through future Festivals: the basic touring set, enhanced by a
few old favourites and a couple of surprises. That year, they played
seven of the nine tracks from their then new album *The Bonny
Bunch of Roses* – released two days earlier – alongside two tracks

apiece from *Rosie*, *Nine* and *Full House*, and 'Limey's Lament' and 'Cropredy Capers' from *Gottle O'Geer*. Of the 15-song set, five were instrumentals, and ten were arrangements of traditional songs or tunes.

A couple of reviews appeared in the music press, and word about Cropredy began to spread.In 1978, just as press pundits and record companies were writing the band off, 1,800 people turned up at Prescote Manor for a Fairport concert that saw Dave Swarbrick and Dave Pegg reunite with the Ian Campbell Folk Group. Even as Fairport's time as a working band seemed to be drawing to a close, the band was laying the foundations of its future.

SIMON: By 1978, it was clear that the festival at Cropredy was beginning to pick up its own momentum. It was obvious that it had outgrown its original location in Anne Crossman's garden. Because more people were coming from outside the village, it seemed appropriate to run it for the band's benefit rather than just as a local fundraiser. The band, of course, continued to make its financial contribution to the village hall. So Christine and Dave Pegg started running it. After trying out various fields and various ways of approaching it technically, by 1979 we were on what we considered a permanent site up at Peewit Farm. You can see it from the current auditorium site; it's now one of the fields we use as a campsite. That was where we came to do our Farewell gig on 4 August, 1979.

However, they would have to play to a very different crowd earlier in the day. Before getting to Cropredy:

SIMON: We played Knebworth that same afternoon on a slightly bigger stage, to a somewhat larger audience, with most definitely a larger PA system. It was a huge contrast. Certainly, it was the biggest PA system I had ever used up to that point, something like 120,000 watts. That was about 1 watt apiece for the audience. These days, that would be considered hopelessly inadequate. We were there as guests of Led Zeppelin, with whom Fairport have always had a good relationship, partly through Peggy's involvement in the Birmingham music scene alongside Robert Plant and John Bonham.

268

PEGGY: In June 1967, Roger Hill and I had left The Uglys and formed a group called The Exception. Together with Alan Eastwood we were a trio, whom people compared to Cream. Our first single was 'The Eagle Flies on Sunday', on which Robert Plant played tambourine. That was his recording debut!

Among the many items pasted into Peggy's band scrapbooks is a clipping concerning John Bonham's birthday.

PEGGY: A couple of years before he became famous as Led Zeppelin's drummer, Bonzo had played the drums in Way of Life. I was the bass player. We were famous for being loud.

Fairport – at Led Zep's request – opened proceedings at Knebworth. Between them and Zeppelin taking the stage were Commander Cody, Southside Johnny and the Asbury Jukes, and Todd Rundgren's Utopia. Demand had been so great for tickets that the entire show was repeated the following week – but with Chas & Dave replacing Fairport Convention on the bill.

Fairport's page in the programme had a definite end-of-an-era feel about it. There was no photo of the current line-up, only solo shots of Swarb and Sandy – the latter having died the previous April. There was a posed shot of the *Rising for the Moon* line-up, and a picture of the rehearsal for the *Top of the Pops* appearance in 1969. Two short paragraphs were devoted to a thank you with a list of everyone who had been a member of Fairport and a plug for the forthcoming album recorded live on the Farewell tour: 'available for a minimum donation of £4.00 (there is no upper limit) from Woodworm Records, Chapel Row, Cropredy'.

SIMON: We went from there to our little gig. The pictures from Cropredy that year are definitely interesting: a stage made from tractor-trailers, rough wooden frames, scaffold poles, and bits of tarpaulin pressed into use. Even the PA system was pretty ramshackle. Something like 3,000 people turned up, essentially to say goodbye to the band. Everyone, including ourselves, believed that was the end of the line: we had a couple of outstanding commitments in Europe, but so far as the UK was concerned that day of contrasts was going to be

Fairport's swansong (no pun intended). Fairport were all set to nail the lid down and say "This far and no further". We'd worked our socks off all summer.

SWARB: There was a lot of affection and loyalty from the audience on that last tour, and even more so when we got to Cropredy for our last hurrah. Sadly, however, experience had shown us that no amount of affectionate loyalty translated into record sales, which is what the industry was about. Every time we went back to the well, it seemed to be a little emptier.

PEGGY: Playing in front of Zeppelin's crowd and then coming back to our own little Festival – our home turf, with less than a fifth of the audience – was very emotional. It worked both ways. You could feel waves of affection coming back from the audience as we played.

The following year, a little-known jazz-rock fusion group called 2nd Vision would release an album called *First Steps*, the opening track titled 'August 4, 1979'. The song would be written by an electric violin player who had been among the 3,000 people at Cropredy on that date.

RIC: Like everyone else, I had really believed that was the last time I would see Fairport. That's what inspired me to write the piece as a sort of 'thank you and farewell'. The trouble was, no one got the point of the title: fans of 2nd Vision, which for those who don't know had a sort of Weather Report / Mahavishnu Orchestra vibe, were hardly likely to be aware of the final gig of a folk-rock group. Lots of people asked me why I had written a piece in honour of the 79th birthday of the Queen Mother!

Also in the audience was Chris Leslie. A little earlier, he had appeared with Steve Ashley. In those days, there was no large secure backstage area and he had simply wandered round to join the crowd.

CHRIS: I was less interested in electric violin than Ric would have been, but this could have been the last time we saw Swarb play one. I was born and raised in Banbury, and was

270

in my late teens when Swarb and Peggy moved to Cropredy. I had already been aware of them and their music, but now they'd become local. They were suddenly real people you could bump into in the street or at a club and have a conversation with.

Both Ric and Chris would in time become Fairport members, of course, although it had then seemed unlikely there would *be* another Fairport after August 1979.

ASHLEY: It was around this time that I wanted to move back into touring. The Albion Band had been resident at the National Theatre for a few years. One of the things that made that appealing was being able to work with Simon. If Fairport had to call it a day, he would become available.

I noticed a change in the kind of venues you could play, though. The old student circuit had virtually vanished, and a lot of the university and college venues had been converted for other purposes. The smaller music venues had gone, too: several had become discos with no facility for playing live music – or if they did, they were interested in punk and new wave acts.

PEGGY: Ian Anderson had heard that Fairport were about to wind up and offered me a job, playing bass with Jethro Tull. Financially, quite apart from everything else, it made a lot more sense than trying to struggle on with Fairport.

SIMON: The music business had moved on. Nobody seemed to want to buy our records. The obvious decision was to put the whole thing to bed and say, "That was then: this is now." As we now know, that was not to be. A year later we were doing the same thing. This time, to a still bigger crowd. More people turned up for our reunion than had for our Farewell, and even then we were wondering whether we could keep it that way. By the end of the [1980] weekend, we were already talking in terms of the following year and maybe other possibilities beyond that. It was a case of loyal support enforcing our continuance in the face of a mighty combination of circumstance, received wisdom and precedent.

There was indeed talk during the day, not only backstage but among the crowd too, about the possibility of a reunion concert a year on. One enterprising fan spent much of that day taking a straw poll. Walking around the field, he accosted Festival-goers with his clipboard: "Would you come if Fairport were to get together and do this next year?"

Fairport's 'annual reunion' was taking shape.

SIMON: It was a literal description. Fairport did not exist outside the Festival.

PEGGY: We began asking ex-members of the band – and friends of the band – to join us on stage from the second year on. It helped to make it a unique event. So we ended up playing again with Richard, Jerry, Trev, Judy, Iain and Ashley.

ASHLEY: 'I'm gonna see all my friends' – Richard had no idea when he wrote those words that one day Fairport and Cropredy would make them come true.

TREVOR: Cropredy has lots of special memories. Returning for each Festival brought them back.

PEGGY: It's something we are aware of the whole year round. We are always watching out for acts we think would work – and really that means acts the audience will like.

SIMON: The curious thing was, Fairport were a band that people were coming to see in fewer and fewer numbers. Then we effectively said, "OK. We're not coming to see you any more. You can come and see us, if you like." And they did, in steadily increasing numbers every year.

30 AUGUST, 1980
SPITTALLS FARM, CROPREDY

Fairport reconvened for their first reunion. Although several aspects of the event that one now associates with Fairport dropped into place then, it was still a long way from the Festival it was to become. Most obviously, it was a one-day event at the wrong end of the month. There was no real structure for camping, and some had to pitch their tents at the top of the performance field.

On the other hand, the set extended to include guests: Richard Thompson and Dave Mattacks, Linda Thompson on a couple of songs, and Ralph McTell for a sequence of songs that took them further out of their comfort zone – a slow version of Dylan's 'I Want You', 'The Night They Drove Old Dixie Down', 'Diddy Wah Diddy', and 'Save the Last Dance for Me'. In the midst of this, Richard Thompson stepped to the mic for a blazing version of Jerry Lee Lewis' 'High School Confidential'. The set closed with a very emotional 'Meet on the Ledge' which sounded that night like a prophecy come true: one had seen Fairport play again – more than that one had seen the *Full House* line-up back together, playing 'Sloth'. It did, indeed, all come round again and Simon caught the mood of the moment when he rounded off proceedings with what would become his Cropredy catchphrase, "Same time next year?"

Finally, the redoubtable Jonah Jones hushed demands for an encore by telling the crowd, "We wouldn't be able to follow that: and we have reached the time we agreed we would stop playing." He then advised everyone to leave steadily and drive safely.

SIMON: At that stage, putting on Cropredy as a one-off event each year was perhaps more straightforward than people might have thought. It had grown both as an event and in terms of audience numbers each year. Everyone had learned from experience. Under Chris Pegg's careful stewardship, it had turned into a really nice little event that we really wanted to do. It had gradually grown longer, to the point where we were considering a two-day event. The catering had improved. The practicalities of the organisation of the performance area, the audience area and the campsites had become easier. The loos were no worse.

At that point, the band was living locally: the Peggs and Swarb were still in Cropredy; Bruce Rowland was in Eydon, not far from Culworth; I was just down the road in Abingdon before I moved to Chipping Norton. Peggy and Swarb were entirely integrated into the community; the rest of us knew it pretty well. It was very much a local event for us, but one that now attracted more and more people from outside the area. It was also the place we'd become used to doing our summer gig. If Fairport was going to exist for one day a year, then it was a pretty good day and a worthwhile occasion for all concerned.

We'd increased the number of support acts, too. In '78, it had been just John and Chris Leslie who were a well-known local folk act at the time. Chris, of course, would become something of a Cropredy regular, appearing with various acts, including Fairport, until the time we actually asked him to join the band. By 1980, we had John Kirkpatrick and Sue Harris and Richard and Linda Thompson and Ralph McTell joining us for a few numbers.

Towards the end of September 1980, a postcard arrived through the letterbox of Fairport fans. One side showed scenic views of Cropredy, the other was a handwritten note from Dave and Chris Pegg, thanking fans for attending Cropredy 1980 and asking if they had any suggestions for what they'd like to happen the following year, 'if we decide to have another reunion'.

For a band whose career has been littered with uncertainty, speculation and unpredictability, there are two great 'ifs' in their career. The first was 'If (Stomp)', the band's first original song, written by Iain Matthews and Richard Thompson – the B-side of their debut single, without which fans might never have had their first 13 years. The second was the 'if...another reunion', written by Dave and Chris Pegg, without which the Fairport story would lack a large number of recordings and some very significant individuals.

PEGGY: No matter where you come from, Cropredy's location is such that you will be going past somewhere with definite Fairport connections: Byfield, Adderbury, Chipping Norton, Barford, all those places. Everyone recognises The Brasenose Arms from the picture on the album.

Peggy was thinking particularly about the places where members and ex-members of Fairport had lived. But there is a second list that would include Banbury, Eynsham, Stanton Harcourt, Abingdon and Brackley – places that are directly or indirectly celebrated in song by Fairport.

SIMON: Because Chris Leslie is very much a local chap, the songs he has written for Fairport include quite a few that are Oxfordshire-based. He draws a lot of inspiration from what goes on around him.

CHRIS: Some are obvious – 'Banbury Fair' has it in the title. Others are more oblique. 'The Dancer' related to my involvement in Adderbury morris, and was inspired by three local musicians who had influenced me as a young man: Mont Abbott, who was a shepherd from Church Enstone; and two dancers from Bampton Morris – Frank Shergold and Arnold Woodley.

The Wood and the Wire began life when Chris found himself staring into the window of the Banbury music shop shown on the sleeve. It would become the title track of Fairport's most Banbury-biased release. Chris has continued to celebrate local people and places. 'I'm Already There' was inspired by a stained-glass window in Banbury Church and, of course, 'Festival Bell' is in part the story of the Cropredy peal. It is also a celebration of the bond between a rural community and its rock residents.

Fairport is very much part of the village. Walking around its streets with Peggy as we planned the box set *UnConventional*, we seemed to stop every few yards to chat with a local resident and exchange the latest gossip. One remarked, "Be sure to tell people we still have a village shop because it makes enough in Festival week to keep going the rest of the year."

Eventually, the village would express its gratitude to Fairport in a unique and highly original way.

CHRIS: 'Festival Bell' was inspired by the village's tribute to the band. We were all very moved by the gesture. I wanted the song to be about Cropredy, and show how much a part of it Fairport's festival is.

24 NOVEMBER, 2006
WHITECHAPEL FOUNDRY

The Fairport Convention Festival Bell is cast. One of the bonus videos on Fairport's Cropredy DVD for 2007 records the event, and the bell's subsequent installation in the village church. Based on empirical evidence, it is likely to remain there for the next couple of centuries. Chris, whose song celebrating the installation of the bell would become the title track of a Fairport album, says, "It's a remarkable tribute and one which is humbling. Who knows how long Fairport will survive. It's defied all predictions to date and could easily continue by recruiting younger members. One thing is certain, in the 23rd century when that bell is still making music in Cropredy, the name on that bell will remind people that once we existed."

GERRY: Bands and musicians get all kinds of awards – gold discs, Grammys, BRITs and so on. Richard Thompson has even had a couple presented by the Queen! But I don't think there is another rock act anywhere that's had a church bell named in their honour.

Each year, as Cropredy Festival begins in the late afternoon of a late Thursday in August, the bells ring out. They will be ringing down the years beyond our imagining.

PEGGY: Cropredy accepts our yearly invasion because it's en-demic to the village. It's grown bigger and bigger each year, but problems haven't grown bigger for the village.

The local community has more than accepted the annual 'invasion'.

PEGGY: They don't just accept it – they do everything they can to accommodate people, including things like the breakfasts which help raise money for the village.

Cropredy breakfasts have become something of a tradition. Local organisations use every available location – the school, the village hall, the canoe club, farms, the cricket club – to provide a range of comestible delights that help Cropredy campers start the day right. Each morning sees an exodus from campsites towards the heart of the village.

PEGGY: Nobody is doing those things to put money into their own pockets. All the money raised goes back to support some aspects of the village. It's one way the Festival supports the community indirectly. I can't imagine anywhere else where that happens, where the locals have become part of the event.

SIMON: Involving and including the residents of Cropredy was something that Dave and Chris Pegg put a great deal of effort into. Over the years, it has made a massive difference to the smooth running of the Festival.

CHRIS: The level of goodwill and the friendliness that comes with it is amazing.

Making its visitors welcome and allowing them to feel safe has always been uppermost in the minds of both the host village and the Festival's organisers.

SIMON: Each year, we try out different things. If they benefit the festival, we try to keep them there. We get a lot of feedback – praise, suggestions and criticisms – and they definitely shape future Festivals. The first year we installed toilets at the bottom of the field – logistically nothing like as simple as it might seem – and got very favourable feedback. They are now very much part of advance planning; the only way we wouldn't have them would be if the conditions in the field made it impractical or unsafe.

Chris Pegg, Dave's former wife, ran Cropredy alongside her other responsibilities for Fairport.

CHRIS PEGG: One rule we had on site during the Festival was 'no blue flashing lights'. That's mainly because it's frightening for the audience. One year, an ambulance had to go through the crowd during Fairport's set and it was very disturbing for everyone. Then, another year, I saw a police car leave with its lights on. I called the local policeman to find out what was going on: it turned out the chief inspector had spotted Billy Connolly in the audience and had despatched a squad car to his home to fetch his Connolly video so he could get it signed!

The programme for the Festival began with a curiously self-contradictory statement: 'Once again we have pleasure in staging the second Fairport Convention Reunion Concert…'. The venue, for the first and only time, was not Cropredy but Broughton Castle near Banbury. The home of Lord and Lady Saye and Sele, it might have been familiar to some festival-goers because of its use as the location setting for a large number of TV and film productions.

SIMON: I recall there was a lot of brainstorming beforehand. We felt we had to offer something more than just the same old Fairport set if we were going to 're-une' again.

PEGGY: It was still very much aimed at Fairport fans in those days. It was also very folkie.

MARTIN CARTHY: Brass Monkey played at Broughton Castle. It was one of our first big gigs and at that point we were still called something like the John Kirkpatrick/Martin Carthy Band, which is a fair indication of how early it was.

In an advance interview, Peggy stated: "Fairport will be doing a lot of things throughout the Festival, including playing on both Friday and Saturday nights. Richard and Bruce and DM will be joining Swarb, Simon and me, so we have two different eras of the band – *Full House* through to *Angel Delight*, and then the band that made our last three LPs. We've also got two new groups – one formed by Martin Carthy and John Kirkpatrick, and the other by Bert Jansch. Steve Ashley will be playing: he's in a duo with Chris Leslie now. There are a couple of local folk acts as well."

Peggy was keeping a few secrets up his sleeve. Friday's performances took place in a huge marquee – more Cambridge than Cropredy – and the whole thing ran from 7.30 pm to 10.30 pm on the Friday, and from 2.00 pm till 11.30 pm on the Saturday. It was made to seem like a three-day festival by including the Broughton and North Newington Sports and Social Club's annual gymkhana and village fete on the Sunday, and a late night 'Bonfire Singsong with the Mothy Band' on the Saturday.

In One End and Out the Other, with music by Fairport, was screened on the Friday and, following this, the GPs (McTell, Thompson, Pegg and Mattacks) played one of their few live gigs. Captain Coco's Country Dance Band, which opened proceedings on the Saturday, included both Simon and Peggy. Fairport were also on hand for a brief guest appearance with Steve and Chris. Finally, the Saturday night set lasted four hours.

The programme, replete with jokes, became essential reading matter for those calling round to find out 'how the Fairport Festival went'. Herein were a multilingual biography of Bert Jansch; the announcement of Chris Leslie's retirement as a professional musician; and Richard Thompson's identification of his musical influences – his parents ("remember Bob and Betty Thompson and the Swing-airs?"), and Wally Swinburn whose Anglian Crosscut fiddle playing was emulated by Richard on his first four albums for the Pompadour label.

RICHARD: Ah yes, I remember Wally Swinburn. Pretty hard to find that on the record racks. I was asked about Wally in a radio interview just the other week, not for the first time.

The Broughton Castle event produced the first officially released Cropredy recordings (not only Fairport's *Moat on the Ledge* but also The GPs, many years later) and the first Cropredy video which captured the majority of Fairport's set. Unfortunately, the remarkable long version of Richard's 'Wall of Death' was not recorded. For the 2,000 people who were able to get tickets, it was a memorable event. For everyone else, there was the documentary evidence.

SIMON: In '81, it expanded into a two-day event.

Fairport played an extended set of 38 songs in total, with guest appearances by Dave Mattacks, Richard Thompson and – performing with Fairport for the first time in 13 years – Judy Dyble.

1982 was the year of the return of Trevor and Jerry.

1983, the year documented by the semi-official release called *The Boot*, saw a flurry of Fairport activity: Dave Pegg's solo album; the last in Swarb's series of solo albums, *Flittin'*, which featured at least one Fairport member on every track; the first Winter Tour (13 nights, beginning at Kendal Leisure Centre); and Ashley Hutchings' return to Fairport's ranks after 14 years. Fairport's ball was rolling once more. That year's Festival programme included an advert for 'Chris Leslie, maker and restorer of the Violin Family'.

CHRIS: I was local. I knew how people felt about visitors clog-ging up our country lanes. Somehow, because Fairport kept it local, even when the scale got huge, everyone accepted it.

CHRIS PEGG: The thing you have to realise about Cropredy is that, in an area where villages and hamlets tend to be out of the way, it was *more* out of the way than most. It's one reason why it never developed into a place that commuters would choose to live.

Harold Wells, a long-term local friend and fan of the band, offered an astute description of Cropredy village when I interviewed him at the Festival: "The big change for Cropredy was when the canal came through. I think at that point the village decided that was the pace of life it wanted."

14 AUGUST, 1987
'VENI, VIDI, IMBIDI'

The Cropredy Festival was so closely associated with Fairport that their name did not need to be included on billings. To mark Fairport's 20th anniversary, they declared the event to be 'The Aristocrat of Festivals', and emblazoned the programme with a crest subscribed with a Latin motto (I came, I saw, I drank). For the first time, Fairport announced in advance that one of the special guests joining them would be Dave Swarbrick.

SIMON: Swarb had formed Whippersnapper and it was obvi-ously a bigger deal than his solo gigs or the things we had done as a duo. So 1987 was the year that ruled a line under Swarb's membership of Fairport, even more than the *Gladys' Leap* album had. Fairport were making it clear that Swarb was not part of the band any more.

Swarb was not the only guest to join the newly convened Fairport on stage. Their guest list amounted to a 'What We Did on Our Holidays' account of the time between the first Cropredy reunion (in 1980) and the last.

SIMON: To use an oxymoron, at Cropredy people expect surprises. It was a matter of surprising them with a more amazing rock 'n' roll rabbit every year.

On the demise of Fairport, Simon, DM and Peggy had become part of Richard Thompson's big band, recording and promoting the *Hand of Kindness* album (1983). Two blocks of RT songs in the Cropredy set served as a reminder of those times. Simon played songs from his solo album and his time in a duo with Swarb. Sandy Denny's solo years were commemorated by Cathy Lesurf and June Tabor, who led the band in a version of 'A Sailor's Life'.

RIC: For anyone who plays electric violin, Fairport's 'A Sailor's Life' has a very special place. So far as English folk-rock goes, that is where it began.

ASHLEY: Its importance cannot be overestimated – in terms of Fairport's development, and in the way it broke down the door and let folk-rock in. Swarb's presence on the recording made it more acceptable to the folk community. It was almost a case of him giving it a seal of approval. It's sad we played it so few times. In fact we *never* played it live with Swarb.

The song that had brought Swarb into the band was also there to see him out. The new line-up of Fairport – Ric, Maart, Simon, Peggy and DM – provided backing for this performance. June sang lead vocals, Richard played lead guitar.

9 AUGUST, 1997
HOME FIELD, CROPREDY

For their 30th anniversary concert, Fairport decided to tell their story in full on stage. Ashley Hutchings offered to narrate.

SIMON: I would say the most successful experiment we tried

at Cropredy was when we decided to use both the Friday and the Saturday night to tell the whole story of Fairport in roughly chronological order. It's been described as splitting the band's set, but that is not accurate and this is as good a place as any to correct it. We still did the full, epic, four-hour set on the Saturday and added to that a set of 90 minutes or so on the Friday.

It was a sort of live essay, read by Ashley, in which we visited every era of the band – if not every single album – in sequence, with as close an appropriate line-up from the time as was possible. Since it was chronological, the cut-off point, on the Friday night, was 1970, the time between *Liege & Lief* and *Full House*. That was where Ashley had left the band; so while he had played as part of Fairport throughout the Friday evening, as Saturday's performance began, he was sitting on stage at a side table and told, in his own words, the story of what the band did next. That in itself was fascinating because it provided essentially an outsider's point of view, albeit the view of someone who had been an essential part of Fairport's early history and has, of course, remained closely connected with the band ever since. His commentary was illustrated by players joining to represent certain line-ups as the band evolved. It brought the story right up to date and ended with everyone who had taken part singing 'Meet on the Ledge'. I thought the whole thing was a successful, original and typically inventive Hutchings-based idea. There have been requests both from people who were there and people who missed it for us to do it again, but the whole point is that it was a one-off event.

We have tackled telling the band's story on other occasions, but each time we have found a different approach. That's part of what Cropredy is about. It's important that everyone who attends in a particular year takes away something special and unique from Fairport's set.

One moment that registered with everyone in the audience was a particularly effective leap of imagination.

ASHLEY: It had to be a balanced account of Fairport's history – the funny with the fantastic, the music and the memories, the triumph and the tragedies. For most fans of Fairport, the greatest tragedy to hit Fairport was Sandy's death. This is true even in the light of the deaths of both Martin and Trevor…

SIMON: We had somehow to mark that moment. Sandy's death occurred during that period when Fairport were not recording studio albums, so we had a natural hiatus.

CHRIS: This was my first Cropredy as a full-time Fairport member. So it was the first time I had been involved in the planning. I remember Dave and Chris Pegg saying, "At this point we are going to play 'Quiet Joys'." Naturally, I wondered who would sing it – the performance everyone knows by Sandy is *a capella* and would be a hard thing to pull off. Peggy then explained we were going to leave the stage and just play the record. It seemed insane, but Peggy just said, "Don't worry, it will work." And it did. Quite an indication of how well Peggy knows the audience.

ASHLEY: We'd no idea how it would go down. People could have struck up conversations or wandered off. There was nothing visual to hold their attention. But what they did – thousands of them – was stand respectfully silent, listening. The track ends with Swarb's multi-tracked fiddle…and as that started there was a roar…

RIC: We came back on as the track finished, the post-Farewell Fairport – Si, Peggy, DM, Maart and I – and played the songs from *Gladys*. It was a moment that marked all kinds of changes in Fairport's story.

SIMON: It was the moment Fairport rose from the ashes: the loss of Sandy; the start of Cropredy; our return to the studio; Swarb's departure and Ric and Maart's arrivals; all bound up in that one song.

ASHLEY: Just playing a recording of a song over the PA – yet it was a brilliant piece of theatre.

So much so, in fact, that when I asked Fairport members, friends and fans to nominate their favourite Fairport Cropredy moment for the box set, *Cropredy Capers*, it was one of the most requested individual moments. Naturally, it didn't make it on to disc: at best it would have been the inferior sound of a song recorded a quarter of a century earlier with some faint ambient sound. In fact, the desk tapes from that year's Cropredy are silent. The track was played in but there was no need to patch it through to the DAT recorder. It's one of very few lost moments from Cropredy which has otherwise, over the years, been meticulously documented in audio and often video formats.

PEGGY: We started with reel-to-reel recordings – big, ten-inch spools – which were reduced to cassette for storage. Later, we moved on to direct, DAT, and finally more complex multi-track digital formats. What's not there is where a tape has gone astray, though there are few that are missing. Most of the gaps in Cropredy recordings happen where a tape ran out mid-song and had to be changed.

Enter Ken Russell

Ken Russell, the *enfant terrible* of English cinema, made his name making innovative TV documentaries before moving on to the big screen, where he made a series of films that included some of the greats of British cinema – *The Music Lovers*, *Women In Love*, *The Boy Friend*, *The Devils* and *Tommy*, rated by many as the greatest rock movie ever made. Two decades later, his star was on the wane and he was once more looking at less ambitious, lower budget productions for television. In 1997, he made a film called *In Search of the English Folk Song*: it was an odyssey to find the Copper Family (whom he never got to, incidentally); on the way, though, he had encounters with significant distractions, including Martin Carthy singing a hymn siren-like in a graveyard, Donovan being as self-obsessed as the lotus eaters and June Tabor, a veritable Circe, on a rooftop with a song about a racing pigeon. At the heart of the film, however, was footage shot at Cropredy – Eliza Carthy, Osibisa, The Albion Band and Fairport. The start of Fairport's Saturday set was delayed by the famous director shooting them performing '17 Come Sunday / Sherriff's Ride' as Chris Leslie's son Samuel performed a Morris dance: it was a song they had learned specially for the film, at the director's request. Three separate takes were required, with full set-ups each time. Ken also took time out to direct the assembled Cropredy audience of 20,000; ever a man for excess, he was clearly in his element briefly taking on the mantle of Cecil B de Mille. That footage wasn't used however, and instead Ken made a madcap music video with Fairport at Woodworm, leaning out of windows swinging tankards, capering on the grass and miming rather obviously in the studio.

KEN RUSSELL: I loved working with Fairport who were co-operative and supportive and incredibly welcoming. Being at Cropredy was an amazing experience and the crowd were the friendliest and most attentive bunch of extras I've ever dealt with.

SIMON: It was a pleasure, indeed an honour, to work with someone of Ken Russell's calibre. But he was certainly a man who knew exactly what he wanted.

CHRIS: I was a very proud dad. There was my son dancing in front of 20,000 people and Ken Russell directing three camera crews filming him. He was too young to know who Ken Russell was and certainly too young to see most of his films, but I remember thinking that one day he would find out and realise what a high spot in his young life it was.

10–12 AUGUST, 2000
CROPREDY 2K

To celebrate the start of a new millennium, Fairport typically organised a Festival that looked both backwards and forwards. It featured big names from the past as well as upcoming acts. The Festival, which began as a late afternoon / early evening event, expanded to three days.

SIMON: When you make a major change – an improvement – to the way Cropredy runs, it has to be something you can stand by. You can't add a big screen, more toilets, an extra day or whatever one year and then decide to go back on it. To do so immediately would look like you'd got it wrong; after a couple of years, it becomes part of what people expect.

In celebrating the millennium, Fairport did not display quite the perversity of Richard Thompson who, when asked by *Playboy* to select 'The best popular songs of the past 1,000 years' did precisely that: his list reached back to 'Sumer is Icummen In' and the hymns of St Godric, though he knew full well that most lists would limit themselves to the last century at the most.

Richard didn't make it to Cropredy that year, but a good percentage of Fairport's past appeared on stage over the three-day event. Iain Matthews, Andy Roberts and Mark Griffiths preferred not to be introduced as Plainsong because some of the band were not with them. Their set included some of Iain's solo material, but drew mainly on the Plainsong repertoire including a version of Richard Thompson's 'From Galway to Graceland', which they had recorded for a tribute album and relearned especially for the occasion.

Keith Donnelly gave over his allocated slot to introduce various artists who had been 'Fairport supporters' (the opening acts on their Winter Tour): – annA rydeR, Bob Fox and Eddi Reader whose rendition of 'Perfect' was one of the weekend's highlights.

Other guests over the weekend belonged to the era that Fairport had just come through. Here were The Incredible String Band, Stackridge, All About Eve (newly reformed and using Cropredy as their relaunch), and festival crowd-pleasers The Hamsters.

On the Saturday night, after Show of Hands completed their set, Fairport took to the stage for a performance bristling with guests.

Opening, unusually, with 'Good Fortune' (consisting of four good tunes), they broke with precedent by having a guest on with them for their first number – actor, raconteur, compere and friend of the band Geoff Hughes. Each subsequent guest seemed to add to Fairport's credentials. Jerry and Kristina Donahue reminded us of the recent appearance of unreleased Sandy material by performing the title track, 'Gold Dust'. Ashley brought on Iain Matthews to perform what he described as "songs from the *Heyday* era" ('Tried So Hard', 'Reno Nevada', 'Suzanne'). Martin Carthy, whose 60th birthday concert Dave and Chris Pegg had organised that year, joined Ashley for 'Postman's Knock', and then performed 'Sovay' as a duet with Swarb. Bob Fox came on for two songs from his latest album, recorded at and released on Woodworm, with Fairport providing backing. Roger Hodgson from Supertramp was the real surprise guest, performing 'Breakfast in America', 'The Logical Song', 'Open the Door' and 'Give a Little Bit' – reminding the audience of Fairport's parallel existence as part of the Excalibur project. He departed the stage leaving Fairport with time for just three songs in that millennium year Cropredy – 'John Gaudie', 'Matty Groves' and 'Meet on the Ledge'.

SIMON: The new century was to bring a change of management at Cropredy. Fairport Convention Ltd. would continue the tradition begun by Dave and Chris Pegg. We would also face some of the biggest threats the Festival has ever had to overcome – floods, drought, foot and mouth, and health and safety.

There are very few festivals in the world that can boast a member of Led Zeppelin as a 'regular guest'. In 2000, Robert Plant used Cropredy to unveil the short-lived Priory of Brion. In 2011, John Paul Jones also appeared at Cropredy accompanying Seasick Steve. Plant has returned to the Cropredy stage several times and his appearance has always been a surprise.

PERCY'S SONGS
CROPREDY: 1986–2008

PEGGY: Planty has appeared at Cropredy a few times, mostly doing a guest spot with Fairport, once with his own band. The first time he played – though he had attended previously – was in 1986, which was the first year Swarb didn't play.

It was also the year that Iain Matthews made his first, welcome, return to Fairport. His presence dominates *The Other Boot*, a two-cassette souvenir of the Festival. Anyone hoping to have a permanent record of Robert Plant's contribution to the evening would however be disappointed.

PEGGY: As the name suggests, those Cropredy cassettes were semi-official bootlegs – although they were released by the band through Woodworm, they weren't given formal release numbers. It was OK to ask friends and fellow-Fairporters if they minded being included, but Robert was in a rather different league – and came complete with a no-nonsense manager.

Plant joined Fairport for three songs on his first visit – 'Mess of Blues', '19 Years Old' and 'Mystery Train'. It would be another seven years before he returned.

RIC: By the Nineties, people had come to expect surprise guests – which is a very self-contradictory statement. Returning ex-members is something they have come to take for granted. People now want to be surprised… wowed… *we* like to hear the sound of 16,000 people all going, "Blimey!"

SIMON: For me, the real coup with Robert Plant was in '93. We'd already included a bunch of Move songs with Roy Wood, and then Robert came on and did nine songs. It was mainly Led Zeppelin material – 'Whole Lotta Love', 'Misty Mountain Hop', 'Thank You' and so on. He was really going out on a limb there. He certainly hadn't worked with us, beyond very informal things, so he was taking a huge risk, because this was, to many, hallowed material that wasn't currently being played, particularly not by the band who had created it. Maartin Allcock was like a dog with two tails, having the opportunity to play all those Jimmy Page guitar parts. Dave Mattacks was very into it too, drumming in a style that was quite a ways removed from the way he normally does.

   For Robert to agree to do those was a bold decision. I remember how he went from good grace, to confidence, to actually taking pleasure in performing those songs again. That, to me, was a real tip of the hat in the direction of Fairport.

If Robert Plant's 1993 appearance was a surprise, it was nothing compared to the next time he joined Fairport during their set. There is something of a tradition about keeping the identities of surprise guests reasonably secret so as to not spoil the impact of their appearance. Word has usually leaked out, following an appearance for a rehearsal, a chance remark on the radio, or a song during a warm-up gig. What was to take place at Cropredy 2008 was in a different league: the festival's best-kept secret ever.

SIMON: We wanted to do something to commemorate the 30th anniversary of Sandy's passing, and wanted it to be special.

CHRIS: Over the years, lots of people have joined Fairport to perform Sandy's songs. Some of the greatest singers in British folk, in fact. But we wanted to avoid any one person coming on with a 'Tonight, Matthew, I am Sandy Denny' approach.

SIMON: Within the band, there had been a lot of discussion about how best to tackle the tribute to Sandy. We knew it had to be both special and memorable: it was definitely a one-off event. In the past, we had guest singers on separate occasions do a Sandy set-within-the-set. I didn't think we should simply repeat that formula. Everyone who has done it has been great. Cathy, Chris, Kristina, Vikki – they have all brought something different and special to the performance. If one person was going to take on Sandy's mantle for that evening, it would have been someone who had done it before… and that was something I felt we should avoid.

GERRY: What we decided on was to have a sequence of singers, all doing one song – their favourite song by Sandy. I don't know who thought of it, but it was a brilliant idea, partly because the only place you could pull something like that off – getting all those ladies up for one song – is Cropredy.

The level of anticipation had been increasing all weekend. Some kind of Sandy Denny tribute was imminent. It had been alluded to on page 48 of the programme, ahead of an article by Dave Mattacks in which he had said: 'Dave Pegg and I did an inordinate amount of session work as a kind of "folk-rock rhythm section for hire." Though there were sometimes sessions which stood out – John Martyn's and Nick Drake's immediately come to mind – it was only when we worked in the studio on Sandy's solo albums that I began to realise what a truly exceptional talent she had.' There had been rumour and speculation, fuelled by stage announcements, remarks in press and radio interviews. But the truth is that barely anyone in the crowd of 20,000 in that field that August evening, could have had the remotest chance of predicting what was about to happen.

On the screen behind Fairport, an image of Sandy dissolves into a backdrop of castle walls. Ashley Hutchings joins the band about to play a song from early 1969. He dons his bass unannounced with a kind of reverent ceremony: a problem with his instrument prevents him playing, he leaves as discreetly as he came on. The band exchange anxious glances. Is it all about to go wrong? Was that an omen? Simon introduces Vikki Clayton.

SIMON: Vikki is one of these singers who have regularly joined us on stage at Cropredy to do Sandy songs. There was even an occasion when she put together a Sandy tribute band called The Nerve, who played at the festival. She is so closely associated with Sandy's songs at Cropredy that she was the natural person to start the tribute.

PEGGY: Vikki had travelled over from Australia to be at Cropredy. She is a singer who truly embodies the spirit of Sandy when she performs her songs. She was our starting point – and exactly the right person to begin our tribute.

Vikki starts 'Fotheringay', the first track from Sandy's first album with Fairport, the perfect beginning. Although Vikki, like Chris While, is very much associated with 'singing Sandy' at Cropredy, the first time she had done so as part of Fairport's set had been as late as 1990. Prior to that, the role had been undertaken by Sheila and Sheryl Parker, Julianne Regan, June Tabor and Cathy Lesurf, who had begun the whole thing with an epic set in 1983 – including most of *Liege & Lief* plus songs from all the other albums Sandy had recorded with Fairport.

SIMON: That had been the first Cropredy at Home Farm. The Albion Band had been on the bill, as had Richard Thompson with his band – with me playing with both of them, somehow contriving to be in three different bands at once. That had made it possible, for the first time, to reconstruct the pre-*Full House* line-ups. To do that, we needed a female singer, naturally. So Ashley and I had prevailed upon Cathy to take on the task. She'd always been a big admirer of Sandy. She did an amazing job.

PEGGY: Would Sandy have come to Cropredy? I think we'd have had a hard time stopping her. Once there, it would have taken men stronger than the Fairport chaps to keep her off the stage!

SIMON: It's easy to forget that I had been in the band with Sandy for only 18 months: when she rejoined in the mid-Seventies, I wasn't part of the band. There had been other occasions when I'd played with her, in the main pretty informal. So far as recording with her, my only connection had been dubbing some backing vocals on a posthumous release of a live album.

PEGGY: There was something about Sandy that made you feel you'd known her all your life.

SIMON: It's very hard to speculate as to how the chemistry would have worked had she rejoined Fairport for a second time. Certainly, we'd have been two very different people from the young rhythm guitarist and the amenable singer who'd worked together in '69. Had she lived, it's impossible to say which direction her career would have gone in. She might have had that lucky break and found mainstream success, which at times she clearly wanted very much. It's hard to speculate how her songwriting might have blossomed. She'd really only just resumed her solo career after being back in Fairport. Certainly, her last album had some very strong songs on it. She might even have lost all interest in music.
   Would *she* have wanted to rejoin Fairport? That's another impossible question. Whatever happened, I know she would have wanted to be part of what goes on over the weekend at Cropredy. She'd have liked the general vibe of the event.

Sandy herself had commented on this shortly before her death: "Would I ever consider joining Fairport again? I joined twice and left twice. The answer, I suppose, depends on one of the reasons I left both times." Her comment, made in a radio interview shortly before her death, was followed by her singing a couple of lines of 'Stranger to Himself' which ended with her laughing.

Back at the 30th anniversary of her death, there are those, including Sandy devotee Vikki Clayton, who sings the first song of that day's tribute, who claim that Sandy's presence is there: "Although Sandy never actually set foot on it, what happens on the Cropredy stage evokes her spirit."

Vikki's song comes to a close. She bows and leaves the stage, replaced by another of the weekend's stars, Celtic folk singer Julie Fowliss, who delivers a sublime vocal on 'Farewell, Farewell'.

SIMON: The idea of a sequence of female singers each doing one song made it feel more like a tribute. Technically, of course, it creates its own problems because of the regular changeovers, but in the end it went amazingly smoothly (we even covered up the glitches) and it was obvious the crowd loved it.

Julie's performance is faultless, bringing something new to the song. It is ethereal and evanescent, imbued with a tangible sense of loss. It is respectful as well as sensitive, never allowing her own performance to upstage Sandy. She finishes; her eyes sparkle in the stage lights; she smiles almost nervously and gives a slight curtsey before she leaves.

Her place is taken by Chris While who regularly joins Fairport at Cropredy. Over the years we've heard her perform a wide range of the songs Sandy sang including, the previous year, the first complete sequential performance of the classic album *Liege & Lief*. As she introduces "a song from Sandy's second solo album", a cheer goes up for the appearance of two ex-Fairport members – Maartin Allcock and Jerry Donahue.

SIMON: Jerry is very closely associated with Sandy, of course. He was Fairport's lead guitarist when Sandy rejoined. Before that he had been lead guitar in her band Fotheringay. He had played on all her solo albums.

Ironically, Sandy's original recording of the next song had not featured Jerry – the impressive guitar parts on 'It'll Take a Long Time' having been provided by Sneaky Pete Kleinow and Richard

Thompson. Simon's acoustic guitar leads in – then Chris's voice soars over it. The song is unexpected. The audience, captivated.

SIMON: Chris is a great mate of long standing. There's a great version of her doing 'Who Knows Where the Time Goes' from '98. Outside of Fairport, we've both worked together in a couple of Albion Band line-ups, so we're very comfortable together on stage. All in all, I have spent a lot more time on stage performing with Chris than with Sandy.

This is clearly an emotionally difficult set. Performing evokes memories, often very different kinds of memories, for each individual involved.

SIMON: Sandy was a complex individual and someone who often defied expectations. I know that when Joe Boyd thought about her joining Fairport, he expected her to eat us for breakfast. As it turned out, she fitted in and was even quite shy about pushing her own stuff forward. She was a curious mixture of strength and fragility – like that Dylan line, 'she breaks just like a little girl'.

PEGGY: She came across as tough, a boozy, sometimes sweary, rock 'n' roll chick…

SWARB: I used to call her Boadicea – though not to her face, usually.

PEGGY: …but actually, she was very insecure and quite mixed up, a 'Crazy Lady' as she called herself.

ASHLEY: Sandy was a curious mixture of opposites, someone who was the most fun in the world to be with, but also someone who could make you feel an unbearable sadness. It's that sense of sadness that imbues a particular ethereal beauty to her best songs. 'Who knows where the time goes?' – what a great line that is, a real stroke of genius.

SIMON: The success and acclaim Sandy achieved were remarkable. She won the *Melody Maker* Female Vocalist of the Year award two years running. That was odd when you consider the more prominent and commercially successful females she was competing against. She wasn't being played on the radio – at least not on mainstream daytime radio. She wasn't on TV all the time, and most definitely didn't have her own weekly TV series, which almost every prominent female singer seemed to do – Cilla, Lulu, Dusty, Sandie Shaw and even Nana Mouskouri. It didn't really work like that, of course, because *Melody Maker* was a specialist weekly music paper and its readership certainly had interests outside the mainstream. The fact that the voting form included things like 'Best Bass Player' showed the level of awareness that was expected in the readership. It is important to remember, and I know this mattered to Sandy, that it wasn't an insider's thing with a limited panel or an industry-only thing: the acknowledgement reflected the opinion of the public or at least that part of the public with more than a passing interest in music. The respect, admiration and loyalty towards Sandy which those votes showed is still there today. Despite being up against mainstream singers who were selling truckloads of singles, here was Sandy, who had not even released a record under her own name at that point, shining through, despite being tucked away in a musical backwater singing with some little-known band.

When something like that happens, it's easy to see it as a big breakthrough. Record companies and managers tend to think that way for obvious reasons. The reality is, what Sandy achieved was all the more remarkable because that breakthrough hadn't happened and would never really happen for Fairport or for most of the people who have been part of the band. If you work from that premise, such accolades are an achievement; working from the opposite direction it becomes immensely frustrating.

Of course, Sandy wanted that other kind of success; being honoured without profit is never easy in this business.

One thing I have learned about job satisfaction in the music business is that it's more important to want what you have than to have what you want.

Sandy's yearning for commercial success was reflected on her albums – the sparse, singer-songwriter approach of *Sandy*, the overwrought MOR arrangements of *Like an Old Fashioned Waltz*, the soft rock of her final album *Rendezvous* with its ill-judged bolt-on single – a version of 'Candle in the Wind'. Each reflects the musical trends of its time.

SIMON: I suppose most people are happy to have a job they enjoy that provides them with a comfortable living; that's been true of my career. Sandy was always striving, feeling she was missing something, both personally and professionally.

Chris While leaves the stage, her spot taken by her daughter Kellie who has chosen to sing a song from Sandy's first album. But as she explains, it's a song that has come to be associated with Fairport

KELLIE WHILE: 'John the Gun' is a very edgy song, very hard to pin down. Sandy recorded two or three very different versions. I suppose I did 'the Fairport version'.

SIMON: It became part of Fairport's repertoire after Sandy rejoined, and we've revived it a few times at Cropredy. It's almost an honorary Fairport song, though the only recordings of the band playing it are live.

There are four live recordings of the song with Sandy: they were made in Sydney, Denver, LA and Uxbridge. It also appeared, performed by Cathy Lesurf, on *The Third Leg*, Fairport's 'official bootleg' of Cropredy 1987. Just as she had the first time, Sandy brought her own songs with her when she rejoined Fairport.

SIMON: Sandy didn't push her songs when she first joined. Of course, by the time she rejoined, her songs were already out there, released on album. I wasn't around, but suspect it was a matter of which of those to add to the repertoire. 'John the Gun' fits in perfectly with Fairport's style.

As Kellie While's powerful version draws to its hard-hitting conclusion, she is joined on stage by her mother Chris. As part of different Albion line-ups, Simon has played with both of them. Chris was a part of Albion Acoustic in the early Nineties; Kellie, having initially appeared as a guest with the band, was to join full time in

2001 (when Simon was no longer a member). She would go on to share vocal and guitar duties with Simon on the Albion Christmas tours each December.

SIMON: Chris and Kellie are so close that we refer to them as 'the sisters'. Certainly, I never sit on stage beside Kellie and think, "I used to be in this band with your mum!" I doubt if she would thank me for pointing out the fact, either. They share so much of the same mindset that I find it impossible to not think of them as being of the same generation.

The two of them have now been brought together to recreate a one-off performance of Sandy's most famous song. The first time they performed it, it was captured off the desk at a gig and so impressed were Fairport with it that they released it as their first-ever download single.

SIMON: It struck me as slightly odd that during the Sandy set we should find ourselves performing a version of our latest single. That's not a concept that often relates to Fairport's activities! During the Winter Tour, we had played St Anne's and Chris and Kellie had come along to see us so we'd invited them to join us on stage for a song. They offered to sing 'Who Knows Where the Time Goes'. Their voices have a special rapport and when we heard the desk recording we knew we had to make it available.

Rumours persist that the track holds a record as the song with most failed attempts to download in the first week of release – a reflection of the unfamiliarity of most Fairport fans with the system of buying songs 'off tin-ternnet'.

SIMON: The download release wasn't a huge success. I think the band had some rather ambiguous advice about how to go about doing it. It was a one-off and what we were told was certainly incomplete, if not entirely wrong-headed. So, if there were failings, they were probably on both sides. The whole download thing is something I haven't really got round to looking at in terms of the Matty Grooves [label] material. There is a lot of Fairport on iTunes, but nearly all of it dates from the first ten years, in effect the Island catalogue. So, while all the early Fairport material is available to download legally, for latter-day and current Fairport material, you are still rather reliant on old technology.

In my experience, the vast majority of Fairport fans prefer their music in a tangible form, packaged as something they can hold, look at, and put on a shelf. Indeed, forget about CD, a good many of them would prefer it on vinyl. It is something we are looking at, particularly after the *Fotheringay II* album – issued on vinyl – sold well. Apart from anything else, it would be good to have Mick Toole's artwork shown off to its full advantage.

In fact, the desire to own a vinyl copy of a record has been registered at either end of the age spectrum: of nostalgic value for the more senior fans, while younger fans regard it as the cool way to own music.

Back at Cropredy, the understated twin fiddles of Ric and Chris complement perfectly the interweaving voices of Chris and Kellie While. It is a long way from the plashing guitars of Sandy's first recording with Fairport or the later live version, its keening fiddle a distant kittyhawk. We have heard five songs from Sandy's repertoire, each tinged with a sense of loss, an aura of missed opportunities. On stage and off, emotions run high. But while Simon, Peggy, Chris, Ric and Gerry know what's coming next, the fans have not the faintest idea.

SIMON: We didn't want to spoil the surprise, and for that reason Robert didn't join us at the public warm-up gigs before Cropredy. We had done one very low profile run-through of the song, two weeks earlier, in a village hall not far from where he lives and for whom he supports a charity. It was a nostalgic thing to do, in a way, because it was very much in the original spirit of Cropredy – totally within the village, with no publicity outside, done as a fundraiser. Fairport were booked for the evening performance. He came along, unannounced. Like Fairport at the early Cropredys, that was considered unremarkable because of him living locally. He got up on stage and joined us for the song, which gave everybody the opportunity of playing it together.

Kristina was there, too, and it gave them a chance to sing together. That was important, because if anyone was likely to be in the firing line of any criticism, it was her. She had the biggest ball to drop. I have to say Robert was totally charming and really put her at her ease; he obviously realised how out of her depth she must have been feeling. After that one run-through, we all felt confident it could be great on the night. We didn't include the song at the Woodford House warm-ups: that would have been one very large cat let out of the bag. So we did a good job of keeping at least one surprise up our sleeves. It's always good to be able to do that – to be able to give the audience more than they are expecting. It was his idea to use a pseudonym on the setlist. It was also his own choice of alter ego.

Fairport's Cropredy setlists consist of song titles – sometimes abbreviated, occasionally obtusely cryptic, followed by the key and often a note about instrument changes. To remind the band when a guest is due on, names of additional performers are clearly indicated in block capitals and usually in full (aside from the obvious such as RT, DM or MAART). On the next song 'B of E' – the setlist announces – Chris will play 'mand', while 'vcls' are by Kristina Donahue and 'Michael Fish'.

Michael Fish is a legend among British weathermen. With over 30 years before the map, he was the nation's longest-serving TV climate forecaster. Yet he is best remembered for the one time he was caught out. In response to a viewer's enquiry in October 1987, he assured the nation that there was no chance of a hurricane; that night, the worst storm to hit Britain in almost 300 years devastated much of the southern countryside. Michael Fish immediately became an eponym for something which takes people, especially people who should know better, totally by surprise.

As 'Time Goes' finishes, Simon Nicol glances as he often does (a kind of unconscious nervous habit) at the setlist. There he sees that the next song is to be performed by Kristina Donahue, Jerry's daughter, and 'Michael Fish'.

SIMON: He wasn't around over the weekend. He was smuggled in during Fairport's set, which we knew would allow the best chance of his arriving unnoticed. He was very much up for it and, I think, enjoyed all the subterfuge.

As has happened with each of the four singers to appear in the night's tribute to Sandy thus far, Kristina Donahue is brought on to a great Cropredy welcome. Then Dave Pegg decides to go off at a tangent. He talks about Sandy having been in the Strawbs for a while... and then "helping out Fairport for a bit". Kristina looks on, unable to start her song.

He mentions Sandy had helped out another band: "She was the only female singer to sing on a Led Zeppelin track." Cheers and cries of "Yes" from the audience as they realise they might be about to hear 'The Battle of Evermore'... but Peggy has more to offer: "We're really honoured to have Robert Plant here."

The crowd roars, Robert Plant walks to the mic, behind him Simon's guitar and Chris Leslie's mandolin begin the familiar folkie riff of the Led Zeppelin classic.

Because it had been recorded as a duet, 'The Battle of Evermore' remains one of Led Zeppelin's least-played songs. Live performances are singularly rare. Lacking concert footage to illustrate it, even a documentary DVD on Led Zeppelin's fourth album almost entirely omitted the song. On the sleeve of the album, where each member of the band was represented by a rune, Sandy's credit put her on a par with Page, Plant, Jones and Bonham by granting her a signifier – three pyramids. Given that Robert Plant's chosen symbol was not actually a rune but the feather of the Egyptian goddess Ma'at, identifying Sandy with an Egyptian symbol had an obvious relevance.

SIMON: You certainly felt the audience response when they realised what was about to happen. You knew it was something special. Then everything about it worked. The band played well, especially Chris taking that long lead part. Robert and Kristina's vocals were exactly right and their voices blended perfectly.

This was a pared-down Fairport. Chris with his Martin mandolin, an image of concentrated playing, stage left. Peggy on bass and backing vocals. Jerry, subdued on drums, cymbals whispering beneath his felted hammers. Simon playing Fender, doubling Chris's mandolin part and moving on through chords and lead lines that should be cited if ever anyone dares say he's "not really a lead guitarist". Stage right, almost in the wings, clad in white, Ric clutches his fiddle to his chest, occasionally strumming a soft chord – the simplest of tunes – across its strings.

RIC: I wasn't really playing on the song, but there was no way I was going to miss it. What a moment! What a thing to be a part of! Those six minutes epitomised what Cropredy is all about.

Up front, standing close, Robert, leonine and ragged, and Kristina, elegant and slender in a maroon evening dress, allow their voices to weave in the song which, in Planty's words, "was the only Zeppelin song where somebody else sang lead vocals. To do that you had to be good. Sandy was very, very good."

SIMON: Just doing the song was significant in itself. Doing it so well was a real bonus. I think that is almost a maxim for Cropredy as a whole event, actually. He [Plant] may be god-like to many people, but he's a bloke; he enjoys performing; he likes working with people he knows he can trust, as we all do; he simply likes being on stage in front of people. We're just glad that he chooses to do that with us sometimes – it's always a great experience.

'Evermore' finishes. Astonished at what they have just witnessed, the audience breaks its rapt silence with rapturous applause. Fairport leave the stage. Only Robert Plant remains. Informally, intimately, he addresses the crowd, sharing personal memories of Sandy. Then he introduces the video tribute that has been put together. He turns and faces the screen… and stands on stage to watch. It's a hair-on-the-back of the neck moment, pure stagecraft. Just as during 'Meet on the Ledge', the stage seemed to spill into the audience making them all Fairport members momentarily, so now it feels like the audience is taking over the stage and Robert Plant, no longer the rock god, is merely the frontrunner in a vast throng of Fairport fans.

SIMON: His tribute was pretty impromptu. And then he chose to stay on stage. That definitely wasn't in the script, so to speak. There is a great photo, which we used in the booklet of the CD of the Festival. He looks lost in the moment. You can see it was a genuine response – unknown to anyone else and unplanned. He definitely wasn't up there preening. It's moments like that, genuinely unique and particularly unpredictable, that make Cropredy what it is.

PEGGY: I know lots of people in the crowd expect surprises – the icing on the cake, the free cocktail at the end of the expensive meal, or however you like to think of it. But it isn't something we're obliged to do. Of course, most of our guests have a direct relationship to the band in that they are ex-members, and whether they are included is largely a matter of availability. Others are people we've met either professionally or personally in the course of the year, and asked whether they'd like to join us. It's an informal invitation, and they are not obliged, even if they say "Yes". If a paid gig were to come up or something else get in the way, then so be it. It would be wrong for several reasons to use such an appearance as advance publicity to promote an event.

Backstage, as Fairport's set drew to a close, Jerry Donahue was the epitome of the proud dad – his daughter's achievement lighting up his face.

JERRY: One of the proudest moments of my life!

RIC: What was really amazing was it didn't just stop the show. Robert Plant's performance was a peak in a long set. Importantly, it was still all about Sandy.

So outstanding was the performance that Fairport released it twice, first on the CD *Live at Cropredy '08*, which included all but the second song of that Sandy tribute, and a year later as a bonus track on *Off the Screen* – the DVD taken from Cropredy 2009. For many, it is those surprise performances that stick out as special memories. It may be an unexpected song: Richard doing The Beatles' 'I'm Down'; Ashley singing 'Nadine'; Simon, Julie and Chris performing an *a cappella* 'Some Old Salty'. Or it may be one of those guests whose appearance is totally unpredictable.

SIMON: Some guests have been totally unexpected. Roger Hodgson's set surprised many. That really came out of the blue. I doubt if many people had any idea who he was when he came on and sat at the piano. Then he started playing and suddenly, it was "Blimey! It's that bloke from Supertramp." I'm referring to the audience here, but there have been times when even band members have been caught unawares by certain turns of events.

A different Cropredy was to make one of those songs a surprise even for the band. A couple of years later, a momentary lapse in concentration would cause someone to list 'Breakfast in Mayfair' as 'Breakfast in America' on the photocopied setlists that appeared at the foot of each mic-stand just before Fairport took to the stage.

RIC: We never noticed until we got on stage! Luckily, everyone realised what it meant really.

PEGGY: One of the great things about Cropredy is the fact that even though we organise the whole event, things can still surprise us in a nice way.

A guest appearance by Frank Skinner, a Cropredy regular in the audience but never an onstage performer before, was intended to be a brief introduction to the presentation of an award. Instead, it turned into 20 minutes of hilarious, but schedule-unsettling, stand-up. Frank would also be a guest on Fairport's recording of 'Ukelele Central' when Fairport played it in their acoustic set at the start of Cropredy 2011. The other guest player on the album version, Joe Brown, joined them for that one number.

SIMON: It's certainly not something we have any obligation to lay on as part of the entertainment. One year, in fact, it turned out that we had very little in the way of surprise guests. It is a nice thing to do – you feel the response from the stage and it is gratifying to know what you have done is well received. Then to do it well adds to the sense of getting it all right. The first time Gary Brooker joined us on stage he sang the third verse of 'A Whiter Shade of Pale' that no one had ever heard before. I'd no idea it was coming and can still remember standing on stage, playing along and realising the words he was singing were totally unfamiliar to me; that quickly transformed itself into thinking "Wow! This is good." Moments like that are when you glance at the few faces at the front that you can make out by the light from the stage, to see whether they are getting it, too. But no one out there should expect one of those moments every single year.

In much the same way, it would be morally wrong to capitalise on appearances by people we have invited to appear – actual guests rather than booked artists.

If someone is listed on the poster or in the programme, it means there is a contract signed and it's a done deal, they are obliged to turn up and give a performance. Anyone else is appearing because they are willing to and want to. If we were to book Robert Plant, we simply couldn't afford him. We're lucky that he – and people like him – are prepared to turn up year after year and be part of what goes on. He was particularly gracious in allowing us to use the recording of his performance on the CD, too.

AUGUST 2002
CROPREDY

In 2002 annA rydeR composed a tribute to Fairport. Titled 'The Crowd', it is about the 20,000 people who congregate annually in Oxfordshire for Fairport's Festival.

ANNA: I wanted to capture the idea that everyone in the field is part of a 'whole' thing. There's no 'us and them' about it. It's one of the things that makes Cropredy so special and totally unlike any other rock festival.

annA's song begins with the idea of looking into someone's eyes and seeing reflected there the whole field of people. Intimate and universal brought together in the same instant. Fairport's recording of 'The Crowd' is a similar coming together of disparate elements. To achieve the result they wanted on disc, Fairport embarked on an unusually complex production, involving three different versions of the song, guest musicians and a cast of thousands.

They gathered at Wormwood on 18 April, 2001, with chord sheets and lyrics, to start work on annA's song. Simon sat at the foot of the carved stairway leading to the control room. Peggy faced him across the room, sitting on a high bar stool. Chris and Ric, on mandolin and fiddle, sat facing each other. Gerry, lost in a haze of cigarette smoke, had clear eye contact with Peggy.

As Simon tried out the lyric, Fairport's rhythm section developed the song's musical architecture – a looping, liquid bass line, drum patterns evolving from simple rhythm into fills, and surging percussive explosions. Ric adapts a lead mandolin line developed by Chris, and plays it on the fiddle.

As the arrangement progressed, Simon reminded the lead players "to leave space for annA's accordion part". From basic play through to first complete performance, in three-quarters of an hour, Fairport developed the arrangement one would recognise from their next album.

Five days later, Fairport recorded the first version, and at Cropredy that year they added the final parts to the song, using the crowd as an extra chorus, which can be heard on *xxxv*.

Over two pages in that year's Cropredy programme, annA in her idiosyncratic way explained what she expected of the crowd. (For example, "When you hear 'you are happy, you are loud' can you be loud please? Eg cheer, clap, go wooooh! etc".) On stage that night she and her brass section assembled stage right at 9.00 pm as the sun was almost down. The audience was a-flicker with torches and lighters as people tried to make out their instructions in the programme. Fortunately the chorus and key lines were printed bold and big. annA then took on the daunting task of rehearsing the entire crowd. "It's a brave move," commented Simon at the side of the stage. "The last person to try this was Ken Russell."

When she was satisfied, some "wooohs" and "aaahs" were recorded. Then, because the first time was "a bit unenthusiastic and rubbish" and the last "just for good luck" she tells her chorus, the entire song was recorded three times. Parts of it would grace the final released version. At the close of that night's performances, Fairport's set concluded as always with a star-studded, emotionally charged version of 'Meet on the Ledge', and the crowd made their way towards to the exits or a still-open food franchise. Unusually though, the speakers began sounding Fairport performing 'The Crowd' and people turned to listen. Many recognised the song and were tricked into thinking that it was the finished version of the live recording they had made earlier.

One kaftan-clad fan announced in astonished tones, "Bloody hell, it's that song we were all singing to!" – and dropped the entire contents of his newly purchased hog-roast sandwich. That night, as every night at Cropredy, he and his fellow spectators were more than just punters; they were part of Cropredy, as much as any 'star' has ever been.

Fairport's 'no stars – just talent' approach also applies to a rather different aspect of the arrangements at Cropredy. It is certainly one that sets it apart from every other festival.

PEGGY: For security reasons, if no other, we have to have 'backstage areas'. Basically there are three zones: one allows general backstage access to the larger area – the artist and guest campsite. We restrict access to the crew area now because of the large amount of equipment. Then there is the immediate backstage area, which is quite small and has dressing rooms and so on. Finally there is the stage area, where your pass will only let you through if you have a reason to be on stage.

CHRIS: I've always liked that aspect of Cropredy, the idea that artists shouldn't closet themselves backstage. Even though there's a huge crowd, everyone respects that.

PEGGY: If someone wants a drink, they go out into the field to the bar. Since I don't have as much responsibility for actually running Cropredy, I am able to spend much more time out in front of the stage, watching the acts. There's a great photo which I really think sums up the event: it's the one of Robert Plant in the middle of the crowd with no one hassling him or treating him like a star.

SIMON: It used to be a facet of that London underground scene; it's always been part of the folk scene, where the evening's guest normally sits among the audience – even that doesn't seem quite the right word – and then gets up to perform a set. It has worked really well for us and, frankly, I wouldn't have it any other way. It is a personal relationship. We have an audience who feel they can come up to you and say things like: "You won't remember but you signed this for me years ago, would you mind signing it again?" or "We've just got a new grandson and he's been named Simon after you," or "Why don't you do so-and-so any more?" or even more constructively, "You've done that song the last three times we've seen you: can you give it a rest for a while?"

That's the kind of feedback you just can't buy. We owe it to them to listen. You can't do that if you are in a little private bubble somewhere.

We never made a conscious decision to avoid the whole rock-star mystique thing. It just didn't seem relevant. That's why we always make ourselves available after gigs. That's why we don't hide backstage at Cropredy, and why we encourage others not to do so either. In fact, in all the years of Cropredy, I think the only person I ever saw with an old-fashioned showbiz head on was Lulu. I think her rider said she wanted pink Champagne. I should say, some bands do have backstage riders in their contract. For example, we did spend quite a bit on Jools Holland's rider, but there were a lot of them. I don't think Lulu got her pink champagne, however, poor girl. There was talk of a bottle of Cava and some cassis. As soon as she finished her last number, she was off down the stairs, into the back of the limo and whizzing up the field while the band were still playing on stage. I don't blame her for that. That's her world. It's just not ours.

Fairport have always been approachable: that's what works for us.

RIC: Almost every act at Cropredy, unless they are the last on, has a signing session shortly after their set. Fans appreciate it and it's good for the artists too, in terms of sales. Sometimes there'll be an act not so well known who do a really good set and they'll draw a massive queue of people wanting to get hold of their CD. It applies to big names too, of course.

I recall seeing a queue for Richard Thompson, who happened to have a CD newly available. The line went right up the field. When I did a signing with Peggy for his *Box of Pegg's* box set, we were there for the better part of an hour. Everyone was patient, pleasant and positive.

PEGGY: That's the thing. Treat people well and they'll do the same for you. That's always been the philosophy at Cropredy and we've never had any trouble or problems.

SIMON: We have continued to go from strength to strength. When *The Guardian* said we were as much part of the British summer as Wimbledon, we sold out in advance for the first time. As you prepare to go on stage at Cropredy you might look back at the last few hours, days, weeks, and think "Never again". Three hours later, I always say, "Same time next year?" and I always mean it. I am looking forward to it just as much as anyone else in that field.

CHAPTER NINE

Nineties

The Nineties saw Fairport's new line-up – Simon, Peggy, DM, Ric and Maart – go from strength to strength. They were a fully functioning, full-time band playing large venues on UK tours when not performing in Europe, Australia and America. They released new albums on a regular basis and made Cropredy an annual event with a worldwide reputation. They played together for more than 11 years, until December 1996.

PEGGY: As we moved into a new decade, it was nice to feel that we were very much in control of Fairport. We knew what we wanted to do and where we were headed.

SIMON: Our audiences had been building year on year, most notably at Cropredy. We were also attracting younger people, some of whom probably hadn't even been born when Fairport first started.

One aspect of Fairport's career, however, was very much out of their hands, as indeed it was for hundreds of bands and singers who had made music in the Fifties, Sixties and Seventies. The CD almost totally dominated the market in the Nineties. Despite the expectations of the music industry, reissues of older, often long deleted material, took the lion's share of the market.

As the decade began, there were very few Fairport vinyl albums available. *Gladys' Leap* and *Expletive Delighted!* were unlikely to be found in record shops, although they could be bought via mail order. The band's most recent releases on other labels, *Heyday* and *In Real Time*, were still available, as were *Liege & Lief* and *History of...* (both on CD). The rest had gone 'out of print' or been deleted. The first album had appeared on a budget label which then ceased to exist. Phonogram stopped pressing their two albums as soon as the band left Vertigo in 1979. The lavish and expensive packaging of *Babbacombe Lee* made it an early casualty. As stocks ran out, each Fairport album simply ceased to exist. Several record companies had terminated vinyl production altogether to make way for the CD. *Red & Gold* and *In Real Time* were released on CD at the same time as their vinyl versions

The Beat Goes On, a label specialising in reissues, leased *Tipplers Tales* for CD release, which might seem an odd choice until one remembers that four of its tracks were still in Fairport's current repertoire – 'John Barleycorn', 'Three Drunken Maidens', 'Reynard the Fox', and 'The Widow of Westmoreland's Daughter'.

In 1990, when transfers of Fairport original albums to CD became available, there was no bonus material and no re-mastering for them. Even more oddly, though the albums came out at the rate of one a month (it was an expensive year for fans), there was no logic to the sequence of reissues. *Full House* was the first CD reissue, before Joe Boyd's Hannibal label reissued *House Full: Live at the LA Troubadour*. The Hannibal running order dropped three tracks from the Island original, including 'Poor Will'. The third album to come out on CD was also live, the non-essential *Fairport LIVE Convention*. Next came *What We Did on Our Holidays*. And so it continued randomly through the year, as Fairport took time out from touring to work on their new album, *The Five Seasons*. When it was released in December 1990, the CD version included one bonus track, 'Rhythm of the Time'.

PEGGY: Most people had moved on to CD by then, and the CD version outsold the vinyl.

The album's most (some might say only truly) memorable track was a setting of 'The Wounded Whale'.

MAART: It's an epic by Archie Fisher. There's a long tradition

of songs about whaling, and of books that gather them together, like *Songs the Whalemen Sang*, for example. Archie
wrote something from the other point of view so one could
see what the whale was going through. It would be a bit like
rewriting a fox-hunting song – and there are loads of those,
too – from the fox's point of view. Or *Moby Dick* turned on
its head.

Maart's words above (from an interview in 1990) were to prove
prescient when his successor, Chris Leslie, wrote a new conclusion
for 'Reynard the Fox'.

MAART: Fairport's version of 'The Wounded Whale' is appropriately epic. I've used the keyboards to create a soundscape
while Ric pulls some suitably whale-like noises from his
fiddle. The live version takes it beyond that.

Enhanced with an atmospheric setting – one performance would
make use of concealed lighting set among the pipes of a vast concert
organ, making it seem part of what Maart was playing – Fairport's
live version was spectacular. It began with Maart performing solo
variations on Erik Satie's *Gymnopédies*. Many fans, however, were
voicing concerns about the way the band's music was becoming
more keyboard-based at that time. *The Five Seasons* never fares well
in polls of favourite Fairport albums and Fairport rarely revive its
songs. Yet, that year had begun with a very different mood, with
the setlist for the tour subjected to a revamp.

PEGGY: (speaking just prior to the tour) We've been working
as a full-time band for a few years now. We thought it was
time to go back and look at the setlist and cut away some of
the dead wood. I think it's going to be the strongest set this
line-up has ever played.

That setlist was duly transferred to the opening of Fairport's
Cropredy performance for the benefit of those who may have
missed out on the tour. Kieran Halpin, guest support on the Winter
Tour, who had been in a duo with Maart, was there. While folk-
rock was still very much in evidence, Cropredy began to broaden its
scope. Ralph McTell, Richard Thompson and The Albion Band all

played sets on the Friday, but fans were disappointed that neither Richard nor Ashley joined Fairport on stage on the Saturday. Ralph, however, did – along with stalwarts Vikki Clayton, Gerry Conway and Jerry Donahue.

SIMON: The only thing that the acts appearing at Cropredy in any given year have in common is the fact that we like them. It's our ball and we can choose what game we want to play when we take it out. It's the same reason we always put ourselves top of the bill.

Once you are satisfied that you have got the balance right, that there is something for everybody, then you have to arrange things to take into account factors like changeovers between acts, the overall flow of events and, of course, the sense of things building to some kind of climax each day.

We also try to consider the fact that everyone wants some time to go back to the campsite, visit the stalls, take a stroll along the canal, walk into the village or whatever. Most people want to meet up with old friends at some point – maybe people they only see at Cropredy. Recent years have, of course, seen it become an opportunity to meet online friends in the flesh. You should be able to look at the programme and think, "Oh I don't really want to see the next two acts – so I'll do such-and-such instead." The crowd always increases steadily through the day, and day by day. With very few exceptions, you don't get a sudden mass exodus or a sparsely populated field – that would be a sign you've got something wrong. That applies even when there are sudden downpours. Obviously, many make for cover, but a lot more arrive prepared with some kind of shelter and those down the front will often just brave the weather.

Simon was certainly right in 1990. Headline act The Bootleg Beatles took the audience on a costumed magical mystery tour of the Fab Four's career and, as trad arr gave way to Lennon-McCartney, the heavy cloud cover did its worst: the rain came, but the crowds didn't run and hide their heads. Surprises in Fairport's set included some unique and unexpected performances, as they were joined by Julianne Regan of All About Eve, followed by Procol Harum's Gary Brooker.

MAART: The Fairport set at Cropredy pushes you, perhaps in ways people don't think about. Obviously it's a long set, which presents its own challenges. It's about 40 songs – sometimes more, like when we've done both Friday and Saturday nights. We try to bring in things from the back catalogue that we haven't played before. Anything before the Woodworm era is going to be new to me and Ric as performers, although it's stuff we know as fans. The main thing though is accompanying guests, not just on songs you haven't played before but often in styles you're not used to. I like the fact that not everything in Fairport's Cropredy set necessarily sounds like Fairport.

One might have expected Fairport to have spent December 1990 plugging their new album or preparing for the Winter Tour. Instead, they were back in the studio, acting as backing band for Beryl Marriott who was recording *Weave the Mirror*, her album for Woodworm. They followed that with their Winter Tour, beginning in the New Year and gradually increasing in length from the planned month of nightly dates. There were also European tours, and they were soon to be back in Australia and the USA.

PEGGY: We'd learned from past experience. We made sure that any tour we arranged, whether it was the UK or overseas, didn't turn out to be a loss-making activity.

Although there was no new Fairport album in '91, *Farewell, Farewell* was reissued on CD, and both Ric and Maart found time to record solo albums, with little or no contribution from the other Fairport members. They were all involved in work outside Fairport. Maart had joined Peggy in Jethro Tull, DM did a considerable amount of session work, including sessions with XTC that he would describe as "some of the most enjoyable I've ever done". Ric and Simon formed an acoustic duo to tour folk clubs, their sets focusing more on songs than previous gigs with Swarb. Playfully, they billed themselves The Travelling Banburys.

RIC: With Fairport, people are used to seeing me playing loud and electric, lots of effects pedals, very much in the tradition of late-Seventies Swarbrick. Playing with Simon allows me the chance to reveal the other side of what I do.

Cropredy 1991 featured a line-up that could almost be called Fairport's roots and branches: the Steve Gibbons Band, Dan Ar Braz, the Richard Thompson Band, and Whippersnapper now minus Dave Swarbrick, who had moved to Australia ("Ever determined to seek out far-away places with strange-sounding names," as Simon put it), but still featuring Chris Leslie, who returned to the stage during Fairport's set as part of Beryl Marriott's Ceilidh Band, which played three tunes. Their appearance was an example of the set-within-a-set. Another example of this was to come during Richard's guest spot, which amounted to an overview of his career to date. Andy Fairweather Low was the surprise guest, with Fairport backing him on his biggest solo hit 'Wide Eyed and Legless', and on a version of 'Mystery Train'. Jerry Donahue, performing 'East/West', proved a real treat for hardcore Fairport fans; that being the piece played by Richard Thompson that persuaded Joe Boyd to manage the band.

Out Of Control

At Cropredy 1991, Peggy mentioned Woodworm's current project, a 'Best of Fairport' drawing on recordings since the mid-Eighties. In time for Christmas wish lists, *The Woodworm Years* came out that December. It included tracks from all of Fairport's Woodworm studio albums: three from *Gladys' Leap* and *Red & Gold*, two from *The Five Seasons*, and 'Portmeirion' from *Expletive*. It also carried three tracks from Simon's solo album, and one apiece from Maart's and Peggy's. Most of the tracks were part of Fairport's current set.

It turned out to be a very satisfying collection – which was not always the case with many later compilations and reissued recordings from their Woodworm era.

PEGGY: When you run a small record label, there is a point beyond which an album is no longer selling. One way you can continue to make money from it is to lease the tracks to another label for a period of time. Unfortunately, that also means you lose control of what happens to those tracks for that period.

RIC: Any CD by a band like Fairport will reach a point of critical mass. Basically, everyone who is likely to buy it will have done so. You then have to decide what to do with it.

ASHLEY: Compilations and budget reissues have always been part of the record business. They made music available to people who weren't prepared to pay full price for every album, but maybe wanted to own something by a particular band.

SIMON: Then Dave said to himself: "The market has definitely dried up. We're not going to sell any more of these. I've still got 150 in the garage, anyway. I'll do a deal with somebody." So the rights to the albums were sold to another label for a period of time. Eventually, they owned a bunch of stuff, and that's when the razor blades came out, as it were. People started lumping things together or restructuring an existing album, adding a couple of tracks and giving it a different title and artwork. That's inevitably going to cause resentment to someone who buys a CD in good faith and subsequently feels cheated because he already owns everything on it. If someone feels short-changed or misled, ultimately that falls back on the band. Naturally, people don't see the broken chain in the connection between musician and purchaser. I cannot defend it and equally I cannot do anything to stop it. People turn up at gigs with Fairport releases we didn't even know existed. Sometimes, the material has gone through yet another pair of hands after being sold on by Woodworm. Other times, the records are most definitely bootlegs; Italy is a great place for discovering records you never knew you'd made. I would say that at every gig you play in Italy, at some point you'll be presented with a completely rogue CD to sign.

PEGGY: I understand how people feel. Sometimes what has happened is as annoying and upsetting for the band as it is for fans. I think now that we're Fairport Convention Ltd. with our own new label Matty Grooves, we have learned to be more careful about letting the kids go out and play on their own, so to speak.

SIMON: Reissues of later Woodworm material were entirely

the responsibility of Dave and Chris Pegg. I know they did what they thought was best in terms of keeping the band's profile high and the material available. Some of the repackaging is excellent. *The Woodworm Years*, for example, really stands up as an album in its own right.

The compilation was released just as the band's silver anniversary year was upon them. Fairport set about celebrating their 25th birthday from the start of 1992. As Peggy was to explain in an interview at the time: "Cropredy is our main focus, and we wish to pay tribute to Trevor who died a couple of years ago. We have lots of old Fairporters joining us, and some very surprising guests. It's all being properly recorded and we hope to bring it out next year. We also plan to do more touring than ever before. Of course, it's also Tull's 25th, so I'll be doing a lot with them as well."

What he couldn't have known at the time of that interview was that an accident would put Ric out of commission for a series of summer gigs and, more importantly, two nights of Cropredy. Nevertheless, an excellent two-CD set of Cropredy '92 was issued in May the following year – the first time recordings from the Festival had been issued in what was by then the standard audio format. *25th Anniversary Concert* also marked Chris Leslie's debut as a member of Fairport, although it would be Fairport's 30th anniversary before he actually joined the band full-time.

With a record nine different lead vocalists featured on the album – Simon, Richard, Ashley, Swarb, Vikki Clayton, Julianne Regan, Chris Leslie, Ralph McTell and Robert Plant – it begins with six songs that are *not* from Fairport's back catalogue. Three had migrated into the setlists from the solo albums where they had begun, while the other three featured guest performers. The album concluded with the unexpected revival of 'Si Tu Dois Partir', surprisingly inserted between 'Matty Groves' and 'Meet on the Ledge'.

The almost contemporaneous release of Richard Thompson's 3-CD retrospective *Watching the Dark* was an obvious topic of interest among Fairport fans, not least because it included the previously undocumented acetate of 'A Sailor's Life', recorded before Swarb had been brought in.

RICHARD: I think everybody had forgotten it existed. I know
    I had. Any attempt to say exactly why it was recorded would

be supposition, certainly on my part. I think it's good to let people hear the song the way we played it on stage, though.

Being a Fairport guest had by that time become so prestigious that, where once Fairport had requested people to join them – almost as a favour – now they had a list of willing volunteers. In 1993, Vikki Clayton was on hand to fulfil her regular 'singing Sandy' function; in addition, the guest list included Bryn Haworth, members of Feast of Fiddles, Everything But The Girl, Heather Wood, Roy Wood and Robert Plant. They were *all* unscheduled and unadvertised surprise guests. Roy and Robert both contributed half a dozen songs apiece, EBTG played a couple of their hits, followed by a fiddle extravaganza and a sea shanty. There was something for everyone – or almost.

PEGGY: We actually got complaints about Cropredy in 1993. Not just someone having a whinge on the Sunday, but actually written complaints. You know, "Dear Sir, I must say how disappointed I was by Fairport's sets… from Mr Angry of Chipping Norton."

The complaints were, surprisingly, about the lack of Fairport material. Of the 38 songs Fairport played that night, only a dozen were from their back catalogue. There were two lengthy sets within the set. The first featured Roy Wood playing hits from his solo career and his time with The Move, which ended – on a warm August night – with 'I Wish It Could Be Christmas Everyday', complete with an appearance by Santa.

CHRIS PEGG: We thought it would be a good joke to have a Santa, fake snow, gifts from the sack thrown into the audience. Sourcing Christmas crackers and the like in July turned out to be one of the most complicated things I have ever undertaken for Cropredy.

The other set within the set was from the previous year's surprise guest, Robert Plant, who took the stage at 10.50 pm and played for 40 minutes. He sang classics from the Led Zeppelin catalogue and a couple of his personal favourites: 'Jesus on the Mainline' and 'If I Were a Carpenter'. Bootlegs of the gig – of which there are many

– are highly prized by Zeppelin fans. Some Fairport fans, however, were less than delighted by the performance.

LETTER TO DAVE PEGG: Dear Peggy, I hope this gets to you (in more ways than one). Robert Plant is all well and good. But for two years running? And for nearly an hour! Bloody hell!

PEGGY: In '94, we hardly had any guests, just Gerry Conway and Danny Thompson, plus Vikki Clayton and Chris While – the latter's first Cropredy – to sing Sandy's songs. We got complaints about that as well.

Vikki Clayton would also be part of the support on the Winter Tour at the start of 1994.

RIC: That was the first time there was a female singer to do Sandy's songs outside of Cropredy.

A month-long UK tour was followed by dates in Europe. In April 1995, the band set aside all other distractions to work on their next album.

PEGGY: I even got leave of absence from Tull for that. My son Matt deputised for me. I suppose that was the moment I realised that Fairport was in fact the most important thing in my life, outside of family. Since 1970, I'd been a part of the band and had put a lot of energy, at different times, into making sure the band didn't die. Being in Tull had been the source of income that had allowed me to do that when Fairport really wasn't in a position to pay for itself. Now things had changed; I knew my days as a full-time Tull were numbered. I've never been a part-time Fairporter.

Jewel

From April 1994, Fairport gathered daily at Woodworm to select material for the album, arrange, rehearse and record the songs; and to mix, master and sequence them. The result was an album that would come to be regarded as a Fairport classic.

In August 1994, the rock magazine *Mojo* was still finding its feet. A new publication, it was hitting a target audience whose tastes ranged from Sixties' folk and psychedelia to emergent Americana. The cover of issue 9 featured The Clash; and topping the list of other artists featured within were 'Fairports' (ranked below them were 'Spin Doctors, New Stones CD, Eagles live').

PEGGY: That article was well-timed, because it came just as the band was getting into its stride. *Mojo* was to become very supportive of Cropredy and Fairport over the years. They came to have a stand at Cropredy.

The article, which included quite a thorough history for those unfamiliar with this particular family tree, was advance publicity for the album *Jewel in the Crown*.

SIMON: By far our wordiest album. Aside from the title track, it has both 'Slip Jigs and Reels' and 'The Naked Highwayman'.

Simon was full of praise for the composer of those two songs, Steve Tilston.

SIMON: Steve can write new songs that sound like traditional songs. I love it.

Fairport would regularly receive demos from aspiring songwriters, as well as cassettes from friends and fans suggesting things they believed might fit in the Fairport framework.

SIMON: Without wishing to denigrate anyone else's work, I suppose the most significant cassette of potential material to arrive was Steve Tilston's. Two copies arrived around the same time. It included Steve's original versions of 'The Naked Highwayman' and 'Slip Jigs and Reels' – both of which were big, challenging songs with lots of words (very typical of Steve's writing style) and great stories. They represented a challenge for me as a singer, but more importantly they were ideal Fairport material, as their popularity with audiences clearly proved later on.

I was aware of Steve as a writer and guitarist before that,

but those two songs were the start of a fruitful and continuing relationship between him and the band. He and Maggie Boyle recorded their next album at Woodworm Studios. I wasn't directly involved – I was somewhat surplus to requirements when you have a guitarist like Steve in the studio. We took 'Here's to Tom Paine' from that album and made it part of Fairport's set. Since then, we've done a number of Tilston songs, including 'Over the Next Hill'. There aren't many live Fairport sets that don't include one somewhere along the way. Top chap and great songwriter!

PEGGY: Steve's 'Rocky Road' has become a Fairport standard – by which I mean one of those songs we do and then rest for a bit, but always return to. For a band that spends most of its time touring, the song has words we relate to. It's another of those songs that gives everybody a turn at lead vocals.

Jewel in the Crown featured an impressive array of contemporary songwriters. As well as Julie Matthews and Steve Tilston, there were also songs by Jez Lowe, Ben Bennion, Rob Beattie, Huw Williams, Clive Gregson, the indefatigable Ralph McTell and Leonard Cohen – whose number was chosen for a particular reason.

PEGGY: We had a meeting with Wadsworth's Brewery about the bar at Cropredy. I think it was about brewing a unique Cropredy ale. Their managing director Fred West – no not *that* Fred West – was at the meeting and recommended a Leonard Cohen song to us. We wouldn't normally look for Fairport material on a Leonard Cohen album, but 'Closing Time' Fairport-ised perfectly. We added a few sound effects: Tracy from the office calling time, and the sound of Friday night at my local, The George at Barford St Michael.

Fairport had performed Leonard Cohen songs in their earliest incarnations, though these had not been officially released.

ASHLEY: We did 'Suzanne' and 'Bird on the Wire' before they became well-known. I believe we were the first act in the country to play Leonard Cohen songs, although people like Judy Collins had been playing them in the States.

The album also included 'The Islands' by Ralph McTell. Over the years, Ralph has "been more than generous, not just giving us songs but also employing us as session players,' says Peggy. In this case, the song came via a circuitous route. Ralph had been asked to provide music for *World Tour of Scotland* by his old friend Billy Connolly. The TV series, which had been a great success and was followed by similar *World Tours* of England, Australia and USA, as well as more specific personal travelogues, would 'use folk music in much the same way as rock was used in *Easy Rider'*. Ralph chose to record the songs at Woodworm, with Fairport as backing band. 'The Islands', co-written with Maart, would recur throughout the series, at one point being sung by Billy. Later series would again feature members of Fairport with soundtracks created by Chris Leslie.

BILLY CONNOLLY: Cropredy is great. I played there a couple of times. Fairport are sterling chaps, every one of them to a man. I can never see the phrase 'airport congestion' without thinking of them.

'Jewel in the Crown' is a subtle satire on the legacy of imperialism. Simon first encountered the song doing his 'other job'.

SIMON: The title track was one I had acquired through a period with The Albion Band. Julie Matthews is a remarkable songwriter and since she was already creating material for her solo albums, for her albums with Chris While and for The Albion Band, I think Fairport were lucky to get the song. It's both subtle and angry and that's quite an unusual combination. It makes the song challenging to perform. Certainly, it's one you don't want the audience to misinterpret.

Like all satires on British attitudes to the rest of the world, 'Jewel in the Crown' is open to being misunderstood, in the same way as the pronouncements of Alf Garnett or Noel Coward's 'Don't Let's Be Beastly to the Germans'.

SIMON: I was pleased fans rated the song so highly that they put it into the top 15 that we re-recorded for *By Popular Request*. It's the most recent song to have made that list.

PEGGY: The fact that there is nothing after *Jewel in the Crown* on that CD is because re-recording anything after that would effectively be asking the same line-up to do a song again. The results wouldn't be as interesting.

The *Mojo* article is a revealing piece, capturing Fairport in a candid mood as they began to tackle 'Slip Jigs and Reels' for *Jewel in the Crown*, which they knew would be an important album for them.

PEGGY: We'd barely rehearsed the song. Simon was still reading from the lyric sheet. As you know, it's a song with a lot of words and it cracks along at quite a pace – a real tongue twister. We were working on the arrangement, trying different approaches.

This is not how bands normally like to be seen, but this was not the first time Fairport had been reported on in the raw. Back in 1969, they had allowed *Rolling Stone* magazine open access to Farley Chamberlayne to observe the creation of *Liege & Lief*.

PEGGY: We just arranged a date [for *Mojo*] and went about our normal business.

'Normal business' starts in one of Fairport's favourite watering holes, the Joiner's Arms at Bloxham. Peggy isn't there; he's back at the office making phone calls to keep the forthcoming Festival on track. DM is away on tour, drumming for Everything But The Girl. Food and drink consumed, Ric, Maart, Simon and *Mojo* reporter Johnny Black take the short drive to Woodworm Studios where rehearsals and moments of grabbed informal interview begin.

The article describes four takes as the song takes shape. The session then breaks up. Peggy, studio-owner and *de facto* band manager, sets about securing cassette copies of the final take while Simon reads his *Daily Mail* and Maart tries to make the next level of Tetris (he's got as far as 13). That is a perfect snapshot of mid-1994-era Fairport Convention.

To his later embarrassment, the article then describes Ric's dad turning up to transport him home to Birmingham, as Peggy reminds him to take a cassette and "work on your fiddle part".

RIC: Not very rock 'n' roll, was it? It sounds like the school run, with me being given my homework!

Jewel in the Crown was released on Woodworm Records in January 1995. Not only had Fairport taken great pains recording the album, but post-production had also been meticulous. Fairport and Woodworm's Mark Tucker had done the original mix of the album before Fairport brought in the highly respected producer Gus Dudgeon to remix six tracks: 'Jewel in the Crown', 'Diamonds and Gold', 'The Naked Highwayman', 'The Islands', 'Red Tide' and 'Closing Time'. For those who enjoy comparative studies of folk-rock, the original mix of the last track is available on *A Box of Pegg's*.

The album is generally acknowledged as the best from the Woodworm era line-ups. The press release issued to the media implicitly confirms this by carefully setting the album in the context of their long career, effectively inviting comparison with what had gone before. One reviewer remarked that it was 'certainly their best album since *Nine* and possibly even better than that'. The press release, in typical Fairport style, ended by pointing out that Jewel in the Crown is also the name of their favourite Indian restaurant, which is shown on the cover.

Acoustic Routes

While Fairport worked on *Jewel in the Crown*, there was an unexpected renewed interest in the folk-rock genre. Not for the last time, *Mojo* magazine profiled it on one of its cover discs. Island Records released *Folk Routes*, a compilation which offered a succinct overview. Fairport past and present naturally dominated it: two tracks from the band, one apiece from Richard, Fotheringay, and The Bunch, two from Sandy's solo career, and four from Ashley Hutchings' various projects for the label. Ashley began the release of his *The Guv'nor* series, which brought together outtakes and other unreleased material from his different bands including, of course, Fairport.

On 12 January, 1995, Fairport Acoustic headed for Italy on a short tour. This latest permutation of the band – dismissively described in an early review as 'Fairport lite' – was a practical response to external pressures.

MAART: Touring as an acoustic four-piece had begun as a way of allowing the band to gig while DM was tied up with other commitments. It's a lot cheaper and easier to tour with just acoustic instruments. On a more creative level, it let us find a new way of doing some Fairport classics – as well as giving us space to play songs that might not have made it into the electric repertoire.

SIMON: The decision to go out as Fairport Acoustic was partly practical, but it also gave us a chance to revisit some old songs in a new way and play certain things we might not have with the full electric line-up.

They recorded their new acoustic material at Woodworm in September and October 1995, straight after Cropredy.

PEGGY: Partly, we were using the studio to try things out, using it as a convenient rehearsal space. It was obvious it was working, so we decided to record it.

Rather than record the older material they planned to include on the album in the studio, they chose to record it during an acoustic concert in Banbury on 30 December, 1995. Fairport performed one of their shortest ever Winter Tours at the start of 1996, which included a mere 17 dates. They nicknamed it The Tourette.
   Because it was easier and much cheaper for the acoustic line-up to tour, 1996 saw Fairport Acoustic playing not only a tour and one-off dates up and down the UK, but also taking their music further afield to Europe, Australia (documented on a live CD) and America.

PEGGY: Fairport Acoustic has proven very flexible. There was a time when I couldn't play with the band and so the acoustic line-up toured without me. We've also toured with the full five-piece. In 2011, Fairport Acoustic Convention opened proceedings at Cropredy.

CHRIS: A lot of people who come to see us at Cropredy may not have caught us during the year on tour so we always play a section of the Winter Tour set. In 2011, we realised that there were people in the field who had never experienced Fairport Acoustic and would have liked to.

SIMON: It's another of those Cropredy innovations. It felt good to be on first, and late afternoon on Thursday is not when you expect a big crowd: we were surprised how many people were already settled in, out on the field.

RIC: There's something of a tradition of opening proceedings at Cropredy with a local act – which is exactly what we did in 2011, if you think about it.

PEGGY: The acoustic set worked – and we'll be keeping it in as the Cropredy starter for a couple of years at least.

Old New...

In March 1996, Fairport Convention released a new album made up of acoustic live and studio recordings.

MAART: *Old New Borrowed Blue* would turn out to be my last album as a member of Fairport Convention.

Maart left in December 1996, although he has joined the band at Cropredy almost every year since then.

MAART: Once you've been part of Cropredy... been on that stage, in front of that crowd... it's something you miss. I'm lucky that Fairport ask me back year after year.

Chris Leslie joined the band, although not as a replacement for Maart.

SIMON: I don't know whether it was a different direction so much as a return to the approach we had had after Swarb had joined.

PEGGY: In a way, Chris was like a delayed replacement for Swarb.

This should be seen *not* as a criticism of Ric, but as a reflection of the many roles Swarb had fulfilled in Fairport. Aside from playing his fiddle, Swarb had played viola and mandolin, was one of the group's lead vocalists, and their main songwriter. That could just as easily be a description of the various roles Chris Leslie has come to fulfil within the band. In March 1998, Fairport had its third (and, to date, last) line-up change since regrouping in 1985. Dave Mattacks left the band, in order to move artistically and geographically into new areas.

SIMON: DM has the unique distinction of being the only person to have joined and left Fairport three times. Eventually, he moved to Boston, Massachussetts, which would have been inconvenient even by Swarbrick standards.

PEGGY: When DM decided to leave, Gerry Conway was his natural replacement. It seemed as if both he and Chris were obvious choices. You kind of thought, "Why aren't they in the band already?"

GERRY: It was Sandy Denny who first introduced me to folk music. That was in 1970. I'd only been playing a few years and had played all kinds of music – pop, soul, light rock. I was in Eclection who played soft rock, but you couldn't really say there was any major folk influence. Then Sandy asked me to join Fotheringay and suddenly we were playing the folkie songs she and Trevor were writing, and arrangements of full-on, honest-to-goodness trad arr.

Fotheringay's only album (their second would not be released until 2008) has only one traditional track, an epic version of 'Banks of the Nile' which *Rolling Stone* summed up with the words 'quite simply the best rock arrangement, ever'. Their unreleased recordings included much more traditional material: Australian songs like 'Bold Jack Donahue'; Scottish ballads such as 'Gypsy Davy', 'Eppie Moray', and 'Wild Mountain Thyme'; plus the English ballad 'Lord Bateman'. The band played even more trad arr numbers live, including some that Sandy had recorded or sung with Fairport.

GERRY: Fotheringay was short-lived, and I went back to playing other kinds of music. That included a long period in Cat Stevens' band. So, 30 odd years later, I found myself back playing the same kind of music and in some cases the very same songs. It felt like a complete circle – and a very nice one, too.

Gerry had, of course, maintained a close association with Fairport and its various offshoots over the years. He had been a session drummer on a couple of Fairport albums, as well as having played with Sandy, Richard, Simon and Ashley. He was a regular, on and offstage, at Cropredy.

GERRY: Dave Mattacks and I go back quite a long way. Of all the drummers I've known, I've spent the most time with DM. We go for a drummers' night out to see Billy Cobham or Elvin Jones, someone like that at Ronnie Scott's. Whenever I was at Cropredy, DM was gracious enough to invite me on stage to play.

One naturally thinks of the powerhouse sound of twin drums, and there were certainly plenty of those. However, it was a very different style of double drumming that would provide Gerry's personal highlight.

GERRY: I remember particularly a version of 'Who Knows Where the Time Goes' that we played on.

That was one of the key moments of Gerry's first Cropredy as a band member. With Chris While taking lead vocals, it appeared on the *Cropredy '99* CD. Before that, there had been a UK tour during which Gerry had been thrown in at the deep end.

GERRY: One of the first gigs I did with them was at Birmingham's Symphony Hall. Peggy thought letting me introduce the special guests would be a good way to introduce me to Fairport's audience. I didn't like to say I had never spoken in front of a microphone before. I had never said anything from the stage. They said, "It's simple, just walk up and introduce Steve Gibbons and P J Wright." As I left the drum-kit, my legs turned to jelly. I did make it to the microphone but then said something like, "Please welcome P J Proby and Steve Wright."

Drawing In

As the century drew to a close the final gaps in the CD reissue of Fairport's back catalogue were plugged. The 'reissues of reissues' compilations that would annoy many of their fans began to appear then too. *Close to the Wind* was comprised of tracks from *Red & Gold* and *The Five Seasons*, released by Mooncrest who had leased them from HTD, who in turn had leased them from Woodworm. It was also released in a short-lived format – the audio DVD – which allegedly, if not audibly, provided better quality and space for additional data such as track notes and lyrics (which were woefully inaccurate). There was nothing to indicate the tracks had been issued before (in some cases on four separate occasions), leave alone where they came from.

PEGGY: Someone once complained to me about having been diddled into buying exactly the same stuff twice. I asked him if he hadn't realised it when he looked at the tracklist and he told me that he hadn't realised because he doesn't listen to our newer albums much. I leave you to draw your own conclusions.

In total contrast, *Fiddlestix*, a careful Australian compilation from exactly a year later (May 1999), made it clear that it was issuing previously available material. Essentially, it plugged the gap between *History of…* and *The Woodworm Years*, but also added some rare tracks and a lengthy unreleased live instrumental. Those two releases – *Close to the Wind* and *Fiddlestix* – represent the way things would go with Fairport's recorded output over the next decade. There would be some thoughtful and often indispensible compilations, some of which were so well put together that they were worth having even when one already owned most of the tracks. Then there would be others sequenced in a way that is best described as arbitrary and whose packaging was, to be kind, lackadaisical, though some might say it was consciously deceptive.

PEGGY: It's a sore point and I don't think those Nineties' compilations can really be said to be part of the band's history. If anything, they would be part of the history of Woodworm as a small record company.

RIC: There is one simple answer: buy the proper albums and you won't need to get anything else.

SIMON: The random reissue situation is one we hope to avoid with the Matty Grooves-released recordings. Between *Who Knows Where the Time Goes* in June 1997 and 1999's *The Wood and the Wire*, 12 different Fairport albums appeared: two recordings from Cropredy, an in-depth retrospective and a more economical *Introduction to...* issued by Island, and other straight reissues on CD. If nothing else, it was proof positive that Fairport were truly a going concern.

Violins

Violins are a key aspect of Fairport's sound, played solo, in duet, and multi-tracked. They have been featured as acoustic, electric, and processed through a battery of effects pedals. Fiddles have been heard low in the mix and leading the sound. It all began, of course, with Dave Swarbrick.

CHRIS: Hearing *Liege & Lief* sent me down to Osborne's music shop in Banbury where I bought an Egmond guitar pick-up to attach, somehow, on to my fiddle. I know this must have been happening to fiddlers all over the country.

The violin had always been an integral, if not central, part of Fairport's sound, even before Swarb joined. Martin Lamble had listed his 'instruments played' as drums, percussion, piano and violin, and Simon Nicol played fiddle on Fairport's first two albums.

SIMON: All right, I admit it: I was Fairport's first fiddler. I was experimenting then, more or less successfully, with a number of instruments, because being a multi-instrumentalist was the thing to be at the time. Richard made a jokey reference to it in the *Full House* credits. I wouldn't claim to be a true player of anything but the guitar, and there are few other instruments I have ever played seriously outside a recording studio where, of course, if you get it wrong you can go back and do it again.

ASHLEY: Simon does some experimental scraping on the first album. It's low in the mix, generally, and pretty easy to miss. You can hear him playing a kind of drone part on 'Nottamun Town', which really contributes to the feel of the track.

SIMON: All right – I could do atmospherics. When we wanted proper fiddle playing, we hired in a proper fiddle player. I didn't play fiddle with Fairport after that.

This is not strictly true: Peggy, Simon and Swarb all played fiddles on an odd instrumental entitled, for the purposes of release, 'Bridge Over the River Ash'.

SWARB: It was a live thing really. We started playing it when Richard was in the band. It had a certain impact when you saw people you expected to play guitar picking up a viola or a violin. It was a sort of joke, and if the playing went wrong it really didn't matter. We recorded 'Bridge Over the River Ash' after Richard left, when we were looking for things to include on *Angel Delight*.

'Bridge Over the River Ash' is unlike Fairport's other instrumentals in that its roots are not in folk tunes but in chamber music. This has been picked up in various stage announcements over the years. Simon has claimed it shows "Our Bach is worse than our bite"; Swarb has claimed it was originally composed by "Alfred, Lord Mozart"; while Maart once pointed out it is one of Fairport's two connections with Vivaldi.

MAART: At the end of the Eighties, Nigel Kennedy made a recording of *The Four Seasons*, which became the biggest-selling classical album of all time. It was top of the [classical] charts for months. So we called our next album *The Five Seasons*, which was one better.

The title 'Bridge Over the River Ash' was arbitrary, designed to be modified to suit the place where it was being performed.

PEGGY: Most English towns and cities are built on a river, so we'd try to remember to find out what it was and use it during the performance. Sometimes, we'd end up asking the audience before we played it.

The River Ash of the title flowed through the Hertfordshire village of Little Hadham, where Fairport had been living at the time of its composition.

PEGGY: The river ran past the back garden which you can see in the photo inside *Full House*. Not, it has to be said, the best-tended property in the area. The bridge itself was about 15 yards down the road from our front door.

Fairport reintroduced this little fiddle extravaganza on their Farewell Tour, a version of which can be found on the live souvenir album of that tour. It had occasionally resurfaced at Cropredy where it has been introduced by a brief excerpt from a familiar piece of music: a snatch of Mozart, 'Air on a G String', 'Whole Lotta Love' or 'Barwick Green' – the theme from The Archers.

SIMON: Once we had two actual fiddle players in the group, it became a bit pointless to play it. It was never intended to be performed by people who knew how to to play it properly.

Once Fairport discovered their distinctive, fiddle-based sound early in 1969, however, they were keen that it be considered as an essential part of the band's music.

ASHLEY: When we did the session for *Top Gear* [in 1969], Swarb wasn't available, so we asked Ric Grech to play.

Ric Grech was the bass player with Family, a band which had come into prominence around the time Fairport played their first gig. He also played the violin, viola and cello. When he stepped in to play that radio session with Fairport, he had been in a somewhat confused state.

RIC GRECH: I've seen it in biographies of Fairport that I had been considered for the band. That couldn't be further from the truth. I had quite enough on my plate as it was. I was in Family and wanted to get out of that to join Blind Faith; *they* were keen to start rehearsing and I was worried that if I wasn't available they'd find somebody else. Also, my drinking was starting to be a problem for me.

ASHLEY: There were lots of things we could have played [on *Top Gear*]. In fact, it was very unusual for us to be playing things on the radio that we were about to release. The fact that we picked two of the songs Swarb had played on rather than something else off the album indicates how committed Fairport were to making the fiddle part of its sound.

RIC: There were very few people playing fiddle in a rock setting then. There were David LaFlamme and Jerry Goodman, but they were both Americans. Swarb was somebody I could relate to. That was what inspired me to start playing the fiddle.

LaFlamme played with It's a Beautiful Day, Goodman with The Flock. Along with Papa John Creach of Jefferson Airplane, Fairport introduced the electric violin into rock music in the late Sixties – a rare and relatively arcane instrument. Most of its exponents were blues and country musicians who, at that time, were more or less unknown to British audiences. While Stuff Smith is usually reckoned to be the first person to play one, Arkansas fiddler Eck Robertson (who wrote the 'Brilliancy Medley') deserves mention too. A great innovator who spent months developing devices to produce special effects on his fiddle (including a tube positioned to make it appear to talk), he embraced the idea of amplifying his instrument and modifying the sound. "I play the fiddle, but I also play with the fiddle," he once told Mike Seeger. His attitude quite obviously applied to the approach of both Swarb and his successor Ric.

ASHLEY: What was fascinating about the way *Liege & Lief* developed was Swarb's process of discovery. People might assume that because he came from a folk background he was on familiar territory. In fact, he had to learn all manner of things, not least what could be done with the electric violin and how it fits in with the other instruments in a rock band.

RIC: Swarb was quite an influence on a nation of aspiring folk-rock fiddlers. We'd all gone back to his album *Rags, Reels &*

Airs. It was like a masterclass – every tune you needed to know. Each new album with Fairport seemed packed with things that made you ask: "How's he doing that?"

Swarb and Fairport triggered Ric's lifelong love of the violin. He even got himself a job in Thomas Smith Violins in Birmingham.

RIC: It was here I first met my hero. One quiet afternoon Mike Burnham, my boss and friend, was out and I was minding the shop. The door opened and in walked Swarb, with the longest hair anybody I'd ever met had had. He tried a few fiddles and I ended up selling him one. The bridge was not to his liking so he asked me to change it. Mike had shown me how to fit a bridge, but I'm no Chris Leslie and my hands were shaking. My three failed attempts resulted in bridges that looked as if they had been fitted by Salvador Dali. Swarb was very understanding and agreed to take a couple of blank bridges away and do it himself.

ASHLEY: When Swarb joined, Fairport discovered a distinctive sound that was entirely new. It was a true electric folk element, which has been much imitated since although, in my opinion, no one has got it more right than Fairport did in the last six months of 1969.

CHRIS: *Rags, Reels & Airs* was the ultimate fiddle reference work. No songs and a huge collection of tunes, all played by the best contemporary player. *Liege & Lief* was voted the most influential folk album of all time, quite rightly. In a more focused way, Swarb's album was to be just as influential.

The album had 18 tracks, ten of which were medleys. Fairport fans would recognise many of the tunes instantly, not from the ceilidh context Swarb had found them in, but from the Fairport tune sets in which he would reset them.

SIMON: Bands playing sets of jigs and reels are now so commonplace that no one really remembers what a radical step it was when Fairport did it for the very first time on *Liege & Lief*. That was Swarb's single greatest contribution.

BERYL MARRIOTT: The set of tunes on that LP actually caused more of a stir than the songs. The dance side of the English Folk Dance and Song Society has always been more conservative than its singers. Swarb had already raised eyebrows when he played with my Ceilidh Band because of his jazzy approach. When he played those revered tunes with a rock band on an amplified fiddle, it was too much for some.

CHRIS: The *Liege & Lief* medley, 'Lark in the Morning' and the rest – that was the first time that had been done. It's been imitated countless times since, including a dozen or so by Fairport, but never bettered.

MARTIN CARTHY: Swarb and I used to play sets of tunes, especially if we were doing long late-night sets at the Troubadour or a folk festival. It's what always happened in sessions where players could go on for hours moving from tune to tune. With Fairport, Swarb took that whole concept into a rock context.

RIC: It was a time when lots of self-indulgent jamming took place. But listen to Cream or the Grateful Dead or Ten Years After and you'll see what Swarb was doing was entirely different. It was precise controlled musicianship.

When Joe Boyd asked Swarb to record with Fairport, it wasn't assumed by anyone who knew the fiddler that he'd agree to do any more than that one recording.

MARTIN CARTHY: I was surprised he did it. His first reaction, typically Swarb, was "I fuckin' 'ate rock music." He agreed, I think, because the money was good. He returned so impressed with Richard Thompson that he knew he wanted to carry on playing with him. I think the hyperbole in this case was "I want to play with him for the rest of my life."

Dave Swarbrick became such a dominant figure in the story of Fairport through the Seventies that it is easy to overlook the fact that there was, briefly, another fiddle player in the band.

SIMON: It was the line-up just before I rejoined the band. It tends to be forgotten about because it never recorded. There are a couple of live recordings doing the rounds among hard-core fans, but that's about it.

SWARB: I was looking for a six-piece band and I thought, "What's better than a fiddle? Two fiddles!" To be honest, until we started playing together, I'd had no idea how it would sound.

Swarb had met Roger Burridge at the Sidmouth Folk Festival. Impressed with his obvious talent, he agreed to give him some violin lessons. Eventually Swarb decided his protégé was good enough to join the band. An interviewer at the time raised the awkward subject of the band's live debut at the Southend Festival, which had coincided with the release of a new album on which 'half the new band make a very limited contribution'.

Gottle O'Geer, the album in question, gave absolutely no indication of what the new Fairport sounded like. Bob and Roger provided backing vocals on one track; Dan Ar Braz did not appear at all. Their debut gig at Roots Hall, the home of Southend United FC, was followed by an eight-night tour of venues in the south of England, interrupted by five nights playing in Holland.

Very few Fairport fans ever got to see that line-up. Geography and bad publicity were an issue, but equally so were some of the gigs they played – three were festivals, two were Oxbridge May balls, three were in small clubs with limited capacity, two of which made Fairport's appearance members-only nights.

So Roger Burridge became Fairport's 'forgotten fiddler'. The line-up lasted less than six months, with a couple of radio broadcasts being all we have to remember them by. Anyone expecting spectacular fiddle duets (such as Ric Sanders and Chris Leslie would later perform) would be disappointed. Burridge played lead violin in order that Swarb could concentrate on vocal duties. Half the band's set was instrumental and Roger played second fiddle to Swarb on those.

SWARB: No reflection on Roger. If we'd had more time we'd have done more things that allowed him to display his talent.

When that version of Fairport fell apart, as it inevitably did, Roger accepted Dan Ar Braz's suggestion that he join him in becoming

334

a member of Alan Stivell's group. So Roger ended up playing the fiddle parts that Swarb had provided on the previous occasion the Breton harpist had toured the UK. Meanwhile, being a member of Fairport hadn't ended Dave Swarbrick's solo career.

SWARB: I wanted to make another solo album. Not just an instrumental set but one with a couple of songs as well. There was a point where I began to feel trapped. It seemed everyone else in the band had quit to do their own thing and there was I stuck with being Fairport.

Swarb had had two shots at making a solo album. On each occasion the project had been hijacked part way through with the record company insisting it become a Fairport Convention album.

SWARB: When the contract with Island came to an end, I made sure I was in a position to make my own LPs. I signed a deal with Transatlantic.

Topic, Transatlantic and Island were the three most successful British labels for folk music in the UK. They had proper distribution deals and access to airplay on national radio. Topic was the purist label, recording significant singers who were firmly rooted in the tradition. Swarb had contributed to Topic albums by A L Lloyd and Ian Campbell.

Transatlantic had signed the Ian Campbell Folk Group while Swarb was still a member. Its folk catalogue consisted mainly of singer-songwriters, but it acted as distributor for Trailer and Leader, two labels offering more traditional, and credible, fare.

Island moved into the rockier end of the market and signed up some of the country's coolest singer-songwriters like Nick Drake and John Martyn.

Under his deal with Transatlantic, Swarb made six albums, although the changing ownership of Transatlantic over those years resulted in their being released on four different labels.

The first two releases, *Swarbrick* and *Swarbrick 2*, brought together many of Swarb's influences and collaborations, including his long-standing duo with Martin Carthy, his more recent duo with Simon Nicol, and Beryl Marriott's Ceilidh Group (enhanced by Dave Pegg and Bruce Rowland). They also offered a glimpse of the work he was doing in Scotland with the clarsach player Savourna Stevenson.

SWARB: The albums were recorded in pairs. All the sessions for both albums at one time. That meant I could have a bigger selection of musicians joining me. Fairport were obviously part of that.

The subsequent pair of albums, *Lift the Lid and Listen* and *The Ceilidh Album* were by Dave Swarbrick and friends. Those friends included the three other members of Fairport, uncredited, on some tracks. Finally, the sessions for *Smiddyburn* and *Flittin'* were dominated by Fairport. In fact, two versions of Fairport appeared – the current Rowland, Pegg and Nicol line-up, and the *Full House* line-up with Pegg, Nicol, Richard Thompson and Dave Mattacks. Those six albums contain only one vocal track, which was the final song on *Smiddyburn*, named after Swarb's new home in Aberdeenshire. A reconvened *Full House* line-up, with Swarb singing, performed a version of Sandy Denny's 'It Suits Me Well', which is so close to being a lost Fairport track that it has appeared on a couple of compilations as a release by the band.

Swarb And After

SIMON: Swarb and I began playing as a duo whenever there was a gap in Fairport's schedule, but it became a more serious partnership in the Eighties when Fairport had temporarily ceased to exist.

SWARB: One of our gigs at The White Bear, Masham, was recorded for transmission by the BBC and would become the first Swarbrick/Nicol LP.

SIMON: The pub had a loyal following, not just local people, but people like Swarbrick and me who would have the opportunity to visit it once or twice a year. Among them was a fiddle player from the BBC Northern Chamber Orchestra called Baz Barker, who also did a bit of production work for BBC local radio. He and Swarb used to get on really well, swapping tunes and so on. So he borrowed a Revox and a couple of mics and recorded our gig there. He thought it would be nice to make a little programme out of what we did. It was broadcast and well received. Somehow the tapes found their way into Neil Cutts' hands. He had a few hundred LPs pressed up, and used to sell them over the bar. I think it was the only release on White Bear Records. It was most definitely a fun night, as you can tell from the album.

Because the album – little more than a bootleg – had very limited availability, Simon and Swarb went into Peggy's Woodworm Studios and recorded a very similar set, based around Swarb's solo albums and the last Fairport studio recordings. Confusingly, it came out (on cassette only) under the punning title *In the Club* – giving the impression it was live.

PEGGY: The fact that Fairporters and close friends had things they wanted to use the studio for gave us the chance to try it out and make sure everything worked correctly. We'd moved from Cropredy to Barford St Michael, which is on the other side of Banbury. The new property gave us a chance to build a proper studio in the disused chapel. Swarb and Simon's album was the first thing recorded there.

The duo would return to the studio in 1994 to record *Close to the Wind*.

SIMON: Really, this was our first album. This would be a properly recorded, properly released LP on a proper record label.

Close to the Wind was the sixth release on Woodworm Records, by now releasing albums by acts not directly connected to Fairport. Most recent releases were by Carrig and The Hookey Band, which included Chris Leslie. The album was produced by Simon and engineered by Peggy. Peggy and DM, who played drums, keyboards and washboard, joined Simon and Swarb on a couple of tracks.

SIMON: Peggy might have played on it more, but he was busy operating the desk.

337

SWARB: It was the last time Fairport worked together in the studio. Those tracks, to me, are the end of Fairport.

The album's title track migrated into the new Fairport's early set and eventually appeared on *In Real Time* (1987).

SIMON: Stuart Marson is a local songwriter from Northamptonshire. I recorded his song 'Close to the Wind' with Swarb and it's been added to Fairport's live repertoire. I used 'Over the Lancashire Hills', his tribute to Kathleen Ferrier, as the opening track on my first solo album. The band on that track is Peggy, DM and me – essentially the Fairport line-up that had made *Gladys' Leap* – an example of a song I kept back from the band's repertoire. It's one of the songs that Fairport could easily have recorded – though in a way, I suppose they did!

SIMON: By 1985, Fairport without a fiddle player was proving impossible. So, yet again, Fairport brought in a guest fiddler who immediately became one of the band.

RIC: People assume that my Albion Band connections with Simon was the reason I was asked to play on *Gladys' Leap*. In fact Peggy and I go much further back and I was also a big Fairport fan. I didn't need to be asked twice!

SIMON: In that gap where the band was having a lie down – between the Farewell gig in '79 and the release of *Gladys' Leap* in 1985 – Fairport were increasingly busy. Although Swarb participated in short tours, he and the band were drifting apart.

PEGGY: We didn't consciously exclude Swarb. He had other commitments.

RIC: It was obvious that Fairport should exist in some form now the band had a new album out. As I played on the album I was asked whether I would like to join. Of course, I was delighted, but I was also nervous. Being asked to play fiddle for Fairport is rather like being asked to replace Miles Davis on trumpet.

Having honed his skills playing along to Swarbrick's jigs and reels, Ric had at least got a working knowledge of core Fairport material.

RIC: At first Fairport played stuff from the late Seventies. I was delighted when eventually they decided to go back and play more of the old stuff. I didn't think it was right that all that classic back catalogue material should only ever get played at Cropredy.

As a member of both The Albion Band and Soft Machine, Ric was at once a graduate of Ashley Hutchings' academy of folk-rock and a prog improviser suited to the rockier direction that Fairport were about to take.

RIC: Swarb is a great folk fiddler, but he also loved his toys – his effects pedals. I'd listen to him play and try to figure out how he was doing it. Then I'd add it to what I played.

Ric quickly stamped his own impression on Fairport's sound. His playing might be understated and consciously folkie, as in 'The Hiring Fair' and his own gentle airs like 'Portmeirion'. On the other hand, phasing and wah-wah could distort his sound beyond recognition, while adding delay allowed him to play layered fiddle parts live, effectively becoming two fiddlers. There are several Fairport instrumental breaks which sound like a lead guitar but actually emanate from Ric's four strings and a bow; his use of effects is best heard in the piece usually referred to as 'Cosmic Intermezzo (PDC)'.

RIC: One of the great things about Fairport fans is how open-minded they are. They'll sit and listen to jazz improvisation right after a fairly straight take on an old folk song.

SIMON: If you look at the stage, it tells you a lot about Fairport. DM behind his kit at the back. Over stage left is Maart, with his keyboards and guitars and gizmos, neat and orderly and packed into a relatively small space. Then centre left is the space occupied by Peggy and myself. But the right-hand side of the stage is left clear for Ric, who needs more room than the Concorde for controls and pedals, but also likes to move around a lot. He has to be able to get to the drum riser, which he likes to leap off at some point, and uses the full depth and width of half the stage. It's a sort of fiddle player's adventure playground.

PEGGY: He injected a lot of energy into Fairport, which we needed at that point. We had to change gear from being the band that met for this great gig once a year to a real, functioning, working rock group. He also really believes in Fairport – he's never stopped being a fan. He is, of course, the first Fairport you see at a gig because he's the one that comes on, welcomes people and announces the support act. Finally, he's the only one of us that's any good at telling jokes on stage.

MAART: Ric and I had grown up with Fairport and neither of us minded admitting we were fans. We were the lead players and, being musical experimenters, we filled out the sound. Some of the stuff Ric used to do was jaw-dropping, confusing but brilliant.

PEGGY: Ric's a great fiddle player – exactly the right person to have come in after Swarb. There are probably lots of people who could have joined and done a great Swarb impression, but Ricky made sure we moved forward.

26 JULY, 1992
CHIPPING NORTON

Somewhat the worse for wear late one night, Ric lost his balance and fell through a plate glass window. Putting out his left arm to steady himself, he cut several tendons. Faced with what could well have been career-ending injuries, he did his best to remain optimistic. The piece he wrote for the programme – "Well, dictated, under the circumstances," as he put it – explained why he was the right person to be Fairport's fiddler:

RIC: 'Even though I can't play this year, I wouldn't be anywhere else but at Cropredy, just as I always was in the years before I joined the band. Whether on stage or off, it's great to be part of the wonderful family, the band and the audience, that has made Fairport Convention what it has been for the past 25 years.'

Ric developed one-handed keyboard parts, including one for 'The Rose Hip', which he had "written as a fiddle duet for myself". At Cropredy, he had taken to bringing on Chris Leslie so that it could be played as intended. He also, as he later remarked, "perfected the one-handed tambourine: highly appropriate when the person standing in for you is a Buddhist". Finally, he took on the role of compere for both evenings.

RIC: I had to brush up on my Fairport history. When you're speaking to the Cropredy crowd, you don't want to attribute a track to the wrong album 'cos you'll get several thousand voices correcting you.

The expertise of his surgeon, David Coleman of the Radcliffe Infirmary, saved Ric's hand and eventually he was able to return to playing fiddle.

RIC: It was good therapy, in fact. I knew what my fingers had to do and I had to make them do it.

As usual, Ric's approach to dealing with this near disaster was to resort to wry humour. For a time, it became a key element of his stage patter. The fact his surgeon shared a name with a famous sports broadcaster was one obvious source of humour: "They thought it was all over, but it isn't now." It was a "pane in the glass"; it allowed him to conjecture on a song called 'The Window [*sic*] of Westmoreland's Daughter'; he even told of an encounter that night in the hospital with someone similarly injured: "I was sympathetic and asked what had happened. He replied, 'I'm a glazier. Some silly bastard fell through a plate glass window and I cut myself trying to fix it in the dark.'"

Naturally polite and courteous, though driven by a fireball energy which can make him seem abrupt and staccato, Ric concluded his piece in the Fairport programme with a sincere set of thanks to his parents, his friends, his medical team, and also 'My special love and thanks to all the other members of Fairport and their wives and, of course, to my dear friend, Chris Leslie.'

Chris Leslie had gamely stepped into the breach, joining Fairport for a gig three days after Ric's accident. Playing a few gigs was one thing. Cropredy was quite another, though.

This was no ordinary Cropredy either, of course. The setlist included 61 songs spanning the band's entire career. As well as Fairport classics, there were songs rarely heard and tracks from solo albums, including Simon's recently completed second LP *Consonant Please Carol*. Playing them would be an impressive assemblage of ex-members – Swarb, Richard Thompson, Jerry Donahue and Ashley. DM, Gerry Conway and Bruce Rowland created a powerhouse of three drummers. There was also a stunning array of guest singers.

CHRIS: Was I nervous? I was glancing from the enormous setlist to the list of guest players, of which I was one. It was incredible. I was just glad that Swarb was going to be there for a big chunk of the Saturday set!

'The Rose Hip' became a solo performance after all, with Ric gamely accompanying on one-handed piano.

PEGGY: Just to pile on the pressure, we'd planned to record both nights for the first-ever Cropredy Fairport CD.

RIC: It was a weird year. Just take a look at the photos and see the expression I am wearing half the time. I was a sort of continuity announcer: I love chatting to the audience, but you can't simply chat to an audience that size. Still, it was very kind of Peggy. I was grateful he gave me something to do and kept me part of the one Cropredy I wasn't able to play.

The 25th Anniversary Concert was Woodworm Records' 22nd release. It featured Chris on just under half of the album's 25 tracks. It included a dozen songs that Fairport would return to and re-record in the studio, after Chris joined the band. The album was 'dedicated to Chris Leslie with much thanks from Fairport for saving our festival'.

For Chris's Sake

Chris was back with Fairport in '92, performing a duet with Ric and playing a track from Fairport's last CD, 'I Wandered by a Brookside'. In 1995, he put on his cocktail cowboy hat for one last time, before which his featured fiddle duet had been a lovely version of Ric's 'Summer in December'.

The following year was to be Chris's last as a Cropredy guest. As well as a brief appearance with Fairport, he also appeared with Beryl Marriott on the Friday afternoon. Their set was an unexpected treat as the stage gradually filled with guests from Fairport.

Later in 1996, following a demanding American tour, Maartin Allcock returned to the UK determined to leave Fairport, just as Simon Nicol had done almost a quarter of a century earlier.

MAART: I realised I was missing my family and I had my own projects that I wanted time to work on.

PEGGY: We'd been all over and everywhere and worked real hard. I'm afraid it took its toll. We had some strained relationships.

SIMON: There were individuals in the band that Maart simply wasn't getting on with. The feeling was mutual. By leaving, he was able to stay friends with the band and we've worked closely with him on several occasions, especially at Cropredy which he attends every year.

Chris joined Fairport as an official full-time band member for their Winter Tour.

RIC: Fairport's sound had changed. It was heavier and more dominated by keyboards. Bringing Chris in took us back to the more typical Fairport sound. Partly, that was to do with instruments, but also his folk background.

SIMON: Local lad, you know. Fairport became a bit less Brum and a bit more rural Oxfordshire.

PEGGY: When Chris joined, a lot was made of the fact that

Fairport had a twin fiddle line-up – not for the first time. More importantly, Chris is a great multi-instrumentalist. He's also a really good songwriter and that naturally made a difference because we could start recording our own songs again.

SIMON: On a purely personal level, it meant the burden of singing lead vocals was shared. It was an added bonus when we discovered, a couple of years in, that Chris's voice was perfectly suited to Swarb's songs. That was great because it opened up a whole new area of our back catalogue to us.

PEGGY: When Maart decided to leave [in 1996], we wanted to take the opportunity to change the sound of the band, to become more 'folkie' again. Chris had played with us so often as part of Fairport and on other projects, he was an obvious choice. He was also a great friend of Ric's and they were, and are, brilliant when they play together.

SIMON: I don't think we so much asked Chris to join Fairport as simply assumed he would. It was that natural.

Chris joined Simon, Peggy, Ric and DM in the band at the end of November 1996, and his influence on the direction Fairport has taken subsequently cannot be overestimated.

PEGGY: Chris is a very prolific songwriter. Having an in-house songwriter made it feel almost like being back at The Angel. Whenever Chris turned up you wondered whether he'd have a new song with him.

Although Chris's writing would dominate Fairport's later albums, on his first with them, *Who Knows Where the Time Goes*, he provided only two – 'John Gaudie' and 'Spanish Main' – which he had written with Maartin Allcock. Both were old songs. In an interview given in 1996, Maart also mentioned "a song on *Old New Borrowed Blue* that I wrote with Chris Leslie," meaning 'Lalla Rookh'. Its inspiration was the story of the last native Tasmanian, the subject of a poem by Thomas Moore, loosely based on an ancient Persian legend.

    By the time he became a full-time member of the band, Chris had been on the fringes of Fairport for two decades. In 1977, he and his brother John had appeared at the village fete at Prescote Manor with the band. Fairport had collected 'The Eynsham Poacher' from John and included it on *The Bonny Bunch of Roses* that same year. It remained part of their repertoire from that point on and Chris can be heard playing it with them on the live album from Cropredy, 2008 – 30 years later. Chris had also been back at Cropredy, supporting Fairport, in 1979 as part of a duo with Steve Ashley. Simon, Bruce and Peggy had joined them on stage for a couple of numbers while Ric Sanders had watched from the audience. The duo returned in 1981, promoting Steve's new album, *Demo Tapes*, recorded at Woodworm Studios; Chris joined Simon, Peggy and Bruce to back Steve on the cassette-only release. From 1980 onwards, Chris became a regular member of Captain Coco's Country Dance Band at Cropredy.

It was not until 1983, however, that Chris would fulfil his dream of becoming a full-time professional musician. He did so via Dave Swarbrick who, after setting up home in Preston Capes, a small village south of Daventry, formed an acoustic group. Martin Jenkins, Kevin Dempsey and Chris joined Swarb to create Whippersnapper.

CHRIS: Peggy had introduced me to Swarb in 1977, and we had played some tunes together. From time to time he would invite me to play with Beryl Marriott's Ceilidh Band, and Fairport. Eventually, he told me he was thinking of forming an acoustic group and asked me whether I would like to join full-time. We rehearsed together for nearly a year.

Whippersnapper's debut performance had been at The Burnt Post, Coventry, on 15 January, 1984.

SWARB: We had a good first year. We played both the Cropredy and Cambridge Festivals. The Cambridge gig was filmed and released as a video, before our first album came out.

CHRIS: Whippersnapper was a great band. I was playing with three top class musicians and got to play fiddle duets with Swarb in front of some huge crowds. It was great apprenticeship for when I joined Fairport.

It was during Whippersnapper's set in 1984 that 'John Gaudie'

345

made its Cropredy debut. The band returned the following year and again in 1987, just before Swarb left the band.

CHRIS: We carried on as a trio for another couple of years, and then for a couple more as a duo with Kevin, before I was invited to join The Albion Band, who were an all-acoustic quartet at that point. I joined as Simon Nicol's replacement.

All along, Chris was moving ever deeper into Fairport's orbit. He would occasionally be asked to play on a number of recordings made at their home studio.

PEGGY: After Fairport's *Moat on the Ledge* and Steve Ashley's *Family Album*, Woodworm Records' third release was my solo LP.

The Cocktail Cowboy Goes It Alone (1983) was a truly solo album. Despite having a whole crowd of friends he could call on, Peggy's album was a do-it-yourself affair, recorded on Woodworm's eight-track TEAC.

PEGGY: I played every instrument. Partly I was teaching myself how to use the studio. If I messed it up, it wouldn't matter. The problem was, there was no way I could play it live. I needed a band to go out and play the stuff live. I had the same problem as Mike Oldfield – rather a different level of sales, though.

Peggy's Cocktail Cowboys played only a handful of gigs and reunited briefly for one song at Cropredy in 1995: aside from Peggy, the band included guitarists Andrew Loake and Neil Gauntlett, Simon Graty on keyboards, and Chris Leslie. Trevor Foster was the original drummer: when he left to join The Albion Band, Gerry Conway took over the drummer's stool.

RIC: The year that we brought on Chris at Cropredy and were able to play 'The Rose Hip' together, I think I knew as we played that if ever there were any way of Chris joining the band, it would be what I wanted. When he did eventually join, a few years later, I wrote a duet called 'The Bowman's Retreat' in celebration.

Maart's parting gesture upon leaving Fairport was to 'Wish my best to my replacement Chris Leslie, one of the finest musicians I have ever had the pleasure to meet.' His remarks appeared in the Winter Tour programme, which marked Fairport's 30th anniversary.

Fiddlestix

Chris came to the band with a great song. Fairport's *Who Knows Where the Time Goes?* album, released in June 1997, opened with his 'John Gaudie'.

CHRIS: I first recorded it with Whippersnapper [in 1984]. It's a true story, though it's acquired something of a legendary status.

SIMON: 'John Gaudie' has got a strong story – 'based on actual events' – and blinding instrumental passages which head off in all kinds of directions to include tunes which allegedly John Gaudie wrote. It's a natural for Fairport.

CHRIS: I love biographies. The story of John Gaudie caught my imagination the first time I heard it. He was hit on the head by a rival in love, and suffered epileptic fits after that. He had a fit while visiting the town of Lerwick and ended up in jail. Somehow he broke free, ran home and, as the song says, wrote a tune. According to legend it was 'Jack Broke the Prison Door', which is the first of three of his tunes that are worked into the song.

PEGGY: Because *Time Goes* – like *Old New* before it – had a song that Chris and Maart had written together, it gave a sense of the continuity of the band.

SIMON: It [*Who Knows Where the Time Goes?*] was an album that everyone brought songs to. 'Sailing Boat' was from annA rydeR's album recorded at Woodworm. I found 'Dangerous', which is one of Fairport's poppier tracks. Chris brought 'Wishfulness Waltz'. I am sure Peggy brought 'Life's a Long Song' from Tull.

PEGGY: It became another of those shared songs where everybody sings a verse.

Meanwhile, Fairport fans' attention shifted from their new fiddler
to their old one, as the band led a campaign dubbed 'SwarbAid' to
support Dave Swarbrick, who had become seriously ill with em-
physema, which eventually left him housebound. The campaign
peaked with a concert in July 1999 at Birmingham City Hall, at
which you could buy a CD of Fairport's appearance there earlier
in the year, when Swarb had made a rare appearance as a special
guest. On 26 April, 1999, when news had broken of Swarb's illness,
The Daily Telegraph had mistakenly published his obituary. Wittily,
the programme for the concert was named *The Daily Epitaph* and
took the form of a mock newspaper. News of his death, like that
of Fairport years before, was seriously exaggerated: in fact, he was
well enough to laugh at the whole thing.

SWARB: As I said at the time, it wouldn't have been the first
time I died in Coventry.

The Fairport Convention line-up that celebrated its 45th anniversary in 2012 first came into being in March 1998. In November 1999,
Fairport released *The Wood and the Wire*, the release proving to be
the beginning of a new era in their history. As it had been before,
it was a period when a fiddler was a driving force within the band.

SIMON: I think that's where Chris really put his stamp on the
band. We suggested he try writing with Nigel Stonier and the
partnership really worked out well.

The album included 14 tracks, nine of which were written by Chris
either alone or in collaboration. It was a very good way to round off
the millennium.

CHAPTER TEN

End of an Era

As the end of the second millennium approached, Fairport found themelves looking backwards, towards mythical events of the first millennium. Alan Simon was one of Fairport's many overseas fans. He had grown up in Nantes, where his English teacher used rock music to stimulate his students' interest. One of the albums in his collection was *Babbacombe Lee*. Not only did it turn young Alan into a Fairport fan, it also sowed the seed of creating a concept album of his own. In 1998, he completed the first part of a trilogy – an epic work called *Excalibur* based on the legend of King Arthur.

In October 1999, Fairport were in Rennes, Brittany, taking part in Alan Simon's vision of a multimedia production of *Excalibur*, its first live performance. Also performing were the Prague Symphony Orchestra, a Breton pipe-band and a choir from Bulgaria.

SIMON: It's hard for British Fairport fans to appreciate the scale of the *Excalibur* project. It has gone on for years, producing several albums and increasingly spectacular live performances.

PEGGY: My second home is in Brittany, as most Fairport fans know. Being part of the *Excalibur* project helped cement my bond with that particularly lovely bit of northern France.

RIC: The thing that fascinates me about *Excalibur* is the way those Celtic myths permeate European cultures. It might seem odd that a series of concept albums and mega-concerts about King Arthur should be big in France but he is as much a part of their mythology as ours.

The project expanded over the following decade and more, producing three albums and two further CDs with themes related to the main narrative, alongside live recordings and DVDs. Because activities surrounding it were Continentally-biased, Fairport's English fans had little access to performances and developments of the project until well into the 21st century – 2009, in fact.

PEGGY: While the whole *Exalibur* thing had massive cult status in France and Germany, we knew most of Fairport's British fans were only dimly aware of it. The CDs weren't readily available in the UK and no British TV companies had taken up the rights to screen it. So we negotiated with Alan to release a compilation of Fairport's contribution on a CD, which we called *Fame and Glory*.

SIMON: It's not exactly a Fairport album. Although some or all of Fairport feature on every track, there are lots of other featured musicians and singers on it as well. It's an example of what Fairport do when they are not exactly being Fairport – hey, we could have called it *What We Did on Our Vacances*.

Among the artists appearing with Fairport on *Fame and Glory* are Jacqui McShee, Martin Barre, John Wetton, Didier Lockwood, Flook and John Helliwell from Supertramp. Other performers who appeared on the show but not on the album include Johnny Logan, Les Holroyd, Roger Hodgson, Gabriel Yacoub and Alan Parsons. As so often happens with things Fairport, all roads led ultimately to Cropredy, of course, when Supertramp's Roger Hodgson made an appearance there in 2000.

SIMON: We didn't have time to rehearse with him, so it was all done on trust. He'd never heard us playing their music until the downbeat. From the first notes, you could see him thinking, "Hey, this is good." That's good for us, too, of course. He was obviously expecting to go through the motions of doing the songs and yet when it happened it was larger than life.

We know we can do that. You can often tell that guests are genuinely pleased. That drives them a little more. So you get a better performance because they're happy, and comfortable and confident with what's happening behind them. That in turn makes for a great experience for the audience.

Being a rare event, Fairport had seen in the new millennium (despite knowing better they, like everyone else, did so at the start of the year 2000) not at Cropredy, or even close to it. Instead they'd shared celebrations with an audience of hardcore fans at the Picture Playhouse in Beverley, East Yorkshire.

PEGGY: It was quite a change. Normally, our seasonal festivities are closer to home. Fans came from all over the country to see in the new century with us. Someone came all the way from Saudi Arabia.

There was no let-up in Fairport activity as a new millennium began, of course. While planning their next album, they'd repackaged and reissued their early live Cropredy albums on CD. They were also involved with the compilation and production of Free Reed's archivist box set *UnConventional*, and toured the UK with Bob Fox and Steve Tilston. The new album became more of a priority as 2001 wore its way on.

Once In A Lifetime

As any Roman schoolboy could tell you from its title, *xxxv* was released to celebrate Fairport's 35th anniversary. Five of its songs were new versions of songs from some of the dustier corners of Fairport's back catalogue. Here, for the first time, Fairport got about the serious business of revisiting their back catalogue in the studio, just as they had done for years on stage. Included is a song from Simon's solo album which had passed into the acoustic setlist and then into the repertoire of the electric line-up. Alongside it is a studio version of the first song we ever heard Chris sing with Fairport on disc; Ric's most-requested instrumental; an old Thompson / Swarbrick-penned single; and a definitive slice of trad arr from the same era (even though we had first heard it on *Angel Delight*).

XXXV

Woodworm Records
1 November, 2002

TRACK LISTING:

'Madeleine'   'The Light of Day'
'My Love Is In America'   'I Wandered by a Brookside'
'The Happy Man'   'Neil Gow's Apprentice'
'Portmeirion'   'Everything But the Skirl'
'The Crowd'   'Talking About My Love'
'The Banks of Sweet   'Now Be Thankful'
    Primroses'   'The Crowd Revisited'
'The Deserter'

'The Happy Man' is a Morris song from Adderbury whose refrain about smoking without fear was yet to become un-PC. There were two versions of annA rydeR's celebration of Cropredy, 'The Crowd'. Chris contributed three new songs. *XXXV* was a well-rounded portrait of Fairport – past, present and future – performed with a little help from their friends.

The album reminded people of what the band had achieved, how long they'd been a part of the British music scene, and how much they had influenced traditional, folk and rock music in the UK. Not only were their fans taking note of Fairport's place in British musical history, but others were too. On 11 February, 2002, at London's Barbican Theatre, Radio 2's Folk Awards presented their Lifetime Achievement Award to Fairport Convention.

ASHLEY: It was a proud moment for me to see the band being recognised in such a prestigious way.

Co-recipients of the award were The Chieftains and Ralph McTell (in recognition of his contribution to songwriting). Two years later, Swarb's lifetime achievement was celebrated, and in 2006, the award went to Richard. That same year, Ashley's contribution was recognised when he received the Good Tradition Award, given to those whose work preserves the traditions of folk music.

While compiling their first box set *UnConventional*, a large amount of unreleased recordings from most eras of the band would come to light. The box set prompted (and partially informed) a serious reissue programme of their albums from Island. Each album was fully remastered and appropriate unreleased material was added as bonus tracks. Simon and Ashley were involved in the reissues, writing informative notes for the CD booklets as well as providing archive photos and recommending bonus recordings to be included. At the same time, parallel reissue schedules were being created for Richard and Sandy's albums.

The research work on Fairport's history revealed how alike their two bass players were, even if temperamentally Ashley is the serious academic and Peggy the jolly party animal.

ASHLEY: Well, there's the hairstyle, of course.

PEGGY: The premature baldness which is the curse of folk-rock bass players.

Both became, in effect, the leader of the band, though they tended to lead from the rear. Both are perceptively astute businessmen, and each has been responsible for some remarkable innovations that have affected business models throughout the industry. Both provided a physical and spiritual home for Fairport Convention. Both are obsessive archivists with a wealth of well-organised press cuttings, photographs and recordings in their collection: there exists almost a complete archive of recordings of Cropredy.

SIMON: There were years – and I think it's pretty obvious which they are – when we said: "We really should make sure we get a good recording of Cropredy. Then, if it turns out well, we should release it."

PEGGY: Other times, we simply thought we'd played well and went to the tapes to see how it had recorded. Actually, let's be honest, to see whether we were as good as we thought we were.

While *UnConventional* would include some Cropredy material – some expressly *because* it was Cropredy material – it avoided using

Cropredy recordings as a substitute for cuts found deeper in the archive. Cropredy itself was represented by a bonus CD which attempted to summarise 'Fairport's bit' of Cropredy, from the opening announcement to the Sunday cricket match (courtesy of a particularly fine performance by Roy Harper).

PEGGY: That left the way clear for our next Free Reed box set, which chronicled Cropredy, mainly using the recordings from the 'unreleased' years.

There were some released recordings that were so important it would have been wrong to have omitted them from a four-CD history of the Festival, so these were naturally included. In the two-year gap between the box sets, a wealth of Fairport material was to be released.

SIMON: The start of this century saw proper reissues of a lot of Fairport's back catalogue. They were the albums as we had made them – including *Full House* restored to the album we'd originally planned it to be – with lots of bonus material. Universal, who now owned the Island, Polydor and Phonogram catalogues, really took pains to get it right. They also did a lot of promotional work, which benefited the 2002 Fairport, as much as the earlier versions of the band it was promoting.

Internal Affairs

While compiling *Cropredy Capers*, the four-CD box set which drew on the unreleased archive tapes from the first 20 years of Cropredy Festival, it suddenly seemed like it might have to document the Festival's demise. Dave and Chris Pegg, the husband and wife team who had run Cropredy and Woodworm, were involved in a well-publicised divorce: one national newspaper carried a half-page article about how Peggy was being 'forced to sell his collection of classic instruments'.

SIMON: It was the end of a chapter. As things stood, it was inevitable that Chris Pegg should withdraw from matters Fairport.

She had never had an official managerial position, but she was the organised person in the Pegg household. Peggy was the *de facto* boss of the band and as a result Chris became central to the band's operations, particularly as far as Cropredy was concerned.

To continue, we had to find a way of achieving the manifold tasks that over the years she had made her own. The biggest job was the stewardship of the Festival. I choose the word carefully because it sums up a multi-faceted and highly complex responsibility.

The future was in the balance. Fairport's own continuance was assured, though there would be a short period when Peggy took time out from the band to deal with the situation. Cropredy Festival, though, was less assured. The name belonged to Woodworm and, thereby, to Chris Pegg who could, had she so wished, have simply continued to run the event without Fairport's involvement.

SIMON: She gave us her goodwill to continue. She could, of course, have taken the Festival as an ongoing asset and even sold it on to another business. But she gave us her blessing to take it over and let it continue in much the same vein as it had previously. Of course, the same was true of *all* the day-to-day matters of running Fairport – processing the income from the records, setting up the tours (though Chris didn't book the tours, the money would all pass over her desk), all contracts (always issued from her office). The Festival has its own momentum, and in many ways is absolutely central to the band's existence. Quite simply, it energises the other 11 months of the year. Cropredy *had* to continue.

For Simon and the band, this was an economic decision. The event mutated nominally into Fairport's Cropredy Convention, otherwise things continued as before. The years of 2003 and 2004 involved a lot of stock-taking, in every sense.

PEGGY: Simon has said some very kind things regarding the overseeing of Fairport's affairs during the 25 years that Christine and I ran the company. It really was a 'cottage industry' and to my knowledge we were the first independent,

355

band-run, label and festival organisers. Christine has an amazing ability in this department and at one point, for example, was looking after three different VAT accounts – for Woodworm Records (the Festival and record company), Woodworm Music (for the studio), and my own account. She would also prepare all the accounts before sending them off to Grant Thornton for approval. She was responsible for setting up the Cropredy site and hiring crew, etc.

We did all of this in the early years pre-faxes and mobile phones and God only knows how it worked! We asked anyone we thought could help us, and that is how our mailshot list arrived, courtesy of Doug and Maggie Lake, two lovely peeps who still attend Cropredy. We would print and stuff and label our own letters to send out – a three-week operation when the list got up to 25,000. Mick Peters, a star electrician who is our site manager and Wintour manager and driver, was a friend of Wayne Averill's. He was 'collared' by me in the Red Lion one evening in the late Seventies and, luckily, still works on events today.

My role was booking all the bands and doing deals and costings to ensure that, unlike many Festivals, ours didn't lose money. I was also the publicity department and did all the PR work. Only on one occasion did we employ an outside company – to promote *Jewel in the Crown*, which I thought was an album worthy of some extra help. I was also the A&R department for the label, and responsible for finding songs and artistes that I thought were worthy of our help in getting more recognition. I was also playing and recording with Jethro Tull at the time, so my life was somewhat busy.

When Christine and I parted, it was obviously going to be a difficult time for all concerned and I came close to cracking on several occasions. She remained a saint and could not have been more helpful in her assistance when we set up the new company.

The name 'Matty Grooves' came from a good friend, Graham Post, who used to do all our printing. Woodworm was not legally able to pass on the names that we had accrued for our mailing list, as we needed permission from those on the list to do so. We started a new list that Simon now meticulously keeps up to date. We had several offers from companies who were interested in buying the Festival from us. Christine wanted Fairport to keep control of it, for obvious reasons; to protect the nature of the event and the goodwill that we had built up in the village. A large chunk of my divorce settlement to her was in order to enable this.

It is great that, subsequently, Christine has been able to attend Cropredy, sometimes with our grandkids Austin and Ava, and enjoy it as an event, which without her dedication and hard work for all those years would certainly not have ever taken place. Fairport thank her enormously.

Over The Next Hill

After Fairport Convention Ltd. came into being, the label Matty Grooves' first release, in June 2004, was Fairport's *Over the Next Hill*. The title track was written by Steve Tilston, who would also contribute 'Willow Creek'. The album concluded with Fairport's new version of 'Si Tu Dois Partir'. Ric, as usual, contributed a couple of tune sets, one of which, 'Canny Capers', was an oblique tribute to Rob Braviner's Canny Productions, which took a lot of the responsibility for Fairport's tours and certain aspects of Cropredy. Chris Leslie contributed three of the album's 11 songs.

CHRIS: 'I'm Already There' is about the doomed voyage of Lord Franklin [to the Arctic in 1845]. The brother of one of the crew was the vicar of Banbury and the song was partly inspired by a memorial stained glass window in Banbury Church. It's a song that has stayed in the set and developed. It's had a couple of different introductions. At the moment, I begin it by singing a verse from the 'Lord Franklin' ballad, unaccompanied.

SIMON: Chris singing that introduction is probably Fairport's most 'folkie' moment ever; traditional song done in traditional style, with not an instrument in sight or sound.

In 'The Fossil Hunter', Chris provides another portrait of another historical figure, Mary Anning. During the first half of the 19th century, she established a worldwide reputation through her fossil discoveries in the chalk cliffs around Lyme Regis.

CHRIS: Her story is remarkable – all the more so because she was a woman at a time when women were not at the fore-front of scientific discovery. I remember being struck by the statement that she 'laid the foundations of our modern un-derstanding of prehistoric creatures'. She is like a bridge be-tween that forgotten age and now.

Mary started young. At 12, she discovered the first plesiosaur skel-eton ever found. As if to show this was not a fluke, a few days later she unearthed another. Although she came from a humble back-ground, she was able to support herself and continue her explora-tions by selling examples of the more common fossils she found.

CHRIS: She was a determined, driven woman. She pursued her life's passion even though everything was against her.

Creating a bridge between the present and the forgotten past, suc-ceeding against the odds, finding a way to earn a living precisely by following one's childhood dream – Mary Anning could almost be a symbol for Fairport Convention. Despite its historical frame of ref-erence, 'The Fossil Hunter' is almost a parallel image of that boy in 'The Wood and the Wire'.

CHRIS: 'The Fossil Hunter' was one of the songs that would become a video for Cropredy. As we played the song, it un-folded visually behind us. It was quite a strange experience, seeing on the big screen what had previously only been in my mind's eye.

In May 2012, a live recording of 'The Fossil Hunter' (from 2004) became the first of the weekly free downloads offered on Fairport's official website.

Despite post-9/11 restrictions having increased the complex-ity for professional musicians wishing to visit the States – "Not to mention having greatly diminished the chances of making a profit at it," as Simon Nicol put it – in 2005, Fairport travelled there for a month of gigs. The tour took them from Pennsylvania and New York to four nights in California.

Having gone through another period of reappraisal and consol-idation, Fairport were now securely back as a working five-piece, with space in their diaries for independent projects and session work. The band's introductory programme note summed it up best: 'With the new office and new label, we've made a few changes to streamline the way we do things… Fairport is, of course, primarily a live band. That means we spend a lot of the year on the road. We love that, but it does mean we're out of the office rather a lot. To help us, we've brought in a couple of long-standing friends who have the skills to keep the admin side running smoothly.' They also plugged their new electronic mailing list and website.

RIC: The general feeling was, things had run fine. They had grown from a very small start to the point where a home-based business was running an international company. Fairport were the prototype of the 'mega-cottage industry'.

SIMON: While the circumstances behind it were unfortunate and unpleasant, the fact that a point came when we had to decide how to continue meant that we could make some changes, become more of a business. Don't infer any criticism of the way Chris Pegg had handled things for Fairport: she did a wonderful job and continued to be supportive. It was simply a matter of different people electing to do things a different way.

PEGGY: Woodworm – studio, record label, management company – came about naturally. It started small. We made mistakes and learned from them. As Fairport grew, so did Woodworm, expanding its activities and skills base to match what the band needed.
    Looking back, you realise how impressive that was. Christine wrote the book on how to run a community-based festival. Look at how Cropredy developed and that, in a nutshell, was what happened with Fairport as a whole.

ASHLEY: The tree symbol on the *History* family tree is an oak. Mighty oaks from tiny acorns grow. That's Fairport, and every band that owes a debt of gratitude to the work of the people who were part of that band at the end of the Sixties and the start of the Seventies.

When Woodworm was no longer available to handle Fairport's affairs, it was suddenly obvious just how much it had done for the band. Replicating it – and indeed revising and reinventing it – was a massive undertaking, but one which had to be done and done quickly, for the sake of Fairport's survival. Again, Cropredy represented a microcosm of the larger situation.

SIMON: There was a lot to be done – alongside simply being a working band that was out on the road frequently. We knew it was impossible to do it ourselves without an extra person to take things on board. That person was Gareth Williams. He had the steepest learning curve on the planet – finding out how the Festival was run and making sure it happened without a break in the continuity. He gave up his touring job as a monitor engineer and really applied himself. After the first Festival, I know he needed a very large lie-down.

When that first Festival had taken place under the new regime, we counted the chickens that had come home to roost and breathed a huge sigh of relief because we had proved it could be done. It's fair to say that there are many aspects of the Festival that are better run now than they were under Chris's tenure. That's not to say that she was doing anything wrong. It's just that in any business where you are doing a lot of repeat stuff year on year, things get done in a certain way because they've always been done in that way.

It was very much a case of a new broom and that led to a number of real improvements. A blast of fresh air blew through. Since then, it's continued to grow and grow: there's some fine-tuning – each year there are more things we take into consideration. One thing that has been outside our control are the increased health and safety regulations that have come in, and we have had to find ways to respond to them. Every year, you learn a little bit more about how it's done.

The first time ever it sold out ahead of time was in 2011, and we had to say to people, "If you haven't got a ticket, don't just turn up. You won't get in." That's always been the case at Glastonbury and as a result they know what they are dealing with. At Cropredy, in any given year, we didn't know how many people we were going to be looking after until mid-afternoon on the Saturday. That was roughly the time we could be certain how many people would be there for the night; it's a bit late to start ordering extra toilets or laying on more water or getting more camping organised.

It's now even more important for it to be seen to succeed in future. It would be nice to think we could sell out again each year, but we'll see.

With the passing of time, friends, collaborators, spouses and commentators come and go. As many friends and fans of Fairport were of a certain age, the new century inevitably brought its share of bad news.

SIMON: We have lost some very good friends. In 2003, Johnny 'Jonah' Jones, whom many Fairport fans will remember as compere at early Cropredy Festivals, passed away. He was the personification of the loveable rogue and we shall certainly not see his like again. He was corny, totally London, and always smoked a roll-up cigarette in his cupped hand – a sign of an old lag. He sported self-made tattoos, a memento from his time in jug. He was the authoritarian figure at The Half Moon (where we first met him) and he became a friend and ardent supporter of the band. He loved being a part of the Fairport family. He took a special kind of pride in watching Cropredy grow year on year and being part of that development. It was a genuine affection and it went both ways. He was a fantastic bloke. I can't think of him without smiling.

He was always funny, even though he gave the impression of being someone you definitely wouldn't want to mess with. Even his passing was not without humour: this may sound odd, but his cremation in Putney was ludicrously funny. Even though it was conducted by a Church of England vicar, it was about as unreligious as it could possibly be. Ralph McTell gave the most wonderful eulogy, a work of art. The place was completely packed, so much so that there had to be an overflow into the courtyard and they had to erect a couple of speakers so people outside could hear. Six of us were selected as coffin-bearers; we carried his coffin in and put it on the dais. I was teamed up with Paul Smith, who is the same height as I am, so that was OK – we were in the middle. As we slid the coffin from the hearse, I heard him yelp – he'd got a huge splinter in his finger from the bottom of the coffin. We both wanted to laugh, despite the circumstances, because that was Jonah all over – he'll get you in the end.

He was much loved, and is much missed.

Like Sandy, Martin, Trevor, Neil Cutts and Rob Braviner, Jonah Jones is one of those people you remember as you sing 'Meet on the Ledge'.

Neil Cutts, who ran the bar at Cropredy, died in 2006. He owned The Brewery at Masham (so was responsible for releasing the first Swarbrick/Nicol LP). A couple of years after that, Rob Braviner passed away. Rob had gradually progressed from tour manager to the point where he was taking a major hand in the running of all Fairport's affairs.

Missing from Cropredy for the first time in 2011 was the near-legendary LHM (Long Haired Mick), whose authoritative control of the backstage area and seemingly every point on every surrounding field was remarkable. After Christine Pegg relinquished the reins of the event, his role became even more significant. He did not suffer fools gladly, but was helpful to anyone who needed assistance. I have a very specific memory of standing beside him as he a) tried to track down Peggy, b) sort out a problem with stage passes of a support act, c) deal with an issue happening at the main gate (discreetly enough to prevent one knowing what the actual issue was), d) casually berate another support act for a minor infringement, e) direct a late-arriving journalist to the press tent, f) locate a batch of programmes for a seller who had run out, and g) smoke an ever-present Marlboro while chatting, offering me a bottle of water, and "making sure you're not getting bored". How could I have been? He was a marvel to observe.

If some of these names sound strangely familiar, listen again to Fairport's recording of 'The Card Song'.

An Occasion

Fairport's links with the BBC were commemorated in the four-CD set *Fairport at the BBC*, scheduled for release in April 2007. They had returned to the Beeb to mark their 40th anniversary, and also to launch their latest album. The guests included friends, fellow musicians and those in the media who had supported the band over the years. It was quite a star-studded gathering.

PEGGY: We should do a group photograph of this crowd – it would look like Fairport's *Sergeant Pepper*.

The band played a short set featuring tracks from the new album and a couple of Fairport classics.

CHRIS (interviewed at the launch of *Sense of Occasion* in 2007): It's been three years since our last studio album, and like our recent releases it's on our own label. I've written five songs for it and Ric's written three tunes – one of which is a kind of sequel to 'Bowman's Retreat'. There're also some interesting cover versions.

The "interesting cover versions" included a version of XTC's 'Love on a Farmboy's Wages' and a post-Squeeze Glenn Tilbrook song ('Untouchable'). Long-time friend and musical associate of the band Steve Ashley donated 'Best Wishes', though Fairport rapidly discovered they had little need of another end-of-the-show song. P J Wright's 'Galileo's Apology' had been the title track of the album he had made with Peggy, almost released on Matty Grooves. The pair did a number of hit-and-run gigs and then toured briefly. *Sense of Occasion* also included new versions of 'Polly on the Shore' and 'Tam Lin'.

GERRY: Ah yes – you've listened to the albums – faulty ears of Fairport Convention.

It was a year of parallel activities, as usual. Dave Pegg became the latest member of the Fairport family to have his career documented in a large format box set. It had already happened to Fairport (twice), RT, Sandy (several times), Swarb, Iain and Ashley. It was a fascinating set to compile. In 2007, the day after Fairport finished their 40th anniversary Winter Tour, he headed off on tour in a duo with P J Wright. In November 2007, Peggy celebrated his 60th birthday with an all-star concert at Birmingham Town Hall.

PEGGY: Like the box set, I wanted to show a big range of what

I'd done and so we had all kinds of friends and musicians along, as well as a set from Tull and Fairport. I even got to play lead guitar!

Peggy's box set was released to coincide with Fairport's Cropredy Convention. Fairport appeared twice, on the Friday playing *Liege & Lief* right through and on the Saturday shifting the focus from the turn of the Seventies to the post-Nineties. Take out a detour into *Full House* and what we had was a set that featured songs from the Woodworm / Matty Grooves era together with the current repertoire of the early Cropredy Fairport. There was even a foretaste of the next album. Having turned the spotlight on their finest hour (or at least 42 minutes) on the Friday, Fairport reaffirmed the legacy of the current line-up.

CHRIS: That was the year we introduced the big screen at Cropredy. I know it is great for everyone in the field to be able to see, but sometimes turning round and looking up at yourself 20-times lifesize can be a bit startling. Purely personally, the big screen has meant that videos have been made for a number of my songs – not the MTV sort of video, but things to be screened when the song is played live. There was a great one for 'South Dakota to Manchester', which had lots of fascinating archive footage in it.

At the start of 2009, Fairport took the unusual step of releasing two new CDs: this was timed to coincide with the Winter Tour. Both were left-field Fairport albums. *Live at Cropredy '08* featured 16 recordings from the Festival. It tied up a few loose ends – 'Reynardine', the rewrite of 'Reynard the Fox', and the three-song *Reader's Digest* version of *Babbacombe Lee*. What dominated the album, however, was something everyone remembered from that Cropredy – the sequence of guest female singers performing their Sandy Denny favourites: with only Julie Fowlis' 'Farewell, Farewell' missing. By way of an explanation, Simon Nicol offered: "It's unfortunate, but when we listened to it back, it didn't quite work. It is a deceptive song and the backing needs to be subtle and very understated." The other release was *Fame and Glory*.

In 2010, Fairport brought *Excalibur* to Cropredy where it occupied an hour of their set. Aside from Swarb, the musicians playing that day were the only guests in Fairport's set. The set included a dozen songs, eight of which had been on *Fame and Glory*. Preceded rather incongruously by 'Ukulele Central', the set came over as pomp rock. The uncertain reception given it was not helped by the fact that what had been a rainy weekend throughout turned torrential, becoming a Cropredy storm unlike anything anyone could remember, as thunderclaps rivalled the huge sound coming from the speakers. As Jacqui McShee came on stage to perform the beautiful 'Morgane', forked lightning crackled through the sky. "That'll teach me to do songs about arch-witches," she said afterwards. For an audience who had already experienced an hour of Rick Wakeman's English Rock Ensemble, it all got a little too much. The spirit of the event was summed up by one disheartened fan, dashing for shelter: "This is what it would have been like if Spinal Tap had played Krumlin." That was also the year Fairport played the condensed *Babbacombe Lee* set and half a dozen tracks from the album they had recently started work on, to be released on 18 January, 2010. Which all left little room for Fairport oldies.

Festival Bell

Early in 2011, *Record Collector* raved about *Festival Bell*, describing it as an 'album of maturity and depth'. The album began with the impressive 'Mercy Bay', in which Chris Leslie again tackled the Lord Franklin story, but from a different angle. Simon took the lead vocal on the tale of the ill-fated and near-fatal rescue attempt by HMS *Investigator*. It was the first of five songs written by Chris on the album. The one which attracted most attention was 'Ukulele Central' – partly because it was so left-field, with all the band except Gerry playing ukes, and partly because additional strumming was provided by comedian Frank Skinner and the legendary Joe Brown, an unlikely brace of guest instrumentalists if ever there was one. The song had been written in collaboration with Ric, who had also teamed up with Peggy to create 'Albert and Ted'.

PEGGY: We didn't write it together. I had a new bass – an Ibanez 505 – and, as I often do when I acquire a new instrument, I wrote a tune as part of getting used to it. Somehow Ric heard it and said he had a new tune that would fit perfectly with it.

RIC: They weren't obvious partners, but when they were put together they really worked. We named the result in honour of our Dads who had worked for years in the same school.

PEGGY: Yeah, Ric's Dad was the Head of English and mine was the caretaker!

Ric also contributed two tunes, 'Danny Jack's Chase' and 'Danny Jack's Reward', which he described as being "a bit piratey".

RIC: They should have a co-composer credit as they were both written in collaboration with Jack Daniels.

With two songs donated by Ralph McTell, the album certainly had a sense of 'old times' about it. Listening to them one realised the old times were what we once called the new era. Time trod its diurnal course and Fairport's thoughts drifted towards their forthcoming anniversary.

CHRIS: Fairport's fans tend to keep track of things. I remember someone asking us what we were planning to do for our 45th. "We haven't quite decided yet," is really another way of saying "Oh! Is it really? Thanks for reminding us."

SIMON: In 2011, we toured with a set that featured songs from *Festival Bell* and the whole of *Babbacombe Lee*. We knew *Babbacombe Lee* was going down well and decided to go through the tapes to see whether we could put together a live version of the original album. We knew it would be sufficiently different to merit there being a second version.

PEGGY: Anyway, what's the problem with there being two versions – how many different recordings of *Tommy* are there?

As Fairport travelled the country on their Winter Tour, playing their complete *Babbacombe Lee*, friends and fans were invited to take part in a poll to select songs from the band's back catalogue to be re-recorded for their 45th anniversary album – and naturally, to form the basis of the setlist for the Winter Tour of 2012.

SIMON: We deliberately didn't simply ask for people's favourite Fairport track. It was very clear exactly what they were voting for.

The most-nominated tracks were rearranged and re-recorded by the current line-up and released as Fairport's next studio album.

By Popular Request

Matty Grooves
January 2012

SIDE 1:

'Walk Awhile'
'Crazy Man Michael'
'The Hiring Fair'
'The Hexhamshire Lass'
'Red and Gold'
'Sir Patrick Spens'

SIDE 2:

'Genesis Hall'
'Farewell, Farewell'
'Rosie'
'Matty Groves'
'Fotheringay'
'Meet on the Ledge'

Many of the choices were predictable: some were classic Fairport, others songs they had revived and were playing live but had not yet taken back into the studio. Perhaps the biggest surprise was the absence of 'Who Knows Where the Time Goes' or any instrumentals. Rarely played songs like 'Farewell, Farewell' and 'Fotheringay' were unexpected vote winners and forced the band to consider how to perform songs from their back catalogue that they had, for various reasons, avoided.

There were two songs from the post-Cropredy era (both, as it happens, written by Ralph McTell), two from the mid-Seventies, two from *Full House*, three from *Liege & Lief*, one from *Unhalfbricking* and two from *What We Did on Our Holidays*. Traditional material was well represented, as were the songwriting talents of Richard, Sandy and Swarb. By popular request, Fairport's fans had put together a thumbnail representation of what the band had achieved in four and a half decades, and the new recordings are convincing evidence of what Fairport were still capable of achieving.

CHAPTER ELEVEN

In Keeping with Tradition

'Once upon a time ...' are the opening words of a fairy tale, the one element of traditional storytelling most people recognise. These four words (like the 'all lived happily ever after' closing) are a formula, part of a structure that we expect within the genre. All traditional genres – by which we mean musical, literary, terpsichorean and dramatic forms that have been shared orally and therefore did not depend on the written word for their preservation – rely on formulaic structures, some of which are quite alien to literary genres. Whether we are dealing with fairy tales or folk songs, Homer or *Beowulf*, the Bible or the big ballads, we encounter the same techniques and devices such as repetition, refrains and reiteration. There will be interchangeable names and locations (which allowed the big ballads to transplant from the English Downs to the Appalachian Mountains), embedded symbolism (maidens with 'comb and glass all in their hand', exchanged love tokens, ladies 'buried... on the top'), and an unquestioning acceptance of both the reality of the supernatural and the harshness of reality.

The magical yet brutal world of the fairy tales collected by the Brothers Grimm, Perrault and Hans Christian Andersen is the same as that of the ballads and folk songs collected by Child, Sharp and Vaughan Williams. Little Red Riding Hood is clearly cut from the same cloth as Reynardine; the strength of true love is tested through strange magic as much in the quest of the Prince in *Sleeping Beauty* as in the events of Hallowe'en in 'Tam Lin'.

Tolkien talks about the collectors ("or some would say 'authors'") of folk tales "fixing the form" of the existing narrative. In a sense, they create a definitive version. When Fairport invented the English form of folk-rock, they went against the views of many in the folk revival who felt that these 'fixed forms' were somehow untouchable.

SWARB: It's an artificial concept. Someone collects a version of a song. Lots of other people know it and have slightly different versions. Probably the chap who sings it will do it differently next time. Yet that version becomes the 'right' one.

When Fairport first applied rock instruments to traditional music, people were still debating as to whether it was right to accompany folk songs on non-indigenous instruments, such as the guitar, and indeed whether it was appropriate to accompany ballads at all. On his visits to Cecil Sharp House researching *Liege & Lief*, Ashley might well have found an article in the *Folk Song Journal* that discussed 'Ballads and the Bardic Tradition', which speculatively delved back as far as ancient Greece to show that narrative verse should be chanted and not accompanied. It is not difficult to imagine the adverse reaction in some quarters to a group of North London rock musicians taking on music which some regarded as sacrosanct.

Of course, the versions of the songs that they created became, in several cases, the new 'fixed form' – the one which two generations of folk singers would then perform. A simple check of the versions of songs like 'Matty Groves' and 'Reynardine' on YouTube will confirm the pervasiveness of the band's influence.

LYNDA HARDCASTLE: When Grace Notes recorded 'Reynardine' for our first album, we based our version on Sandy's. There are other recordings of the song but that was the one we took as our source.

SIMON: I wouldn't say what some have claimed – that Fairport are source singers. Our versions of those traditional songs are very accessible to people, and obviously memorable. That means that people may have learned a traditional song from the Fairport version. What's important is that they realise the song goes beyond that, and ours is only a version.

There is nothing unusual about ownership of a traditional song being attributed to particular performers. Dylan was cold-shouldered for years by Dave Van Ronk in a dispute over 'House of the Rising Sun'. 'Scarborough Fair' should be considered Martin Carthy's song, rather than Paul Simon's, although Carthy would disarmingly defuse that debate thus: "Though in both cases we only had squatter's rights." 'The Hexhamshire Lass' is still Bob Davenport's, whether it's sung by Dave Swarbrick or Chris Leslie.

Fairport became *the* folk-rock band, but ask most people what kind of music Fairport play and the answer will be folk.

PEGGY: Fairport were never just a folk band, just like Cropredy was never *only* a folk festival. There is a huge folk influence in both cases. I like to think we have used the best of what folk has to offer but we mix in a lot of other things.

If you wanted a band that almost exclusively played electric-folk, there was Steeleye Span who took folk-rock into the charts and on to TV in a way that Fairport never achieved. Similarly, The Albion Band had a broader approach to folk music, including dance and ceremonial traditions. They took folk-rock to the National Theatre and community centres in a way that Fairport never did. Fairport never were, and never have been, a folk act. They've played folk tunes. Various band members have worked on the folk scene. Nor did Fairport discover folk in 1969, despite the Damascene epiphany described in some biographies of the band.

In this chapter, we look at how much of what Fairport have done is truly folk music. It's always been a key part of what Fairport were and are.

When reviewing Fairport's first release, 'If I Had a Ribbon Bow' in *Melody Maker*, Chris Welch remarked on its 'melodic folkie quality'. It was a prescient comment. The band had included folk material from its early days. One of the many bands from which Fairport was forged was the Ethnic Shuffle Orchestra. Only one fragmentary recording of that group exists, a version of 'Crazy Words, Crazy Tune', which the band called 'Washington at Valley Forge'. It had come from the repertoire of Geoff Muldaur (via a recording by Jim Kweskin's Jug Band). He'd collected it from a 1927 recording by the California Ramblers. Like that song, a lot of what that embryonic incarnation of Fairport played drew on American folk music.

Sandy Denny directed the band to include British traditional music. She had made several solo appearances on radio and TV performing songs like 'The Wild Rover' and 'The False Bride'. Her first album with Fairport included a couple of songs associated with the tradition: 'She Moves Through the Fair' was written by the poet Padraic Colum to a traditional Celtic tune; 'Nottamun Town' was a song with obvious English roots that had been preserved in the family repertoire of Appalachian singer Jean Ritchie, who was more than a little displeased when Dylan appropriated the tune for 'Masters of War'. It was 'reclaimed' by Shirley Collins and Davey Graham. Fairport's version developed it further. While the LP version restricts itself to a simple setting of the song, on stage it opened out and became what, at the time, was known as raga rock, the most famous example of which was The Byrds' 'Eight Miles High'.

The Byrds had come to prominence with an electric version of Dylan's 'Mr Tambourine Man'. Byrds' mainman Roger (or Jim, as he was then) McGuinn was a respected player on the New York folk scene, contributing acoustic guitar or banjo as a session musician for artists in America's folk revival. Then he went to see *A Hard Day's Night* and everything changed. He got a new hairstyle and sunglasses (like Lennon), a 12-string electric Rickenbacker guitar (like Harrison), a new chart-friendly vocal style (like McCartney), and started The Byrds.

Their manager got hold of a Dylan outtake, an early version of 'Mr Tambourine Man' which Dylan had recorded with Ramblin' Jack Elliott for inclusion on *Another Side of Bob Dylan*. Stripping down the visionary poetic song to a single verse and catchy chorus, The Byrds added jingle-jangle guitars and lush, layered harmonies and inadvertently invented a new genre, which the American music press dubbed folk-rock. Dylan purists were outraged at what had been done to his song. Dylan himself, happy to join The Byrds on stage by way of thanks, drew inspiration from that and The Animals' electric version of his (stolen) arrangement of 'House of the Rising Sun', to create his own "wild mercurial sound" on his trio of classic albums from 1965 and 1966: *Bringing It All Back Home*, *Highway 61 Revisited*, and *Blonde on Blonde*. *Cashbox*, reviewing the second and finest of this trilogy, stated that, 'folk-rock has truly come of age on this LP'.

However, the term folk-rock, when applied to 'Mr Tambourine Man' or any of those Dylan albums, doesn't really make sense.

While Dylan might have come from an acoustic music scene, he was never really 'folk'. Moreover, by any definition of folk beyond those used by PR men trying to market music, Dylan's songs, or indeed any direct singer-songwriter material, are not truly 'folk'. The term implies an uncertainty of authorship caused by the dissemination of a song via the oral tradition which makes a song's authorship anonymous or (as some would have it) 'unknown'.

Because singer-songwriters often adopt a consciously 'folk' style though, their output can be mistaken for folk songs. 'She Moves Through the Fair' is an obvious example where even traditional singers have assumed the song was handed down through the generations.

For record company marketing departments, classing anyone who sang to a folk guitar as 'folk' was a convenient bit of categorisation, whether the performer in question be Dylan or Donovan, Bert Jansch or Gordon Lightfoot. One of Sandy's first boyfriends Jackson C Frank, the composer of 'Blues Run The Game' and 'You Never Wanted Me', was consistently described as a folk singer in press coverage at the time. Many of the songwriters whose work Fairport have covered fall into this category – McTell, Taylor, Williams and Tilston, not to mention the in-house folk-rooted talents of Denny, Thompson, Swarbrick and Leslie.

Of course, every song has an author. What the folk process does is to make that irrelevant. So at the time when Fairport were formed, songs by the likes of Woody Guthrie, Ewan MacColl, Stephen Foster and A P Carter were becoming 'folk'. The same would happen later with songs by Dylan and Richard Thompson. Someone once criticised Ewan MacColl for altering the words of 'Shoals of Herring', which he had written, because the complainant was convinced it was a traditional Scottish song called 'Shoals of Erin'. One still smiles at the singer doing a floor spot in a local club who introduced a "Traditional song I learned from Fairport Convention. I think it must be the only Irish folk song to include Red Indians." This was incorrect, and not just politically so, because the song being introduced was 'Slip Jigs and Reels' by Steve Tilston.

So half of that American definition of 'folk-rock' fails. As for the rock part, it has to be said that when the term was first coined no one was thinking in terms of rock music *per se*. Many have argued that rock as we know it was invented by Dylan and The Band on their 1966 world tour, almost two years after music journalists had first started using the term. Indeed to this day, Americans still define what we would call rock music with the umbrella term 'rock 'n' roll'. The problem was that 'rock 'n' folk' didn't sound like a genre (at best it might be a style of playing, such as Conway Twitty's approach to songs like 'Danny Boy') and 'folk 'n' roll' had obvious pitfalls in terms of mishearing. So it was some marketing executive at CBS who came up with 'folk-rock'.

What Fairport did back in 1969 was to take the marketing term, turn it on its head, redefine it and ultimately create 'the first British folk-rock album'.

RICHARD: Fairport gained something of a reputation for extended jams. We weren't into improvisation in the same way as Pink Floyd, though. The simple fact was, when you had to play four or five sets in an all-night session, you simply didn't have enough material. It was easier to jam off the back of a song for six or seven minutes than learn two new songs.

Richard is being slightly disingenuous. His improvisations, displaying guitar virtuosity that gave him legendary status, were a key part of the early appeal of Fairport Convention. One of the songs which regularly benefited from the approach was Richard Farina's 'Reno, Nevada' which the band never released in their official canon (Iain Matthews would record it shortly after going solo). However, a short version, recorded for the BBC, appeared on the bootleg *Heyday* and then a highly extended version, recorded for French TV, surfaced and was subsequently made available on *Fairport UnConventional* and the extended CD version of *Fairport Convention*.

Spoonful

What Fairport were doing was exactly the same approach Cream had adopted with old blues songs – turning 'Spoonful' into a 12-minute, three-cornered battle among bass, guitar and drums – or what the Grateful Dead had done with old Americana and rock 'n' roll songs. What if Fairport were to apply this rock approach (and by '69 one could use the term legitimately) to a traditional English folk song? The raga-rock take on live versions of 'Nottamun Town'

373

was certainly a toe in the water. The real *eureka* moment came when Sandy happened to sing the old ballad 'A Sailor's Life' backstage before a gig.

SIMON: In those days, we did stretch out a bit more. It was a normal thing to take one song in your set and improvise off the back of it. I'd just noodle around and Richard would go off on one. Richard was particularly good at it. So we decided to try it with a traditional song, without consciously thinking, "No one has ever done this before."

ASHLEY: It came together so easily. It felt natural. We barely changed it, aside from inviting Dave Swarbrick to add fiddle. This helped in terms of folk-credibility. It also created that partnership between Richard and Swarb. For me, though, it stands as a real testament to the creativity of Martin Lamble's drumming.

JOHN PEEL: Everything about that track is the way you would want it in an ideal world, but nothing more so than Martin Lamble's drumming which ebbs and flows, like currents rolling stones beneath the sea.

Fortunately, one can actually retrace those steps. A very lo-fi cassette recording of the original experimental performance can be heard on *Fairport UnConventional*. A slightly later studio acetate, whose precise purpose is long forgotten, was included on Richard Thompson's first career retrospective *(guitar/vocal)*. Other changes, including a very obvious and biomorphic one, were about to take place in the development of the band's approach to this simple narrative ballad. This acetate is lacking one key element of the *Unhalfbricking* version – Dave Swarbrick's fiddle.

SANDY: I'd been singing 'A Sailor's Life' in the clubs for years. It was one of the first real folk songs I learned. I think I probably got it from Bert Lloyd's Penguin. [Despite the wonderfully surreal image this creates, Sandy is referring to *The Penguin Book of English Folk Songs*, which certainly includes the version of the song Sandy performs.] It was actually quite well known. [Martin] Carthy had recorded it and there are a lot of variants. Because they are known by different titles, it's not obvious that they are the same song, but clearly all the elements were there.

I wasn't involved in the rock arrangement at all. It was a bit like – here I am with my old ballad and here's the band I joined and what they have done with it. At least, on stage. On record, of course, it's 'new, improved, with added Swarbrick'.

Unhalfbricking concluded with their groundbreaking recording of 'A Sailor's Life', which was totally new to most people who bought the album and markedly different to anyone who had been lucky enough to hear them play the song live.

With it, Fairport had created a track which provided a valid and exemplary definition of the misused term folk-rock. Here was a song that was most definitely traditional: more than that it was a song with themes right at the heart of English folk music. Technically a ballad in that it was a narrative written in quatrains, it also complied with the romance, brevity and simple humanity of folk song. Of the six people performing on the track, two were well-established through performing in folk clubs and at festivals and were highly regarded as folk musicians as a result. The remaining four, while having a keen appreciation of and growing affinity towards folk music, most definitely belonged to the second generation of British rock musicians, the natural successors to the likes of The Stones and The Yardbirds who had wrested music away from the sole possession of chart-friendly boy bands, including The Beatles and The Hollies, and given it a new dimension.

The American writer Ralph Gleason provided a succinct image for the history of British pop: 'It began as High School with singers like Cliff Richard and Adam Faith, big names in Britain but meaningless over here. Then along came The Beatles to the Senior Prom. After that The Stones and The Yardbirds took it to College. With no native heritage of black music to draw on, graduate pop turned to its own roots. British folk music provided the edge in the music of Ray Davies of The Kinks and the Fairport Convention.'

While 'A Sailor's Life' was treated with respect, almost with deference, it also served as a springboard for the most fashionable rock approach of the time, the extended improvisation (*aka* jam, previously freak-out).

What makes Fairport's recording totally unlike the extended

jams that they and other bands were indulging in at the time is precisely what happens in the second half of the recording. In a very structured and significantly understated way, the band retells the story instrumentally. It is almost symphonic and reflects precisely the structure of the lyric Sandy has just sung. The opening movement sets the scene and mood with cymbals crashing like waves on a harbour wall. Then comes development and form, the instruments combining in much the same way as the boat being built, then the central journey, full of conflict and competing elements. Finally, disaster and resolution and a coda which returns the improvisation to the point where it had started.

SANDY: I was amazed when I listened back to the recording. We were all young, after all. There were older musicians, established performers, people we admired, who weren't attempting anything as bold as that. Maybe in jazz or classical music or someone *avant garde* like Frank Zappa. Not some little rock band from North London!

Hearing the studio version was a revelation in another way. We hadn't played it live many times. I recall there was always a big decision as to whether we'd include it each night. We used to try to see whether the audience would take it on board. I can't be certain but I think there were even times when we got all democratic, and took a vote!

Normally, if you have a jam of some kind, the lead singer will dance or at least sway about a bit. You couldn't do that with 'A Sailor's Life'. It didn't have that kind of feel and it seemed wrong to do anything which distracted from the playing, which was always pretty intense. It became a chance for me to sneak offstage for a quick drink or a fag.

SWARB: I don't know how many people realise that 'A Sailor's Life' was an experiment and very much a studio creation. It might have turned out to be the way the band went – performing electric versions of traditional songs, which is how most people seem to think of Fairport – but it was a one-off. I was only a session player and I never played it live with the band, though they had done it a few times before I joined. But when I did join, the first thing I did was help decide whether we were a band any more! We then all focused on the 'traditional project', which became *Liege & Lief*, with Ashley Hutchings taking charge, assuming his natural bandleader role, which was something I didn't take to naturally.

ASHLEY: What is absolutely remarkable about Fairport's version of 'A Sailor's Life' – aside from the fact that no one had done anything like it before – is precisely what the instruments do. During the song itself, everyone held back. I think it's one of the most appropriate and understated examples of backing that Fairport ever played. Then, in the second part, everyone is interpreting the song, and that includes me on the bass and the wonderful Martin Lamble on drums. The rhythm is essentially down to Simon Nicol who is without doubt one of the very best (if not the best) rhythm guitar players in this country.

MARTIN CARTHY: When Swarb came back from the Fairport session, he was in a totally different frame of mind to when he set off. He was really buzzing.

Carthy and Swarbrick were without question the biggest folk act in the UK at the time. In effect, they were a two-man supergroup. Martin was respected the world over for his guitar-playing, regularly voted Britain's best male folk singer and even then with an astounding repository of traditional songs. Swarb had played with Beryl Marriott before joining the Ian Campbell Folk Group which he left to team up with Carthy full time in 1967; before that he had been the guest fiddle player on Martin's LPs as well as playing on sessions for Ewan MacColl, Bert Lloyd, Nigel Denver and Julie Felix, among others.

Martin, with typical generosity, said that if Swarb felt that playing alongside Richard was what he wanted to do, then that's exactly what should happen. The duo had bookings in their diary, and obviously they would need to be fulfilled. By July, however, Swarb would be free to join Fairport full time.

The improvisational skills that Swarb brought to bear in this new electronic context had been honed in long late-night sessions at the Troubadour, one of London's most revered folk clubs. Sessions would go on into the small hours, often not ending until dawn was breaking over the capital. To fill time and give Martin's vocal chords a well-earned rest, the two would improvise medleys of traditional tunes that could last anything up to half an hour.

Fairport's recording of 'A Sailor's Life' was seen as a one-off experiment by everyone at the time and could easily have remained so. Since May 1969 Fairport have played it live only once, in an ill-fated attempt at Cropredy with June Tabor on what can best be described as uncompromising vocals, followed by an instrumental that strove to replicate the content but sadly not the spirit of the original. Significantly, most of the performance of this key song in the history of the band was omitted from the subsequently released video documentary and vanished totally from the concert video that was released.

SIMON: It's fair to say that we've tackled 'A Sailor's Life' twice in our history. One time it was an experiment that worked and produced things beyond our wildest speculations. The other it was just an experiment, full stop.

Without the recording of 'A Sailor's Life', there would probably have been no Steeleye Span or Albion Band. Thin Lizzy might never have recorded 'Whiskey in the Jar' and it's unlikely we'd have ever had The Levellers, Horslips or Bellowhead. It also ensured that Fairport continued to exist.

Fairport's next album *Liege & Lief* saw the full flowering of the seeds sown with 'A Sailor's Life'. Variously described as 'the greatest folk-rock album, 'Fairport's finest achievement' and 'the most influential folk album of all time', it defined Fairport for the rest of their career.

Five of *Liege & Lief*'s eight tracks are traditional and after the album's success, everyone thought of Fairport as *the* folk-rock group. What is surprising is how little traditional material they have actually recorded since that time. The subsequent release of *Full House* in 1970 indicated their approach as being clearly folk-influenced, although the only actual folk song is 'Sir Patrick Spens'. 'Flowers of the Forest', which is listed as traditional, was written by Jane Elliott in 1776. There were two tune sets and everything else was the product of the Thompson / Swarbrick song-writing partnership.

'Sir Patrick Spens' condenses into a single narrative two maritime tragedies from the end of the 13th century. To consolidate a political alliance, Alexander III, King of Scotland, despatched his daughter Margaret to be married to Erik, King of Norway. On their return voyage, the courtiers who had accompanied her were lost in a shipwreck. These documented historical events are conflated in the song with a slightly later event. Alexander died in 1286 and his granddaughter, also called Margaret, known as the Maid of Norway, became heir to the Scottish throne. To forge an alliance between England and Scotland, Edward I proposed a marriage between her and his infant son. But tragically, the Maid of Norway died too on the voyage back to Scotland in 1290, her first visit to the country of which she was briefly the uncrowned Queen. She was the last Scottish monarch descended from the house of Dunkeld, founded by Duncan I who was briefly usurped by Macbeth, and later murdered. Following her death, Scotland was without an effective monarch for a period of 16 years until Robert the Bruce seized power. Some have therefore seen the ballad as an allegory for the captain-less ship of state.

Although his name survives in the ballad based on the events of this tumultuous decade, Sir Patrick Spens is not mentioned anywhere in historical records relating to either event.

If, as planned, Fairport's epic version of 'Bonny Bunch of Roses' had also made it on to the same album, it would have changed the balance enormously. It would have added a second ballad, which rivalled 'Sloth' in length. Moreover, unlike the supernatural ballads of *Liege & Lief* ('Matty Groves' may be based on actual events but the narrative approach gives a gloss of fiction which places it somewhere between soap opera, revenge tragedy and animated cartoon), both ballads were historical epics with heroic and tragic central characters – the stuff of tragedy and Greek myth.

In the end, as the extended CD version of the album and the tracks on the live Troubadour CD show, *Full House* was an album with a precarious balance. Tipping one way it could have been even folkier than its predecessor; a nudge in the other direction would have moved it closer to *Unhalfbricking*.

RICHARD: A lot was going on musically at The Angel in terms of creating music. We were discovering traditional songs we wanted to do. We were also writing a great deal.

SIMON: I used to observe Richard's songwriting process and I was very aware of the small percentage that finally made it anywhere near completion. His wastepaper basket – or box, if we are to be accurate – was always full of screwed-up sheets of paper representing abandoned ideas. I know Ashley rescued a few that Richard was intending to scrap. Seeing the amount of effort required to write a song quickly convinced me it was not a route I wanted to follow.

SWARB: Someone once told me the art of being a great record producer is largely about making good editorial decisions. That's certainly something we were conscious of doing with *Full House* – not that those decisions were by any means unanimous.

RICHARD: What finally made it on to the album was largely down to timing. By that I mean what we felt was ready when we made the record. A few months later it would have been quite different.

We might therefore postulate a version of *Full House* that included 'Walk Awhile', 'Sloth', 'Doctor of Physick' alongside 'Now Be Thankful', 'Poor Will and the Jolly Hangman', 'Sickness and Diseases' and 'Journeyman's Grace'. Who knows, it might even have included a couple of the songs that appeared on *Henry the Human Fly*. Fairport did, after all, record 'Poor Ditching Boy' years later. In other words, very much a band-composed creation, somewhat akin to *The Wood and the Wire*.

On the other hand (or, given that it's a *Full House, in* the other hand), we could have had 'Sir Patrick Spens' and 'Flowers of the Forest' with 'Bonny Bunch of Roses', 'Banks of Sweet Primroses', 'Staines Morris' and 'Bonny Black Hare'. That would certainly have consolidated the view that Fairport were primarily an electric folk act.

As it turned out, the songs that didn't make it on to *Full House* were either put on the back burner or held over for the next LP.

Angel Delight offered four traditional songs: two heroic ballads, which opened the album; 'Banks of Sweet Primroses', which is a great folk standard; and 'Bonny Black Hare', a bit of bawdy *double entendre*.

SWARB: *Double entendre* is quite generous: it's more a *single entendre* song!

'The Woods In Search Of Some Game'

May 14 is known to Fairport fans as BBH Day – Bonny Black Hare Day – because of the opening line of the song. It's a song that threads its way through Swarb's career. He first recorded it in 1966 when he accompanied A L Lloyd's version on the Topic anthology of erotic songs *The Bird in the Bush*. The same album included 'The Widow of Westmoreland's Daughter', recorded by Fairport in 1978 and performed by them regularly ever since. The following year, he accompanied Martin Carthy's recording of it on *Byker Hill*. This in turn became the title track of a compilation of the Carthy / Swarbrick recordings. Fairport included a live version on *Farewell, Farewell*. It had remained in Swarb's solo repertoire and the only time it was performed in Fairport's set at Cropredy was as a solo performance by Swarb.

The song was collected in 1938 in Walberswick, Suffolk, from Mr Morrow, an immigrant potato picker. It is, as Swarb once described it, "grade A traditional English filth", with deft symbolism and a neat pun on the word 'hare'.

'Banks of Sweet Primroses' was very much a folk standard by the time Fairport recorded it. The Welsh traditional singer Phil Tanner recorded a version for commercial release in 1936 (and on two separate occasions after that). The Copper Family recorded their version in 1952 for the BBC's archive of traditional music: members of the family would record it again on four subsequent occasions. It was also in the repertoire of Fred Jordan and Harry Cox. Louis Killen and Shirley Collins both recorded it as the title track of an album in the Sixties – Shirley, for some reason, added an 'e' ('The Sweet Primeroses'). Martin Carthy recorded it, with Swarb, on *But Two Came By*. While many of Fairport's versions of trad arr songs can justly claim credit for widening the reputation of the song in question, their version of 'Banks of Sweet Primroses' is but one in a long line of variations of this great pastoral idyll. It's worth noting that an earlier version, with Richard Thompson leading the melody line, was recorded live and released on the various LA Troubadour albums. Swarb, too, recorded the song with Whippersnapper on the album *Promises*.

Fairport revisited 'Sweet Primroses' in 2002 on *xxxv*. Between Fairport's two studio versions it had also been recorded by Eliza Carthy, Brian Peters, Blue Murder, Robin and Barry Dransfield, Maggie Boyle with Steve Tilston, The Dubliners and Tony Rose. It has since also been recorded by June Tabor, Martyn Wyndham-Read, Martin Simpson and Jon Boden.

Fairport chose to open *Angel Delight* with two traditional ob-scurities. 'Lord Marlborough' can claim to be one of the first folk recordings since Percy Grainger recorded George Wray singing it in 1908. Along with other wax cylinder recordings from that year, it was released on the LP *Unto Brigg Fair*. Nic Jones recorded it for his first album *Ballads and Songs* in 1970. They called it 'Lord Melbourne' and 'The Duke of Marlborough', respectively.

'Sir William Gower' had appeared in *The Penguin Book of English Folk Songs* under the title 'The New York Trader'. The song is also known as 'William Glenn' and 'Captain Glenn'. Although there are many similar stories of ships cursed because of a sinner aboard (from Jonah to the Ancient Mariner) this particular version was overlooked by British revival singers until Fairport's version.

It is part of the cycle of life of all folk-rock acts that eventually they move further and further away from a trad only repertoire and Fairport set the precedent very quickly. The follow-up to *Angel Delight* consisted entirely of original Fairport compositions, aside from 'Sailor's Alphabet'.

The only traditional track on *Rosie* was the instrumental medley, though Trevor Lucas' 'The Plainsman' did borrow a traditional tune, 'Come All Ye Tramps and Hawkers'. Like *Angel Delight*, *Nine* opened with settings of two traditional songs. 'The Hexhamshire Lass' was first published in 1813 in *Rhymes of the Northern Bards* col-lected by John Bell.

For 'Polly on the Shore', Peggy created an arrangement that re-called 'A Sailor's Life' – an understated accompaniment to the sung version followed by a musical retelling of the story. The singer usu-ally credited as the source of the song is Pop Maynard, and before

Fairport created their version, it had been recorded by Martin Carthy and Dave Swarbrick (on *Prince Heathen*), Shirley and Dolly Collins (*Love, Death & the Lady*), and Trees (*On the Shore*).

While the band continued to play traditional songs on stage, *Rising for the Moon* in 1975 was their first 'trad.-less' LP since their debut.

The next album *Gottle O'Geer* had only one traditional song (plus a heavily overdubbed and remixed instrumental). 'When First To This Country' is a version of 'Lakes of Ponchartrain', a song which Mike Waterson had unearthed in the late Sixties and set to a variant of the tune for 'Jock O'Hazeldean'. He passed the song on to Christy Moore (being an Irish song set in America's southern states, it did not suit Mike's Yorkshire repertoire), who recorded it with Planxty in 1974. At the time Swarb recorded his variant it was being performed by Paul Brady and Martin Simpson in remarkably different versions, both of which would subsequently be recorded. It came out at a time when Fairport's live work had shifted into a more folk context. The song had links to 'The Banks of the Bann', which Fairport fans may know through Shirley Collins' recording in which she is backed by Richard Thompson, Simon Nicol, Ashley Hutchings and John Kirkpatrick (on *No Roses*) – and is a version close to that collected from the Gant Family of Austin, Texas, by John Lomax in 1934. It was, however, common to the repertoires of several American singers – Joan Baez, Ian & Sylvia, Dylan, Peggy Seeger, Happy Traum, etc – all of whom are likely to have learned it from the version by The New Lost City Ramblers.

Back In The Club

SIMON: Swarb, Peggy, and I had already started doing some folk club gigs. Really, that was out of friendship and desperation – we even called ourselves the Three Desperate Mortgages. We all had time in our diaries so we would go off and do a few gigs and find it was 'a right hoot'! In those days, folk clubs were featuring a lot of live comedy performers – people like Billy Connolly, Mike Harding and Jasper Carrott. As a result, we were able to take a light-hearted approach to the whole thing since back then people expected to go to a folk club and laugh! Club audiences were quite used to going home with their jaws aching. We got into that mode and it was very easy to work together again. That in itself was very liberating.

By the late Seventies, folk-rock was becoming distinctly unfashionable. Punk had kicked a hole in the structure of the music industry. Prime targets for punk venom were the various sub-genres of rock which had grown out of the underground scene – glam, prog, heavy metal, Brit-blues, folk-rock.

BILLY BRAGG: The irony was that folk musicians, like everyone else in the music establishment, felt threatened by punk. If they'd looked closely, they'd have seen that punk was directly linked to folk. A few, like Peter Bellamy, realised that.

The Bonny Bunch of Roses is Fairport's most traditional album. Framed by two sets of tunes, its nine tracks include a new Swarbrick song and one apiece from Richard Thompson and Ralph McTell (both writing at their most 'folkie'). Everything else was traditional. The sea shanty 'General Taylor' is one of the very few songs in the repertoires of both Fairport and Steeleye Span.

SWARB: Generally, when we looked for traditional songs to arrange, we tried to avoid the obvious and anything which someone else had done before us.

'The Eynsham Poacher' was an Oxfordshire song, so local to Fairport. It had been collected by Dave Arthur and quickly became popular among local musicians, which is where Fairport got it.

PEGGY: I collected it off John Leslie. He left it at my house – and I refused to give it back!

'Adieu, Adieu' dates from 1750 and comes from the singing of Jumbo Brightwell, though Fairport are more likely to have got it via The Watersons. It's another song of failed criminality, with the perpetrator expressing regret at being captured but little remorse for his crime or his victims. It's likely to have been written as a warning to those considering burglary, as it makes reference to Fielding's gang – an early name for the police force created in 1749 by the novelist

Henry Fielding, who was also Justice of Westminster. Today they are better known as the Bow Street Runners. Both songs have remained an active element of Fairport's repertoire.

The album's title song is a cryptic ballad from the Napoleonic era. Fairport first performed it around the time of *Full House*, recording it for the album and for a BBC radio session. Like 'Banks of Sweet Primroses', this 'lost' traditional song from the Richard Thompson era is found in the repertoire of Phil Tanner. Both were included in the 1968 EFDSS collection of his recordings and Swarb certainly owned a copy of the LP. The track, an epic, takes around six minutes to perform. Fairport's arrangement is almost 13 minutes long.

They followed *Bonny Bunch* with *Tipplers Tales*, an album as uncertain about its sense of direction as the location of its apostrophe (there is none). The only non-traditional content of the album are a song by Allan Taylor and three tunes written by Peggy, which come across as fillers. The album dances around the twin themes of seduction and the effects of alcohol. Given the LP's title, it could almost be classed as a concept album. Peggy's tune titles – 'Bankruptured', 'The Hair of the Dogma', and 'As Bitme' – deliberately picked up on the theme. Allan Taylor's 'Lady of Pleasure' is a fond celebration of women of easy virtue and easy terms. It's an LP of sex 'n' drink 'n' folk 'n' roll.

Only one song breaks the mould. It opened side two of the original LP and comes conveniently halfway through the CD version. 'Reynard the Fox' is a hunting song and is written as an intriguing dialogue between the account of the hunters and the thoughts of their prey. The song was collected by Vaughan Williams in Norfolk, which happens to be the home county of folk singer Peter Bellamy, who naturally had a particular interest in songs that were 'mainly Norfolk'. As a result, 'Reynard' appeared on the debut album by the group with whom he had made his first recordings, The Young Tradition. A slight adaptation of the lyric enabled Fairport to sneak in a discreet namecheck for one of the group's other members. This was not their only modification. YT's version was called 'The Foxhunt'. In 2008, Fairport would make a more significant modification to the narrative of this traditional song.

CHRIS: We decided to revive 'Reynard the Fox', and times had changed with the foxhunting ban having been introduced. I decided to write a new final verse in which Reynard gets away. It fit in with my own views on the subject as well. To avoid confusion we printed the new version in the Cropredy pro-gramme, the year we introduced it.

Like *The Bonny Bunch of Roses*, *Tipplers Tales* included an extended version of a ballad, taken to extreme lengths by Swarb's fiddle playing. The Child ballad 'Jack Orion' is given the epic treatment on this occasion. A song about the seductive power of a maestro fiddler, it had an obvious appeal for the multi-matrimonial Mr Swarbrick. He had recorded the song with Bert Lloyd and Martin Carthy; for Fairport's version, he punctuates the narrative with original Swarbrick tunes.

CHRIS: When Swarb's Whippersnapper recorded the first ver-sion of 'John Gaudie', we used an approach similar to what Swarb had developed in 'Jack Orion', using tunes to punctu-ate and illustrate the story.

Jack's ballad had added original tunes to a traditional song; John's reversed the process. The story of Jack Orion can be traced back to legends concerning the Greek demi-god Orpheus. These have at-tached themselves to various musicians over the centuries. One of these was the Bardd Glas Geraint, whom Chaucer names as one of the greatest Welsh musicians. The song 'Glasgerion' records his ex-ploits. Child included it as number 67 in his ballad collection; with the title anglicised (or perhaps one should say Americanised), it became 'Jack Orion'.

'Three Drunken Maidens' most neatly combines the album's two themes. It is another song that came to Fairport via Bert Lloyd. It dates from the early 19th century when the Isle of Wight was 'a great pleasure garden of wantonness and debauchery, lubricated by the prodigious availability of untaxed alcohol'. When Fairport recorded it, it was ahead of its time, but today its drunken maidens (who specifically aren't maidens by the end of the song) would fit in nicely with the gaggles of garrulous girlhood inhabiting inner city hostelries most nights of the week.

PEGGY: There's a lot of bonking on that album. We should have called it *Live in Maidenhead*.

Further sexual misadventure can be found in a song that became a firm Fairport favourite – 'The Widow of Westmoreland's Daughter' is yet another song to be found in the recorded works of Bert Lloyd. John Kirkpatrick recorded it on his first album with backing from Ashley Hutchings and Richard Thompson.

PEGGY: We certainly knew of John K's version, but I am pretty sure Swarb got it from Bert Lloyd.

SIMON: It's a song with probably the most gynaecologically unsound advice ever made public. It's great fun to sing and has a tune that really rocks and fits the story perfectly.

RIC: Pure unadulterated filth – just the way we like it [stage announcement, 1989].

SIMON: I like the fact there's a twist in the tale, too. Honesty wins out in the end. She might have been gullible but at least she gets her man.

Framing these sagas of sozzled seduction are two of the great traditional drinking songs. 'Ye Mariners All', also known as 'A Jug of This', was a folk-club staple and would certainly have been known to both Peggy and Swarb from their days with Ian Campbell. It appeared in that handy repository of English traditional song, *The Penguin Book of English Folk Songs*. Bert Lloyd included the song in his recording of a selection of songs from the book in 1960. Martin Carthy recorded it for his first LP, but a glance at the first two lines makes it clear that it is Bert's version that Fairport are following. Bert used 'A Jug of This' as the closing song on his 1960 LP, *English Drinking Songs*. The track was preceded by the song Fairport used to close *Tipplers Tales*, 'John Barleycorn'.

SWARB: 'Barleycorn' is a really well-known folk song. It's the kind of thing that Fairport normally avoided, but in the context of the LP, it was exactly right. We found a different way of doing it.

Swarb had recorded the song previously with Martin Carthy, who would release a total of six different versions.

MARTIN CARTHY: Forget the academic stuff about death and re-
    birth, fertility symbols and corn gods! The reason that this is
    one of the best known and most popular of all ballads – and
    one which has crossed a great many musical thresholds – is
    that it's actually about that other activity which most com-
    monly accompanies the singing of traditional songs: drinking!

The "academic stuff" involves the idea that the song is a relic of a
pagan celebration of the corn god. Although it is old – the earliest
record of the song being from 1635 – it is unlikely to reach back into
mythic territory. More likely, it is a pastiche from the early 17th century when writers first began to take interest in folk songs as valid
creations and inspiration. Its unknown author stands at one end of
a line that has writers like Richard Thompson and Chris Leslie at
the other.

    Not only was it a well-known traditional song, it broke another
of Fairport's codes of practice. Mike Waterson's definitive 1965 recording inspired Steve Winwood to create a version which became
the title track of a Traffic album in 1970. Steeleye Span had also created a folk-rock version in 1972 on *Below the Salt*.

    Fairport's "different way of doing it" involved setting the old
pagan song to the tune of 'We Plough the Fields and Scatter' from
Hymns Ancient & Modern. The song works particularly well at
Cropredy, where surrounding fields are usually a-sway with amber
waves of grain waiting to be harvested. Naturally, Fairport have
performed it there on a number of occasions.

    Tipplers Tales was released exactly ten years after Fairport
Convention released their debut LP. In that time they would record
26 different traditional songs. It would be over a decade before
Fairport released a studio version of a traditional song they had not
recorded before. *Red & Gold* came out in December 1988 and included one traditional song, which Roy Harris recorded in 1975 on
his album *Champions of Folly*.

PEGGY: We like to have a song in the set which allows each
    band member a verse on the vocal mic. That started with
    'Walk Awhile', which is probably still the best song to do it.
    There have been others like 'Angel Delight', 'Rocky Road'
    and 'Life's a Long Song'. Maart did an arrangement of 'The
    Beggar's Song' that worked like that.

MAART: We didn't stop playing traditional songs. That would be like not being Fairport! But with so much great stuff to choose from, we didn't have to hunt around for new folk songs to include. The old stuff was easier anyway, because Peggy, Si and DM had been playing it for years, while Ric and I knew it from being fans. You've only to look at all the live albums that came out to see how much trad arr Fairport were actually playing. It's just we were playing *old* old songs as opposed to new old songs.

SIMON: As we began to release albums from the mid-Eighties onwards, there were murmurings in some quarters about the lack of traditional material on them. The old traditional stuff was expected when we played live, so there was no need to start looking for folk songs to record. But it was what people expected from us and in the end we had to make the effort and do it.

Broken Token

By the Nineties, there were lots of folk-rock groups, most of whom clamoured for a slot at Cropredy. Folk itself had become cool again and a new generation of artists was emerging. Eliza Carthy was certainly at the forefront, followed closely by Kate Rusby, The Corrs, Spiers & Boden, Damien Barber and Chris Wood, who joined the old guard of established acts like The Oyster Band, June Tabor, John Tams and Martin Simpson. All were looking for new old material. The pickings were getting thinner.

PEGGY: We stopped trying to find folk songs that no one had done before and began to 'Fairportise' more familiar traditional songs.

The opening track of Fairport's *The Five Seasons* released in December 1990 was effectively a statement of intent. It was a traditional song, but it was one of the most famous of all traditional English songs – the broken token saga, 'Claudy Banks'. The song originates with the Copper Family of Rottingdean, Sussex, and is their best-known number. The family and individual members have recorded six versions of it. Shirley Collins learned it directly from them and included it on her folk-rock classic *No Roses* as the opening track.

The Young Tradition placed their version of 'Claudy Banks' as the opening track of side two of their eponymous first album. Their recording also crops up on a number of compilation albums. From that recording, it found its way into the repertoires of countless groups and choirs specialising in harmony vocals, among them Coope Boyes & Simpson, Mountain Ash, Regal Slip (great group name – read it backwards) and Muckram Wakes.

Besides being associated particularly with the Copper Family, 'Claudy Banks' (or 'Banks of Claudy', as it is also known) was in the repertoire of many important source singers: their recordings, long since deleted, were to reappear around the time Fairport recorded it. The CD revolution would make available once more recordings by Pop Maynard, Fred Jordan and Frederick White (recorded in 1909 by Vaughan Williams on a wax cylinder).

'Broken token' songs are a very specific genre of English folk music. They are tales of separation (often as the result of military service), mistaken identity and ultimate recognition. It has to be said that the genre does stretch credulity in that the fact one's own true love is overseas and unseen for a number of years is hardly going to make him totally unrecognisable. Various devices have been employed to justify this – battle scars, physical alteration through hardship on hard ships, facial hair, failing vision, the assumption that the person is dead and, of course, 'being all in disguise'. As a symbolic gesture before parting, the couple have 'shared a ring' and recognition comes when the returning lover produces the matching half – this is the 'broken token'. Anyone with a mental image of the semi-circles resulting from this severance should remember that puzzle rings in which two or three rings are designed to lock together are still a common item of romantic jewellery in southern Europe, the Middle East, Africa and Ireland. A medieval English version is what is being recalled in the song. 'Claudy Banks' follows the conventions of the genre perfectly, except it is a 'broken token' song without the token.

Given the subtlety of the song, Fairport's approach was rather heavy-handed, with Simon striking the rhythm emphatically on acoustic guitar and DM providing a strict march beat. Acoustic guitar, accordion and a very clean fiddle make it hard to think of this as folk-rock. One reviewer called it 'a dutiful recording', which perhaps says it all. However, it was not the album's only traditional track. 'The Card Song' was a fondly remembered song from Peggy's days with the Ian Campbell Folk Group.

PEGGY: It's an old musical drinking game. You named the person who had to sing the next verse. We stuck in the names of some of our mates.

IAN CAMPBELL: It's an army song, designed to encourage drinking. No one knows who wrote it, so it must be a folk song.

Released in 1995, *Jewel in the Crown* contained just two traditional songs, 'Kind Fortune' and 'She's Like a Swallow'. Both were taken from *Folk Songs From Newfoundland*, of which Maartin Allcock acquired a 1970 reprint (he gives this date in his sleeve notes). The book, originally published in 1934, consists of songs collected by Maud Karpeles in 1929 and 1930. She was carrying out one of the last wishes of Cecil Sharp, with whom she had worked closely for the last decade of his life. Like Sharp, she believed that songs (and dances) should be collected from a living tradition, which, they both believed, was facing extinction. The First World War seemed not only to confirm their worst fears, but accelerate them. The slaughter on the Western Front wiped out precisely the class of people who had served for generations as song-bearers. Just as community-based workmates from the Northern mills were recruited for 'Pals' regiments because they were already a disciplined team, in the South recruiters targeted Morris sides.

In 1916, Sharp and Karpeles headed off to America to collect songs preserved by singers in the Appalachians. One of Sharp's earliest discoveries was the great ballad singer Jane Gentry of Hot Springs, Madison County, North Carolina. He collected over 70 songs from her. One of them was the American version of the Child ballad 'Little Musgrave' re-titled 'Matty Groves'. When Fairport created their banjo arrangement of 'Matty Groves' in 2012, they were in fact returning it to source, just as Ashley Hutchings had on his album *As I Cycled Out on a May Morning* (2003).

When 19th-century settlers in America decided to move away from the eastern seaboard, they encountered the great barrier of the Appalachian mountain range. It stretches from Canada

(Newfoundland is formed by its mountain peaks thrusting above the sea) to Tupelo, Mississippi, the birthplace of Elvis Presley. The range is largely impassable and its southern transit, the Cumberland Gap, was so famous that it is celebrated in several songs. As a result, small landlocked communities developed and existed in remarkable isolation for decades. These people had brought with them the folk songs they had sung at home in England, Ireland and Scotland – which were passed down through the generations and preserved in the oral tradition. Fairport's 'Nottamun Town', for example, was preserved in the family traditions of the Ritchies of Kentucky.

In the Twenties, Ralph Peer, the man who invented the term 'record producer', began collecting the music of Appalachian residents. Most famously, he spent three days in 1927, recording local musicians in Bristol, Tennessee – those sessions becoming the starting block for the careers of Jimmie Rodgers, the Carter Family, Blind Alfred Reed and Pop Stoneman. It was, in essence, the birth of country music. Four decades before Fairport shot adrenalin into the body of traditional music, country artists recast the British tradition as America's first white pop music.

Sharp and Karpeles arrived before commercialisation had occurred and collected hundreds of different songs that had originated in British traditional music. Sharp died in 1924, but not before he heard about the treasury of traditional music that Newfoundland had become. Maud Karpeles arrived in 1929, armed with a tape recorder. Like Sharp, she saw herself as preparing for a 'folk revival'. Others preserved songs as pieces of folk literature, ignoring the tunes that were an integral part, or they collected them in order to rework the tunes as classical pieces.

In the introduction to his second series of *Folk Songs From Somerset* (1904), Sharp wrote: 'My main intent in preserving these songs was not that they be kept like museum exhibits under glass, but that they could continue to be sung, when and howsoever people might wish to.'

Words Pete Seeger was to echo in 1980: "Some people handle old songs like museum exhibits or ancient manuscripts: they have to put on special protective gloves and deal with them very carefully. Songs were meant to be sung. If songs were animals, they'd roam free and wild; they wouldn't belong in a zoo and you certainly wouldn't send them to a taxidermist."

MARTIN CARTHY: In the end, there really is only one bad thing
     you can do to a song, and that is not sing it.

The two traditional songs on *Jewel in the Crown* seemed overshadowed by the rest of the album, and never became a key part of
Fairport's stage repertoire. Maart had left by the time Fairport released *Who Knows Where the Time Goes?* which contains only one
traditional song, a version of 'The Golden Glove' with a setting by
Sally Barker. The song, allegedly based on an actual event during
the reign of Elizabeth I, belongs in a category which Bert Lloyd described as 'lower class aspirational' – songs where romance, kindness or diligence are rewarded with land, love or lucre by some up-
per-class *deus ex machina*. Among the best known are 'Matt Hyland',
'The Honest Labourer' and 'Willie O'Winsbury'.
     Sharp and Karpeles collected versions of the song in both
Appalachia and Newfoundland, where new variants continued to
turn up right into the Seventies. In 1901, it was published with full
illustrations as a graphic novel in the short-lived London magazine
which gave the genre its name, *The Graphic*.
     In 1972, the Derbyshire folk group Muckram Wakes (Roger and
Helen Watson plus John Tams) heard there was a traditional singer
called George Fradley who sang in the pub in the village of Cubley,
where he lived. They arranged to meet him, with the intention of
collecting songs. Unfortunately, he offered them the more popular
elements of his repertoire – early pop, music hall, comedy songs.

JOHN TAMS: We were a bit in awe of him, but eventually I
     plucked up the courage to ask him, "'ave you got owt a bit
     older?" In response, he sang 'The Ballad of the Squire of
     Tamworth'.

This is the version of 'The Golden Glove' Fairport recorded in 1997.

HELEN WATSON: It was an absolutely superb version. Of course,
     we were delighted. George, on the other hand, couldn't un-
     derstand why three young people should be interested in the
     song. We were bowled over by it and all he could say was
     "That old thing – I didn't think you'd want to hear that old
     thing." It was ironic really because that is exactly what we ex-
     pected from a traditional singer.

New Tradition

The second generation of the folk revival held singers from whom they collected directly in particular esteem. The revivalists of the Fifties liked to perpetuate the idea that folk music was dead, killed off by industrialised society, mass media and the world wars. Bert Lloyd, Ewan MacColl and their contemporaries believed their job was to revive the music in Britain, like some kind of folk Frankenstein's monster.

EWAN MACCOLL: We were able to reverse the process and use modern society to revive folk music. The new cities allowed for the formation of folk clubs, designed to perform and preserve the music. Both radio and television were used to bring folk music to a wider audience.

PETER BELLAMY: We were actually persuaded that there no longer were any real folk singers. When we began to discover that there were still people performing the music the way it had been played for decades, perhaps for centuries, it was like American kids in the Sixties discovering that the old country blues singers, like Son House, were still alive.

SHIRLEY COLLINS: The songs collected by our generation are part of an unbroken oral tradition. They did not go through the process of being written down, tidied up, edited or 'improved'.

There were suspicions that some of the folk music performed by Ewan, Bert and co. had been rewritten to fit in with their own views. When Shirley collected from the Copper Family, Pete Coe from the Legg Family, Peter Bellamy from Walter Pardon, or Muckram Wakes from George Fradley, they were perpetuating a valid, established folk process.

When Fairport recorded 'The Golden Glove', they tapped into that rich seam. It is held in high esteem by the folk revival; aside from source recordings by Frank Hinchliffe, George Fradley, Bradley Kincaid and the wonderfully named Esau Fudge, it has also been recorded by most of the big names in traditional music, among them Muckram Wakes, Nic Jones, Peter Bellamy, Shirley

Collins, Damien Barber, Spiers & Boden, Chris Foster, Ruth Notman, John Wesley Harding, Sally Barker and Mike Seeger.

One cannot leave the song without quoting Harry Smith's typically idiosyncratic headline for it in his *Anthology of American Folk Music*: 'Lady Spurns Squire Preferring Dairy Chores to Aristocratic Leisure'.

A radio DJ attending Cropredy 1997 was heard to remark: "I really hope they play that folk song from their new CD." It wasn't 'The Golden Glove' he meant, though. He was referring to 'Who Knows Where the Time Goes'. That year's Cropredy was the indirect source of another Fairport recording of a traditional song. *The Cropredy Box* includes a studio recording of 'Seventeen Come Sunday'. It was a one-off recording to which Fairport would 'lip sync' (the preferred euphemism for 'mime') for a sequence in the film Ken Russell was making about folk music. The song was an interesting choice. It was collected by Vaughan Williams, Cecil Sharp and Percy Grainger, and would have been hard to miss as it was widespread in several different variants. In the Fifties, a version of the song called 'As I Roved Out' provided the title for the first folk music series on the BBC. Paul McCartney heard it being sung in Liverpool in 1960, which inspired him to rewrite it in a modern context as 'I Saw Her Standing There'.

PAUL MCCARTNEY: There was an old folk song about a guy who meets a girl on her 17th birthday. He tries to chat her up but she is having none of it. He ends up having to admire her from a distance. Most of The Beatles' audience were young girls and 17 was, let's say, a significant age. So I borrowed from that old song to make my own – that and a dash of 'Sweet Little Sixteen'.

Steeleye Span beat Fairport in adapting the song to folk-rock and their versions feature Martin Carthy and John Kirkpatrick, who both recorded it individually and with their other group Brass Monkey. Rearranged by Vaughan Williams for his *Folk Song Suite* and Percy Grainger in a choral setting, it was an early instance of a song wrested from folk and harnessed to a different genre.

Composers like Grainger, Holst, Butterworth, Delius and Vaughan Williams had co-opted folk to meld into their musical milieu at the start of the 20th century, just as Fairport was to do in its final quarter. Their next album included a traditional song, which showed the process of folk-hijacking went back even further.

SIMON: It's a song that puts together courtship and hunting. I don't know whether gory descriptions of slaughter were ever actually a good chat-up line, but Robbie Burns seemed to think so.

PEGGY: It's known Burns was fond of a tipple. Maybe his mind was wandering.

'Western Wind' is often attributed to Scotland's national poet. Much of his writing was based on traditional songs – he wrote a version of 'Tam Lin', for example. In this case, the source of the poem is a fragment of a medieval song, 'Westron Wynde' which in the mid-16th century was 'modernised' and published under the title 'The Lover in Winter Plaineth for the Spring'. The original fragment is the first verse of Fairport's version, and is the oldest piece that Fairport have ever recorded.

Fairport's *xxxv*, which provided a snapshot history of the group at 35, added yet another traditional song to the Fairport canon.

CHRIS: When people talk about Morris music, they tend to think of tunes but there were also lots of Morris songs. 'The Happy Man' is one of those, from the Morris tradition of Adderbury.

Chris plays fiddle for the North Oxfordshire Morris side, where he lives. The song was collected in 1917 from William 'Binx' Walton, but was familiar to many Fairport fans thanks to its inclusion in 1976 on Ashley Hutchings' album, *Son of Morris On* – where it is performed as a stick dance by the Adderbury Morris with guest musicians.

Simon continued to keep an Ashley / Albion connection via his annual appearances with The Albion Christmas Band. At the same time, Chris continued as a part of St Agnes Fountain, whose Christmas shows include original songs and reworkings of more familiar carols. One might think the traditional song on Fairport's next album came from those connections.

SIMON: The Albion Band perform a number of wassail songs
    in the Christmas Show. Fairport's 'Wassail Song' is from the
    same tradition.

The wassail is a mid-winter song which predates what we refer to
today as carols. Many of the songs are remarkably similar, as indeed
are the many American variants. Phil Tanner's 'Gower Wassail' is
usually seen as the definitive source recording, of which Steeleye
Span created a folk-rock version for their third album. Fairport's
wassail, included on *Over the Next Hill*, has a very similar lyric set
with a rather more spritely tune. Chris, Peggy, and Simon take a
verse each in the song.
    Although Fairport have since released new studio versions of
traditional songs they had recorded earlier in their career, that 2004
release was the last new traditional song of their first 45 years. With
Chris Leslie as songwriter-in-residence and a wealth of strong new
material from outside the band, finding and recording traditional
songs was to become much less of a priority for Fairport.

PEGGY: There are so many great Fairport folk-rock songs that
    we really don't need any more. People want to hear the old
    ones.

CHRIS: There are lots of bands continuing the tradition of play-
    ing electric folk that Fairport started. I think most of them
    have played at Cropredy over the years.

Certainly, if you wanted to hear a set that was almost exclusively
electric trad during that second weekend in August, there often
is plenty to choose from. The Home Service, The Oyster Band,
Steeleye Span, The Albion Band, Bellowhead, Demon Barbers and
so on continue what Fairport began.

SIMON: There's always some traditional material in the set.
    You have to have something to keep 'Matty' company! A great
    song is a great song, whether it comes from someone in the
    band, a track you've heard on someone's album, or good old
    trad arr. In a way, it's a false division, all those folk songs must
    have been written by someone, we've just forgotten who . . .

Meet on the Ledge

At the close of every Cropredy festival, the ranks of Fairport swell by some 20,000 members, all joining in heartily and flawlessly on 'Meet on the Ledge'.

SIMON: The lights come up on the audience and it's as if you can see every face individually. Fully lit, they are an amazing sight. There is no embarrassment. They sing it lustily. They are not like a family gathering embarrassedly mumbling the tune of 'Happy Birthday' to Grandma. Some of them are really belting it. They sing like they mean it, because they do, because it's all come round again. It's the climax of their weekend – not in a sense that they've looked forward to this moment, they may not even have given it any thought. But I know, as the lights come up and they sing, loud, clear, heartfelt, as one, that everything good about that weekend, everything they've ever liked about Fairport, is focused in that particular moment. You can see it in their faces. You can hear it in their voices. You can feel it in the great wave of sound that comes back at you. There is nothing like it.

You've stood there, so you know what it looks like and what it feels like. What you don't have is the sublime privilege of singing the verses of the song that build up to that moment or the sensation of being the one to toss the song into the audience and feel them catch it and throw it back. It is a very good place to be, at that moment in time.

It's not just that same moment at every Cropredy over 30 years or so. It's a whole history, right back to the first time Richard turned up with his guitar to play us a new song he'd written that we might like to record. It's every time we've played it since, all the places, all the circumstances.

When Richard Thompson wrote 'Meet on the Ledge' he was 17 years old. The song articulated an adolescent's feelings about drifting apart from old friends and moving into the mysteries of adult life. On the one hand it's about putting away childish things; it's about those 'blue remembered hills'; and it's also about looking ahead, towards unimaginable horizons.

Within months of its composition, the meaning of the song had been transformed, of course. The catchy chorus that everyone thought was a potential hit became a lament, a pop pibroch, a rock requiem – 'When my time is up I'm going to see all my friends.' Those lines became not some vague future appointment but rather a hope of an almost spiritual kind.

A decade on, when it seemed Fairport's own time was truly up, it became what it has remained, their anthem.

PEGGY: Of all the songs we felt we had to include in the Farewell set, that was the most important. I know Simon still found it hard – you can hear that in his voice on the album. If you look at the faces on stage in the Cropredy finale, especially people who were in Fairport at the time, you can see the emotion ringing down the years. It's impossible to believe that such a great song was destined to sit on the shelf for a decade.

RICHARD: It's become an important song for Fairport. That's both flattering and gratifying. To me, like any juvenilia, it's somewhat embarrassing. I still play it from time to time, not just with Fairport but at my own gigs. It always seems to go down well.

RIC: I remember singing 'Meet on the Ledge' in the audience at the Farewell Cropredy. It takes a lot to make me sing it. I had tears streaming down my face. It's always an emotional song to perform.

CHRIS: Standing on the left of the stage, looking across at Simon, and sometimes a guest vocalist who's sharing the lead with him, you can see that every word has meaning. I am there, waiting for the mandolin break, thinking, "Wow! How do I follow that?"

It's been claimed that the idea behind the song came from a tree that Richard and his friends used to climb as youths; as they did so they imagined themselves to be intrepid mountaineers. This interpretation seems woefully literal for a song of forlorn optimism.

SIMON: It's far more than just Fairport's song. It's a song, for example, that a lot of people have chosen to have played at their funerals. It was played at Sandy's. On some occasions, I have played it as part of a funeral service. It's a fair measure of the greatness of the song that it can be an anthem and a celebration at an event as large as Cropredy, and yet is just as valid sung quietly – almost as a meditation – to a small gathering of people sharing their grief.

The original recording of the song and contemporary radio broadcasts of it included extra voices on the chorus. The original recording credited Richard's friends Marc Ellington, Paul Ghosh, Andrew Horvitch and Kingsley Abbott. On tour, Fairport always bring on supporting artists plus backstage guests to join them. The lead vocal on the original recording was, of course, shared between Iain Matthews and Sandy Denny.

RICHARD: Obviously, it wasn't written as a duet, but at the time some of our versions of songs shared the lead vocal. 'Meet on the Ledge' gave us the opportunity to do it with one of our own songs.

Fairport continue the tradition of sharing vocals on the song, which is today led by Simon, by inviting guest vocalists to take the second verse at Cropredy, and sometimes on tour, too.

SIMON: It is like having your friends round. You're glad to see them and want to make the occasion special, to make them feel welcome. You want to give them little treats and surprises.

PEGGY: Things happen every year that could not take place anywhere else. It's a bit like pulling a rabbit out of a hat but, like any good magic trick, it takes a lot of setting up. 'Meet on the Ledge' is always reliable – our "Goodbye, thank you, see you soon!"

One of those treats was a unique overture, an instrumental arrangement of the song by Maartin Allcock, played as Fairport began their set in 1990.

MAART: It was nice to be able to do something different with such a classic – 'Variations on a theme by Richard Thompson'. It's always been the last thing Fairport play in the set: just that once it arrived three hours early.

When the song was released as a single in December 1968, the record company, reviewers, radio DJs and even the band were convinced it would be a hit. It was lost in the Christmas rush and achieved neither the airplay nor the sales it deserved. Despite that, the song has enjoyed a wider familiarity than anything else by Fairport. It was helped initially by its inclusion on a compilation album released in January 1969. The cover of Island's first rock sampler *You Can All Join In* featured a shot of the label's artists, gathered in the early hours in Hyde Park. Members of Fairport stand alongside Traffic, Free, Jethro Tull, Spooky Tooth, Wynder K. Frog (whose drummer and future Fairport member Bruce Rowland stands just to the left of Richard Thompson), Nirvana Clouds and Ian A Anderson, a folk musician and today editor of *Folk Roots*, who does not appear on the album. The 12-track set cost 12 shillings and 6 pennies (62.5p) and sold well.

IAIN: They found the best possible way of bringing together all those members of different bands for the photo. They threw a big party and, as dawn broke, they were ushered into the park where the photographer was waiting. That's why we mainly look cold, weary and the worse for wear.

SANDY: That horrible photo. A right bunch of scruffs. It was very early, the cold grey light of dawn. I had a hangover waiting to happen.

In a break from their normal practice, Fairport included 'Meet on the Ledge' in a number of radio performances at the time. It was first broadcast on John Peel's *Night Ride* show on 25 November, 1968. A week later, they played it again on Stuart Henry's show. The latter version appeared on the cassette of *Heyday* and is reckoned by many to be the best. It is included on the *Live at the* BBC box set, too. The week after that, they played it on John Peel's *Top Gear*. It also featured on the TV show *How It Is* on 13 December, 1968, and early in the new year on a short-lived BBC youth programme *From the Roundhouse*. Still hoping to push it into the charts, Fairport played it again on *The Radio 1 Club* in January.

SIMON: Like so many of Richard's songs, it is obscure and sometimes intangible. Then suddenly its meaning becomes crystal clear, but you know it is only one of many possible meanings. It's a mighty song for such a young man to write. It matures with you; like a great book or well-crafted poem it takes on new significance every time you return to it.

It's simultaneously universal and deeply personal, about loss and nostalgia, but also a song of optimism and the simple joy of being. When I sing it, particularly at Cropredy, I am aware how virtually everyone hearing it will be bringing their own meaning to the words.

MARTIN CARTHY: I learnt it for one of the benefits held for Fairport after the accident. That would have been the first time Swarb played it – though I doubt he remembers.

SWARB: I think Martin and I considered learning it for one of the benefits we played after the crash. Martin sang it with Fairport at Pebble Mill on a TV appearance to promote an early Cropredy.

NORMA WATERSON: It really is a wonderful song. It reminds me of that line in the carol, 'the hopes and fears of all the years are met in you tonight'.

ASHLEY: If the shock of the accident in 1969 made everyone in the band grow up quickly, it did the same thing to 'Meet on the Ledge'. The song took on new meaning for so many people. For those of us in the band, it was an impossible song to perform for many years.

SIMON: After Martin Lamble's death, I think we all felt too traumatised to return to the songs we had been playing before. Nowhere is that more true than in 'Meet on the Ledge', whose layers of meaning were suddenly revealed. Lots of those songs took on new resonances and ironies: they dealt with loss, forced partings and death itself. They felt too close to home – almost prophetic, if that's not too grand a term.

RICHARD: I cannot tell you what it's about. I wouldn't even if I knew. It would spoil it for too many people. It's one of those songs better left open-ended so people can bring their own interpretation to it.

SANDY: Any regrets? Having so little time to sing 'Meet on the Ledge' is an obvious one. It is such a great song. After the accident, there was an agreement that none of us would sing it. It was never discussed – it was something we all just knew. It was laid to rest with Martin. When we formed Fotheringay, Trevor and I wrote a song called 'Peace in the End', which we very consciously modelled on 'Meet on the Ledge'.

ASHLEY: The recording has so many things in it – the friends brought in to swell the chorus, the way Iain and Sandy let their voices play against each other in the alternating verses, Richard's guitar cutting through the fade. More than anything, whenever I play it, I marvel at the way Martin Lamble's drumming drives the song along, full of hope and enthusiasm… full, dare one say, of life.

DM: Of course, during my first stint with Fairport, I never got to play it. As a drummer, for me, it's a post-Cropredy thing. Because it's a song that builds subtly, it offers some genuine challenges for a drummer.

GERRY: There's a moment when the song comes to a sudden halt for a couple of beats, and then with a crash on the drum the chorus soars back in. That moment, especially when I've played with more than one drummer, is totally electric.

SWARB: The song was never really part of my time with Fairport, but when we sang it on the Farewell Tour those lines about too many friends being 'blown off the mountain by the wind' had a special resonance because we had so recently lost Sandy.

GERRY: One year at Cropredy, we projected on screen pictures of friends of the band no longer with us as we played it. They were right behind me, and even without being able to see them I was very aware of them – Martin, Sandy, Trevor, Rob Braviner.

PEGGY: The song became linked to the accident before I joined. So it was years before I played it. It is strange when you think about it – joining a band and then not playing a song which is one of their classics. It had too many memories attached to it even then. Every year, there are sadly more people in your thoughts as you sing it.

RICHARD: I was asked to sing it at my mother's funeral. It is the hardest thing I have ever done.

CHRIS: 'When my time is up, I'm gonna see all my friends.' That is a statement of hope. It's a very profound statement for a teenager, no matter how much Richard tries to dismiss it.

PEGGY: Every year, that moment when the lights come on and shine on the audience for that chorus of 'Meet on the Ledge' is an emotional one.

RIC: The field is full as far as the eye can see. Despite baking heat or winds or thunderstorms or whatever the English summer has thrown at them, they have stood their ground.

SIMON: They have stayed with us, stayed with Fairport, through the Festival, over the years. They are our friends, just as the song says.

CHRIS: I usually have a solo, just before the crowd are due to sing. You can feel them building up for it – 20,000 people drawing breath, ready to perform their bit.

SIMON: 'Meet on the Ledge' is a piece of work that belongs in the category of genius. It wasn't immediately obvious. I always knew it was a good song. It's always been great to play and to sing. But its layers, its depths, its power, its potential, its significance to so many people in so many ways, emerge and unfold over time.

As a finale and a conclusion, it is perfect. It became the last number at Cropredy in 1983, when the late Johnny (Jonah) Jones stepped up to the mic as Fairport completed a particularly stunning version (with two drummers, Cathy Lesurf providing duet vocals, and Richard Thompson on backing vocals and lead guitar). "That's got to be it," he announced. "You simply cannot follow that. Fairport Convention, ladies and gentlemen, the greatest folk-rock band in the world. It all comes round again."

At that moment, the song's place as the inevitable conclusion to a Fairport set was ensured. All that remained were four words we once thought Fairport would never be able to say: "Same time next year?"

No song represents Fairport as succinctly as 'Meet on the Ledge'. For more than 30 years, it has been the only way to end a Fairport concert. It is the natural way to end their story or, to be precise, their story thus far.

Post Script

As work on this book neared completion, we heard the sad news of the death of Geoffrey Hughes. Known to millions through the memorable characters he created on television, he has, for years, been both a fan and a friend of Fairport. He was compere on several occasions at Cropredy and often joined the band on stage with his bodhrán. Like Fairport, he was a true survivor in a notably fickle industry.

It's said you can work out someone's age by asking them to name their favourite *Blue Peter* presenter. You can do the same thing among the Cropredy crowd who identified Geoff by one of the roles he played on TV – binman Eddie Yeats from *Coronation Street*, Mr Lithgow in *The Bright Side*, relative-from-hell Onslow in *Keeping Up Appearances*, Vernon Scripps in *Heartbeat*, or nefarious Twiggy in *The Royle Family*. Younger members of the audience might recognise him from appearances as Uncle Keith in *Skins*, while pop obscurists will know that he was the voice of Paul McCartney in *Yellow Submarine*. Whovians feel a need to remind you that he played Mr Popplewick in *The Trial of a Time Lord*.

I recall a Fairport gig in 2004 at Leeds City Varieties. Geoff was in the area, doing some work with Yorkshire Television, and as usual turned up to see his mates, arriving backstage before the show with a couple of large bottles of Champagne so that we could all help celebrate his birthday. Fairport were shortly due on stage, and so the drinkers among the band exercised restraint but suggested we, "save some for after the show". Geoff popped the first cork and declared, "That's not going to stop us, though, is it, Nige?" Three-quarters of an hour later, we watched Fairport from the wings of the old music hall, suitably refreshed.

I wish he were still around to read this history of his favourite band, told in their own words.

Fairport Convention – A Selective Discography

1997   *Who Knows Where the Time Goes?* (Woodworm WRCD 025)

1999   *The Wood and the Wire* (Woodworm WRCD 033)

2001   *XXXV* (Woodworm WRCD 038)

2004   *Over the Next Hill* (Matty Grooves Records MG2CD 043)

2007   *Sense of Occasion* (Matty Grooves Records MGCD 044)

2009   *Fame and Glory* (Matty Grooves Records MGCD 049)

2011   *Festival Bell* (Matty Grooves Records MGCD 050)

2012   *By Popular Request* (Matty Grooves Records MGCD 051)
Almost every Fairport studio album has been reissued in
expanded form on CD with additional tracks. The in-depth
multi-CD version of *Liege & Lief* is highly recommended.

LIVE ALBUMS

Fairport have always been, essentially, a live act. There is a
daunting array of live releases of varying quality and legitimacy.
This list selects key live albums referred to in the text.

1970   *House Full* (Island 586376-2)

        Released in 1977 as *Live at the LA Troubadour* (Island
        HELP 28) and subsequently repackaged under this title.

1974   *Fairport Live Convention* (Island ILPS 9285)

        Also known as *A Moveable Feast* and *Fairport Convention
        Live '75*. Three further CDs of live recordings from this era
        have been issued since 2000.

1977   *4 Play* (Shirty Records SHIRTY3)

Compiled and released by Dave Swarbrick in 2012, this captures the 'final' line-up in fine form.

1979   *Farewell, Farewell* (Woodworm BEAR 22)

Audio souvenir of their final tour.

1982   *Moat on the Ledge: Live at Broughton Castle* (Woodworm WR 001)

The first live album from the Cropredy Festival. There have been several subsequent releases of Cropredy recordings. The box set *Cropredy Capers* brought together highlights from the Festival's first 25 years over four CDs. Other Cropredy albums include *The Boot*, *The Other Boot*, *The Third Leg*, *25th Anniversary Concert*, *The Cropredy Box*, *Cropredy 98*, *Another Gig–Another Palindrome*, *Live at Cropredy '08*.

1986   *Here Live Tonight* (Fiddlestix FOFC1)

This was the first in a series of fan-produced albums from Australia. There are many semi-official (and sometimes totally unauthorised) live Fairport release, not all reach high standard of this set.

2006   *Off the Desk* (Matty Grooves Records MG2CD 043)

Compiled by Ric Sanders from dozens of hours of Winter Tour recordings, this was a serious attempt to re-present the live sound of 21st-century Fairport outside their extensively documented Cropredy performances.

2012   *Babbacombe Lee Live Again* (Matty Grooves Records MGCD 052)

Rather than release a single live performance of the complete Babbacombe Lee, Fairport remade the album selecting the best performances from 30 nights of Winter Tour performances.

Ironically, while Fairport have benefited from some of the best compilation releases ever, they have been victims of some of the worst and most opportunistic of all time. The simple rule is to approach any Fairport compilation with care and remember that it is never the album they intended to release.

It can become confusing: there are at least three CDs, from different eras of the band, entitled *Meet on the Ledge*. Bizarrely, Universal decided to call one of their compilations *What We Did on Our Holidays* (though the album's 16 tracks included only two from the originally titled album), and there is also a set called *What Else We Did on Our Holidays*.

These are – to my mind – the best of the readily available compilations:

1972   *The History of Fairport Convention* (Nov '72, Island ICD-4)

An exemplary overview of the band's released material to date. Sadly, the CD reissue upset the balance by omitting a couple of tracks and dispensing with the excellent packaging.

1975   *Heyday*
(Oct '76, private cassette)
(LP Sept '87 Hannibal HNBL 1329)

Ashley compiled the set from tapes of BBC sessions. The album was groundbreaking in this respect. Originally only available via mail order on cassette, it was subsequently issued on vinyl (with slight track changes) and CD (ultimately in an expanded form). Superseded by *Live at the BBC* (*qv*).

1981   *The Airing Cupboard Tapes*
(Aug '81, Woodworm cassette, no cat no)
(CD Nov '02, Talking Elephant TECD 046)

Compiled by Dave Mattacks, this documents the period from Simon's departure to DM's decision to follow in his footsteps. It consists of live recordings, though the versions seldom equate to the released studio version in terms of line-up or musical approach.

1992   *The Woodworm Years* (Dec '91, Woodworm WRCD 47)

A very listenable compilation of tracks by Fairport members individually and collectively in the first five years of their return to recording.

1998   *Fiddlestix* (Oct '98, Raven RVCD 47)

A well-judged compilation of released, rare and previously unavailable material, put together by Australian fans and designed to bridge the gap between *History of* and *The Woodworm Years*.

2002   *UnConventional* (May '02, Free Reed FRQCD 35)

A big box set (four CDs, book, family tree, Cropredy guide book) that traces Fairport's entire career via unreleased or extremely rare recordings.

2007   *Live at the BBC* (April '07, Universal Island 9845385)

This four CD set brought together all the surviving recordings which Fairport made for BBC Radio 1. Where tapes had been lost, off-air recordings were sought out. It provides a fascinating alternative history of the band. A compilation drawn from it, *Best of the BBC*, is less interesting as it includes only radio versions of songs included on official albums.

This pioneering set was so successful that it led to other sets on the same model including 'BBC complete' sets of Sandy Denny and Richard Thompson.

Significant Fairport recordings can also be found on compilations credited to its various members. The first of these deserves special mention because its approach was so groundbreaking.

Richard Thompson's *(guitar/vocal)* included, alongside unreleased solo material, outtakes from *Liege & Lief* and *Full House*, a very rare Fairport b-side, a live recording from the legendary LA Troubadour season and a BBC session. At the time the BBC had a policy of not allowing their recordings to be used anywhere but on their own record label and the version of 'Mr Lacey' on *(guitar/vocal)* was the first to be leased by them.

Big box sets tracing the careers of Sandy, Richard, Swarb, Ashley, Iain and Peggy have all included rare or unavailable Fairport recordings as has Ashley's continuing, occasional archivist series *The Guv'nor*.

VIDEO / DVD

As Dave Pegg pointed out when I said I planned to include a brief guide to Fairport videos, "We're not the most visually-orientated of bands. Our videos tend to be film of us playing live."

The early years of Cropredy were documented on videotape, though today these efforts look primitive and are of archive interest only. Of particular interest in later Cropredy video releases are the bonus tracks featuring the videos made to be shown on the big screen behind Fairport as they play.

Sadly, some of the best Fairport videos are no longer commercially available (though like most things videographic, YouTube may have the answer). Island's *It All Comes 'Round Again* (VHS only, 1987) is an in-depth, well-illustrated documentary. The BBC's *Babbacombe Lee* programme has sadly never been released commercially, but the film of the *Full House* line-up live in Maidstone made by Tony Palmer is available on DVD (Neptune, 2008). As this book was being completed, the BBC transmitted *Who Knows Where the Time Goes?*, a documentary about the band's first 45 years.

Publications

Back issues of magazines like *Mojo*, *Rolling Stone* and *Melody Maker* have been regularly cited in the text. Original copies would need to be sought out, as none of these publications has chosen to include Fairport pieces in anthology volumes they have published. There have been many in-depth studies of folk-rock and these naturally include extensive sections on Fairport. The first of these was *The Electric Muse* (Eyre Methuen, 1975) by Dave Laing, Karl Dallas, Robin Denselow and Robert Shelton.

Also recommended, as being partially about Fairport:

White Bicycles (Serpent's Tale, 2006), Joe Boyd's autobiography.

Ashley Hutchings: The Guv'nor and the Rise of Folk Rock (Helter Skelter, 2002), by Brian Hinton and Geoff Wall.

No More Sad Refrains (Helter Skelter, 2000), Clinton Heylin's biography of Sandy Denny.

Richard Thompson: Strange Affair (Virgin, 1996), by Patrick Humphries.

Electric Eden: Unearthing Britain's Visionary Music (Faber & Faber, 2011), by Rob Young.

Books specifically about Fairport include:

Fairportfolio (private printing, 1997), by Kingsley Abbott (detailed account of their early years by a close friend of the band).

Meet on the Ledge (Eel Pie, 1982), by Patrick Humphries. Updated and republished as *The Classic Years* (Virgin, 1997).

If You Really Mean It (Star Cluster, 1999), by Walter Heger (an obsessively detailed history in German).

The Woodworm Era (Jeneva, 1995), by Fred Redwood and Martin Woodward.

Fairport UnConventional (Free Reed, 2002) by Nigel Schofield, a companion volume with CD box set.

The history of Cropredy Festival is told in the annual programmes for each Festival and also in:

Cropredy Capers, by Nigel Schofield.

Festival Folk (This Way Books, 2005), by Joss Mullinger and Catherine Hayward.

annA rydeR and David Hughes have both published journals of their tours as support for Fairport.

Websites

Fairport's official site
    www.fairportconvention.com
Expletive Delighted
    www.musikfolk.co.uk/expletive-delighted
Talk Awhile, a web based discussion group
    www.talkawhile.co.uk
FC list, an email based discussion group
    www.fclist.org
Friends of Fairport, publishers of *The Ledge*
    http://homepage.ntlworld.com/unhalfbricking

Roll of Honour

The publishers gratefully acknowledge the contribution of everyone listed below, whose generous support has helped bring this project to fruition.

Kingsley Abbott
Lizzie Abraham
Mark Adams
Mike & Linda
    Adams
Sally Adams
Paul Ager
Sam Alexander
Darren Allen
Gerry Allen
Stephen Ambrose
Jens Andersen
Adam Anderson
Alan Arnold
Pete Arrowsmith
Brendan Ashton
John Aspinall
Clive Attwood
Pete Auckland
Bob & Jane Austen
Geoff Austin
Sue Auton
Bob Ayton
Graham Bailey
D. E. Balfour
Paul Ballard
Bryan Bance
Ian Bancroft
Marcus Banks
Nigel Banks
Ray Barber
Matthew Barbier
John Barlass

Hugh Barr-Hamilton
Adrian & Chrissy
    Bartlett
Andy Bassett
Phillip Bassill
Mike Batchelor
Stefan Baumeister
Richard Baxter
Jez Beacham
Andrew Bean
Gary Beard
Paul Beard
Marinus Beers
Richard Bennett
Tim Bennett
Yvonne Bennett
Steve Bennion
Helen & Eric Benton
John Berresford
David Best
Mike Betteridge
Ian Beveridge
Jim Bickhart
Graham Bickle
Terry Bidle
Richard & Carol Bird
Simon Bishop
Drew Black
Rebecca & Ralph
    Blackbourn
David Blackmore
Jon Blacow
Steve Boat

Mike Bodinham
Paul Anthony Bond
Joachim Bongers
Paul Booker
Jonathan Bore
Greg Borgartz
Michael Botho
Jean Bouguennec
Rob Bousfield
Ray Bowden
Richard & Tricia
    Bowden
Ray Bowers
Malcolm Bowie
Martin Bowie
Bridget Box
Tom Brazier
Michael Brien
Howard Brindle
John Brindle
Mandy Broadbent
Steve Broadhurst
Richard Brock
David Brooks
Jerry & Eleanor
    Brooks
Heather & Ian
    Broom
Adrian Broome
Les Brown
Tony Brown
Bob Bruce
Tristan Bryant

Ian Burgess
Trevor & Selina
  Burgess
Mike Bursell
Geoff Burton
Hugh Burton
John Burton
John Bushby
Phil Cadman
Dr Clive Calcutt
Tracey Cameron
Victor Campanile
Jim Campbell
Tamzen Cannoy
Pete Carpenter
David Carter-Green
David & Ruth
  Cartlidge
Trevor Casbolt
Tom Casey
  & Lisa Equi
Alan Casselton
Derek Caudwell
Paul Goode
  in memory of
  Michael Chalmers
Paul Chalmers
François Chaussy
Dave Chick
Keith Chick
Roger Childs
Ken Chitty
Gregory Chludzinski
John Christian
Jill & Richard Clapp
Martin Clark
Susan Clark
Mark Clarke
Nick Clarke
Peter Clarke

Debby Clayton
Pat & John Clayton
Paul Clemons
Chuck Cobb
Richard Cocking
Dave Collins
Sonia Collins
Finn & Rowan
  Collinson
John Collinson
Ian & Dianne Collis
Steve Connolley
Stuart Cook
Robin Coombes
Julian Cooper
Brian Cope
Tim Copeland
Chris Corble
Mike Courtney
Peter Cowley
David & Glynis
  Cracknell
James Crawford
Bernie & Mary
  Crease
Roi Croasdale
Keith Cronshaw
David Crowther
Patricia Crozier
Patrick Curry
John Czyzyk
Richard Darby
David Darvell
Karen Davies
Lizzie Davies
Martin Davies
Chris Davis
Stella Davis
Keith Davison
John Dawson

S. John Dawson
Simon Day
Airt de Buitléar
Andrew Deards
Arjan den Boer
Andre Denis
Jeff Dent
Pete Devine
Leon H. Dicks
John & Janet Dillon
Jon & Jan Dixon
Rosemary Dixon
Thomas Dixon
Martyn Dixon-Jones
Rick Dodderidge
Mark Donmall
Nic Dowding
Peter Doyle
Martin Driver
Inger Duberg
Steve Duggan
Nancy & Wayne
  Dunham
Kenneth Dunkerley
John Dunne
Richard Dunne
Stephen Dunne
Daniel Duvall
Tor Dybo
Louise Edis
Trevor Edlington
Tim Edmonds
John & Olive
  Edwards
Bosse Ehnsiö
David Eisener
Peter Elliot
John Elliott Ford
Chris Ellis
Janice English

Arie Euwijk
Richard Eyre
Ric & Karen
  Fairburn
Craig Falconer
Val & Steve Fermer
Adrian Ferris
Brett Field
Jon Fielder
Gordon & Margaret
  Findlay
Kat Fisher
Lorraine Fitchew
Keith Fletcher
Steve Fletcher
Alan Fludgate
David Foley
Anders Folke
Richard Forsley
Lindsay Foulis
David Francis
James Franey
Giampiero Frattali
John Freeman
Ian Fry
Alistair Fyfe
Aysel Gafarova
Tim Galley
Raffaele Galli
Paolo Galloni
Blaise Gammie
John Gardner
Nick Gaze
Paul Ghosh
Benjamin Gibbs
Neil K. Gibbs
Geoff Gilborson
Edgar Gleim
David Glennie
Christian Globisch

Dawn & David
  Good
Stanley Goodhew
Simon Goodwin
John Gorringe
David Gosling
Gerry Gough
Tom Gough
Stuart Grant
Bill Green
Brian Green
Nigel Green
Mark Greening
Ray Groves
Elizbeth-Anne
  Grummitt
Geoff Haigh
Ruth Hainsworth
Chris Hall
Norman Hall
Peter Hall
Richard Hall
Richard &
  Marianne Hall
Anne Hallam
Dennis Hamer
Peter Hamilton
Gary Hampton
John Hanson
Chris Harding
Oz Hardwick
Bill Harrington-
  Stewart
Keith Harrison
Paul, Lucy &
  Eleanor Harrison
Raggyphil Harrison
Richard Harrison
Annie Harrison-
  Brooks

Simon Hartshorne
David Haslam
Steve Hasson
Thor-Rune Haugen
Graham Hawkins
Yasuo Hayashida
Ian Haydock
Richard Hazlewood
Robert Heath
Ken Heathfield
Jean Henry-Allen
Mark Hepburn
Willie Hershaw
Jon Heyes
Steve & Sheila Hill
Tim Hills
Peter Hines
Wolfgang Höhl
David Hoffman
Roger Holdcroft
John Hollington
Richard Holme
John Holyome
Andrew Hood
Derek & Karen Hood
Chris Hope
Stephen Horner
Davis Hornsby
James Howard
Peter Howarth
Mike Howlett
Tim Howlett
Adrian Hubbard
Simon Paul Hughes
Steve Hulbert
Graham Hunt
Dr. Oliver Ilgner
Carl Iredale
A. James Sr.
David James

Ian James
Phil James
Dan Jennings
Jenny Jennings
Mike Jervis
Jezwald
Darren Johnson
David & Erica
    Johnson
Ian Johnson
Alan Jones
Bill Jones
Howard Jones
Tom Jones
Keith Jordan
Peter Jordan
Perry Julian
Matthew &
    Helen Kean
Mike Kearney
Janet Kearns
Graham & Cathy
    Keevill
Michael Kemp
Ian Kenny
Rosemary Kerr
Richard Kinder
Shane Kirk
Jim & Tina Kirkham
Gary Kirrage
Jeff Kluckers
Brian Knowles
Peter Kühn
Mark Kulkowitz
Michael Kutapan
Brian & Lyn Lacey
Shane & Margaret
    Lagor
Phil & Lorraine
    Lambert

David Lands
Charles Lane
Kevin Lansdale
Stefan Laubi
Darren Lawbuary
Malcolm Lawrence
Jean Lawton-Day
Peter Leighton
Andy Leonard
Andy & Wendy
    Leslie
John Lester
Diana Lettice
John Leversuch
Stephen Lewin
Henry Lewis
Jon Lewis
Richard Lewis
Graham Ley
Shirley & Amy
    Leyshon
Peter Lukacs
Jesper Lund
Maralyn Lunney
Alex Lyons
Sue Lystor
Carol Macleod
Michael Madden
Gary Maiden
Carole Marsden
John Marsland
Roy Martin
Bill Mather
Dave Matthews
Paul Matthews
Ian Maun
Stephen Mayo
Ian McBride
Jamie McCoan
Joseph McCord

Sheena McCormack
Ian McDonald
Eoin McDonnell
John McGettigan
Ian McGregor
Neil McIntosh
Alan McPhail
Alastair McSporran
Trevor Meadows
Andy Meagher
Emma Melville
Rui Mendes
Rog & Jane Mercer
Sandie Middleton
Graeme & Janet
    Middleyard
David Miles
Michael & Pam
    Miller
Robert Miller
Clifford Milner
George Mina
Paul Minett
Paul Minkkinen
Brian Minshall
John Mitchell
Steve Mitchell
Clifford Mockett
Hans Hermann Moll
Les Moll
Simon Mollart
Dale Monette
Claire Moore
Pat Morgan
Rodney Morgan
Malcolm Morris
Steve Morris
Tom Morris
Andy Morton
Gail Moyle

Iain Muir
Robert Mulford
Joss Mullinger
Kevin Mulrooney
Stephen Mummery
Liz & Brian
    Musselwhite
Michael New
John Newton
Paul Nicholls
Karen Nicolaysen
Jan Niezgoda
Athan Nistal
Tom Noble
Jeffrey Norman
Tony North
Derek Nurse
Mick Oates
Adam Officer
George Onslow
Ewan Organ
Larry Orme
Robert Osman
Helge Ottesen
Hajo Otto
T. P.
Philip & Pip
Richard & Grace
    Palmer
David & Linda
    Papworth
Jacques Paquet
Lyn & Ollie Pardo
Phil Parker
Stephen Parkin
Bob Parkins
Keith Parry
Linda Parry
Roger Parry
Ian Partridge

Nick & Russ Patrick
Cheryl Pawelski
Ron Pearsall
Kevin Pearson
Steve Peek
Stephen Pegum
Martin Perry
Mick Peters
Michael Peterson
David Philips
Tom Phillips
Allan Pickett
Dave Pickup
Michael Pietsch
David Pollard
Philip Polley
Alastair Poole
David Potter
Matt Powell
Anil Prasad
Sarah Pressland
Dave Preston
Kurt Prinz
Massimo Pulleghini
Carol & H. Rainbow
Maggie Ramage
Jenni Randall
Stephen Randall
Jeroen Ras
J. Ravenscroft
Alan Rawle
Simon Raymonde
John Rea
Michael Read
Robert Renton
Peter Revell
Andreas Rewitzer
Steve Rhenius
Mary Richards
Dave Richardson

Tina Rickards &
    John Beddowes
Warren Rigg
Simon Riley
Stuart & Jane Riley
Duncan Rippon
Ian Ritchie
David Roberts
Iain Roberts
Les Roberts
Philip Roberts
Sue Roberts
Martin Robinson
Lee Robson
Alan Rogers
David Roper
Tony Rose
Jeremy Rutter
Annice Ryan
Mark Salt
Paul Sampson of
    Ebbesbourne
Richard Sanderson
Paul Sandy
Chris Sansome
Stephen Saunders
Glenn Savegar
Hasko Schmidt-
    Kliemann
Olaf Schmidt-Rutsch
Rainer Schobess
Howard Schofield
Ton Schuringa
John Scothern
Simon Scott
Michael, Georgie,
    Elouise & Samuel
    Scrivens
Barry Seward
Dean A. Sewell

Ian Shaw
Peter Shaw
Paul Sheath
Ron & Alyson
  Shepherd
Graham Shield
Mark Shimmin
Melanie Shoemark
Paul Siddons
Philip Silvie
Carole Simmonds
John Simmons
Greg Sinclair
Alan Skingsley
Elliot Smaje
Graham Smart
Nic Smith
Scott Smith
Roly & Val Smith
Adrian Smith
Evan Smith
James Smith
John & Davina
  Smith
Leslie Smith
Martin Smith
Martin Smith &
  Kirsty Thorpe
Wayne Smith
Nick Smithers
Betty & Roger
  Snowden
Lee Soden
Tim Sparrow
Martyn Spence
Graham Spencer
Peter Spooner
Mike Stafford
Doug Stammers
Alan Standing

Martin & Indra
  Starnes
Andreas Steurer
Mike Stilton
Ian & Margaret
  Storey
Peter Storey
David Stuart
Donald Stuart
Keith Styles
Mark Sullivan
Patrick Sullivan
Gustav Susaa
Annie Sutcliffe
Anne Sweetman
Suki Swindale
Chris Sykes
Christopher
  Taberham
Andy Talkington
David Tasker
Stephen Tautz
Chris Taylor
Col Taylor
Mark Taylor
Rebekah Taylor
Ray Teagle
Chrissy & Paul Teale
Gary & Eileen
  Thomas
Lin Thomas
Roger Thomas
Kevin Thompson
William Thompson
Peter Thomsen
Alastair Thomson
Alan Thornsby
Michael & Linnet
  Thornton
David Todd

Howard Toussaint
Steve Truman
Brian Tubb
Paul Tuck
Paul Turner
Paul Turner
Geir Tvera
David Tweedie
Steve Valentine
Hans Valk
Peter van Burg
Piet & Carol van
  der Westhuizen
Eric van Maaren
Anne & Derek
  Van Ryne
Ian Van Ryne
Ali Van Ryne
Simon Vernon
Bart Verpalen
Paul Vodden
Paul Vyse-
  Widdicombe
Martin Walker
Bill & Claire
  Wallace
Edwin Wallage
Murray Walters
Barbara Walton
Ian Walton
Paul Walton
Stephen Wankling
Graham Warren
Janet Waskett
Gary Waters
Malcolm Watson
Jeremy Way
Dave Weedon
Nick Weinreb
Andy Weller

Tony Wells
Staffan Wennerlund
Paul Wesseler
Jack Westwood
Michael & Fiona
  Wheeler
Dave White
Mark White
Stan & Gillian
  White
Chris Whitefield
John Whiting
Fiona & Deon
  Whittaker
Keith Whittington
Frits Wielens
Kevan Wildy

Robin Willcocks
Darren Williams
Graham Williams
Jeff Williams
Kev Williams
Philip & Christine
  Williams
Stuart Williams
Sue Williams
Angela Wilson
Ian Wilson
Bill Windsor
Arild Winnberg
Simon Withers
Patricia Wollen
Kevin Wood
Rich Wood

Michael Woodage
Neil Woodcock
Paul Woodhouse
David Woolven
Ron & Lesley
  Woolven
Alan Wormwell
Stef Wouters
Christer Wredlert
Phil Wyborn-Brown
Shigemasa
  Yamashina
Pete Yates
Peter Yeates
Kevin Young